KEELE
UNIVERSITY

7 Day Loan
40p per day Fine

Please return by the

D1435018

5 166 410 0

Imagined Diasporas
among Manchester Muslims

World Anthropology

Series editors Wendy James & N.J. Allen

*forthcoming title

Imagined Diasporas
among Manchester Muslims
The Public Performance
of Pakistani Transnational Identity Politics

Pnina Werbner

Professor in Social Anthropology
Keele University

James Currey
OXFORD

School of American Research Press
SANTA FE

James Currey
73 Botley Road
Oxford OX2 0BS

School of American Research Press
Post Office Box 2188
Santa Fe, New Mexico 87504-2188

Publication of this book was assisted by
a publications grant from the University of Melbourne

British Library Cataloguing in Publication Data
Werbner, Pnina
    Imagined diasporas among Manchester Muslims : the public
performance of Pakistani transnational identity politics. -
(world anthropology)
    1. Pakistanis - England - Manchester - Social life and
customs
    I. Title
    305.8'914122'042733

ISBN 0-85255-920-8 (James Currey paper)
ISBN 0-85255-921-6 (James Currey cloth)

Library of Congress Cataloging-in-Publication Data
Werbner, Pnina.
    Imagined diasporas among Manchester Muslims : the public performance of Pakistani
transnational identity politics / Pnina Werbner.
        p. cm. -- (world anthropology)
    Includes bibliographical references (p.) and index.
    ISBN 0-85255-921-6 (J. Currey) -- ISBN 0-85255-920-8 (J. Currey: pbk.) -- ISBN
1-930618-11-5 (School of American Research Press) -- ISBN 1-930618-12-3 (School of
American Research Press: pbk.)
       1. Pakistanis--England--Manchester--Politics and government. 2.
Pakistanis--England--Manchester--social conditions. 3. Manchester (England)--Politics
and government. 4. Manchester (England)--Ethnic relations. 5.
Muslims--England--Manchester. I. Title. II. World Anthropology (Santa Fe, N.M.)

DA690.M4 W46 2002
305.891'4122042733--dc21   2002019212

Typeset in 10/11 pt Monotype Photina
by Long House Publishing Services, Cumbria, UK
Printed and bound in Great Britain
by Woolnough, Irthlingborough

This book is dedicated with love to
my friends Majid and Shaheen, Munir and Shahnaz,
to my beloved mother and to my father,
whose generosity, optimism and commitment
to tolerance and peace seem boundless.

Contents

Illustrations

PLATES

TABLES

FIGURES

Acknowledgements

This book has been in preparation a very long time. I first presented a version of Chapter 7 at the Pakistan Workshop at Satterthwaite in 1988. Virtually all the different chapters have had many audiences and readerships, and I would like to thank all of these for sharing their ideas so generously with me.

The research on which the book is based was conducted between 1986 and 1994, out of which 3 years were funded by the Economic and Social Research Council, UK, and a further period of 4 months by the Leverhulme Trust. I wish to thank both bodies for their generous assistance. Many of the chapters were first presented at the Pakistan Workshop's annual meeting at Satterthwaite, and I am particularly grateful to the participants, including Peter Parkes, Wenonah Lyon and Hastings Donnan, for their useful comments. Sonia Khan, Khawar Ghaznavi and Nyla and Arshad Ahmed between them meticulously transcribed and translated the speeches for me, and I am very grateful to them for their careful and painstaking work. Munir Choudry helped me with the fieldwork and his assistance has been quite invaluable; my debt to him is beyond repayment. His wife Shahnaz, and Majid and Shaheen Khan, also helped me understand the rationality behind the Muslim offence during the Rushdie affair. I am grateful to them for their lasting patience with me. Hajji Bashir Ahmed introduced me to his Sufi order and supported my research with endless generosity.

Various chapters of the book were commented on by others as well. Chapter 1 was presented at University College London, and I am grateful to Bruce Kapferer and Ruth Mandel, as well as the other participants at the seminar, for their comments. Chapter 4 was presented at the Manchester University Social Anthropology seminar in May 1991, the Delphi Forum Conference on 'The Unification of Europe and its Impact on the Third World' at Poros, Greece, in June 1991, and at the John Logie Baird Centre of the University of Strathclyde's ESRC workshop in October 1991. I am grateful to Caglar Keyder, Sophia Mappa, Marilyn Strathern, Nigel Rapport, Tim Ingold and the other participants at these meetings for their comments, and to Richard Fox, as editor of *Current Anthropology* and Richard Werbner for their incisive comments. Chapter 5 was first presented at a meeting of the Observatoire du Changement Social en Europe Occidentale at Poitiers in 1991, and at Oxford University's South Asian Studies Centre. In revising the chapter I benefited greatly from discussions with Joyce Miller and Don and Leah Handelman. I would also like to acknowledge my indebtedness to David Martin for his notion of a 'buried intelligentsia', and to Hastings Donnan for his helpful comments on Chapter 5. Chapter 6 was first presented at a Conference on

Muslims in Europe convened by the Agnelli Foundation in Torino, and at Oxford University's Anthropology Department's Ethnicity seminar. Michael Fischer made additional useful comments for which I am grateful and thanks are also due to various anonymous readers. A version of the Conclusion was presented at the Pakistan Workshop in the Lake District in 1997, and I would especially like to thank Pritam Singh for his very helpful comments.

During most of the research, I was a single woman in public meetings composed entirely of men. Despite that, and despite the fact that I was a Jew among Muslims, I was always treated with the greatest respect. This in itself is a tribute to the tolerance of British Muslims, especially so because the research was on hot political issues from the protagonists' point of view. There was a good deal of speculation about my possible hidden motives and agendas, and now and then I became the target of malicious gossip. It was thought that I might be a spy, although for whom was never quite spelled out. I accepted this slander as an anthropological occupational hazard, natural in the politically charged atmosphere of factional politics in which I was working, though I always defended myself hotly if and when the gossip reached me. Despite these persistent rumours, the men at the centre of this study continued to help generously with the research, and to give me of their time and thoughts. I am particular grateful to Mr Manzur Ahmed, Maulana Baig, Chaudhri Amin and their colleagues for their friendship and willingness to let me record their meetings. Finally, I would like to thank my husband, Richard Werbner, and my father, Philip Gillon, for helping to clarify and illuminate the obscurities of my work and thinking.

All of the chapters in the book draw on earlier published work. Chapters 1 and 9 draw on Werbner 1991c, Chapter 2 on Werbner 1996c, Chapter 3 on Werbner 1990c, Chapter 4 on Werbner 1991d, Chapters 5 and 6 on Werbner 1996d, Chapter 7 on Werbner 1994, Chapter 8 on Werbner 1996e, and Chapter 10 on Werbner 1998.

Introduction

On September 11, 2001, the New York World Trade Center's twin towers collapsed under the impact of two fuel-laden passenger planes, leaving more than 3,000 men and women dead. The death toll included ordinary citizens from across the world working in the buildings, air passengers and tourists. The skyline of Manhattan, the scene of so many thrillers and apocalyptic movies, was shattered as if by a special-effects visual illusion. As it emerged that an elusive Islamist, Usama bin Laden, and his al-Qaida clandestine global network were the source of the devastation, it seemed that the clash of civilisations predicted by Huntington (1993) between Islam and the West had finally materialised.

Global images of terror invaded every Western home. For Muslim viewers they underlined the terrible vulnerability of Muslim diaspora communities. In the past, as this book discloses, British Pakistani Muslims had always been a vocal minority, demanding equal citizenship rights, never afraid to speak their minds even if their opinions – support for the Iranian *fatwa* against Salman Rushdie or for Saddam Hussein during the Gulf War – were out of line with British popular sentiments. They felt sufficiently secure in Britain to express their political opinions, however contentious, without fear. Indeed, in their own public arenas, in the diasporic public sphere they had created for themselves, Manchester Muslims articulated familiar visions of apocalyptic battles between Islam and the West, especially the USA, the source of all evil. So too, they used Islamist rhetoric to attack Muslim regimes, criticising them for their corruption and weakness in the face of the West.

Michael Ignatieff has argued that faced with autocratic regimes which suppress all dissent, Muslim

> ... political opposition takes the form of apocalyptic nihilism, a rejection of the world as it is – the existence of the state of Israel, the failure of Arab leadership and its elites, the miserable inequalities of modernisation in the Arab world. Modern jihad seeks escape in fantasies of violent expulsion of the infidel, the driving of the Israelis into the sea and mortal strikes against the Great Satan.[1]

By contrast to the Middle East, however, in Manchester Muslim diasporic flights of rhetoric were rooted in a political imagination that made no serious attempt to implement its millennial fantasies. As I argue in this book, in imagining their different diasporas, local Pakistanis tended to position themselves imaginatively as the heroes of global battles. Now came the moment of real apocalypse, beyond the imagination, and with it a self-silencing by a people who were in the position to feel tangibly the potential rage and terror of the West.

[1] Michael Ignatieff, 'What Will Victory Look Like?' *The Guardian*, 19 October 2001, G2, p. 4.

1

2 Imagined Diasporas

Unlike the Iranian revolution or the Rushdie affair, the ensuing moral panic against Muslim minorities in Britain was relatively muted. A massive police presence was mounted in vulnerable neighbourhoods to deter possible attacks. Some mosques were daubed with graffiti, an Afghan taxi driver was seriously injured in London the day after the bombings, Asians (not just Muslims) were insulted in streets, buses and pubs as they went around their daily business. In America, there was more violence, with a Sikh man murdered. Above all, Asians and Muslims felt stigmatised as never before, associated with terror and subject of constant surveillance and suspicion. Young Asians moved around in groups. Women stayed home. Men avoided going out in the evenings. Businessmen suspected that customers were avoiding their firms. There was resentment as well as fear, a feeling of being perceived as unwanted outsiders.

Global images of terror, violence and fanaticism are contagious. As the world watched bin Laden and the Taliban condemning the West and calling for its destruction, or Muslim crowds burning American flags and Bush effigies in a violent display of hatred, it was hard for viewers in Britain not to associate these images with their neighbours next door. Nevertheless, a *Guardian* ICM poll found that 82 per cent of Britons had not changed their feelings towards British Muslims, and 88 per cent thought it unfair to link them to the terror attacks, according to an NOP *Daily Telegraph* survey.[2] Tony Blair, the British Prime Minister, stepped in to declare that Islam was a religion of peace and that the Qur'an did not condone suicide bombings. The battle was not, he assured Muslims and the public at large, between the West and Islam, but against a small number of evil individuals, terrorists. By now Huntington's 'clash of civilisations' – or its denial – had become the jargon of politicians and the media.

Akbar Ahmed points out in *The Guardian*[3] that 'The terrible and tragic events of September 11 have opened a Pandora's box of questions about Islam'. Among these, the status of suicide bombings remains unresolved. Arguably, the line between martyrdom and suicide in Islam is highly ambiguous. Nevertheless the Prime Minister and Muslim clergy in Britain invoked a moderate Qur'anic interpretation which was intended to protect local Muslims. They, in turn, condemned the World Trade Center bombings as they gathered in Downing Street for a media and press conference. Dressed in suits and ties, they spoke in rational tones and lucid English bearing only the trace of an accent. Gone were the Muslim mullahs of *The Satanic Verses* affair, with their long beards and foreign accents, declaring death to Rushdie in broken English. The men and women now representing the Muslims of Britain through the Muslim Council of Britain were highly respectable members of their communities and their tone was moderate. Here was an exemplary diaspora; a diaspora that understood its minority status and identified with its newly adopted nation. Yet the usual internecine divisions between Muslim organisations analysed in this book also surfaced immediately.[4] Nevertheless, the representatives demanded a change in British policy for which they had been struggling since the Rushdie affair: the extension of the Race Relations Act to include a clause against incitement to religious hatred. They used the opportunity presented by the global crisis to extend their bid for equal citizenship.

[2] Alan Travis, 'British Do Not See Islam as a Threat to Values', *The Guardian*, 12 October 2001, p. 4.
[3] Akbar Ahmed, 'Veiled Truth', *The Guardian*, 22 October 2001, G2, p. 6.
[4] Bodi, Faisal,'Muslims are a Multitude, Not a Lone Voice', *The Guardian*, 22 October 2001, 'Media', p. 6.

This was indeed a victory, but a bitter and double-edged one. The new law was intended as much to curb extremist Islamist rhetoric in British mosques as it was anti-Muslim racist discourses. London had become a centre of world Islamic terror. Quite explicitly, the envisaged law was not intended to silence pretentious postmodern writers or sacrilegious comedians who spoofed Islam. Yet the existence of such a law would probably have made the publication of *The Satanic Verses* actionable in court, even if the novel might ultimately have escaped banning or censorship.

In the early days of diasporic Muslim silence after September 11, whether sympathetic, pragmatic, or merely enforced, there were some lone voices of dissent. The Shaikh of a Naqshbandi Deobandi mosque in Manchester invited his congregation to raise their hands in support of the Taliban. A young *imam* at the Manchester Central Mosque told his youthful congregation in English that it was not bin Laden but the Jews who had bombed the NY Trade Center. This was proved by the fact, he said, that all the Jews had stayed away from the towers that day. But on the whole, criticism was muted. Muslims in Britain – and worldwide – were genuinely deeply shocked by the devastation and loss of life in Manhattan.

Nevertheless, as American bombing in Afghanistan assumed its fearful and monotonous pounding so familiar from the Gulf War, and as scenes of wounded Afghan civilians and on-the-ground devastation filled television screens, the usual British Muslim transnational identity politics reasserted itself, but with one important difference. This time the diaspora joined a growing British peace movement critical of the war or the way it was being fought. Muslims were able to share the same anti-American, anti-war rhetoric with others in the society. Rather than being seen as deviant and out on a limb, diasporic Muslims succeeded in creating alliances with local activists – CND, the English Left, anti-globalisation lobbyists, pacifists. Muslim, mostly Pakistani, spokespersons were young and articulate. But the sentiments and discourses had not really changed.

Political commitments can be very long-term and passionate, embedded in moral narratives of self and community. If, as I argue in this book, diasporas are transnational communities of co-responsibility, we need to disclose where their identifications, the centres of their subjective universe, lie. Undoubtedly, the sufferings of New Yorkers touched everyone. But not everyone saw New York as 'their' global city and New Yorkers as compatriots. The Evil Attack on the Free World, in the rhetoric of Western leaders, meant something different to those for whom the Manhattan skyline had a beauty and permanence of its own; who saw its towering skyscrapers not merely as the expression of unbridled capitalism but as cathedrals of modernity, embodiments of the human imagination and its desire to transcend itself. By the same token, while Westerners shared Muslim concern for Kashmiri, Palestinian or Iraqi victims of war, the pain felt by Muslims in the face of this suffering was one of shared selfhood. For Western liberals, the essential fragility of the capitalist economy compounded the horror of the mass murder. For most Muslims this economy was a side show if not an evil global plot. Everyone recognised that the attack was symbolic, but only Westerners fully comprehended its devastating consequences.

While people might agree that an act is heinous, as an aesthetic, embodied experience its impact varies between moral communities. This is a key point of the present book, developed in relation to the global conflict over *The Satanic*

Verses. That conflict, I argue, was above all a passionate argument about the aesthetics of the religious imagination. So too, ideas about politics and leadership differ. For most postcolonial Pakistanis, politics, even democratic politics, evokes a world of self-serving corruption and nepotism. As a result, they are deeply sceptical of all political leadership and state power. Yet they themselves are passionate political actors and so they go on believing that some place, somewhere, the ideal, exemplary political leader will emerge. Inevitably such a leader is envisioned as a charismatic saviour, bearing a religious mantle. In a society where most people are deeply pious, dissent is often couched in religious terms. The Prophet Muhammad was the exemplary leader for all times, legislator, holy man, warrior and statesman. Repeatedly, this book shows, outstanding individuals, from Muhammad Ali Jinnah to Imran Khan, are mythologised in local diasporic narratives as exemplary persons.

This also makes sense of the ambivalence surrounding the figures of Saddam Hussein or Usama bin Laden. A Pakistani survey in October 2001 found that – against the judgement of their own president – 86 per cent of the people of Pakistan believed there was no evidence linking Usama bin Laden to the World Trade Center bombings. In his posture and appearance, bin Laden projects the classic image of a pious, saintly Muslim world renouncer, a man who has abandoned his great wealth to live an austere existence in the desert for the sake of Islam, dedicating his life to the battle against Western domination. He speaks calmly and looks peaceful and almost ethereal. Such a man could not by definition be capable of mass murder. Hence the bizarre but nevertheless widely believed Jewish conspiracy theory, with the Jews accused, simultaneously, of being the evil arm of American imperialism *and* its hidden destroyers. Where a Westerner might see in bin Laden an evil megalomaniac, ordinary Muslims see a courageous *mujahiddin* contending with the evil forces that oppress Palestinians, Iraqis and Kashmiris, and that desecrate the holy lands of Islam.

This discourse of good and evil hides other diasporic vulnerabilities. Pakistanis in Britain are sensitive to the opinions and anxieties of friends and relatives on the subcontinent. They watch Pakistani satellite TV (there are several stations) and read Pakistani daily newspapers. They fear for the fate of their families back home if violence and civil war erupt there. They identify with the plight of the Afghan refugees or the Palestinians. No wonder, then, that neither the smouldering ruins of Ground Zero, still emitting acrid smoke over the Manhattan skyline six weeks after the devastation, nor the deadly and mysterious anthrax attack on the USA, nor even the rational pragmatism of President Musharraf, seem to them to justify the allied war with Afghanistan. The alliance with Arab regimes created so painstakingly by Britain and the US is treated with cynical scepticism.

This divergence of political interpretations, even if rooted in somewhat different political cultures, nevertheless does not amount to a clash of civilisations. After all, within the West too, perceptions of the conflict differ. As I write, in the first month of the air war over Afghanistan, there are reports daily of Afghan civilian casualties, and Americans seem to be fast losing the global sympathy their tragedy elicited. In the British press virtually all commentators, Muslim and English alike, preface their columns with reminders of the sufferings of Palestinians and Iraqis, and of America's complicit role in the rise of bin Laden and the Taliban. It is evident that neither Pakistani nor Western interpretations of the current crisis are uniform. They are *meroscopic*: partial, positioned, sited and inevitably perspectival political visions.

A young British Asian friend of mine, a sociology professor in the USA, by origin a Hindu who was born and raised in the Midlands, told me that she and her Asian friends in the USA were increasingly being subjected to surveillance by the authorities. For the first time in her life she has felt stigmatised as an outsider; for example, when one of her friends tried to board an air flight and was kept back for two hours, or when others were asked to appear before the authorities for no apparent reason. She feared greatly that civil liberties in America were being eroded as massive arrests of Muslims (mainly Arabs) took place both in the USA and in the rest of Europe.

If war were a cricket game, British Pakistanis could support their national cricket team without fear. As this book shows, the ambivalences of diasporic living, marked by multiple loyalties, do not ordinarily require resolution. But war is not cricket. Six weeks after the terror attack, the unacceptable face of British Islam resurfaced in the media, this time in the shape of young Pakistani men with marked English regional accents, who bore placards proclaiming that 'Islam will Dominate the World'. *Al-Mujahiroun*, a virulently anti-American and anti-Semitic Islamist organisation calling for the establishment of *khilafat*, a world-Islamic state, announced that young British Muslims who joined the jihad against the Western alliance, fighting alongside the Taliban in Afghanistan, would die as martyrs, *shaheeds*, for Islam. Young British Pakistani men, interviewed in Britain or in Pakistan – on their way to the Afghan front – affirmed openly on satellite TV that their first loyalty was to their Muslim religious brethren, even if this meant joining battle against their countrymen. In shocked response, the Secretary of Defence and MPs in the House of Commons evoked the spectre of treason and spoke of the failure of citizenship. Muslim leaders protested that the volunteers were a tiny minority. Yet looked at from the perspective of the British Pakistani community, young men's defiant defence of their religion, although mostly confined to verbal statements, underlined the truly tragic predicament of a diaspora caught between apparently conflicting loyalties. By now the vast majority of Pakistanis in Britain were solidly against the bombings in Afghanistan. Parents, afraid of losing their children to a culture of secularism and western consumption, had brought them up never to betray their Muslim identity. If the older generation of immigrant-settlers rejected *al-Mujahiroun*, as most did, they also felt alienated by British policy. The result appeared to be a widening chasm of the kind that occurred during the Rushdie affair and the Gulf War.

In the long run, however, moments such as these are part of a learning process that compels a diaspora to consider what diasporic citizenship really means.[5] The shades of political opinion that the global conflict evoked underline a central theme of this book: that the British Muslim diaspora can only be analysed in all its dialogical and heterogeneous complexity.

The tragedy is, as this book also documents, that in Manchester the majority of Pakistanis had moved on before September 11, away from religious radicalism to more positive activism for human rights. Women and young Pakistanis were increasingly taking their full place in society. With most of the first generation of immigrants on the point of retirement, the days of strangerhood

---

[5] See Werbner 2000b.

seemed to be over for many. True, there were still deprived inner city neighbour-hoods in Britain where unemployed Pakistani youths clashed with police and racist groups. This had happened in Oldham and Bradford in the summer of 2001, causing massive destruction of property and ending in fragile truces. But in the more affluent suburbs of Manchester or London, young British-born Asians, including Muslims, were entering university or embarking on professional careers.

The new global vulnerabilities that were revealed by the intensification of conflicts in the Middle East affected not only Muslims but Asians more generally, and even diasporic Jews living in the West. Such vulnerabilities raise the question whether members of diaspora communities can ever fully cease to be strangers.

Postcolonial narratives of diaspora

Postcolonial narratives of diaspora and exile situate the stranger as the archetypal figure of a globalising modernity. Referring back to works by Simmel (1950) and Schutz (1944), scholars such as Bauman too (1993: 148, 150; 1997) have focused on the ambivalent position of strangers as 'matter out of place' in modern nation-states, and on the correspondingly ambivalent senti-ments strangers evoke. This ambivalence is also seen at times to be a source of creativity. In losing their homeland, it is argued, strangers gain detachment and with it the possibility of aesthetic contemplation and moral integrity (Papaster-giadis 1993b, Chap. 3). The stranger-intellectual is both an objective, reflexive social observer-cum-scientist and an aesthetic renewer-from-the-margins, a producer of counter-hegemonic narratives. In many ways a cosmopolitan, he or she is open towards divergent cultures, tolerant of diversity, commanding what is culturally alien (Hannerz 1990: 239–40).

Hannerz makes a further useful distinction, relevant to the present work, between cosmopolitans and locals or transnationals. It is an opposition which echoes, on a *global* scale, an old anthropological distinction between encapsulated and non-encapsulated networks of labour migrants at the *national* scale.[6] Transnationals are persons who sustain their home culture away from home. They build around them surrogate cultural worlds which serve to shield them from the local culture into which migration or forced exile has inserted them. Unlike the cosmopolitan or stranger-intellectual, their intended project is not one of aesthetic mediation but of aesthetic consolidation and moral renewal. The encapsulated transnational communities formed by such strangers have their own organic leaders and intellectuals but these differ quite radically from the marginal intellectuals, the Salman Rushdies and Homi Bhabhas, whose works gain worldwide acclaim for their innovative originality.[7] Transnational leaders and intellectuals are rarely heard and even more rarely recognised and listened to beyond their own communities. They speak a foreign language or enunciate

[6] Philip Mayer, for example, contrasted 'Red' and 'School' circulatory labour migrants in East London, South Africa (Mayer 1961). The former maintained close-knit networks spanning town and country, and were culturally conservative in their leisure activities; the latter formed wide-ranging, loose-knit networks of friends made in town and explored new forms of consumption and entertain-ment.

[7] On this difference see van der Veer 1997 and Friedman 1997.

alien, widely unacceptable sentiments. They are nevertheless still intellectuals in the Gramscian sense, a 'buried intelligentsia', hidden from the public eye, who emerge only occasionally and exceptionally into the wider public arena.

This book is about the political imaginaries these invisible leaders narrate. It traces the early establishment of a diasporic public sphere and its dramatic visibilisation in response to the publication of *The Satanic Verses*. The movement followed is from a relatively benign sense of gradual integration of Muslim immigrants into British society to what seemed for a moment an almost cataclysmic *Kulturkampf*, and the ensuing struggle for multicultural citizenship which this encounter has generated.

Simultaneously with this global confrontation, the book follows a micro-political battle as it unfolded in a very local social drama: that of the rise and domination of a local *maulvi*, a charismatic religious cleric whose career, and the attempts to remove him from his post at the Central Mosque in Manchester, animated factional politics in the city for over a decade. The two conflicts – the global crisis that came to be known as the Rushdie affair and the bitter local struggle for honour and power – move the book forward to its final denouement.

The dialogics of identity

To narrate is to make sense of experience, to tell a meaningful tale. To make sense of the narratives of others is to construct a narrative of narratives, a fable of fables.[8] Central to my own narrative are the fables of diaspora told by overseas Pakistanis living in Britain in their attempt to understand who they are as moral human beings living outside their natal land. Their narratives are re-presented through their speeches, made at public meetings in Manchester, and in one case in Birmingham, over a period of several years. Alongside their narratives is my own academic narrative, an argument with other scholars debating the issues of ethnicity, migration, diaspora, identity, multiculturalism, cultural hybridity and racism.

The book starts from the insight that cultures, like languages, are produced and reproduced dialogically (Bakhtin 1981), and second, that the outcome of social encounters is critically determined by the social positioning of actors within their own societies. In both senses the book is an experiment in dialogical anthropology, one that goes beyond the postmodern stress on the dyadic encounter between anthropologist and cultural Other.[9] Against that emphasis, the present book seeks to analyse a range of dialogical encounters among Pakistanis themselves in order to disclose broader processes of cultural contestation and hybridisation. It is only by analysing specific social situations, I suggest, that we can grasp the contingency of culture and identity as they are negotiated through ongoing moral, aesthetic and political disagreements and discordant discourses. Just as Westerners carry their debates with them wherever they settle, so too South Asians have carried their political imaginaries and cultural disagreements into the diaspora. Such debates are compounded by divisions between generations of immigrants. Hence each of the two narratives traced here, that of

[8] 'Fable' is the Latin word for 'plot', 'mythos' in Greek, a feature of narrative I develop in Chapter 6.
[9] For an overview of dialogical anthropology as a dyadic encounter see Clifford (1988), Chap. 1.

the anthropologist-scholar debating with other scholars of diaspora and ethnicity, and that of the people at the centre of my study, is necessarily dialogical. Both narratives – the Pakistani and the scholarly – are unfinished arguments debated from different vantage points within two relatively autonomous epistemic fields of discourse.

In anthropology, dialogical strategies were intended to challenge the omniscient ethnographic authority of the anthropologist by exposing the process – and limitations – of fieldwork: the fact that research is conducted fortuitously and piecemeal, and hence that its ultimate representation of a seamless, 'whole', homogeneous culture is necessarily false.[10] Yet the fact that culture itself is dialogical means that the use of this notion cannot and should not be restricted merely to the engagement between the ethnographer and her/his culturally alien interlocutor, a tendency, we have seen, of much recent critical anthropology. For Bakhtin, dialogical language was both hybridised and political. Starting from his notion of the dialogical imagination (1981), the assumption made here is that the dialogical necessarily alludes to a far more pervasive condition of sociality and cultural creativity through argument than that which the individual encounter across cultures can capture.

For much of the book, then, the dialogical narratives, the Pakistani and the academic, are juxtaposed, running alongside one another. Deviating from this general narrative structure is a central chapter on the Rushdie affair. As a fieldworker and ethnographer of Pakistani society, I found that the Rushdie affair became for me a personal moment of crisis. My initial reaction to the calls for the author's death was one of disbelief and shock. The sense of the gulf between myself and the people who for years had been not only the subject of my scholarly research, but close friends whom I trusted and esteemed, was quite devastating. At the height of the affair I was advised to avoid public gatherings of Muslims because my Muslim friends feared for my safety. Muslim anger was a powerfully tangible presence. I could not betray my friends by being openly critical, yet the experience of being 'silenced' was deeply disturbing. From my position within modernity I simply could not comprehend my friends' perspective.

This kind of alienation is both humbling and revelatory for the anthropologist: I learned, first, that cultural differences could be all too real even for the 'tolerant anthropologist', and – as time went by – that understanding and communication across difference is a slow and painful process of mutual learning and persuasion. As an Israeli committed to the cause of peace and Palestinian independence in the Middle East, I had tried to conduct my research from a position of honesty considering who I was and where I came from. A good deal of my fieldwork thus consisted in animated arguments about political events, local, national and international, yet I found that, on the whole, I shared with many Pakistanis both a love of and an obsession with politics, key principles and views about international issues and the rights and wrongs of political conflicts. For the first time I found myself deeply alienated by the apparent irrationality of people who – while espousing the cause of Palestinians against *Jewish* fundamentalists – could appeal to the Qur'an as an *Islamic* endorsement of a death sentence against a novelist.

---

[10] See Clifford and Marcus 1986, Clifford 1988. This is not to concur with the postmodernist critique that realist modern ethnographies did, in fact, always make such holistic cultural assumptions.

It is, perhaps, a test of human friendship that such profound disagreements can be bridged, and it was only my trusting esteem for my Pakistani friends which compelled me to begin to understand the Rushdie affair as seen through their eyes. And, like many other scholars today, I have had to reflect upon the implications of my radical modernist position and its impotence in the face of religious and cultural passions. The resolution of my personal aporia as an anthropologist has been to argue, in writing, in the present book *with* those with whom I most profoundly disagree, rather than turning my back on them.

Chapters 4 and 5 of the book are thus in part a direct dialogical engagement with a Pakistani and Muslim audience. Starting from a neo-Kantian position, I argue that it is possible to explain the rationality of different cultural, moral and aesthetic grammars *across* cultures. Seen from a Western literary perspective, *The Satanic Verses* can be shown to be a great modernist novel written by an enlightened humanist rather than an affront to religion produced by a criminal. Yet I show too why, from the perspective of a high Muslim aesthetics, the novel is both a transgressive and a blasphemous text of the worst kind. My explicit aim is to disclose the rationality of both sides, for only by creating the grounds for mutual respect, I believe, can a resolution of this particular conflict between pious Muslims and a secular 'West', and others like it, be possible. Indeed, one could argue further that the anthropological project is one of discovering and disclosing the rationality of the other (see Asad 1993, Chap. 5), but, I would add, echoing McIntyre and others, that this disclosure can only be undertaken from a position of commitment to one's own values (McIntyre 1988). Starting from a relativist perspective, Richard Rorty has criticised the notion of absolute incommensurability between cultures espoused by Lyotard (1985), and argued that the anthropologist learns another culture by finding commonalities across differences (Rorty 1992a).[11] The problem is nevertheless one of establishing, as he says, the grounds of freedom in which a truly open 'respectful hearing' (ibid.: 63) or dialogue can take place.

I recognise, of course, that this dialogical attempt is itself utopian and is probably doomed to failure. It could also be argued that my utopian hope of mediating such a breach makes this book a constructed allegory of my own complex subjectivity. Yet it is perhaps one of the privileges of exile and diaspora, as the present book highlights, to envision utopian futures.

The massive scale of transnational cultures founded by post-World War II immigrant-settlers and refugees in the postcolonial, post-imperial West has disturbed earlier modernist conceptions of the nation as culturally homogeneous. Most distinctive about these new transnational cultures is, first, that they are free to be creative within a civil society that allows a good deal of space for autonomous voluntary action, and second, that they are able to consume the highly indus-trialised, mediatised and technologised products of a culture industry based largely in their natal homeland. The greater toleration of difference marking the current era of Western nationalism, like the efflorescence of cultural goods, has allowed diasporas to flourish and, indeed, influence world affairs as never before (Tololyan 1996: 21–6; Friedman 1997: 84–5; Melotti 1997). This book is about one such transnational community, at present adopting and, indeed, demanding this tolera-tion of difference, and the creative social spaces and narratives it has generated.

---

[11] A similar argument is put by Strathern 1987b in a critique of feminist scholarship.

By the year 2000, there were an estimated 120,000 Pakistanis living in Greater Manchester and the North West more generally, with the city forming the business and cultural hub of the whole region. In Britain as a whole it is estimated that there will be 750,000 citizens of Pakistani origin, out of a population of some 1.5 million British Muslims who are mostly young, British-born and concentrated in urban areas (Anwar 1996: 131). In statistical analyses, Muslims in Britain emerge as a relatively deprived group (Modood et al. 1997) but the community also has its wealthy members and an ever growing petit bourgoisie, many of them former factory workers. The rise of this class has been particularly evident in Manchester. About 30,000 Pakistani settlers and their children live in the city and its outlying suburbs.[12] Many are affluent and relatively educated businessmen and professionals, a feature of the Manchester Pakistani community which distinguishes it from Pakistanis settled in Bradford or Birmingham, for example, many of whom originated from relatively under-developed rural areas of Pakistan.

The Manchester community is small enough for people to know each other across class and neighbourhood. Networks of friends, family and acquaintances criss-cross the city. People meet on multiple indexical occasions, from weddings and communal Qur'an readings to funerals and public events (Werbner 1990a). The public events described here were organised by activists from a wide range of class and caste backgrounds. Although most of the actors are very local, many are connected to national and international networks beyond the city. Their oratory must thus be understood to be directed to a wider, more global audience.

Peacocks in the jungle

'If peacocks dance in the jungle, who can see them?' asks a Punjabi diasporic proverb, reflecting ironically on the paradoxes of diasporic existence. For diasporans, achievements of wealth and status are hollow unless they can display them before an audience living elsewhere, at home, in the authentic heartland of their imagined collectivity.[13] The fleshpots of the West are in this sense located experientially in a wasteland, a 'jungle', beyond human habitation. If that jungle is to be colonised and cultivated, it has to be remade as a known, significant place on a transnational map. This means, in effect, as the present book shows, that diasporans must constantly confront their invisibility through active acts of mobilisation and hospitality, and through public demonstrations of generosity which reach out beyond their locally constituted territorial communities. They must be seen to contribute real material or cultural goods *across* national boundaries through their political lobbying, fund-raising or works of poetry, art and music. Diasporans create havens of generosity for visitors (especially VIPs)

---

[12] An estimate based on a 50 per cent increase from the 1991 census of 20,000, a figure which includes Pakistanis living in Stockport and Trafford, most of whom work in the city centre or have lived there in the past. By 2000, there were about 75,000 Pakistanis in Greater Manchester (1991: 50,000). A high proportion of Pakistanis in Britain are very young, hence the high demographic increase, augmented by the arrival of spouses from Pakistan in quite high numbers (figures based on Anwar 1996: 17–20).

[13] Tololyan 1996 distinguishes between diasporans, subjects living in the diaspora, and the adjective diasporic which describes their condition.

and travellers, for refugees and tourists. In return, these itinerants bear witness that the diasporic jungle has been settled and civilised.

This stress on an active display of identification in the making of diaspora echoes Tololyan's recent call to analyse the embeddedness of diasporic subjectivities, the sites of 'double and multiple consciousness', in 'structures of diasporic polity and collective being' (Tololyan 1996: 28). These can only be achieved through 'doing' (ibid.: 16) or, more broadly, through *performance*. The invisible organic intellectuals of diasporic communities engage in constant practical ideological work – of marking boundaries, creating transnational networks, articulating dissenting voices, lobbying for local citizenship rights or international human rights – while at the same time they re-inscribe collective memories and utopian visions in their public ceremonials or cultural works.

But not all diasporas are the same and, indeed, the present work considers the entanglement of three quite different diasporic identifications animating the transnational subjectivities of members of one community, that of Punjabi Pakistani migrant-settlers in Britain. My analysis reflects critically on a growing scholarly literature which responds to the evident expansion of the concept and discourse of diaspora, attempting to probe its salient features and limits.[14] At issue is not only the postwar multiplication of new diasporas, as the term is embraced by different transnational intellectuals, but the growing promiscuity of the meanings of diaspora as it spills over into cognate discourses of postmodern multiplicity, border crossings and deterritorialisation.

What are the limits of diaspora? Conventionally, diasporas derive their imaginative unity from sacred time-space chronotopes of shared genesis, homelands, sacred centres and cataclysmic events of suffering (dispersion, genocide, slavery). The spatial and temporal orientations generated by these founding moments-places are those of ever-deferred re-turns or homings as Brah (1996) calls them, articulated, this book discloses, through commemorations and utopian visions of millennial renewal. It is these ideologies of a shared past and common destiny that connect the circuits of travellers and goods, and link diaspora communities to each other either directly, or via an originary centre out there. Yet despite and against these historical imaginings, such communities must be grasped, Avtar Brah and James Clifford remind us, as historically contingent social formations, experienced variably from different subject positions – of class, gender and political orientation (Clifford 1994; Brah 1996).

But the expansion of diaspora also entails, the present book proposes, a more radical conceptual rethinking: a recognition that the imagination of diaspora is constituted not merely by aesthetic products – novels, poems or films – but also by a compelling sense of *moral co-responsibility* and *embodied performance*, extended through and across national boundaries. An example of this is the voluntary labour and philanthropic giving vested for over half a century by British Pakistani settler-citizens in the project of building a diasporic community oriented towards its homeland, Pakistan. The present book analyses the way these sojourners raise money for this homeland, commemorate its founding moments and criticise its defects. Pakistanis in the diaspora mobilise vast sums for their nation at times of

---

[14] The most important contributions have been made by Safran 1991; Tololyan 1991 and 1996; Hall 1990; Gilroy 1993; Clifford 1994; Brah 1996; Anthias 1998; and for a review of recent diaspora discourse, see Werbner 2000a.

disaster and war. They host visiting dignitaries and dream of return. In this respect they form a conventional diaspora focused on a national homeland.

But at the same time Pakistanis have also redefined themselves as a *Muslim* diaspora. There are cogent grounds for arguing that universal religions cannot become diasporas (Cohen 1995: 188–9); above all, because they are philosophically grounded in a transcendence of space and time. To invent a Muslim diaspora against the grain has entailed for British Pakistanis a refocusing on the Islamic peripheries – on minority Muslim communities, often persecuted and displaced, beyond the Islamic heartland. Hence, Pakistanis in Britain have rediscovered their connection to Palestine, Bosnia, Chechnya, Kashmir. In their fund-raising efforts they work with major Muslim transnational non-governmental organisations such as Islamic Relief or the Red Crescent. Indeed, on reflection it seems evident that the Muslims of India have always harboured a diasporic consciousness: in the 1920s, for example, the pan-Indian *khilafat* movement which was founded to save the Ottoman Caliph was animated by a powerful diasporic political consciousness, even though, as Alavi has argued, the movement arose from a gross misreading of the real geopolitics of the time (Alavi 1997). Pakistan, like Israel, is the nationalist fulfilment of a diasporic vision anchored in a religious identity.

Being a *Muslim* diasporan does not entail an imperative of physical return to a lost homeland. It enables Pakistanis to foster and yet defer indefinitely the fulfilment of the myth of their return back home, while asserting their present responsibility for fellow diasporan Muslims – their membership in a transnational moral religious community, the *umma*. The Muslim diaspora opens up a diasporic space of critical dissent against corrupt leaders everywhere: the Arab world, Pakistan and the West. Through their locutionary pronouncements of dissent in public meetings, the book discloses, Pakistani settlers recentre Britain as a significant locus of the Muslim world, and hence also of diasporic action.

But being a Muslim diasporan is not an ontological finality for Pakistanis. It remains in tension with an equally compelling diasporic orientation towards a South Asian aesthetic diaspora: an aesthetic world embodied by the flow of mass popular cultural products from the subcontinent, and by a nostalgic reinscription in ritual and ceremonial of the pungent tastes and fragrant smells, the vivid colours and moving musical lyrics of a lost land. These, more than any diasporic novel written in English, stamp South Asia indelibly on subjects' diasporic bodies. The puritanical intellectual sobriety of Islam is for the majority of Pakistani settlers in Britain countered by the sheer pleasure of South Asian food and dress, films and poetry, comedy and parody, music and dance. Yet the transnational diaspora these performances embody is a *depoliticised* one that demands from its members nothing except enjoyment and consumption. There is no sense here of a moral or politically grounded transnational subjectivity, of responsibility for an other, even of a return. As a transgressive aesthetic, however, South Asia has nevertheless become for marginalised groups – women and youth – a source of powerful counter-narratives to Muslim male elder domination in the diasporic consciousness of British Muslim South Asians. Purity and fun, the book thus discloses, are implacably opposed in the politics of Muslim diasporic communities in the postcolonial world.

Can this transposed aesthetic of desire emanating from South Asia (itself an invention of a pan-Indian culture industry) be said to constitute a 'diaspora'?

Amitav Ghosh argues that South Asians form a diaspora of the 'imagination' (1989: 76), embodied by an 'epic' relationship between centre and peripheries. In extending this definition what needs to be recognised is the power of mass cultural production and trade to underwrite transnational communities in the postcolonial world (see Ong and Nonini 1997). Exported from South Asia (more rarely, from the West), this packaged culture constitutes a South Asian trans-national community otherwise divided politically and morally into national diasporas (Indian, Pakistani, Bangladeshi, Sri Lankan) and religious ones (Muslim, Hindu, Sikh, Jain, Buddhist, Christian), often locked in bitter and intractable con-flicts with one another. South Asia is perhaps best defined as the originary locus of a powerful *counter*-diaspora, transgressively interrupting pure narratives of origin and faith or over-policed boundaries (on such transgressions see Bhabha 1994).

Writing diaspora

One of the key features of the crisis of representation in anthropology has been to question realist anthropological genres of writing as modes of constructing other-ness or alterity. The dangers are seen to be of essentialising the other and inventing reified social entities, whether of community, culture or nation, from a false stance of objectivity, a stance which disguises the necessarily biased per-spective of ethnographers as socially positioned individuals. The crisis has led to a demand for a new dialogical engagement with the Other. At the same time new authenticities have also been evoked: of cultural hybrids, multiple voices, polyphony, contested representations, arguments of identity (see Werbner and Modood 1997).[15]

In this book I argue that Pakistanis create hybrid political discourses, often fusing in surprising combinations the stress on civil democratic rights with Islamic piety. Against simplistic celebrations of cultural hybridity, however, the ceremonials described here also highlight the situational co-existence of many valorised cultural purities, contextually enacted but nevertheless experienced as emotionally compelling. Being 'Pakistani', it becomes clear, far from referring to a reified identity, encompasses a historically produced multiplicity, created in response to diasporic and subcontinental movements: of Islamicisation, Empire, modernism and nationalism, further embedded in quite different regional and linguistic traditions.

The identifications these movements have produced for South Asians are sometimes fused but often kept separate through a series of set apart, 'framed' public celebrations. The narratives performed on these occasions construct fables of identity; they allegorise local power struggles and the predicaments of stranger-hood in a global idiom. But equally important for Pakistani settlers, the book shows, are their all-encompassing factional struggles for local power and honour. If the official message appears to be about the place of Islam in the world, the unofficial, indexical message is performative – a disguised parry in a local battle among male elders for control of Manchester's Central Jami'a Mosque, or

---

[15] For early invocations see Fabian 1983, Clifford and Marcus 1986, Marcus and Fischer 1986, Clifford 1988 and Rosaldo 1989.

between these elders and women for the right to active representation in the diasporic public sphere. Backstage meanings, as Goffman (1959) called them, may be understood only by a core of political activists who read the political barbs or threats and the tell-tale signs of future counter-attacks. In their speeches orators switch codes, even languages, directed at different audiences, especially if local civic leaders or visiting state dignitaries, British or Pakistani, are present. As in many rituals, a formal poetics may be interrupted by unofficial and often subversive interludes (see R. Werbner 1989, Chap. 3; Werbner 1990a, Chap. 9). But even apparently straightforward speeches disguise deeper meanings; replete with double entrendres, they contain ambivalent references to local conflicts and controversial figures that only those in the know, an inner cabal, understand. Hence who the speakers are, and the composition of the audience, are indexical markers in a game of metacommunication about relativities of local power. Seen together, both events and their narratives tell the dramatic tale of a battle for dominance between grassroots local leaders. At the same time what is disclosed is the processes through which collective political subjectivities – of gender, community, nation and diaspora – are reinvented in response to the emergence of new transnational communities and the experience of alien citizenship.

In presenting these public events and the hidden micropolitics of community that move them, my aim is also to elucidate the different kinds of silences with which diasporic Pakistanis are contending. On the one hand are the imposed silences produced by the majority population's social denial or negation. These are the silences of racism and cultural xenophobia. On the other hand are the voluntary 'silences' of submerged identities, highlighted situationally, in social interaction. These highly valued ethnic and gendered identifications – Islamic, South Asian, British, Pakistani, Punjabi, feminist – co-exist for actors, but they are kept apart and elaborated in different public arenas or identity 'spaces'. Racism and ethnicity, I argue, entail different forms of ethnic mobilisation. In sum, then, the book explores the cultural performances staged by members of diasporic communities in the social spaces they create. Through these performances they both respond to racism and xenophobia and also naturalise their multiple identities, vesting them with current value in Britain.

The focus on public events and cultural performances has been theorised most comprehensively by Sandria Freitag (1989a & b) along with other anthropologists and social historians studying the place of popular culture in South Asia (see especially Kumar 1988 and Metcalf 1982). In their analyses, these scholars consider public events as historically significant moments in which relations of class, patronage, identity, community, communal conflict and social protest are articulated. Public events are often structured in debate, in agonistic competition and in dialogue. In British India, Freitag argues, the emergent 'gap' between indigenous South Asian popular public arenas and the colonial state created a 'space' for new leaderships and popular movements, while fuelling episodic moments of communal violence which the state was impotent to control effectively (Freitag 1989a).

In the contemporary world Muslims are more than ever locked in agonising debates among themselves about aesthetics, law and morality, a feature of Islamic society stressed by Michael Fischer and Mehdi Abedi with brilliant insight in *Debating Muslims* (Fischer and Abedi 1990). Whereas that book travels widely, from Iran to Mecca to Houston Texas, the present book is narrowly focused on the openly public and yet invisible politics of dissent. This is not a book about 'hidden transcripts', as Scott (1992) aptly calls informal modes of resistance; although the arguments of identity it traces are mostly performed far from the public eye, they nevertheless take place publicly, in arenas established and sustained by migrant settlers in Manchester, a city of immigrants since its very inception. The passion with which speakers vest their rhetorical performances is hard to capture in a written text. Through gesture and voice, orators attempt to move and mobilise their audiences. They enact dramatically, often with some exaggeration, a whole range of emotions from anger and rage to sorrow, love or despair. In this respect the Punjabi protagonists at the centre of this book differ from the laconic Pathans who, according to Lindholm (1996, Chap. 11) suppress any public show of emotion.[16]

This discussion of public arenas needs to be placed in the broader context of a debate regarding civil society and the emergence of a public sphere in the bourgeois nation-state. Habermas has defined the public sphere as an arena in which private individuals meet to deliberate on matters of public significance (Habermas 1989; see also 1992). My focus here is on the diasporic public sphere, defined as a series of interconnected spaces in which the pleasures and predicaments of diaspora are debated and celebrated. In drawing the parameters of this sphere, my aim is not to reify a substantive division between private and public which feminists have rightly challenged; instead, the present book highlights the fluidity and multiplicity of issues and arenas which constitute the public sphere. Reflecting critically on the modern public sphere, Seyla Benhabib has argued for a need to recognise its increasing 'porousness' and complexity, which arise because 'neither access to it nor its agendas for debate can be predefined by criteria of moral or political homogeneity' (1992: 94). Nancy Frazer (1992), critiquing the narrow definition of the bourgeois public sphere proposed by Habermas, argues that women and other marginalised groups from the beginning created a counter civil society or counterpublics to the official, hegemonic public sphere. A truly functioning democracy, she argues, requires such subaltern counterpublics,

> parallel discursive arenas where members of subordinated social groups invent and circulate counter-ideologies to formulate oppositional interpretations of their identities, interests, and needs. (Frazer 1992: 123)

The Pakistani public sphere in Manchester which is the subject of my book differs from Gilroy's black 'alternative' public sphere of 'story-telling and music-making' (1993: 200) in being non-commercial and discursively focused around public meetings and ceremonials. But it shares with that alternative sphere a sense of opening up a space for dissenting and emancipatory discourses, outside and beyond the official, national public sphere, of being the locus for the mobilisation in social movements. The public sphere is, as Frazer too recognises (1992: 110), a theatre 'enacted through the medium of talk'. In extending this metaphor, I show that the actors in this subaltern drama not only give voice to their views and interests; they act out in public a tragic drama of personal conflict and rivalry, performed in front of a partisan and highly committed audience.

---

[16] For a review of the literature on the affective dimensions of performance more generally, see Kratz 1993.

Invisible identities & social movements

Recent work on social movements has located their existence in invisible networks within the public sphere, emerging suddenly and sporadically, as happened in the Rushdie affair, to resist the encroachment of multinational capitalism, neoliberalism and the state into civil society (Touraine 1981; Castells 1983, 1997 & 1998; Melucci 1989). As Melucci in particular has shown (see Melucci 1997; also 1996a and 1996b), in a world in which planetary codes are beamed through the media and the state the work of identity is one of first discovering and then negotiating shared identities.

In the present book I draw on these discussions to develop a theoretical framework for the analysis of *ethnic* social movements. Ethnic and religious movements resemble other new social movements, I argue, in fostering alternative identities and lifestyles which are submerged in the invisible spaces diasporic groups create for themselves, far from the public eye. Within these spaces they debate and argue over moral, political and existential issues affecting their group. What needs to be further explained is how the small, fractionised ethnic and religious associations which foster these debates are able to mobilise periodically on a much broader scale. This high level of mobilisation was evident, for example, as the book shows, in the British Muslim response to the Rushdie affair and the Gulf crisis. For most of the time, however, Pakistani and Muslim identity-creating associations are engaged in internecine conflicts of honour. Paradoxically, these invigorate and renew ethnic identities, and reproduce the diasporic community in all its dialogical complexity. *Internal conflict and disagreement are thus reproductive of transcendent ethnic identities, a key point of the book.*

If ethnic ceremonials are mainly invisible, they are still constructed symbolically as moments set apart from the flow of the quotidian, of the taken-for-granteds of everyday life. This symbolic dimension of public events has been explored by Don Handelman (1990), who focuses on the *architectonics* of these events. Handelman analyses public ceremonials as crystallisations of particular symbolic complexes and representations of self and community, but also as negotiated encounters or social situations.[17] Complementary to this approach are the works of French theorists such as Lefebvre and Bourdieu on social spaces. They argue that social spaces are imaginatively and materially constructed, yet, unlike institutionalised spaces, they are empowered or negotiated through contestation (Lefebvre 1974/1991; Bourdieu 1985). Because public arenas are symbolically constructed, the 'spaces' they open up are also cultural embodiments of historically situated identities. This points to the fact that the creation of diasporic spaces of identity requires significant material investment and hence also social mobilisation. Social space in this sense may be defined as the nexus of financial, organisational and cultural investment.[18]

---

[17] The analysis of 'social situations' and social dramas was a key feature of the Manchester School of Social Anthropology which began with an original essay first published in 1940 by Max Gluckman on the ceremonial opening of a bridge in modern Zululand (Gluckman 1958).

[18] Increasingly, anthropological studies of performance privilege processes of active contextualisation rather than assuming context (or text) as givens (Bauman and Briggs 1990).

Arguments of identity

As we have seen, Pakistanis belong in a taken-for-granted way not to a single diaspora but to several *different* diasporas – Asian, Muslim, nationalist Pakistani, Punjabi – a *hybrid* diaspora, each with its own aesthetics and ethics, which is imagined and performed rhetorically through cultural events. The need to distinguish between these diasporas is a key theoretical point of this book as a whole. Each chapter in turn examines different types of cultural performance which celebrate different imagined diasporas – the Pakistani 'nation', the Asian 'community', the Muslim *'umma'*, the South Asian 'diaspora'. Intersecting with these visionary narratives are the often clashing political ideas held by actors about the nature of democracy, citizenship, power, morality and identity.

Just as there are two parallel narratives – the Pakistani and the scholarly – which run alongside each other, so too these various cultural performances are juxtaposed in the book in a complex collage. Narrative time is only partly followed; the story line shifts back and forth between past and present to make theoretical points, and follows chronological time in order to highlight the moral plot, the social drama at the centre of the book. In other words, I make no attempt to create through narrative an illusion of transparency, of a seamless whole. Nor do I claim that the range of events reported here is comprehensive in any sense. Every year in Manchester alone dozens of such events take place. The book is quite explicitly a *construction*; the nuts and bolts, the shifts between fieldnotes and interpretation, the *gaps* between events and voices, are evident. Inevitably, the final product is *my* construction. At the same time my aim in adopting this explicitly disjunctive representational strategy is also to make some serious theoretical points. One of these points has already been made, namely, that social life is dialogical and hence culture, identity, tradition, history and community are the products of processes of argument.[19] Indeed, what makes modern Islam so fascinating and remarkable is precisely its members' arguments among themselves about who they are and where they are going. This feature of social life is not, however, uniquely Islamic, but a crucial feature of many postcolonial societies.[20] Cultural objectification in the modern world is a continuous process, not a fixed reality.

One may even go further to suggest that arguments of identity are not simply the product of modernity and postcoloniality. They are the very stuff of culture. Social life itself is dialogical, Richard Werbner argues, even at its most minute, micro scale of human interaction (R. Werbner 1991, 1995). Werbner shows how Kalanga in rural Zimbabwe argue or disagree about the past, about memories and events which affected them, and about how these events are to be interpreted as moral narratives. Indeed, strangerhood, he demonstrates, is not merely a Western modernist trope but a predicament experienced in colonial as well as postcolonial Africa (R. Werbner 1989). Cultural dilemmas and alternative ways of being and creativity 'make' culture, not as a received, museumised object (Friedman 1997),

---

[19] This point is recently disclosed in a whole series of monographs written by anthropologists and cultural historians. They include a host of books on Muslims societies, from the early works of Geertz and Gellner, to more recent ethnographies of a changing Muslim world (e.g. Kumar 1988, Fischer and Abedi 1990, Launay 1992, Asad 1993, Lambek 1993, Bowen 1993; Kepel 1985).

[20] See, for example, Dominguez 1989; Paine 1989; Handelman 1990; R. Werbner 1991; Tsing 1993; Hutchinson 1996. And on contemporary Pakistan, see Ewing's masterly analysis of different encounters between saintly believers and modernity (Ewing 1997).

but as a dialectically emergent reality. Similarly, the present book aims to refute the view that strangerhood, internal difference and the dialogical imagination are exclusively modernist Western tropes of thought and being.

Hence, a central point of this book, one which I believe bears constant repetition, is that none of the social unities we evoke – identity, diaspora, community, nation, tradition – are consensus-based wholes; all are the products of ongoing debates and political struggles or alliances. It is in the rejection of the possibility of debate that violence occurs. This is the second point of the book, one which I develop in Chapter 1 and follow through to the Conclusion. Racial violence is the opposite of everyday ethnicity or multiculturalism – of arguments of identity – because it institutes as truth an absence of dialogue, a silence, a turning away. Instead of mutual recognition and moral responsibility, racism and xenophobia are the products of violation and *misrecognition*.

Honour & the politics of dignity

My third point relates to the issue of identity and, even more specifically, the *public performance* of identity. In a landmark essay, Charles Taylor has argued that the notion of identity was first problematised by the Enlightenment in its envisioning of a shift from a society based on 'honour', rank and status within a hierarchical system, to a society based on the right to 'dignity' – to be respected as a unique individual or collectivity within an egalitarian system. Dignity, the right not to be *mis*recognised, is, according to Taylor, a defining feature of modern citizenship (Taylor 1992: 35). The notion can be traced to the Kantian idea that all individuals are potentially rational moral agents, and to Rousseau's and Herder's views that all human beings have the right to follow the moral inner 'voice of nature' within them, or (in the case of Herder) their authentic collective cultural truths. It is these unique individual and collective claims to be recognised which have, of course, precipitated many modern nationalist movements. *Within* the nation-state the claim to equal dignity implies not simply equality before the law, based on the Kantian appeal to a transcendental individual human rationality, but also the right to have one's culture recognised and its reproduction, its continued identity, assured. Citizenship in the 'decent society', Avishai Margalit has argued, 'must be egalitarian in order not to be humiliating' (1996: 154). 'Symbolic' citizenship implies that symbols directed explicitly or implicitly against some citizens of the state should not be given institutional support (ibid.: 161). The right to symbolic citizenship is at the heart of the aporia we call multiculturalism – the dilemma of how to balance universal equal individual and collective dignities and particularities in the face of the contention that a 'supposedly neutral set of difference-blind principles of the politics of equal dignity is in fact a reflection of one hegemonic culture' (Taylor 1992: 43; see also Werbner 1997a & b).

There are, of course, many pragmatic resolutions of this dilemma. Some of these are spelt out in the following chapters. I have certain doubts, however, whether an evolutionary narrative of progress, marking a radical rupture between societies of 'honour' and 'dignity', is as self-evident as Taylor assumes. True, the metaphysical groundings of the rights of strangers to be different have changed. Cain was condemned to exile from his land, to be 'a fugitive and a vagabond', away from home. But the mark of Cain, let us recall, is the mark not of Cain's dishonour but of God's *protection* (Genesis 4: 15). The tradition of recognising and honouring the stranger is not a modernist one. The Prophet Muhammed was welcomed by the citizens of Medina and ultimately made governor of that city. The *rejection* of the stranger – of Joseph and Miriam – is re-enacted annually in Christian nativity plays as the ultimate sin. I stress these biblical and Qur'anic parallels here to underline the commonalities between the three great monotheistic religions.[21] Rather than the 'clash of civilisations' posed by Huntington (1993), oppositions between Islam and Christianity or Judaism themselves represent arguments of identity and political struggles for 'honour' and 'dignity', not fundamental divisions of dogma.

When I initially read Taylor's essay it seemed to shed light on the narrative structure of the present book. The book was (I thought) a juxtaposition of an internal, *intra*-ethnic 'politics of honour', grounded in Pakistani/Punjabi ideas about honour (*izzat*) and shame (*sharm*) with an external, *inter*-ethnic, 'politics of dignity' in British society. Hence, or so it seemed initially, the moral plot of my book traces the development of this double politics of identity and the dialectical relation between them.

Yet on second thoughts I found this neat dualistic picture to be misleading. The very notion of *izzat* connotes, ambiguously, status, rank, honour *and dignity*. As I have argued in an earlier work, for Pakistanis the dialectics of Muslim caste and hierarchy are played out in constant tension with the egalitarian ethos of Islam (see Werbner 1990a). At the same time modernity too, as Habermas for example has argued, is characterised by a dialectical tension: between the inva-sive forces of modernity, of economic and state administrative 'rational' systems, which determine an unequal allocation of 'honour' in the name of rational efficiency, and the 'lifeworld' – the lived-in world of implicit understandings and personal recognition (Habermas 1987). Undoubtedly, however, these tensions are played out historically in different idioms. At the local, grass-roots political level described in this book, the battle for honour *within* the community differs from the politics of recognition addressed to the state and the wider society.

In a critique of Dumont's construction of Hindu India as a holistic order which allows no spaces for egalitarian individualism (Dumont 1970), and of Marriott's definition of Hindu subjects as 'dividuals' lacking autonomous self-containment (Marriott 1976), Mattison Mines offers an alternative vision of South Asian individuality (Mines 1994). Ambitious men in Tamil Nadu, he demonstrates, aspire to achieve positions of civic responsibility which mark them out as unique individuals, set above ordinary men. Individualism in South Asia is thus not so much absent but achieved as a mark of honour in recognition of public responsibility and service. Sara Dickey's illuminating account of the charitable fan clubs established by Tamil film stars also highlights this drive towards civic recognition, even by the very famous (Dickey 1993).

Mines' insight allows us to bridge the apparently incompatible approaches to South Asian politics exemplified, on the one hand, by Barth's and Bailey's early accounts of the centrality of maximising, networking man in South Asian politics (Barth 1959; Bailey 1969), and, on the other hand, Dumont's structural holism

---

[21] Even beyond the Near East, as Bikhu Parekh reminds us, the Hindu epic *Ramayana* has as its central theme 'exile, suffering, struggle and eventual return' (Parekh 1994: 613).

which posits that only world renouncers may achieve individuality – by placing themselves outside and beyond the temporal world of politics. Civic individuality in South Asian politics can be seen to mediate between political ambition and world renunciation by opening a space for selfless service for the common good which must, nevertheless, be competed for and attained agonistically. Like active citizenship in the West, the achievement of civic individuality implies a transcendence of narrow, selfish, individual interests (Phillips 1993). This explains why *seva* or *khidmat*, selfless communal service, is frequently seen by South Asians as a condition of leadership and honour.

One strand of Muslim politics evident especially in the diaspora is concerned with a defence of the legitimacy of Islamic symbols. Veiling, for example, while not inherently political, becomes so, as Eickelman and Piscatori note, when transformed into a public symbol (1996: 4). Thus Islamists, disillusioned with pusillanimous, corrupt Muslim regimes, call for a global *umma* and a return to a pristine political Islam, an idealised ethical order in which veiling becomes part of a larger symbolic complex which imaginatively re-enacts the foundational moment of Islam. In the Rushdie affair, the perceived vilification of the Prophet, a living presence for most British Muslims, was experienced as a humiliating attack on their symbolic citizenship in Britain.

That recognition and respect in the diasporic public sphere – 'honour' and 'dignity' – are matters of passionate concern for diasporic Pakistanis is a key argument developed here. The book follows the quest of subaltern leaders for dignity in many overlapping struggles: in the battle for honour which often spills over into violent factional conflict (Chapters 1 and 9); in the determination of local-level organic intellectuals to gain recognition for their 'community' and nation (Chapters 2–4); in the protests against *The Satanic Verses*, the battle to get the blasphemy law extended, and the defence of Saddam Hussein during the Gulf crisis (Chapters 5–7). The quest for honour is conducted through charitable donations and celebrations by women, cricketers and young men (Chapters 7 and 8). The same desire for recognition was evident in the welcome given by the British Muslim press to Prince Charles's announcement that he wished to become defender of 'all faiths', not just of Christianity. The analysis traces the way in which different political imaginaries of identity are rhetorically constructed: of nation and of 'community' (in Chapter 3), of the Islamic *umma* (in Chapters 4–6), and of the Punjabi and South Asian cultural diaspora (in Chapters 7–8). In Chapter 2, I show that these different political imaginaries of diaspora can also be fused in the oratory of local subaltern politicians, as they attempt to move their audiences and mobilise their support.

Part One looks at the invisible spaces in which the micropolitics of community are played out. Chapter 1, the opening chapter of the book, sets the scene. It analyses the lines of cleavage – religious and sectarian, by *biradari* (kinship-cum-caste group), class and gender, cultural, political, ideological and personal – which are the elementary social divisions out of which transversal alliances and factional alignments are formed among Pakistani settlers. And it introduces the main protagonists to the conflict whose fortunes are traced in the rest of the book as they appeared at a particular moment in history, through a series of civic and ceremonial events.

Chapter 1 thus tells the story of a community at war with itself. Drawing comparatively on the literature about factionalism in the subcontinent, it raises

the question of why *violence* appears to be so endemic in local-level British Pakistani politics. What makes these politics so passionate, and how does factionalism
serve to buttress and enhance the influence of radical nationalist and religious
ideologies and their proponents among British Pakistanis? What is the relationship
between ethnic diasporic public arenas, the state and global politics?

Chapter 2 raises the issue of identity and the aesthetic-cum-moral construction
of diaspora in relation to the emergence of anti-racist, ethnic and religious social
movements. It also introduces the reader to one of the key protagonists in the
social drama narrated here, and to the moral arguments of identity he raises
against his factional opponents.

Pakistanis *globalise* their local predicaments by interpreting their local conflicts
as moral dramas, analogous to historical and international world-shattering
events. Political mythologies are grasped here as moral narratives, and their chief
characters personify abstract qualities (see also Malkki 1995: 54). Chapter 3
examines the dialogical imaginings of Pakistan as a modern nation-state by
leaders of two rival Pakistani factions vying for political and religious hegemony
in Manchester. The chapter argues that Islamic collective myths are distinctive in
focusing on exemplary, 'perfect' persons. Hence, Muhammad Ali Jinnah is appropriated as an exemplar of national perfection by groups holding *opposing* political
ideologies of state and nation. The oppositions reflect different conceptions of time
and history – of the past in the future. Hence, like most collective myths, I show,
narratives of nation conflate past events and future aspirations or fears in a
visionary unity. The central place of memory and commemoration in these
mythic constructions has to be understood in the light of current debates about
the significance of identity and memory (e.g. Antze & Lambek 1996; R. Werbner
1998).

The conclusion to Part One refers to an event that mythologised the emergence
of a successful and prosperous immigrant community in Manchester. This narrative of 'community' was one created jointly by settlers and their English hosts. The
story told from the podium of this meeting was one of increasing prosperity and
integration into British society. It glossed over a darker reality of racism and
deprivation, and of intractable factional and religious divisions, a reality that
surfaced in other contexts and was articulated from other platforms. The chapter
raises the question as to whether the official representation of Muslim immigrant
integration as a 'success' has survived. Could the congratulatory atmosphere at
the meeting be repeated after the Rushdie affair, or has the affair left an indelible
historical trace which now necessarily permeates all British Pakistani collective
narratives?

Part Two examines the visibilisation of the Muslim community in Britain as it
clashed publicly with the state over the publication of *The Satanic Verses* and,
later, supported Saddam Hussein during the Gulf War. Chapters 4 and 5 deal
with the central historical moment in the book, when Pakistanis moved bodily on
to the 'streets' of Britain. Chapter 5 analyses the speeches made by local Pakistani
councillors to defend Muslims against the charge of being irrational 'fanatics'.
Chapter 6 focuses on *The Satanic Verses* itself, and analyses the gap between a
Muslim aesthetic of the sublime and a modernist aesthetic of imperfection. The
chapter explores the problem of cultural translation, arguing against decon-
structivist and extreme postmodernist approaches, for the possibility of dialogue
across cultures. At the same time, the chapter probes the reasons for the Muslim

outrage in response to the novel. My aim in the two chapters is to expose not only an argument *with* British society but an internal Islamic argument between radicals, calling for the death of the author, and moderates, attempting to find common ground with other religious communities.

Chapter 6 plots the rise of an organically hybrid, 'magical' Islamic radicalism which combines religious ecstasy and a love of the Prophet with a modernist rhetoric of civil rights. It shows how speeches made in Manchester in the months preceding the Gulf War constitute a hybridised discourse of protest. Like early Methodism, the chapter argues, key actors in the drama of contemporary Sufi Islam are lay preachers and community leaders who play an important role in articulating the political frustrations of ordinary Muslims. Such lay preachers fabulate current affairs to construct imaginary nations, communities and diasporas, co-existing in a global space. They create moral fables of good and evil and it is such a moral fable, the chapter argues, which explains why Saddam Hussein came to be regarded as a hero rather than a villain by local Pakistanis and, indeed, by the Muslim 'street' worldwide.

Part Three of the book examines the emergence of new popular cultural spaces beyond the mosque and community elder politics. Chapters 7 and 8 juxtapose a series of popular cultural events as spaces of 'fun' in order to highlight the conflict among the puritanical demands of Islamic reform movements, modernist ideas about nationalism and the aesthetics of South Asian popular culture. Most Pakistanis, I argue, are able to participate in these three aesthetic and moral 'worlds' through the management of situational *separations* or *disjunctions*. In particular, the popular culture of weddings, performed in hidden feminised spaces, and cricket, a privileged domain of masculinity, empower women and young men, often marginalised by community elders and excluded from the diasporic public arena. The globalised reach of the South Asian media has meant that popular culture is all-pervasive, enabling diasporic Pakistanis to embrace a tolerant Islamic vision and creating a bridge to the wider South Asian diasporic community. The centrepieces of these chapters are the visits to Manchester by Imran Khan – on his first visits still the revered and adulated Captain of the Pakistani national cricket team – and the passionate responses these visits generated. Yet the apparently irrepressible dimensions of popular culture as 'fun' raise profound sociological questions: why is the new Islamicism unable to stamp out these moments of effervescence? Why is it the *Asian* public sphere which is most prominent nationally in Britain, institutionalised in the media and press?

Chapter 9 draws together the various chapters of the book by revealing the final fate of the protagonists in their factional battle for honour, while concluding the processual analysis of the structure and organisation of factional conflicts among Pakistanis in urban Britain. The chapter reflects on the rise of Islamophobia and the difference between essentialising discourses of racism and those of a shifting, multicultural 'ethnicity'.

Finally, the Conclusion raises the general question of emancipatory politics and relates it to the need to conceptualise a theory of the *heterogeneous community*. Rather than rejecting the notion of culture and community altogether, the chapter argues, the necessity to recognise that communities are created by arguments of identity, negotiated from different subject positionings and imagined through partial, meroscopic visions. This chapter also highlights the emergent activism of Pakistani women in the diaspora.

The realm of ideology, of politicised religion and culture, is not the only one, of course, in which British Pakistanis (Punjabis, Muslims) participate. Urban life itself is marked for most citizens by intermittent forays into the public sphere which interrupt the routines of daily life. This disjunctive mode of living is captured by the discursive strategy of the book with its gaps and interruptions, and with its shifts in scale. The politics described here point to the fact that the public sphere, regarded in terms of the reach of its audiences and the authoritative impact of its pronouncements, is a highly complex, plural and, indeed, *tiered*, ranked sphere.

In an earlier book on community formation among British Pakistanis in Manchester (Werbner 1990a), I analysed the way Pakistani ethnic identities and moralities were reproduced in symbolic and material relations between households through ceremonial and ritual exchanges controlled by women. This *inter-domestic domain*, I argued there, mediates between the utterly private and the unambiguously public. At its most inclusive, the cultural performances marking this domain – weddings and funerals – mobilise several hundreds, and even thousands, of people connected in durable relationships to a particular household or set of households.

The interdomestic domain remains focused, however, on familial and personal concerns and performances. A real 'ethnic' diasporic public sphere emerges only when the discursive focus of narratives, and the principles of mobilisation, are no longer simply personal but public and political. When the personal *becomes* political. The public sphere is the sphere of politicised culture, of identity politics, of religious ideology, of anti-racist strategising. The narratives constructed within this sphere are narratives of collective rather than individual or familial subjects. This diasporic public sphere is one which ethnic or religious communities must create themselves. They must actively construct the context as well as the poetics for the performance of identity. Pakistanis, I show, have been engaged in a process of discovering how to become an effective diaspora. To be an effective diaspora is not within the gift of the state or the wider civil society. The diasporic condition is one which is learnt through experience and experimentation. Once a public sphere emerges, it serves, despite its restricted reach, as a forum in which the issues debated transcend the personal and familial to engage with global events and national conflicts. From time to time, Pakistanis who are also Muslims, Punjabis and British, mobilise to make these issues, at least temporarily, matters of wider public concern. This book is about those debates, conflicts and periodic mobilisations.

I
Invisible Spaces

1
Villains & Heroes in a Game of Honour

In 1985, a man died in Manchester of a heart attack, following an affray in the Central Mosque (*Arabia* 1985). In 1988 another man died of a heart attack after being punched in the chest during a fight between two opposed British Pakistani neighbourhood-based associations.[1] At certain phases in the history of the British Pakistani community, political violence has surfaced in the public arena. Pakistani public meetings are often confrontational and charged with passion. The intensity of political action is a potent and tangible current running through these events.

If diasporic Pakistanis' local-level politics is often concerned with apparently minor or even trivial issues, why is such politics so volatile and potentially violent?

In a sense it may be argued – as, indeed, local activists in Manchester told me in response to this question – that this is the way politics is conducted in Pakistan as well. In other words, Pakistani *political culture* is a volatile and potentially violent culture. The politics of the subcontinent is a politics of honour and shame, of *izzat*. It could also be argued that the marked encapsulation of diasporic Pakistanis in Britain, their exclusion from positions of status and honour in the national public sphere, makes positions *within* the community prizes of such immense significance that they inspire competition to the point of violence. A man's status derives from his internal communal position, the offices he holds in key local Pakistani associations.

At first glance, most Pakistani associations are of the *'tonga'* ('rickshaw') variety; their active membership is restricted to office-holders and a rather limited number of supporters. What puzzled me and moved me to embark on the intricate study of communal micropolitics was the fact that despite the small size of any particular association, events such as elections or protests could mobilise over a thousand men. What dynamic connected the tiny associations, one-man bands, 'letterhead' groups, which pretended to 'represent' 'the community' to the outside world? What enabled their mobilisation across the broad diasporic political arena of a vaguely demarcated territory called 'Manchester'? To answer these questions, and to appreciate why public events became increasingly confrontational from the 1980s onwards, we need to examine the pattern of *alliances* created between such associations. The political field is a *unitary* one, cutting across class, regional and occupational divisions. Public events are 'testing' occasions within this broader field (see Bailey 1969). It is this crucial feature

---

[1] A report of this fracas appeared in the *Manchester Evening News* at the time (date unavailable).

which allows comparison between the political culture of overseas Pakistanis and South Asian factional alliance politics.

To unravel the complexities of local-level politics within Manchester's diasporic public sphere, I begin with a description of an electoral contest which I witnessed in 1987. What seemed at the time a single, minor event turned out to be determined by a complex patterning of political alliances. It revealed that political blocs in Manchester, as in South Asia, are *composite* alliances of associations active in different political arenas. Yet although such alliances are pragmatically negotiated, they are grounded in long-term historical processes and structural contradictions. The need is thus for a model which shows how political maximising comes to be interpolated by religious and ideological movements.

The Pakistani diasporic public sphere is, of course, a highly restricted one created by British Pakistanis as an autonomous and apparently self-contained network of arenas. The languages spoken in its arenas are principally Urdu or Punjabi, the events convened nationalist (Pakistani) or religious (Islamic), the candidates for office – as well as their supporters – of Pakistani origin. Yet within this arena, resources and accolades offered by the British state and the local government or by the home country, Pakistan, are highly sought after 'external' prizes.

The 'halagula'

In June 1987 the Manchester Longsight Pakistani community held elections for a Community Representative, to serve on the City Council's Race Sub-Committee. There were three main contenders for the position, and each had mobilised his own group of supporters. The election aroused a great deal of interest in the local community, and on the appointed day the election hall was packed, with many people forced to stand, crowded along the walls and at the back of the hall. This made counting of votes almost impossible. An initial attempt to base the count on a simple show of hands ended in confusion. A second attempt to congregate each group of supporters in a different section of the hall, while shifting people from their seats, simply added to the confusion. During the third – and decisive – count, one of the candidates, Chaudhry Amin, along with one of the other two, announced, quite unexpectedly, that they had decided to run on a *joint* ticket (as Community Representative and Deputy). Not surprisingly, this announcement was followed by a tremendous uproar from the crowd; in effect, the two candidates had changed the rules of the game midplay, as they were approaching the goal posts.

The outcome of the voting was as follows: the combined votes of the two candidates, 290; the third candidate, 170.

According to the rules set before the counting, the *third* candidate was the winner. But the *majority* had voted for Chaudhry Amin and his 'new' deputy!

The response to this impasse was chaotic: a tangible electric current of potential violence ran through the packed hall. Bands of supporters surged towards each other and the stage, shouting and gesturing threateningly. The three leaders made no attempt to control their respective groups and it was left to the Pakistani chairman of the meeting and the Principal Race Officer conducting the election to attempt to restore order. They finally managed to announce above the noise that the election had been declared invalid and that new elections would be held at a future date to be announced.

What lay behind this event and its dramatic and unexpected U-turn? I was intrigued and puzzled by the unlikely alliance, apparently created on the spur of the moment, between two men who *I* had thought (obviously quite mistakenly) to be the chief rivals. I decided to probe into the event a little further. The more I probed, the more what appeared to be a highly localised incident within a circumscribed political arena became linked into all the other major political divisions within the community and to several disparate arenas. It was impossible to comprehend this one event without knowing the history as well as the current alliances of different associations and organisations, their leadership disputes – indeed, even their links to Pakistan. I had entered, unwittingly, a complex tangle of blocs, factions and alliances. This book is the product of my attempts to unravel that tangle.

The three arenas

There were, in 1987/8, three major contexts or political arenas (Swartz 1969, Jones 1974) in which Pakistani community politics were publicly conducted in Manchester. Each arena not only followed different selection rules, values and objectives; it also related to different definitions of 'community'. There were, of course, many other more specific – or lower-level – contested arenas, but these three arenas were all marked by their city-wide territorial catchment area and publicly supervised election procedures. Each arena was the product of a discursive formation, with its own rules, ideological articulations, spaces and power-contestations.

In terms of value the most important arena was the religious one, that of mosque politics, with the focus being on the Central Mosque and control of its management committee, the *Jami'at el Muslemin*. The Manchester Central Mosque, built through local donations at a time when the community was still united, is a corporate property owned by the 'community' and subject constitutionally to regular democratic elections. Since the Central Mosque supposedly serves all Muslims in Manchester irrespective of national or sectarian affiliation, it is also the scene of contested Islamic religious approaches. As Islamic religious divisions have multiplied in Britain, the mosque has become a site of regular, often violent, conflict, from shouting matches and fist fights to alleged kidnappings and physical attacks, all of which have necessitated frequent external interventions by the police, the Mayor of Manchester, the Pakistan High Commissioner (who reputedly intervened at one point on the instructions of the higher echelons of the Pakistani government) and the courts.

Since the 1980s the mosque has also been the scene of extended and expensive litigation. It was built entirely from funds raised from within the community (see Werbner 1990a) and is considered by most local Pakistanis to be one of the most beautiful and important mosques in Britain. Officially the mosque of the whole Muslim community, it is effectively controlled by Pakistanis. In recent years other mosques have been built, representing various Islamic sectarian approaches or Sufi orders. None, however, has usurped the symbolic primacy or hegemony of the Central Mosque.

Elections to the mosque have been sporadic and fraught with conflict. Although supposed to be held annually, no elections were held for a lengthy period during the 1970s while the mosque was being built. Two or three elections were then held in succession, the last being the scene of a major confrontation and outside intervention. At this point the constitution was changed and elections are now supposed to be held every three years. The postponement of elections and attempts to change the constitution (rival 'authentic' constitutions are in circulation) are a regular feature of mosque politics.

The Pakistani Community Centre emerged more recently as a second political arena. The Centre was built with funding from Urban Aid and there was a fierce contest to get control of the grant by a united front of the more established old-timer associations (for details see Werbner 1991b). It was ultimately handled by a local literary society. By 1988 the Centre had held only one seriously contested public election, which deteriorated into a *halagula* (a noisy public dispute). The Centre's formal constitution lays down strict election rules which are supposed to ensure that procedures are respected and closely supervised. Membership of the Centre is open to all members of the Pakistani community in the city (and even to interested non-Pakistanis), the boundary of the city being defined in very broad terms.[2] In accordance with the Centre's charitable status, elections are supposed to be held annually as part of the Annual General Meeting at which an Annual Report and audited accounts are presented. The Executive Committee meets every month and is officially open to all members of the Centre. But the constitution has been used in the past by the Executive Committee to disqualify both voters and candidates. The financial mismanagement of the Centre was so serious that in 1994 it was taken over by the City Council in co-operation with the Pakistani Sub-Consulate in Manchester. In 1995 a new management committee was nominated by the local authority.

The third political arena during the 1980s, the Race Sub-Committee, had a relatively short history. Set up by the Radical Left Labour Party group controlling the Council at the time, it functioned as an advisory body composed of elected ethnic community representatives, and was chaired by a councillor. Each ethnic community in the city – West Indian, African, Chinese, Indian, Pakistani, etc. – was allocated a number of seats, and 'Community Reps', as they were known, were elected annually, with the voting supervised by the Council through its recently established Race Unit. The Race Unit (later disbanded and its workload redistributed) had several full-time workers and also served the Race Sub-Committee, prepared lengthy agendas, minutes, etc., advised community reps on matters of procedure and substance, and attempted to carry out policy decisions. The meetings of the Sub-Committee, held monthly in the imposing Council Chamber, were extremely formal and required quite detailed knowledge of the rhetoric of public administration and the functioning of the Council. The Longsight elections for the Sub-Committee were the first to be publicly proclaimed and supervised. The winner, Chaudhry Amin, whose fiery anti-clerical speeches are presented in the next chapter, was the victor in Longsight.

The Pakistani community was allocated four seats on the Sub-Committee, based on four territorial divisions: North Manchester, Longsight, Whalley Range and Central. The first three marked the three main Pakistani residential clusters

---

[2] The boundaries of the Community Centre membership were discussed at an executive committee meeting in which it was decided to leave them deliberately vague.

in the city, the fourth was something of a catch-all and included the business community in the city centre. Although the boundaries of these divisions were initially left vague, pressures increased to define them unambiguously as elections came to be seriously contested.

Elections to the Sub-Committee were thus based on local territorial sub-divisions within the wider community. Pakistanis referred to elected representatives as 'councillors' and appeared to make little distinction between them and official councillors elected at the local authority elections. There was only one Pakistani municipal councillor in the whole of Manchester in 1987, elected the previous year.[3]

Each political arena defined different discursively constructed 'communities': the Central Mosque arena defined a religious community; the 'Pakistani' Community Centre arena defined a 'secular' national community; the Race Sub-Committee defined a local British 'ethnic minority' community. Each arena invoked its own discourse, or episteme, in Foucault's terms (Foucault 1984), and encompassed within it different ideological and political orientations. The Mosque was the scene of religious disputation and competition for sectarian hegemony; the Community Centre revealed the inherent tension in Pakistani national discourses between secular culture, religion and social justice, articulated locally in divisions between religious purists and secularists, 'rich' and 'poor', workers and businessmen, democrats and nationalists. The Race Sub-Committee elaborated a discourse of anti-racism and equal rights. These quite separate discourses disguised the fact that, in reality, associations and their leaders competed in terms of a further discourse – that of individual honour, determined by complex internal arguments and loyalties grounded in district, caste and *biradari* affiliations. In some senses, then, the urban field of political action was the familiar scene of Punjabi 'village politics'. Each election was a test of factional power: elections for Community Reps established alliances; these were further tested in the elections for the Community Centre Executive, which rehearsed the elections to the Central Mosque, the ultimate prize for the winning faction. During mosque elections, territorial divisions, ascriptive links, individual animosities and ideological orientations all converged in a single unifying arena, that of the 'community' as an embodied, multiple and complex reality.

At stake were a series of segmentary oppositions.[4] In the Muslim community these were based on nationality, sect (Sunni/Shi'a), religious approach (Reform versus mystical), and charismatic loyalty (to a particular saint or order). Each segment had its own mosques (Deobandi, Tablighi, Barelvi Sufi orders, UK Islamic Mission, etc.).

Although during the 1970s the major ideological conflict in the city was between the Barelvis and Deobandis, the actual factional division in the Central Mosque was between the 'moderate' anti-*maulvi* (Muslim cleric or legal expert)

---

[3] In 1988 a second was elected. Both are university-educated youngish men originating from Africa, one from Kenya, the other from Mauritius. The Kenyan councillor has, however, lived in Pakistan for part of his life, and speaks fluent Urdu and Punjabi. The third Asian councillor, a woman, is an Indian Muslim Gujerati. All represented the Labour Party. Since then a series of Asian councillors have been elected but their numbers remain relatively constant.

[4] I discuss these in detail in Werbner 1991b. The intricacy derives from the fact that any base (national or regional origin, Islamic denomination, British territorial residence) generates a different set of cross-cutting segmentary oppositions.

group, advocating the preservation of the openness and universal nature of the mosque as a central mosque, equally accessible to all Muslim groups in the city, and the pro-*maulvi* faction, committed to specific traditions, first Deobandi then Barelvi.[5]

Conflicts at the Central Mosque have led over the years to the establishment of separatist mosques in Manchester, each dominated by a different sectarian approach or Sufi cult affiliation. Until his final defeat in 1991, the *maulvi* of the Central Mosque was affiliated to a Sufi Qadiriya order centred on a British saint in Walthamstow, London. Rivalling this mosque was a Naqshbandi mosque affiliated to a saint in Birmingham, while another Naqshbandi order was headed by a local saint. Although ideologically the closest to Maulana Saheb, the *maulvi* of the Central Mosque, these groups were thus major rivals in the political arena.[6]

The pattern is one in which close collaterals sharing the same religious approach are political rivals who form alliances with ideologically more distant sectarian groups (hence the closest ally of the Maulana was a Shi'a, Khaddam Saheb, and he also gained support from one branch of the UK Islamic Mission, affiliated to Jama'at-i Islami, an Islamist party). Such rivalries between close collaterals are the stuff of factional politics on the subcontinent as well.

Like the Muslim community, the Pakistani community as a territorial entity is divided by residence in Manchester according to village or district of origin in Pakistan and according to caste. Three large caste groups dominate the Manchester political arena. The Arain who originate from East Punjab and are settled in Pakistan in the cities and the canal colonies (Faislabad, Sahiwal, Multan, Bahawalpur). Many entered Pakistan as refugees after Partition in 1947. Most Arain businessmen have moved out of Manchester's inner city and live scattered in the city suburbs. They are regarded collectively, along with the professionals in the city, as the wealthy 'upper' classes. The other two major groups are Gujar and Rajput, originating primarily from the Jhelum District and surrounding districts (Gujrat, Gujar Khan, Chakwal). These migrant settlers who, of course, were never refugees, still have deep roots and extensive links in their villages of origin and are intensely involved in Pakistani political rivalries at home. They are also the ones who most universally dream of returning home one day.

All three caste groups call themselves 'Chaudhry' (i.e. headmen) and are regarded as *zamindar* (landowners). While the Arain caste's status in West Punjab, prior to Partition, was quite low, its members' achievements both in Manchester and Pakistan have placed them high within the landowning group. As Chaudhry M. explained in his speech during the Asian Business meeting referred to at the end of Chapter 3, Arain immigrants to Manchester tended to start businesses quite soon after their arrival in the city (cf. Werbner, 1989c) and most of the wealthy businessmen, particularly in the clothing and garment trade, are Arain. Jhelmis worked longer in factories and many are today smaller businessmen: market traders, taxi-drivers, small manufacturers, owners of grocery stores. Although Manchester, a large city, has migrant-settlers originating from all

[5] Briefly, Barelvis follow Sufi saints and traditions; Deobandi are reformist Muslims committed to purifying Islam of what are defined as 'Hindu' or 'syncretic' elements leading to saint worship as a form of idolatry (for a full account of the historical divisions in India, see Metcalf 1982). I define moderation as a tolerance of divergent points of view and an attempt to work within a broad consensual framework. Extremism is defined as a commitment to a specific ideology as the only legitimate truth which others must conform to or be excluded altogether.

[6] All names used are honorifics.

over Pakistan and from a large number of caste groups, it is these three main caste-cum-district groups which seem to count – as groups – in the political arena. Professionals who hold office in associations mostly originate from Pakistani cities and from the higher castes (Pathan, Sayyid, Qureshi, Siddiqui, Mughal, etc.) but they are few in number and seldom have large *biradaris* locally.

Local-level politics are often dismissed by observers as *'biradari politics'* – a term which seems to imply that whole caste groups compete against each other for power. But this reading ignores the architectonics of factional alliances: in reality, caste groups are split internally, with rivals joining opposed factions, so that factional alliances cut across caste affiliations in a pattern well analysed in discussions of factional politics in South Asia.

Blocs & factions

Two major scholarly debates focus on the processes and organisation of South Asian politics. The first arose in response to Barth's model of political bloc formation among the Swat Pathan, the second was inspired by discussions of factional coalitions in Indian politics. On the whole, the two debates have remained discrete, although in reality they relate to a single phenomenon, constituted by the same basic cultural principles of social organisation.

Barth's model is remarkable both for its economy and lucidity (Barth [1959] 1981). He argues that segmentary descent systems, rather than defining 'a hierarchy of homologous groups' and their situational fission and fusion within a merging series (the Nuer model), 'define rivals and allies in a system of two opposed political blocs'. The principle by which the system operates is as follows:

> Closely related descent units are consistent rivals; each establishes a net of political alliances with the rivals of allies of their own rivals. In this fashion a pervasive factional split into two grand alliances of descent segments emerges, with close collateral segments consistently in opposite moieties. (Barth 1981: 55–6)

As Lindholm (1982) and others (e.g. Ahmed 1980) have shown, these principles are given cultural expression: a relationship of enmity between parallel cousins is known as *tarburwali*; the alliances or 'blocs' are known as *dala*. Lindholm notes that these dual parties are spoken of as 'concrete entities' (1982: 79) so that 'each individual sees the tribal world as divided into those who are in his party and those who are against his party'. Each village *dala* 'ramifies in a net of alliances throughout the region' (ibid.).

Barth's model is thus as much a *cultural* model as a sociological one. A major strength of the model is that it relates political alliance to *violence* or potential violence: vulnerability to violence sustains the *dala*. In Swat vengeance killing is the prerogative of individuals and not of larger corporate groups, and hence the groups which make up an alliance can be quite small and genealogically shallow. (This contrasts with tribal groups such as the Bedouin of Cyrenaica which engage in perpetual feuding: feuds encompass much larger tribal segments comprising several hundred people, and it is between these that alliances are formed. See Peters 1959, 1967; Black-Michaud 1975.)

Similar cultural notions animate Punjabi conceptions of cousin enmity and alliance. Enmity between cousins is known as *sherika bazi*. 'Sherika' means family, and 'sherik' is a patrilineal brother or cousin of the same blood. Such enmity arises, as among the Pukhtun, from disputes between close agnates over inheritance, property or leadership. 'Bazi', which literally means 'fun', refers here to conflict. Political bloc alliances in rural Punjab are known as *pattiwal*. Like Pukhtun *dala*, they are made up of coalitions of rival groups determined at the lowest level of segmentation. Close agnates compete through membership in rival factions or blocs.

Barth contended that Pukhtun bloc alliances were remarkably stable despite the intermittent defections of strong leaders from one faction to another (Barth 1981: 166). Defections were risky for minor leaders and were, in any case, unlikely as long as a person's close collateral rival was in the other bloc (ibid.: 169). This persistence of factional alliances has also been noted in studies of factions in Indian politics. In the Punjab, 'some factions, and the strife between them, endure for many decades' (Pettigrew 1975: 65), even, Pettigrew argues, beyond the lives of their leaders. She documents the history of one such factional division in the Punjab which persisted for ten years.

The major difference between Pukhtun and Indian factions relates not to the underlying principle generating factional alliances ('my enemy's enemy is my friend') which is common to both, but to the multiplicity of political arenas in which factional divisions are manifested in the broader context of Indian state politics (see Jones 1974). In Swat society kinship defines both territoriality and individual property rights. Factional opposition is thus articulated by an inclusive idiom (that of unilineal descent) which encompasses the political, economic and personal relationships of group members within a single uniform framework (but see Ahmed 1976: 103–22 for a contrary view). Not so in Indian politics. Factions in the Punjab, for example, manifested themselves in a variety of contexts or arenas: the Punjab state, the Sikh community, the Congress party, the state administration (Pettigrew 1975: 68). Each of these arenas determined a framework of rules, values and ideals within which factions operated (ibid.: 64), whether this be the unity of the Punjab, the Khalsa, or the party, or the need for administrative impartiality (ibid.: 68).

Pettigrew identifies certain key features of factions:

(i)   They are *not* anomic; on the contrary, they operate within the framework of *rules, values and ideals of the larger whole*.

(ii) They are in competition for control over resources and are based, to use Jones's term, on 'distributive policies', i.e. patronage (see Jones 1974: 365). According to Jones, *class* politics, by contrast, is based on 'redistributive' policies.

(iii) They are relatively persistent.

(iv) They consist of persons tied horizontally and linked vertically to one another on a *variety* of bases (economic, kinship, etc.; this is the feature most commonly stressed by other students of factions).

(v)   They are kept alive through *a series of mobilisation events* in *different* political arenas. This is particularly important for an analysis of *urban* contexts.

(vi) They are not simply leader-focused, but leaders embody the power of the faction and the resources under its control.

(vii) The faction, as a coalition, operates through *both vertical links and horizontal ties*. Factions are thus internally divided into *different 'levels'*. *Upward* links are crucial to local leaders if they are to maintain their *downward* links (Pettigrew 1975: 64–74).

(viii) Finally, factions are integrative, in the sense of creating alliances which *cut across villages* (or classes and neighbourhoods), and link together both villages and cities.

This model of factional alliances as vertical organisations linking village and district levels has been attacked by Hardiman in a trenchant critique of earlier analyses of Indian factions (Hardiman 1982). The 'Great Indian Faction' is, he argues, a mythical construct which orientalises India as a 'factious society' (1982: especially 226–31), unable to govern itself according to 'modern', 'rational' agendas. The model fails, he claims, to recognise that village factional politics are relatively insular, while Indian district nationalist politics were motivated by subaltern class protest movements as much as by power struggles between equals within political oligarchies:

> vertical networks of patrons and clients were less important during the course of the nationalist movement than horizontal solidarities of an essentially class nature. (Hardiman 1982: 209)

In response to this far-reaching critique, Sandria Freitag chooses to drop the term 'faction' altogether from her theoretical vocabulary, substituting for it a euphemistic, less transparent alternative, 'relational alliance' (1989a: 223). Freitag argues that the role of such relational alliances can only be appreciated in the light of a further key distinction: between 'community', constituted through the public arenas it fosters, and the 'state' with its institutionalised modes of representation. Communalism (and the key role of relational alliances) emerged, she argues, because of the 'inability to integrate successfully [communal] public and state realms' which had developed separately and autonomously (Freitag 1989a: 223).

These novel insights into South Asian politics highlight the fact that factions, conceived of as vertical pragmatic alliances, are ideologically penetrated, caught up dialectically between a politics of honour and shame, personalised rivalries, historicised local vendettas and utilitarian alliances, on the one hand, and class-driven antagonisms or self-consciously 'primordial' (religious, linguistic) segmental loyalties, on the other. Such a politics is never exclusively and permanently communal, or class-based, or utilitarian. Instead, emergent solidarities (whether of class or community) are fleeting achievements. During the Rushdie affair, as we shall see, deadly enemies buried the hatchet, but not for long. Working-class sentiments articulated in local contests by Rajput and Gujar Mancunians, who originate from small-scale peasant landowner families, do not inspire permanent working-class solidarities (though in national British elections, Pakistanis almost invariably support the Labour Party); this petty-zamindari class is itself split ideologically between secularist democrats, deeply antipathetic to Islamist agendas, and religious nationalists, and is further fractionised by historical animosities and personal vendettas. In their rhetoric, community leaders articulate this complex, conjunctural reality.

Factions, unlike political parties, are not bureaucratic organisations. They mobilise situationally in response to social events: elections, ceremonial celebrations,

Plate 1.1 A factional meeting at the Community Centre

Plate 1.2 An Urdu poet

religious parades, public fights, political demonstrations. It is this piecemeal 'localism' which explains why bloc alliances are composed – and here Barth's insight is crucial – of groups opposed at the lowest level of segmentation. Close collaterals compete directly in local arenas and indirectly, via their allies, in broader contexts. They rarely fuse situationally with their opponents into a single solidary group, in Nuer-like segmentary opposition to more 'distant' or ideologically opposed groups. The ramifying networks which make up factional blocs mean that localism is not tantamount to insularity. Diasporic public arenas are not purely local. They are penetrated ideologically by global tendencies and by factional conflicts and alliances beyond the local; in the case of Manchester, they extend into the north of England, and even to Pakistan itself.

The emergence of new factional alliances

A faction is a network of networks in which the constituent groups at its base are relatively small. The shifting composition of opposed blocs stems not so much from the shifting of whole groups and their leaders from one bloc to the other, as Barth and others suggest, but from internal disputes within the base groups which lead to secessions and splits (see Pocock 1957), with the losing sub-group inevitably shifting to the opposed faction. Quite often these splits occur as a natural response to the growth of constituent groups. The shift of part-groups to the rival faction in response to internal splits was evident in Manchester.

Discussions of factionalism often focus on specific leaders and their maximising strategies and political intrigues. Mancunian communal politics suggest, however, that no single leader really controls a faction. Usually leaders co-operate to form a kind of oligarchy with an internal division of labour. As Seth Saheb, the leader of the dominant faction, explained: 'Khaddam Saheb deals with the Town Hall, he is our "foreign minister"; I am more in the community.' The role of the third factional leader, Maulana Saheb, the *maulvi* of the Central Mosque, was to deal with religious matters. Different leaders are deemed more suited to represent the group in different arenas by virtue of their mastery of appropriate discourses.

Yet communal politics are framed in a discourse of individual reputation and honour. Important leaders are the focus of endless interest and gossip, and their personalities are minutely dissected and analysed in what appears to be a personalised politics of good and evil, trust and treachery, altruism and greed. Such an individualistic gloss is unable, however, to explain the emergence of factions which are, ultimately, the products of broader structural cleavages and contradictions.

The creation of two new political arenas – the Community Centre and the Race Sub-Committee – was associated with the emergence in Manchester of a new factional constellation (see Appendix 1). Although the new factional alliances had certain affinities with the past, and the past was indeed constantly *referred* to, the introduction of new political prizes and institutional contexts introduced a radical break with the past.

During its formative years, from 1950 to 1980, the community was controlled by a group of pioneer immigrants. Of these the most powerful and influential were a large-scale clothing wholesaler and his associate partner. The wholesaler not only had a vast turnover (and thus many suppliers and customers dependent upon him), but he and his partner also benefited from their status as founder-members of the community who had helped many later immigrants to settle or to start businesses. Both partners were East Punjabi Arain and had a large network of relatives and *biradari* members in Manchester and other parts of the North West (particularly Rochdale). The wholesaler was energetic, sophisticated and powerful, while his partner was highly respected for his wisdom and dedication to community causes.

In the early 1970s the partnership split up somewhat acrimoniously and the wholesaler's brother, Chaudhri Ji, became a full partner. Before the split the wholesaler had had a dispute with Seth Saheb, a fellow-villager, also an East Punjabi Arain, then a market trader, who took the wholesaler to court and won his case against him. Seth Saheb was never forgiven for his temerity and was excluded from factional power circles despite his increasing wealth and influence as he too moved into wholesaling. This dispute was to have repercussions in the 1980s.

Clearly then, even at this early stage, cracks and potential lines of secession were discernible in the solidarity of the controlling Arain group. The economic power of the pioneer wholesaler, his clear pre-eminence in the community, and his avoidance of office kept potential dissenters under control. The 1970s was a period of communal construction and relative harmony. £250,000 was raised from within the community (a relatively small one, then only about 10,000 strong), to build a beautiful mosque, and Manchester's reputation as one of the most successful Pakistani communities in Britain remained unchallenged. There were, of course, disputes, since this was a period of religious ferment throughout the country, in which the division between the Deobandis and Barelvis surfaced and caused rifts in many cities. In Manchester a prior *maulvi*, a committed and open Deobandi who refused to allow Barelvi practices in the Central Mosque, was accused of sexual misdemeanours. A distinguished man with an international reputation as an Islamic scholar, he was subsequently appointed head of Pakistan's advisory committee preparing the country's legal transition into an Islamic state. Although he eventually won his court case, he resigned as *maulvi*, and subsequently founded a separate mosque, the Islamic Academy.

Other points of dissension during this period focused on the refusal of the mosque's Management Committee to hold public elections; instead, new groups and associations were co-opted on to the Committee. The excuse for the delayed elections was that these would disrupt the building programme. The ruling Arain faction was itself divided on the religious issue, most members being Barelvi. Some of the other office-holders, in particular the Chairman of the Committee, himself sympathetic to the Deobandi (and its offshoot, Tablighi Islam), felt that the mosque should be open and non-denominational, and refused to support the attack on the *maulvi*.

In any case, the underlying ferment never coalesced into a clear oppositional faction; the disputes and divisions were contained and only rarely erupted into real violence. This was probably due to the economic power and influence wielded by the head of the ruling faction and by the faction's evident contribution to the corporate wealth of the community.

Most remarkable is the fact that, during the whole of this period, resources, power and patronage were *internally* generated. The influence of the state was minimal and it was not regarded as an important source of economic prizes. All this changed during the 1980s. First came the success of the literary society in obtaining a large Urban Aid grant to build the Community Centre (on the disputes surrounding this grant see Werbner 1991b). It later became evident that smaller welfare grants and jobs could be accessed through the local authority. In the meanwhile the wholesaler's financial empire collapsed suddenly and unexpectedly during the severe economic recession of 1981, and no other Pakistani emerged to replace him. Some of the largest remaining wholesalers in Manchester are Hindus, while the most prominent of them all (owner of the 'Joe Bloggs' label), although a Muslim, was not only a newcomer to the city and a non-Punjabi but, as we shall see in Chapter 7, a man willing to openly flout Islamic prohibitions. Lost was an internal source of patronage and power not dependent on outside largesse; the community no longer had a family or group possessing sufficient philanthropic resources to disburse in competition with state grants.

The implications of the collapse of the pioneer wholesaler's empire were not immediately evident. After the mosque building project was completed, the whole committee resigned *en bloc* and did not stand for re-election. Chaudhri Ji, the wholesaler's brother, replaced him on the committee and became its Chairman. Key members of the old committee, including the pioneer wholesaler, remained trustees of the building, responsible also for the handling of the mosque's financial affairs. It was during this period that the divisions within the Arain establishment manifested themselves publicly. The wholesaler's brother was re-elected at the next election before the family firm finally folded up. He abandoned his old allies (and, it would seem, his brother, the original kingmaker) and aligned himself with some of the other old-timers hitherto excluded from mosque politics. Among these was Seth Saheb, the market trader who had taken his family firm to court, who was now himself a successful wholesaler. The brother explained to me that his motives, in abandoning his erstwhile allies, including his own brother, were to save the community and re-unite it. In the event, he failed to achieve this aim.

His 'betrayal' of his former allies was to spell the collapse of the power of the faction which had built the mosque and controlled the community for so many years. The new triumvirate which led the ruling faction for the next decade ruthlessly squeezed him out, while his prior faction was left in disarray. The older brother retired to Pakistan, and the Arain group, which had ruled the community for thirty years or more, was finally split. Attempts to unite it around a newly formed Arain association appeared to have been short-lived. The last stronghold of the outgoing faction – the trusteeship of the mosque – became the locus of litigation over the control of mosque financial affairs. Bitter disputes which periodically erupted into violent conflict marked the following years.

The triumvirate leading the new ruling faction was dominated by Maulana Saheb, the *maulvi* of the Central Mosque, a recent appointment of the former Management Committee. Just as his predecessor had refused to allow Barelvi ritual practices in the mosque, he refused to allow *non*-Barelvi practices there.[7]

For a while it appeared that the power of this new ruling faction was unbreachable. The old trustees, while succeeding legally in maintaining their

[7] On similar struggles surrounding such ritual disagreements in other parts of the Islamic world see Bowen 1989 and Launay 1992.

claims to life-trusteeship, had lost much of their reputation and credibility. Even those opposed to Maulana Saheb criticised them for what was perceived to be a desperate attempt to hang on to power at all costs; they had always been, it was said, undemocratic (had they not delayed the elections for so many years and never held elections to the Pakistan Society which they controlled?). Forgotten was their major achievement of building the Central Mosque. In the meanwhile, the new ruling faction's main achievement was to *lose* a building purchased through voluntary contributions by the prior Management Committee. Unlike their predecessors, Maulana Saheb and his allies seemed incapable of raising the rest of the funds needed to complete the purchase of this building, and were forced to re-sell it at great financial and communal loss (see Werbner 1991b).

In the 1986 elections, an entirely new Management Committee was elected. This followed the intervention of the Pakistani Embassy,[8] which decreed that the twelve leaders of both the opposed 'old' factions (six from each group) should resign and not stand for re-election. The prior ruling faction boycotted these elections while the new ruling factions put up a list of front men they could trust. Or thought they could trust.

By the end of 1986, the new ruling faction was attempting to spread its control to all major institutions in the community. Wherever I went, organisational leaders spoke of the pressures exerted upon them by the Central Mosque faction and its militant *maulvi*. The key targets for control were the Community Centre, on the one hand, and the neighbouring Barelvi mosque, the *Dar-ul-Uloom*, on the other. This predatory attitude was evident for a considerable time, during which the power of the ruling faction was gradually undermined by *internal* divisions and by the creation – perhaps only temporarily – of a new viable opposition.

The unity of the new factional alliance was indeed short-lived. Maulana Saheb created his own group within the main faction, composed of personal followers and disciples of his saint. The internal factional divisions within the ruling faction appear to have emerged when the 'dummy' management committee fronting the ruling faction began to assert its independence from its patrons. The Maulana, a charismatic, ambitious and clever man, worked alongside them, apparently also supported by Khaddam Saheb, an activist and voluntary welfare worker in the community. The Arain businessmen, among them Seth Saheb, began to sense that their dominant position within the faction was threatened. A key figure in the development of the new factional constellation was the elected Vice-Chairman, a Jhelmi of the Gujar caste, who controlled a large *biradari* (kinship-cum-caste group) in the Whalley Range neighbourhood of Manchester and was influential throughout the North West. He reputedly became the ally of Maulana Saheb, and at the same time the unifying focus against which the new faction coalesced.

We can, at last, return to our initial starting-point – the inexplicable manoeuvrings during the Longsight Community Rep elections. The new opposition faction emerged through a classic alliance between groups opposed at the lowest level of segmentation. A major activist in the formation of the new faction was, we saw, Chaudhry Amin. Chaudhry Amin had for several years been a minor but active supporter of the new ruling faction, headed by Maulana Saheb and its Arain kingmakers. But he had suffered a public insult by the Maulana who had mocked and abused him in the mosque in front of several spectators. In retaliation, he

[8] At the time Pakistan had left the Commonwealth to which it subsequently returned.

formed the Longsight Association, in opposition to an earlier association affiliated to the mosque. The mosque then intervened to fractionise his association (with the result that there were three 'Longsight Associations').

The process which took place was thus as follows: the previously existing Longsight Association (A) had a dispute with the Central Mosque regarding the handling of mosque finances (a leader of this association was 'appointed' as a 'new' trustee of the Central Mosque, originally with the intention of mobilising support in Longsight for the triumvirate's new ruling faction during the earlier disputes). The mosque's ruling faction then encouraged and supported the formation of a second Longsight association (B), headed by Chaudhry Amin, to oppose (A). When he too came into a confrontation with the Maulana and his group of supporters (itself a sub-group *within* the ruling faction), he aligned himself with the other 'internal' faction of ruling Arain businessmen (now excluded from office by the Embassy ruling and forming another sub-group) against the Maulana, his Gujar Vice-Chairman and *their* 'internal' sub-group. The mosque then intervened a second time to fractionise this second Longsight association (B). The seceding group (C) then nominated their *own* third candidate for the Longsight Community Representative elections. There were thus three candidates standing for election: a representative of (A) who was also a supporter of the rival Naqshbandi *Dar-ul-Uloom*; a representative of (B) who was initially set up by the mosque to oppose (A); and a representative of (C) who supported the Maulana's sub-faction within the ruling faction, and was set up in opposition to (B) as well as (A) (see Appendix 1).

This is why there were three candidates for the Longsight Community Rep position, and why the leader of (B), Chaudhry Amin, chose to ally himself with a more distant collateral against a closer, more recent, rival. (A) of course could have chosen to ally himself with either (B) or (C) who were equidistant collaterals. He was, indeed, under some pressure from his group to go along with (C); all were Jhelmis, and they all knew each other well. He chose (B) because (C), a Rajput, had insulted him by mocking the low-caste origins of his wife.

It was at this point that Chaudhry Amin, the leader of (B), emerged as a major leader and unifier of the opposition faction, determined to defeat the *maulvi*'s group controlling the mosque. In order to broaden his alliance he contacted a group of Gujars in Whalley Range who were bitterly opposed to the Mosque Vice-Chairman (a close relative) and by extension also to his allies, the Maulana and his radical ally, Khaddam Saheb. The split in Whalley Range had its origins in Pakistan. It centred on a division within a single village in Jhelum. The two village factions in Manchester were part of an 'international' village factional dispute which refracted the unity of the group both in the village and in Manchester and across Lancashire and Yorkshire. The Gujar Vice-Chairman of the Central Mosque in Manchester had for several years been the acknowledged leader of local villagers living primarily in the Whalley Range residential cluster in Manchester. A recent leadership dispute and factional split in the *village*, however, had split the group in *Manchester* into two opposed factions. Chaudhry Amin helped the seceding faction to form an association rivalling that of the Vice-Chairman and his ally, the radical activist who until then had held complete political monopoly in Whalley Range.

In the meanwhile, a cousin and close ally of the Vice-Chairman from the same village was elected as Community Rep, virtually unopposed, in the Central

District, thus strengthening the power of Maulana Saheb's ruling faction (three of the four Community Reps on the Race Sub-Committee were currently from this faction with only one elected member from the opposed faction – Chaudhry Amin, the Longsight Rep). He too, as we saw, was initially selected by the ruling faction, and had only quarrelled with it in the course of preparations for the elections.

This new factional constellation brought Jhelmi men, previously content to provide votes rather than assume office, very much into the centre of the Manchester Pakistani diasporic political arena. Most came from dominant castes in their home villages, which were providing (in Pakistan) more and more elected councillors and members of parliament and of provincial assemblies. They began to realise that in Manchester too they could challenge the Arain business community's hegemony with their superior numbers and organisational talents. Many of them had become businessmen themselves. Others were now unemployed, having retired or been made redundant from manual jobs. In their prime, at an age (around 50) when they would have been active elders and headmen in their natal villages, they had plenty of time for political activity. There was no need for any serious mobilisation: the mosque building was complete, the building opposite had been lost, and funding had come increasingly to be regarded as dependent on state largesse and successful political manoeuvrings in the Town Hall (this, following the astonishing success of the little-known literary society in receiving what was by local standards an enormous grant).

Among those forming the opposition alliance were some with strong ideological commitments to the secular, working-class and democratic platform of the Pakistan People's Party, including the local Pakistani councillor and his supporters and several religious leaders. The first main objective of the group was to win control of the Community Centre. Although the Centre had been built by a group of poet workers strongly opposed to the (old) ruling business faction of the Central Mosque, now that this group had itself become the 'establishment', it formed an alliance with the new ruling mosque faction and in particular its *maulvi*. This was mainly because members of the Community Centre Executive, initially really not much more than a *tonga* association,[9] had only a very small constituency of supporters – literary aficionados (themselves divided between *two* rival cultural associations), along with a few relatives and friends – who might vote for their group, certainly not sufficient numbers to win a major election. They were willing to let the activists of the Central Mosque into the affairs of the Community Centre in order to retain their seats on the Executive. This, despite the fact that the poetry society had explicitly requested the Community Centre from the Council so that it could serve as an alternative meeting-place to the mosque.

During the period running up to the Community Centre elections, paid-up membership of the Centre rose from a few hundred to almost one thousand. Both factions – the mosque and the opposition – frantically enlisted supporters (and paid their membership fees) for what promised to be a closely contested poll. The opposition led by Chaudhry Amin even managed to shift the *maulvi*'s rival association (A) in Longsight to his side (although this alliance proved to be short-lived).

In the upshot, the elections turned out to be a fiasco for Chaudhry Amin and his allies. Initially they had succeeded in disqualifying one of the 'Mosque' group's key candidates, a founding member of the Centre, on a technicality (he

---

[9] A *tonga* is a small vehicle like a rickshaw that can carry very few people.

was two days late in renewing his membership). The 'Mosque' group retaliated about a week later, only a few days before the elections, by disqualifying eight(!) of the opposition's candidates, including the current Secretary of the Executive. By checking laboriously through the membership lists, they found that some of these candidates had not paid their dues at all (in the chaos of registering new members they had apparently, so they claimed, forgotten to do so. Membership was only £2 which makes the claim credible.) Some were disqualified simply for being seconded by somebody else who had forgotten to pay his dues.

All the opposition's work had come to nought. Their list was stripped of most of its key candidates. Their defeat was bitter. Although a compromise was negotiated and only one list was presented at the Annual General Meeting, no elections took place and in effect the ruling faction had won. A public row was avoided because a key member of the disqualified group decided to accept the constitutional interpretation of his group's disqualification and withdrew gracefully. It is noteworthy that he was a 'real' city councillor, and thus one of the few local Pakistanis to have achieved a respected position in the wider society. The Community Centre elections mattered to him deeply: he had worked very hard to make the Centre a success, as had virtually all the candidates from both groups, and election to the chairmanship would have enhanced his wider status. But he accepted defeat stoically, since it was obvious that otherwise there was bound to be a nasty confrontation between supporters of the two groups. Supporters were told that there would be no contest and the majority stayed away. The atmosphere in the hall during the AGM was tangibly resentful but very restrained. Fence-sitters I spoke to approved of the fact that a major confrontation (which could have involved a thousand registered members) had been avoided.

The defeat undermined the strength of the opposition alliance and its credibility. It was composed of several local groups only loosely linked together. Although Chaudhry Amin had created an umbrella organisation uniting them (of which he was the chairman), the alliance had failed to secure the support of any major leaders outside the smaller local associations in Longsight and Whalley Range. The hope that the two Arain businessmen who had founded the current ruling faction would abandon Maulana Saheb did not materialise. In the coming months there was to be a series of further elections, first to the Race Sub-Committee and after that to the mosque. The new opposition's power would ultimately be tested by the mosque elections.[10]

This, then, is a bare outline of Pakistani factional formation in Manchester at one moment in the history of the community. Neither the complexity nor the passionate intensity of political activity can be conveyed by such a brief account. What is evident, however, is that personal ambition or enmity *and* ideology are both important features in the formation and persistence of factions. The disputes of the Longsight Association (A), headed by a Rajput 'Chaudhry', with the ruling faction reflected the resentment of workers towards the business elite in the community, and towards the handling of mosque finances. The division in the Community Centre focused on the right of the mosque to intervene in the affairs of the Community Centre. This was part of a more general division between the *maulvi* and the opposition alliance which attacked the tendency of religious

---

[10] These took place on 18 August 1989.

officials to intervene in communal politics. The mixing of politics and religion, like class cleavages, was an important issue, widely debated and crucially affecting the community's development. In my discussions with the various adversaries it was clear that they felt extremely strongly about these matters, and were willing, at least officially, to make strategic compromises only within the clear limits set by their respective principles.

Pettigrew rightly argues that studies of factions have tended to stress the centrality of leaders and the different constituencies from which they recruit followers. The emphasis is on the utilitarian bases for these groups which seem to cut across ideological commitments and render them irrelevant. But even in Pettigrew's account, factions are regarded as formed in relation to patronage and distributive policies. Thus, the continuing focus on the Machiavellian talents or rivalries of individual leaders and on the instrumental aspects of factionalism has meant that the relation between factional politics and ideology has only recently come to be addressed (Freitag 1988, 1989a & b; Hardiman 1982; see also Asad 1972). In the following two sections I attempt to probe further into this relationship.

Patronage & leadership

There is little doubt that cultural ideas about patronage underlie factional structures. A leader must be seen to provide his followers with tangible advantages. To do so he must be seen to have access, if he is a local leader, to higher sources of patronage. At an even higher level, he may be in a position to disburse such resources himself. Overseas Pakistanis operate their factions, rightly or wrongly, as though such patronage channels are equally significant in the British political context. They *perceive* this to be the case, even though the vertical channels of patronage are by no means as obvious and transparently public as they are in Pakistan. In the hope of gaining patronage, they spend a great deal of time hosting and entertaining both high-level Pakistanis and British officials and dignitaries – ministers, municipal councillors, ambassadors and the like. Their hosting of the Pakistani High Commissioner and visiting Pakistani senior civil servants and politicians will, they believe (apparently with some justification), provide them with patronage in Pakistan (in the form of business licences, state-allocated building plots, etc.).

The relationship between visiting dignitaries and local community leaders is in reality, however, rather ambiguous. Overseas Pakistanis are not part of a dignitary's electoral constituency and the factional power of local leaders is thus of little interest to him. He may be just as interested in a convivial host or in being entertained in the grand home of a wealthy British Pakistani businessman. Pakistani dignitaries clearly enjoy their trips to Britain and the fuss made of them; the symbiotic relationship between local leaders and visiting dignitaries persists, but the prizes are as much symbolic as practical.

Vertical links to Pakistani dignitaries are complemented by vertical links to British dignitaries. These too are fraught with ambiguity. The British system of grants and allocations is hedged with bureaucratic procedures, and direct patronage is rare. This is particularly so for community leaders (as against official black political representatives). Once again, much of the gain in knowing Members of Parliament, Lord Mayors and ministers is symbolic. Nevertheless, acquaintance with councillors and MPs does make some difference, as grants have to be obtained through the different representative bodies and must obtain council sub-committee approval. MPs can help with particularly difficult immigration matters. Hence followers regard good vertical links both with visiting Pakistani dignitaries and with local British politicians as essential for a leader. They also believe that these connections will ultimately bring patronage rewards. Any serious leader is expected to establish upward vertical links, and it is the *level* of these links which is regarded as a test of that leader's status and his ability to disburse patronage. Many aspiring leaders engage in voluntary immigration advice since this ultimately becomes a source of immediate patronage and an excuse for forging links with British MPs and other concerned politicians. The more successful they are in this advisory work, the more likely they are to estab-lish such vertical links.

Of course, wealthy activists possess a more direct capacity for patronage, and especially if they can provide work or markets as some large clothing wholesalers can. This too may create a loyal clientele. A source of patronage during the late 1980s was associated with the Manpower Services Commission which provided wages for workers in the community, recruited from the ranks of the unemployed. In one instance, a local Pakistani office-holder on the Community Centre Executive obtained such MSC jobs for *two* family members, appointed to key positions (albeit low-paid and temporary), and this despite the apparent objectivity of an interviewing selection panel! Such MSC jobs were becoming more common in community associations, providing a fertile source of patronage.

It should also be remembered, however, that running a faction is an *expensive* enterprise. Leaders entertain both dignitaries and supporters at large-scale dinners. They usually pay the membership fees of followers to the Mosque, the Community Centre and, most recently, the Labour Party (registering 500 members can be a very costly affair!). They pay for the printing of embossed invitations to dinners and ceremonial celebrations. Being a leader is thus expensive, and a faction can only be viable in the long run if at least some of its key members have enough reserve capital to afford the constant outlays of funds required. In Britain, these expenses necessarily come out of leaders' own pockets. They are a matter of *noblesse oblige* (see Werbner 1990a).

Leaders need formal associations as bases from which to create vertical links. The Pakistan Society, the Muslim Business Development Centre, the Longsight Association – all organisations active in the late 1980s – have been replaced by other organisations such as Al Masoom (itself now disbanded), which became a key actor in the local-level political arena of the mid-1990s. But the principles of organisation remain the same. Organisations must find bases from which to operate. Dignitaries are often hosted in hotels or restaurants. The Muslim Business Development Centre, for example, while lacking a building of its own, exploited its links to the City Council to use the Town Hall premises for its public events. On several occasions it invited the Lord Mayor to attend these ceremonial events, thus signalling to visiting dignitaries from Pakistan that it was the effective proprietor of Manchester Town Hall and its magnificent reception rooms. The visitors could not possibly guess that the premises are available to the public for a fee. What was most cunning about this strategy was the fact that it is actually cheaper to hold public events in the Town Hall than in expensive hotels; the catering costs are relatively modest and the more expensive entertaining can be done by a small group constituting the inner cabal.

The two neighbourhood associations discussed here (Longsight and Whalley Range) tended to use the Pakistani Community Centre as their base. The Centre is new and impressive, and it fitted these groups' image as representatives of the mass of Pakistanis, the 'working class', living in Manchester.

While factions direct their energies towards winning elections in key arenas, the intervening periods are interspersed with activities, internal elections and public commemoration events and celebrations held by the various associations. Now and then one of these events erupts, there is a *halagula*, a public commotion or noisy argument, which is discussed and gossiped about, analysed and recounted. The potential for violence permeates communal politics. The most violent event in the late 1980s, as mentioned at the outset of this chapter, was a confrontation between the two factions in Whalley Range (a group, it will be recalled, that had only recently split off) in which a great deal of damage was done and an elderly man died of a coronary.

This event was significant for another reason too: it highlighted the way factional disputes within the city and even in a single neighbourhood are 'penetrated', to use Jones's expression, by wider networks and divisions elsewhere. The leaders of the opposed groups in Whalley Range were, as already mentioned, from a single village in Jhelum District, and had previously been part of a single faction there supporting the same candidates for council and provincial elections. The division in Manchester appears to have been precipitated by a division in Pakistan, following the death of a local notable and kingmaker. His sons led the secession and mobilised support among those disgruntled with the current leadership. Following the fight in Whalley Range in which the man died, a petition was organised blaming Khaddam Saheb, one of the triumvirate of leaders of the ruling factional alliance, for plotting and causing the fight. The petition was signed by members of the opposition faction throughout the North West, who were linked to the group in Manchester. In the following council elections *in Pakistan* the ruling faction was routed, 'finished', and this triumph greatly strengthened the political hand of the local opposition faction in Manchester, as they gained defectors keen to join the now successful group.

Links beyond Manchester to the North West are evident in many public confrontations in the city, and a recurrent complaint is that those attending local election meetings were from Blackburn, Bolton or Rochdale. A local leader bragged to me that he could mobilise support throughout the North West, and listed a series of small towns where he had supporters. In 1987, the link between the politics of Pakistan and Manchester was evident in a poster printed by the Whalley Range United Association which had sponsored a large fair, bull competition and racing contest in their village in Pakistan, held in the name of the (Manchester) leaders' father. The event, which cost the British Pakistani promoters several thousand pounds (in addition to fares), was attended by members of *both* opposing Whalley Range factions. Each videoed the event separately, and the two competing video versions were circulated among supporters and adversaries throughout Manchester and the North West. Among men in these groups were several who hoped to return to Pakistan in order to hold political office, and indeed, one local activist appears to have succeeded in winning a place in Pakistani council elections. The complexities of elections in Pakistan are discussed endlessly in Manchester. The leader of the Whalley Range seceding group had his phone cut off after he accumulated an enormous bill during Pakistani (and Manchester) elections.

Apart from such major fights which have long-term implications, there were also minor fights during committee meetings or at the mosque, and these too were publicised by word of mouth. The various communal public events during fieldwork conducted in the late 1980s are listed in the Table 1.1.

Table 1.1 Mobilisation events during 1987–8

Date	Public disputes and elections	Ceremonial events and meetings
May 87	Eid Party public argument	Eid parties (1, 4) Dar Ul Aloom anniversary (2)
June 87	Race Sub-Committee elections	Pakistan cricket team parties (1, 4, 5)
July 87	Race S.C. 2nd elections	Election Victory celebrations (2) Pakistan Day ceremonial dinners (1, 2)[a]
September 87	Whalley Range meeting and violent fight	Outgoing Councillor party (3) Petition Town Hall (2)[b]
October 87		Eid Milad-un-Nabi ceremonials and public processions (1, 2)[c]
December 87	Pakistan provincial local elections	Quaid-i-Azam ceremonials (1, 2, 3)[d]
January 88	Public dispute over disqualification of candidates to Community Centre	Muslim Development Centre Town Hall conference on Asian Business (1)[e]
January 88	Community Centre elections (ended with no contest)	Longsight Association Dinner (2)[f]
March 88		Confederation elections (2) Pakistani minister's visit (1)[g] Pakistani minister's visit (2)[h]

Key
1 Controlling faction
2 Opposition faction
3 Old controlling faction
4 Elite Pakistanis not involved in community politics
5 Youth organisations or initiatives

Notes
a) (2)'s event was attended by the local MP for Longsight and other dignitaries.
b) Involved appeals to the MP and Council Chair and confrontation in Town Hall.
c) (1)'s event held at the Town Hall and attended by local MP and new Pakistani Sub-Consul.
d) (1)'s event held at the Town Hall and attended by the Pakistani Ambassador. (2)'s event held at the Pakistan Community Centre and in Whalley Range, the latter attended by the Pakistani Sub-Consul and several barristers. (3)'s event held at a hotel and attended by the Pakistani Ambassador.
e) (1)'s event held the following day at the Town Hall, attended by the Council Chair (Lord Mayor), several councillors and the Pakistani Ambassador.
f) Attended by a visiting dignitary from the Pakistan Embassy, London.
g) Took place at the Town Hall.
h) Took place at the Community Centre.

Such events keep the associations and factional alliances alive and provide public clues to shifts in allegiances. Some groups do indeed shift, and most people regard acts of betrayal and disloyalty as inevitable. When a group shifts, as mentioned, it is not normally a whole group which moves but a disaffected section of it. Given these underlying utilitarian features of factions and the recurrent fact of defection, the stress put on principles, values and loyalty is striking. Again and again faction leaders stressed to me their constancy, and the fact that they stuck to their side through thick and thin. One leader said of a man who had shifted twice, 'He is not a man of his word. In politics you need to have some principles and to stick to them.' This sentiment was echoed many times by different group leaders.

Ideology & leadership

Every good drama must have its villains and heroes. In Manchester there was general consensus beyond the ruling faction about who the villains were. In the opposition's view, they had destroyed the community and undermined consensus politics irreparably. It is worth devoting some space to a portrayal of the protagonists who have animated the imaginations of political activists in the diasporic public arena in Manchester since the 1980s.

The 'villain' of this drama, Khaddam Saheb, is an enigmatic Iago-type figure. A sophisticated man, his reputation for cunning and cleverness was unsurpassed in the community. It was believed that he and his close ally, Maulana Saheb, the *maulvi* of the Central Mosque, had their spies everywhere, so that nothing happened in the community, even in its most secret meetings, which they did not know about. Although his sharpness and ability to outmanoeuvre any opponent were universally acknowledged, his motives and objectives were less clearly understood. His enemies claimed that he was motivated by greed: he wanted power, economic advancement (from the grants he obtained) and, more subtly, that he was a Shi'a intent on creating divisions among the Sunni. His supporters saw him as a man dedicated to furthering the cause of the underprivileged, selflessly and without remuneration. Outside the community his reputation and status were quite impeccable until the hero of this piece opened the attack against him.

In fact, he was not an unusual figure on the South Asian political stage. He combined true idealism with extreme pragmatism and a measure of cynicism. Much like Kairon, the Chief Minister of the Punjab whom Pettigrew describes, he was a committed socialist, while at the same time he understood factional politics all too well and played them to the hilt. His strategies seemed to be motivated partly by self-interest, whether economic or political, at the same time as their ultimate *raison d'être* was to gain control for the sake of a wider cause. For an outsider – and even for many insiders – the difficulty in understanding his objectives stemmed from what appeared to be an internal contradiction. He was at once radically left-wing and at the same time radically dedicated to the Islamist cause of increasing the power of Islam. This uneasy combination of universalistic and particularistic ideologies made him an enigmatic figure, more in the Shi'a than the Sunni tradition, following in the path of some left-wing *mujahiddin*, an eclectic socialist, anti-colonial believer in the Shari'ati mould (see Akhavi 1983; Fischer and Abedi 1990: 211–21). To further these dual causes he attempted to gain control both of the Central Mosque and of anti-racist and welfare institutions, set up to protect immigrants' individual rights. Yet his adversarial politics continuously created internal division and dissension on a scale hitherto not experienced by Pakistanis locally.

The 'hero' of the present drama, Chaudhry Amin, is an entirely different character. A 'military man', as one of his allies described him, he is the Othello of the drama, a less subtle character altogether. From a village Chaudhri family in Jhelum, he had been a sergeant in the army before migrating to Britain. In his attack on Khaddam Saheb, the radical activist, and his friend the Maulana, he was forthright and often positively rude. He realised that the only attack his opponents could not handle was one which was open, direct and public, especially if such an attack could be mounted in the presence of outside dignitaries. His first aim was to undermine his rivals' unblemished public reputation, while making clear that the community was not totally united behind them. His second aim was to make public his intention to mobilise support against them, to wrest them from office, reputation and power.

In his ideology too this leader was far more straightforward. Since the power of the controlling faction derived from its close alliance with the Central Mosque *maulvi* and his religious order, his main call was for the separation of religion and politics, arguing that *'ulama* have no part to play in contemporary community politics in Britain. In his election victory speech (in Urdu) he made clear, as we shall see (in Chapters 2 and 3), that *maulvis* are mere employees of the community, paid to provide service. He mocked the Management Committee of the Central Mosque for their pusillanimity in failing to restrict Maulana Saheb's meddling in communal politics.

The key, however, to understanding the unfolding social drama which dominated Manchester's diasporic political arena during the 1980s, and which left a legacy of intra-communal hatred, suspicion and bitterness, is the enigmatic figure of Maulana Saheb. A tall, striking man in his early forties with a dark beard and smouldering eyes, he is a tragic villain, like Macbeth, trapped by the contradictory role he occupies, which itself epitomises the central aporia of contemporary Islam, not only in Britain but in South Asia and in many parts of the Muslim world. To put the matter simply: for British Pakistanis Islam is conceived to be the highest value, yet the scholars of Islam, the owners of divine knowledge, the men who hold the key that unlocks that divine message, are mocked and denigrated.

In an oblique and yet far-reaching critique, Philip Lewis describes the position of the *'ulama* in Britain as so dire that those who speak English choose to retrain themselves as Urdu and Islamic high school teachers! (Lewis 1994, Chap. 5). Pakistani *'ulama* train for seven years, during which time they learn Arabic and come to know the Qur'an and Hadith in great detail (ibid.: 135–9). If the methods of teaching are a little archaic, it is important not to underestimate the level of knowledge and professionalism achieved by graduates. Yet they receive a mere pittance as salaries from their congregations (ibid.: 123). The sectarian fights in which they engage diminish their reputations and make them the butts of jokes; they are disdained as ignoramuses or criticised for their extremism. This is particularly so in the case of the Barelvi *'ulama*, caught between saints and lay preachers, but the detailed scholarship of the *'ulama* is rejected by other Muslim believers as well, and especially by the young scientists and engineers who man the Islamist movements both in Britain and elsewhere.[11] But if the real scholars of Shari'a who know Islam for what it is – a loose system of laws and precedents (see Al-Azmeh 1993: 12, 25) – are rejected, then what is left, as Al-Azmeh argues convincingly, is merely a set of symbolic props and highly selective utopian do's and don'ts (such as the much publicised prohibition against usury and the injunction for women to wear the veil). This limited diacritical repertoire needs no learned *'ulama*. It stands, metonymically, for the 'true Islam' (Al-Azmeh 1993: 25–6; Gaffney 1994: 53). Hence Sunni *'ulama* as experts are redundant, apart from their role as *imams*, leaders of the prayers. Not surprisingly these men of knowledge turn in desperation to extremist ideologies and come to be politicised. If they dip into mosque funds or engage in the sale of amulets to augment their miserable incomes, this too is hardly surprising.

The serious outcome of this devaluation of Islamic scholarship is that so far in Britain there has been little serious attempt at independent *ijtihad* (legal innovation by analogy) which would amount to an engagement with Islam as a modern religion practised in British society, although a few exemplary scholars such as Shaikh Badawi point the way towards such a future dialogue. The challenge facing Muslims in the 1990s, Philip Lewis argued, was whether they could mobilise

> the intellectual and imaginative resources within the Islamic tradition to engage with the religious, intellectual and cultural traditions of the West. Islamic traditions developed in South Asia contain a variety of perspectives honed in conflict with British hegemony, ranging from accommodation to isolation and defiance. The need now is for a critical and constructive exchange both within this tradition and with the majority society. (P. Lewis 1994: 208)

Things are changing, however slowly. An article in *Q News* reported that a 'meeting of the Muslim Law (Shari'a) Council – a national grouping of *faqihs* (legislators) drawn from across the theological and juristic schools' – had decided upon the legality of organ transplants by Muslims (*Q News*, 28 July 1995). Real critical engagement seems distant, however, when even attempts to co-ordinate a single date (based on the sighting of the new moon) for the celebration of *eid* by all the sectarian groups in Britain have so far failed abysmally. It seems that the moon hanging over Britain is still hidden behind the clouds of sectarian intransigence.

The following chapters trace some of the public arenas in which the battles for communal honour and power in the diasporic public sphere were fought out during the late 1980s and early 1990s. Such battles, I show, were as much rhetorical and oratorical as indexical;[12] they articulated political imaginaries of diaspora, fabulated by protagonists in their attempts to mobilise support for their cause. I begin by tracing some of these public events which followed immediately upon the *halagula* at the Community Centre. My focus is on the myths of identity, nation and community narrated by the speakers at these meetings.

During much of this time the 'community' was a parochial backwater at war with itself. It was into this scene of parochial rivalry and imaginative creativity

---

[11] For a discussion of this rejection see Werbner 1996a.

[12] The notion of the 'indexical' is traceable to Peirce, and is used by phenomenologists to refer to the particularity and historicity of symbols, tropes and speech events. These may also become indexes or yardsticks of status and power relations, inclusion and exclusion. More generally, indexical refers to the specificity of meaning in particular contexts, including relativities of power and status (see Garfinkel 1967: 4; Bar Hillel 1970; Fernandez 1986; R. Werbner 1989; P. Werbner 1990a: 260–1).

that the Rushdie affair erupted like a bombshell, displacing the factional hostilities and mobilising Muslims in a solidary battle to redeem the honour of Islam and its Prophet. The Rushdie affair invoked for Muslims in the diaspora an intense consciousness of their marginality and powerlessness in their newly adopted society. It also underlined the fact that they were citizens of Britain with all the attendant rights and duties this implied. Related to this, the affair revealed a potentially powerful capacity for cross-sectarian mobilisation on a national scale. The affair was thus both empowering and disempowering; it alienated Muslims while anchoring them more firmly in their newly adopted society. The discourse of multiculturalism and religious pluralism generated by the affair created new agendas for active citizenship.

But even before the Rushdie affair had died down, the Gulf War broke out, underlining further the sense of alienation and impotence Muslims felt vis-à-vis the West. The rhetoric enunciated from mosque pulpits and diasporic public arenas in response to these two global events became increasingly utopian and millenarian. There appeared to be a growing radicalisation and Islamicisation of Pakistanis in the diaspora. In later chapters of the book, I trace these historical developments which, for a time at least, enveloped the local community's diasporic politics of honour and shame in global issues. Looking back, however, we find a surprising break which occurred as the 1990s progressed, *away* from radical utopianism towards pragmatism and tolerance; from purity towards dionysian effervescence and South Asian 'fun'; from a focus on the mosque as the central arena to a diasporic commitment to the plight of transnational Muslim victims of violence. In many senses this has been a move from male elder dominance to youth and women. Yet this, too, has been disrupted by the September 11 bombing of the World Trade Center. Once again, the Muslim diaspora in Britain felt under siege. The penultimate chapter of the book traces this second historical rupture before returning to the final denouement: the fate of Maulana Saheb and his allies in the local battle between good and evil.

2
The Fables of the Blindfolded Ox & the Blue Jackal

On honour and political passion

Some time after the *halagula* at the Community Centre which set me off on the trail of factional politics, Chaudhry Muhammad Amin, the aspiring community leader we encountered in the previous chapter, celebrated his victorious election as an ethnic representative, a 'Community Rep', to the Municipal Council's Race Sub-Committee. The election had been a hard-fought one and Chaudhry Amin had vanquished a formidable foe and personal enemy, Maulana Saheb, the current cleric or *maulvi* of the Central Jami'a Mosque in Manchester.

Chaudhry Amin was a man of honour. He had served for many years as a sergeant-major in the Pakistan army, working his way up through the ranks, before he deserted and emigrated to Britain. He had sweated on twelve-hour shifts in a textile mill before opening a small knitwear factory. A Punjabi of land-lord peasant stock, he was dark, hard and proud, not a man to be slighted in public. Always an aspiring leader, the public offence perpetrated upon him by the Maulana at the mosque had fired him with a sense of mission. He was determined that no servile *maulvi*, nor any of his friends – cunning urban sophisticates and arrogant businessmen – would usurp the rights of the people. He was a repre-sentative of the people and he had triumphed. He savoured his victory. His speech, made to his supporters, mostly ex-factory workers like himself, at a dinner celebrating the victory of their 'party' on 19 July 1987, was a rhetorical *tour de force*. It reveals some of the basic moral ideas which underlie ethnic community diasporic politics.

He began his speech, as virtually all community leaders do, by citing from Muhammad Iqbal, the revered Urdu national poet, and by promising the opposi-tion that he would represent them well, because 'as all our great leaders have told us, in a democratic system it is necessary to have an opposition party'. Hence, he continued, 'Now that the activities of the election have finished, we are all brothers. Therefore I pray ... that Allah will give us unity (*idhad*).' Returning to Iqbal once more he went on: 'As the Eastern poet says:

A man exists only in the unity of his nation
As a wave is in a river,
Beyond the river, there is nothing [i.e. without a nation to lead there is no leadership].

Having appealed to communal unity, he moved to the more serious business of demolishing the opposition faction and its *maulvi* leader, who, he claimed, was wasting public money by travelling around in taxis and watching videos, instead of performing his religious duties. The Maulana had called him an illiterate in public, an unforgivable dishonour and the basis for a perpetual personal feud:

They call us *kolu-ka bail*, an animal without a brain [the ox that drives the oil press round and round with its eyes covered]. And whenever they want to they say: 'If that thing [person] does not remove itself we cannot start the *namaz*' (the prayers) [i.e. Maulana Saheb refuses to conduct the prayers at the Central Mosque in his presence].

It is strange to be called *kolu-ka bail*. You know what an ox of the *kolu* is? The ox that goes around and around [the oil press] all day [blindfolded]. And at night they give it something to eat, grass, and then it sleeps.

We *are kolu-ka bails*. Yes, it means that we work hard all day. Islam does not decree that we should not work. If it did, how could the schools be run? Or the mosque, without paying the wages and expenses of its employees?... This, to work, is not unusual or *haram* [forbidden] in Islam. It is wrong to call us *kolu-ka bail*. The task of the [Mosque] Committee is to supervise [the employees] and Committee members should not shut their eyes or ears [to the corruption of the *maulvi* and his allies]. When I asked one of the [Committee] workers: 'are you listening?' he replied: 'we are using our ears rightly'. 'What do you mean?' I asked. 'Allah created our ears opposite each other', he said. 'We hear with one ear, and clear the sound from the other'. [In other words, we ignore what is going on in the mosque.]

But *we* use our ears ... we listen both from this side and from the other side – which is why we have ears. Today we are not only saying but we are issuing a warning. They [the Maulana and his allies] should not take part in politics. They have a crystal ball and they gaze in it and predict what will happen to this or that [political] 'party'. Then they make propaganda and generate internal conflicts between members [of that group], and thus prevent them from doing anything about matters of real importance.

Today we are making clear that we shall break their crystal ball. Then they will no longer be able to perpetrate these things...

I learnt a lot during the day of my election – who is for me and who against. Who is a true supporter, and who a pretender. Where a person stands [in relation to me].

Having completed the fable of the Blindfolded Ignorant Ox, Chaudhry Amin turned to a new fable, the fable of the Blue Cowardly Jackal:

Now we know about those *neelkanth*. Most of you wouldn't know the meaning of *neelkanth*. There was once a jackal (*gidar*) who was slightly bigger than the other jackals. One day he was hungry so he went to a village. But the dogs all chased him out of the village [at this point in the speech, the audience laughed uproariously]. He saw a man, a dyer, who was dyeing clothes. Because he was confused by what he saw, he fell into the big tub of dye. When he came out, the dogs all stepped back [in fear] so he thought he had become something special now. He went further and saw a lion eating his prey. The lion was surprised to see him. At that time, it was said, animals were able to talk. The lion asked him: 'Who are you?' He said: 'I am a *neelkanth*.' The lion said: 'What is a *neelkanth*?' The jackal said: 'A *neelkanth* is a creature who, when he draws his claws over the earth, he tears it open. If he speaks loudly, all the trees fall down. If he calls once, a thousand voters come. If he clicks his fingers, four or five hundred voters come. And if he waves a big stick, two hundred voters come.' The lion was scared. He thought: 'If he draws his claws on the earth it will split, and where will I go then?' So he gave the jackal his prey – because he was scared. And for about a month the jackal went on eating this way. One day it rained, and the dye was washed away so that his real colour was revealed.

[Shouting] The lion saw the real thing and the jackal ran away in fear. Last Sunday [election day] it was raining and the dyed colour of the *neelkanth* was washed away. [Neel – blue, the colour of evil and cowardice] And they ran away like jackals. Those *neelkanths* ran away.

There is another verse from Dr Iqbal:

Don't fear the strong wind, eagle

For it comes to carry you higher. ['Isn't he a leader!' a member of the audience comments].

We come in truth, and we have the unity of truthful and sincere persons. With the help of these people we formed an organisation. And because we come in truth, people helped us. It is like this. If you do not abandon the truth, there is no power in the world that can overcome you....

Somebody told me: they are reading *dawas* (supplications) against you [in the mosque]... A famous *alim* said once: 'Pilgrimage is true, but the pilgrim is false; fasting is true, but he who fasts is false; *namaz* (praying) is true, but he who prays is false.' So too, those *dawas*, supplications, which are read against us, those are true, but the people who read them are false. That is why they were not accepted [by God]. That is why those *dawas* came to us, came to the truth.

If someone wishes to answer my speech, let him do so in a public meeting and we shall answer in the same manner, in public. And if they answer us in the mosque [a place of prayer] then we have the right to answer them in that same place. And let them not say then that this is a place of prayer since they were the ones who brought it into disrespect [who desecrated it].

Finally, I embrace you all with an open heart and advise you that we should defend (*masba*) our good deeds (*'amal*). That way we shall stay close to Allah. It should not come to pass that a voice descends from heaven [saying] that 'your *imam* is not true (*behazar* – without respect) therefore your *namaz* prayer cannot be heard [when you say your prayers behind the *imam*]. Follow (find) the good *imam*.'

I am so grateful to all of you who have spared your valued time and come here, and granted me the opportunity to thank you.

• • •

The fables of the Blindfolded Ox and the Blue Jackal tell a story of human passion and social morality: of individuals competing for honour and leadership in a battle of strategy, power and rhetoric; and of moral responsibility for the welfare of fellow countrymen and women, and for the cultural reproduction of the community as a moral community, a community of brothers and sisters who are beholden to one another. The passion of the battle is the passion of individuals who, in exile, away from home, seek status within the narrow public arena of diasporic politics. Despite the objective narrowness of this arena, however, it is, for the participants, a central stage in which they act out their passions and rhetorical skills in a mythologised drama of human encounters and social intrigue. As Levinas argues:

Those animals that portray men give the fable its peculiar colour inasmuch as men are seen *as* these animals and not only *through* these animals; the animals stop and fill up thought.... It is an ambiguous commerce with reality ... equivalent to an alteration of the very being of the object. (Levinas 1987: 6–7)

The fabled animal constitutes the man or woman as a coward or hero, as cunning and evil or strong and reliable. It reveals his or her exemplary, archetypal qualities, while retaining the reality of individual social agency. It naturalises their 'true', hidden identity.

What are the consequences of this intensity of political involvement? One obvious consequence is a passionate commitment to the communal political

Plate 2.1 Factional leader

Plate 2.2 Man of reputation

values fostered in the internal debate between contestants; a second is that, as will become evident during the course of this book, the narrow stage of community politics is *globalised* as a world stage. The actors are perceived, and perceive one another, in vivid, dramatic terms. They are acting out a global drama, a drama in which people assemble to talk about democracy, power, nationhood, religion, the state and global politics. Such debates take place almost entirely hidden from the public eye, in a foreign language members of the wider society cannot understand. A third is that actors play on their identities, now fusing them, now keeping them apart.

The fusion of identities

In his speech Chaudhry Amin conflated his different identities as a Punjabi, Pakistani, British, Muslim, Mancunian (i.e. Manchester man), in order to appeal to his audience, themselves Punjabis, Pakistanis, Mancunians and Muslim. The question of *when* diasporic collective identities are kept apart, and when they are fused, is important if we are to escape from a simplistic discourse of 'cultural hybridity'. On the surface, it seems relatively straightforward to argue that migrant or diasporic identities are powerfully 'hybrid'. This is the view suggested by Hall (1990), Gilroy (1993) and Bhabha (1994). Migrants subvert the purity of national cultural boundaries, and disturb the apparent homogeneity of the nation through their hybrid existences. The argument in its simplicity is a compelling one. It appears to describe a grand historical shift from national purity to cosmopolitan hybridity. But it could also be argued that it starts from a frozen understanding of identity and culture, one which fails to recognise the *synchronic dynamics* of identity, their constant shifting between singularity and plurality.

This dynamic has been a guiding truth of anthropological theory, at least since the publication of *The Nuer* in 1940. *The Nuer* demonstrated that collective identities are always relative. If social agents bear multiple (and sometimes contradictory) identities, these are typically highlighted or foregrounded situationally and selectively, in opposition. The further important insight contained in Evans-Pritchard's analysis, and one which bears directly upon current debates about identity and social movements, is that these sited identities are valorised in the last instance not by simple material interests or ecological exigencies, but by the moral values of sociality which *constitute* these interests and constraints within given contexts.

In the critiques of segmentary theory which followed the publication of *The Nuer*, a key point to emerge was that identities (and hence also interests and valorised socialities), grounded in different organisational principles, cannot always be kept separate as the theory had suggested. Men and women may be, for example, and indeed often are, both lineage members and affines, spouses and siblings, and it is the fusion of these identities, with all the tensions and contradictions such cross-cutting ties imply, which shapes modes of mediation and overarching processes of dispute settlement or transversal alliances.

Hybridity theory recognises moments of fusion but it fails to understand when and why diasporic identities are kept separate and apart, why people are willing to defend one strand (e.g. Islam) of a 'hybrid' identity at enormous personal cost. A key aim of the present book is to disclose the dynamic logic of diasporic situational *separations* of (sometimes conflicting) identities – and hence also of loyalties, sentimental identifications and communal imaginings – and their fusion, achieved through creative acts of cultural performance. Beyond segmentary theory, I argue further that what makes such fusings so powerful is their weaving together of different types of identity – moral, aesthetic and political – to create a powerful grass-roots basis for ethnic mobilisation.

In an urban context, segmentary theory was drawn upon to illuminate processes of situational selection among labour migrants on the Zambian (then Northern Rhodesian) Copperbelt. In their dealings with the colonial mine management, Mitchell and Epstein argued, workers highlighted their solidary black identity in opposition to the white management, while in their internal competition for leadership or leisure activities, tribal and sub-tribal identities were invoked situationally and selectively to allow for preferential neighbourly relations, ritual assistance in burials or the suspension of traditional rural hostilities through joking relations.[1]

At the same time, however, low-paid workers also formed tribal dance troupes in which they *fused* structurally disparate identities (of class status and ethnicity) in cultural performance. Hence, rather than display authentic emblems of tribal tradition and assert their distinctive separateness by opposition, the dancers chose to dress smartly in the prestigious European clothes of the town and to sing in Chibemba, the *lingua franca* of the Copperbelt. Tribal oppositions were, however, also expressed – through ribald and obscene joking directed at the spectators, many of whom were women. Mitchell (1956) tells us that the dance was, among other things, a courting dance performed by young bachelors seeking sexual partners.

In theorising Mitchell's case study, it may be argued that this fusing of identities – of urban and tribal aesthetics – was a mode of empowerment. Such a fusing drew its force partly from the improvised and yet taken-for-granted nature of the conjunction. In other words, what made the Kalela dance so effective (and the dancers so irresistible), was the repeatedly renewed act of conjoining – the creative, humorous fusion of identities which remained, in principle, also discrete.

Intentional hybridity of this sort, and its counterpart, cultural essentialism, are thus both political performances. Anticipating current debates, Abner Cohen highlighted the way that 'political ethnicity', the articulation of identities – political, economic and cultural – is played out agonistically in the public arena.[2]

---

[1] Mitchell's (1956) and Epstein's (1958) application here of segmentary theory and its associated principle of situational selection is, of course, an example of the more general approach to urbanism and the colonial encounter which became the hallmark of the Manchester School (for a recent discussion, see Rogers and Vertovec 1995). The sited nature of ethnic boundary maintenance was later developed by Fredrik Barth in a celebrated essay (Barth 1969). In Britain two social anthropologists, Wallman and Banton, have both adopted this approach which stresses the situational nature of ethnicity, and have applied it to local British contexts (see Wallman 1986). Against this, I have argued, however, that the Manchester School's situational approach, as initially formulated and as later developed by Barth, glosses over the problem of how 'new', constraining, communal injunctions and norms are created and actively valorised by migrant groups in town and what implications this has for social theory (Werbner 1990a).

[2] Cohen's interest in diasporas and transnational communities, in the fusion of identities and the responsive creativity of ethnic cultures, raised a set of foundational questions for anthropologists, which have come by now to be part of the taken-for-granteds of the discipline. There is an irony here for the newborn discipline of Cultural Studies, which has tended to claim intellectual proprietorship over cultural politics and the politics of identity while denouncing anthropologists (the 'handmaidens

Cohen's most recent work on the Notting Hill Carnival in London (1993) is especially important, for in it he highlights both the momentum towards cultural fusion in response to changing power relations, and the ultimate irreducibility of culture to politics. If identities are fused and politicised, he demonstrates, the aesthetic and the moral remain as truths in their own right which cannot ever be fully encompassed by the political.

Chaudhry Amin's speech revealed the powerful fusings of discrete discourses and the appeal to different identities characteristic of the political rhetoric of aspiring, grass-roots British Pakistani leaders. In their rhetoric the usual spatial and cognitive separations normally observed between the sacred and the profane, *din* (religion) and *dunya* (the world), the political and the aesthetic, are overridden for the sake of moving an audience. As elsewhere in the Muslim world, Pakistanis normally manage their multiple identifications through 'a radical disjunction between personal piety and [a secularised] public life' (Geertz 1968: 107). Being, simultaneously, British, South Asian, Pakistani, Muslim, Punjabi and modern, the range of incongruous taken-for-granted identifications (and hence of identities kept in disjunction) they embrace is perhaps unusually large. It is, of course, a multiplicity which has its roots not simply in the recent migration process to Britain but in South Asia itself, a legacy of successive imperial regimes and religious movements, of population displacements, the modern rise of nationalism(s), postcolonial wars and religious hostilities – all of which have conjoined to make the subcontinent, seen analytically, a vast, billion-strong 'border-zone' of social actors bearing multiple and often contradictory palimpsest identities, mediating unreconcilable chronotopes of space and time.[3]

The situational management of these multiple identities is, in fact, quite consonant with classic segmentary theory. What creates the postmodernist, postcolonial *differance* is the further fact that the traditional is now essentially also modern: identity only makes sense, in a taken-for-granted way, within the modern. At the same time, as invoked by cultural mediators, it can also become highly reflexive or objectified in cultural goods. As Paul Gilroy argues, black identities are rooted in slavery and in the black diaspora it generated. The cultural narratives created in response to this brutal encounter with modernity are 'deeply embedded' in modernity itself (Gilroy 1993: 190), woven into the very fabric of modernist discourses. This is falsified, in his view, by the black movements which have attempted to deny the experience of slavery by invoking a pure African, pre-slavery genealogy and 'tradition'. Extending Gilroy's point, one may argue even further that the black diaspora itself is a modernist imagining, the creation of black intellectuals seeking a common platform.

If diasporas are imaginative constructions, then there is no reason why exiles should not regard themselves as part of a whole series of quite *different* diasporas simultaneously. In their rhetoric, British Pakistanis evoke at least three diasporas, each of which valorises a different domain of sociality: moral, political and

[2] (cont.) of colonialism') for representing culture as stripped of its political dimensions. Against that stereotype, the movement in Cohen's four monographs (Cohen 1965, 1969, 1981, 1993) reveals an increasingly historicised, performative and dialectical approach to the study of cultural politicisation.

[3] A palimpsest is a piece of writing material or brass rewritten or re-engraved. The notion of palimpsest identities is used by Bauman 1997, Bhabha 1994, Young 1995 and Werbner 1997a to describe the historical overlayering of cumulative identities. Chronotopes are historically experienced time/space unities, as defined by Bakhtin (see Clark and Holquist 1984: 278).

aesthetic (the Muslim, the Pakistani and the South Asian/Punjabi). Nor are these diasporas merely the imaginatively *discursive* products of sentimental nostalgias. The diasporas 'exist' also as observable realities objectified through the global distribution of packaged 'culture' – foods and spices, cassette tapes and Bombay film videos, elaborate designer *shalwar qamiz* – ranging in its pretentiousness from high to mass popular culture. The culture industry supplying these diasporas reaches the very ends of the South Asian and Muslim diasporic worlds.

On the one hand, then, these multiple diasporas exist for Pakistanis as sites of sentimental attachment, imaginatively and actively constructed in local cultural performances; yet it is important to recognise that they also exist *beyond* the subjectivities of diasporic actors – in the aesthetic, political and moral products of a vast and increasingly transnational culture industry. The focus of the present chapter is, however, on the local cultural performance of diaspora, seen as moments leading towards the emergence of a local religio-ethnic social movement. The event presented in this chapter was itself a single episode in a continuing Mancunian social drama, in which local factions mobilised behind a changing constellation of grass-roots leaders. As we have seen, their ultimate aim was to capture the Central Mosque and with it the moral high ground of the Muslim Asian Pakistani community in the city. The performance described was thus typically, like most other such performances I attended, an embattled argument of identities intended both to mobilise support and to contest a range of aesthetic values and moral assumptions imputedly held by opponents. During this period, such performances and the arguments they encapsulated were hidden from a wider public, a fact significant for an understanding of the rise of new social movements.

Social movements

In his landmark discussion of social movements, Alberto Melucci makes the point that

> collective actors invest an enormous quantity of resources in an ongoing game of solidarity. They spend a great deal of time and energy discussing who they are, what they should become and which people have the right to decide that. (1989: 218)

Social movements, he argues, live a 'double existence', performed partly in the 'invisible networks of civil society' and partly in the 'temporary mobilisations through which they become publicly visible' (ibid.: 228). The visible action is thus the other pole of the production of 'new cultural codes within submerged networks' (ibid.: 44, 70). Temporary public visibilisation occurs whenever collective actors openly confront an antithetical public policy (ibid.: 70). Otherwise, much of the activity of members of social movements is directed towards actualising collective values through distinctive lifestyles, within 'submerged networks'. In other words,

> collective action is nourished by the daily production of alternative frameworks of meaning.... Latency does not mean inactivity. Rather, the potential for resistance or opposition is sewn into the very fabric of daily life. (ibid.: 70)

Moreover,

> the forms of action ... are at one and the same time prior to and beyond politics: they are

pre-political because they are rooted in everyday life experiences; and *meta-political* because political forces can never represent them completely. (ibid.: 71)

Melucci draws both on the work of Touraine (1981) on social movements and, even more, on the theory of communicative action proposed by Habermas (1989). In the view of the latter, all forms of power ultimately draw their legitimacy from the everyday, taken-for-granted 'lifeworld'. In the communicative practice of everyday life, according to Habermas,

cognitive interpretations, moral expectations, expressions and values have to interpenetrate and form a rational interconnectedness via the transfer of validity that is possible in the performative attitude. (1989: 327)

Like Touraine, Castells and Melucci, Habermas sees contemporary social movements as attempts to defend the erosion of the lifeworld, and the personalised identities it sustains, from a further encroachment of economic–administrative systems of control and profitability. The issue in such movements, he argues, is not primarily one 'of compensations that the welfare state can provide, but of defending and restoring endangered ways of life' (ibid.: 392).

If for Melucci, however, the present is actualised through alternative ways of living which enact a visionary future (hence he speaks of 'nomads of the present'), more stress is placed by Castells and Touraine on the social movements' imagining of 'reactive utopias' (see Touraine 1981; Castells 1983). For members of social movements, they argue, present identities are rooted in a vision of a perfect future which may be, as in the case of Islamic movements, a recovery of a perfect past. This implies a more unified ideological vision than that found in most social movements. Hence Melucci reports that the Italian movements he studied were composed of disparate social actors with varying agendas. Such internal disagreements are, indeed, in his view, a key reason why public political mobilisation in such movements is usually temporary and issue-centred, rather than sustained and supported by unified ideologies. By contrast, other theorists lay more stress on the broadening of ideological alliances through a 'chain of equivalences' (see Mouffe 1988; Mercer 1992).

The need is thus to identify the organisational processes underlying mobilisation (see Hannigan 1985: 446). The rise of ethnic and diasporic movements reflects a complex interaction between, on the one hand, continuous ethnic arguments of identity which take place in invisible spaces, hidden from the public eye, and, on the other hand, processes of ideological production and organisational mobilisation which reveal the submerged social networks of ethnic activists and broadcast their collective voices periodically to a wider public sphere (see Werbner 1991a).

My argument starts from the fact that ethnic participation is not limited to the spaces allocated by a dominant state. It unfolds in the spaces and arenas created by members of the ethnic community themselves. Top-down theories of multiculturalism or ethnicity which see culture merely as an instrumental product of state control or beneficence[4] fail to recognise the aesthetic and moral dimensions of ethnic mobilisation. Rather than being determined by the state, identity spaces are created by activists pitched against one another in a local micropolitics of honour, in which the stakes are ontological, a matter of defining who 'we' are.

[4] This is a commonplace argument (see, for example, Baumann 1996) which we reject collectively (Werbner and Modood 1997).

Hence, a further feature of performance is highlighted in Chaudhri Amin's speech. Performances reveal the conflicts and divisions preoccupying both speakers and their audiences. Performances are therefore not mere solidaristic events, expressions of a transcendent unity.

But this, of course, begs the question of what is 'community'? Benedict Anderson's work on 'imagined communities' has released the sociological imagination from its fixation on community as *Gemeinschaft* – a traditional, face-to-face group of consociates (1991 [1983]). To refine his heuristic concept further, however, the need is to elaborate on the fundamentally different senses in which community is imagined and, equally critically, is enacted and actualised through cultural performance, or incorporated through organisational mobilisation.

In extending my earlier work (1991a), I want to suggest that in ethnic diasporan groups three dimensions of community are publicly imagined and incorporated: the *moral* community, the *aesthetic* community (or the *interpretive* community) and the community of *suffering*. Each 'community' is a cultural world which is constructed through performative imaginings by networks of social actors continuously mobilised and renewed by these performances.

The moral community

Moral communities are the product, as Bauman has argued, following Levinas, of a sense of responsibility *for* others (Bauman 1993). A central moral idea animating Pakistani activism is that of public service for the common good of the 'community', *khidmat*, service rendered selflessly, with no expectation of return. *Khidmat* is a form of unilateral giving, and may be conceived of as a sacrificial offering in the sight of God, an expression of public responsibility. It parallels the Hindu notion of *seva* which paradoxically, as Adrian Mayer shows, must deny its own publicity: 'true public service, like the true gift or offering, is that which is secretly made; once it becomes publicly known it can be tinged with motives of selfishness or used as an aid to advancement' (Mayer 1981: 157).

Many recent analyses of diaspora stress its communicative, experiential and aesthetic dimensions, objectified in artistic products: novels, poetry, popular music (for example, Gilroy 1993 or Brah 1996). However, if we conceive of diasporas as communities of co-responsibility, we need to seek notions that define the gesture of reaching out, of tangibly acknowledging co-responsibility beyond localism. Philanthropy as a mode of reaching out across boundaries can serve to objectify a scattered transnational collectivity. More generally we may say that *khidmat* objectifies the limits of the moral community set by such unilateral giving, or, alternatively, sharing. Public giving is an act of *identification* which expresses personal commitment stemming from a shared identity. Ethnic fund-raising is thus a culturally generative gesture. Buildings such as mosques and community centres need money to be constructed and managed. No viable ethnic organisation can be run without funding and voluntary labour. To manage an association, convene committee meetings, hold celebrations, respond to welfare needs, show solidarity with victims of wars and natural disasters, requires appeals, fund-raising and voluntary efforts. The victory meeting Chaudhri Amin addressed was hosted by him along with a core of close supporters. Without their donations it would never have taken place. The paradox is that public unilateral giving confers honour and status on the giver, and hence his/her altruistic motives are always subject to doubt. Nevertheless, moral communities are actualised, above all, through performative acts of giving.

Elsewhere I have shown that giving may be competitive or equal, generating different associational forms: hierarchical, in which giving is agonistic and flows from the rich to the poor, with the rich holding important public offices; and sharing between equals according to need, in which it is the organisers who gain status and esteem (see Werbner 1990a, Chap. 10). But whether balanced or agonistic, giving always occurs within recognised limits of trust. The category encompassing donors and recipients is, from this perspective, also conceived to be a moral community. Through his/her donations, an individual expresses membership in a circle composed of mutually trusting others. Moreover, contributions made in different contexts signify an individual's identification with a progressively widening series of moral communities – from a circle of known intimates, 'homeboys', fellow villagers (*grain*), a transnational network focused on a single village, to the whole national or religious community, including many unknown persons, and then further to a scattered diaspora or the home country of origin. After the outbreak of the war in Bosnia, for example, Pakistanis mobilised throughout Britain in a sustained communal drive to raise funds, food and medicine for Muslims in Bosnia, a community whose very existence was, until recently, entirely unknown to them.

Unilateral giving does not necessarily imply a rejection of otherness. Membership in an expanding series of moral communities, all of which are represented in the public domain, endows individuals with their essential, inalienable sense of identity. In claiming public recognition, moral communities may be asserting equal rather than superior moral worth. Through giving, ethnic identity is not merely passively conferred or displayed. Nor is it generated in opposition. It requires an active gesture of identification, of giving, signalling moral commitment or 'proximity' in the sense suggested by Levinas (see Levinas 1989).

Going back to Melucci, it is important to recognise, however, that the moral community is not a unity. It is full of conflict, of internal debate about moral values. Such debates imply fierce competition for leadership. They also involve competition for the right to name: Who are we? What do we stand for? What are we to be called? Are we Muslims? Democrats? Pakistanis? Socialists? Black? Asian? The power to name, to inscribe, to describe, implies a power to invoke a world of moral relationships, a power underlined in the myth of *Genesis*. Naming constitutes a forceful act of leadership in its own right.[5]

Solidarities are achievements, usually ephemeral (yet they are 'imaginatively' critical moments: anti-essentialist arguments attacking the false construction of 'culture' or 'society' fail to recognise the importance for participants in moral debates of an imaginative belief in the reality of such achieved solidarities). Solidarity is, in fact, often a feature of early immigrant sociality. Permanent settlement,

---

[5] For an extended discussion of the debate about the correct 'name' for South Asians in Britain see Werbner (1997b). During the 1970s and early 1980s claims were made for a unified 'black' resistance movement (see, for example, articles published in Sivanandan 1989, 1990) but this was later notably modified by Stuart Hall in a talk given to the British Film Institute (republished in Hall 1992) in the light of critiques by Asian intellectuals (such an early critique appeared in Modood 1988). Like the early socialist movement, feminists attacked all essentialist constructions (for example Brah 1996, Saghal and Yuval-Davis 1992).

however, brings fragmentation as numbers increase and associations multiply and often compete internally for moral supremacy. The factional battle between Chaudhry Amin's faction and Maulana Saheb's faction was an instance of this political and ideological diversification, a moment in an ongoing struggle. Often, ethnic territorial organisations, such as the Manchester Central Mosque, which initially objectified communal unity, split, objectifying communal fragmentation. At the same time, the efflorescence of associations creates an institutional network which enables the urban community to reproduce itself in all its cultural and ideological diversity, leading to a process of increasing communal incorporation and institutional completeness, an elaboration of the moral community in all its complexity.

In his speech Chaudhry Amin articulated the moral dimensions of ethnic voluntary activity by engaging in a moral argument or dialogue with the opposition. He called for unity, truth, sincerity and the values of hard work and professional conduct. He also called for democratic public debate and recognised that such a debate was an essential feature of democracy. He made clear that people were locked in moral interdependency: a person cannot exist outside the community, as a wave cannot exist outside the ocean. He spoke in vivid images and tropes, appealing to Punjabi and Islamic cultural idioms and moral ideas to score his points and carry his audience forward with him. His rhetoric underlined the fact that an ethnic community is not only a moral community; it is also an aesthetic community, a community with a shared fund of tropes, symbols and images, associations and understandings.

The aesthetic community

If the moral community is defined by *khidmat*, unilateral giving or sharing, the aesthetic community is defined by cultural knowledge, passion and creativity.[6] The Pakistani (Muslim, Punjabi, Urdu, English) community, defined as an aesthetic community, has its cultural experts: its orators, poets, priests, saints and intellectuals. It shares common idioms of humour, love, tragedy, popular culture, festivals, cricket and myths of the past: of national or religious exemplary heroes, of great battles and victories, of oppression and freedom. It shares aesthetic ideas of spatial separations between the sacred and the profane, *din* (religion) and *dunya* (the world), sensuality and spirituality, 'fun' and sobriety. To perpetuate and reproduce these, the community has incorporated itself in myriad associations: literary societies, religious organisations, orders and sects, sports clubs, women's cultural associations, and so forth.

Chaudhry Amin's speech contains implicit acts of identification with several different aesthetic communities. The imagery in the speech is Punjabi, perhaps even pan-Asian. The *kolu-ka bail*, the blindfolded ox who grinds the oil seeds, is a familiar village sight; it evokes a faraway home community, agriculture, the dusty hot plains of the Punjab. Similarly, the fable of the blue jackal invokes the spaces between villages, the uninhabited jungles where lions and jackals live on the margins of humanity. The *neelkanth*, literally meaning 'blueneck', is an

---

[6] Bauman (1992) attributes the notion of an aesthetic community to Kant, citing Lyotard (1988). The notion of an aesthetic community is more distinctively grounded, however, in my view, in postmodernist theory than in a Kantian aesthetics (see Geertz 1983, Chap. 5, for a superb account of what makes for an aesthetic community).

oblique reference to incarnations of Shiva and Vishnu, although it is used here quite differently. Iqbal's poetry invokes heroic images of rivers and eagles, but also of the nationalist movement to create Pakistan as a Muslim independent homeland. The moral lessons are Islamic, but also Western-democratic. They evoke images of mosques, prayers and religious aphorisms. Chaudhri Amin and his audience have complex identities: they are Punjabis, Pakistanis, socialists, democrats, British and Muslim. The speech reaches them as an aesthetic performance in all these different dimensions. What Hall refers to as the 'silences' contained in each discrete identity (Hall 1991) are revealed through the rhetorical imagery, moving the audience to passion, touching their sentiments, the nostalgic yearning for another place with its smells and physical sensations. But also, at the same time, drawing *moral* lessons from these images which are much more specific.

The aesthetic community is thus intertwined with the moral community. Ideas about purity and pollution, good and evil, articulate the two and, as we shall see in Chapters 5 and 7, may generate moral conflicts about the legitimacy of aesthetic forms or, indeed, of a morality which rejects these valorised aesthetic forms.

Towards a theory of ethnic complexity

It has become almost a truism in the sociological literature to argue that ethnic divisions 'intersect' with other social divisions: of class, race, nation, religion and gender (see Anthias and Yuval-Davis 1992). People are positioned in terms of the intersection of all their different identities. Often, of course, ethnic or racial groups are relegated to an inferior class position, compounding their marginality, but this is not universally the case: middleman minorities and mobile ethnic groups may achieve wealth and education while still being marked by their ethnic or religious origins. Lists of categorical intersections, however long, cannot capture, however, the shifting and dynamic nature of ethnic complexity. In the case of Pakistani settlers, for example, divisions by class, gender and generation intersect with other significant social divisions and sources of identity which are segmentary and fluid, while positioning needs also to take account of differential location within the ethnic field. Some Pakistanis sustain dense networks of sociality with fellow-ethnics and are positioned close to the core of communal activism; others exist on the periphery of the ethnic group. Each of these socio-cultural axes – segmentary, class, ethnic field and categorical – is the locus of different cultural mobilisations and each generates its own internal and external cultural dialogues.

First, rather than being an 'ethnic' group with a single, culturally marked boundary, Pakistani settlers form a segmentary system of groups. The local community is not bounded by a single boundary, but contains boundaries within boundaries, revealed in situational opposition. Pakistanis form part of one of the largest 'segmented diasporas' in the world today (see Werbner 2000a). Collective identities refer to a series of encompassing moral communities on a rising social scale, defined by language, region, or sectarian affiliation. To be a British-Pakistani-Muslim-Punjabi-Asian-Black-Mancunian-Sunni-Deobandi-Jhelmi-Gujar is not necessarily, as anthropologists have long recognised, to bear contradictory or multiphrenic identities, since all these identities may never come into conflict in practice. Others may share such complex identities, and particular identities may be highlighted in different social situations. Moreover, the most intensely passionate and all-encompassing moral conflicts may not necessarily be between people bearing opposed identities; rather, they may be 'internal' ones, such as that between Chaudhry Amin and Maulana Saheb – both men, both Muslims, both Punjabis, both Sunnis although one less pious and more of a modernist than the other. What actually divides them thus is their political stance regarding the relationship between religion and civil society; the conflict between them as leaders of factions surrounds the growing politicisation of religion and the control of this politicisation, expressed in the argument over democratic procedures at the mosque and the duties of religious officials in voluntary organisations. As we have seen already, neither protagonist would hesitate to mobilise allies *well beyond* his primary identity group in order to strengthen his side in the battle between them.

Second, the community is divided by class. Pakistanis (Asians, Muslims) do not simply form an 'underclass' (see Werbner 1990a). The fact that they are divided by class has important bearings on ethnic organisation. Some of their associations are 'hierarchical': they are dominated by upper-class fractions – by the wealthy, by professionals or by intellectuals. These subaltern groups speak for the 'whole' ethnic community, while representing only a fraction of it. They are often spokesmen to the outside world. They confer identities which 'silence', sometimes deliberately, sometimes strategically, the other identities of the people they speak for. Sometimes these silenced, submerged identities erupt into the public domain, exposing the fictional quality of the self-declared identities displayed by subaltern leaders. 'Black' – no, we are Asians. 'Asians' – no, we are Pakistanis. 'Pakistanis' – no, we are Muslims. 'Muslims' – yes, but these self-proclaimed leaders are Wahabis, not 'real' Muslims... All these different moral communities, which span different social scales, have come over time to be incorporated in diasporic voluntary organisations with shared moral and aesthetic interests. I shall return to this 'silencing' below, in discussing the British debate about the politics of identity.

A major line of cleavage cutting across class and segmentation is gender. Not surprisingly, the position of women in the community differs radically by class and regional origin. Nevertheless, even urban, educated middle-class women, as we shall see, must battle to gain a voice in the diasporic public sphere, dominated by male elders. So too young British Pakistanis are beginning to develop their own lifestyles and agendas.[7]

In addition to segmentary, class and gendered divisions which imply sited social 'boundaries' – identity markers of inclusion or exclusion highlighted situationally – the Pakistani community is significantly also a social field, not a 'closed', bounded group. Its actors, men, women and youth, are positioned differentially in terms of their access to symbolic, cultural and financial 'capital' (Bourdieu 1984). Processes of social exclusion and incorporation which sustain cultural boundaries are less critical to the reproduction of the group than the continuity of ethnic 'centres' (or 'cores'), producing 'high' (or, indeed, popular) cultural products. Hence, modern-day ethnic groups in capitalist societies tend to be defined by their centre or centres rather than by their peripheries. At the

---

[7] Jacobson (1998) argues that young Pakistanis are adopting an increasingly Muslim identity but, while this is true in some contexts, it is also true that in many other contexts the majority follow secular or South Asian popular lifestyles.

centre are the cultural experts and communal activists, the organic intellectuals like Chaudhry Amin and the Maulana. The periphery consists of ethnic consumers, whose knowledge, commitment and identification vary a good deal, and who are differentially embedded in communal networks. These centres (for they are several) are sustained by their constitution as loci of high value, competed for in a game of honour and prestige, and by the continuous efforts of the cadres of intellectuals and experts that form them to achieve moral, cultural or religious hegemony.

As permanent sojourners, Pakistani settlers increasingly come to straddle more than one cultural world and can 'switch' lifestyles. With the maturation of the second generation, born and brought up in Britain, some are increasingly becoming ethnic cosmopolitans or hybrid mixers (see Gillespie 1995). But from the very earliest days of settlement, the community fostered 'bridging' associations, mediating between the group and the wider society. Such associations are Janus-faced, facing inwards towards Britain and its civic institutions, and outwards towards Pakistan, at one and the same time. They invoke universalistic values of citizenship in dealing with the wider society, values which gloss 'silently' over the particularistic cultural and ethical values of the various cultural or religious organisations and the factional politics in which they are engaged.

Despite often very divisive conflicts within ethnic communities, such as the conflict between Chaudhry Amin and Maulana Saheb, the community forms a transcendent unity through the broader coalitions it builds up, centred upon overarching values, cultural icons and organisations – the home country, the Prophet of Islam, the central communal mosque, and so forth. The cross-cutting ties within the community and the dense social networks cutting across factional, class and cultural divisions create the possibility of local communal ethnic mobilisation in response to a local issue about which there is widespread agreement. It is such coalitions which form the basis for the emergence of social movements.

The rise of a British Muslim social movement

The British Muslim mobilisation following the publication of *The Satanic Verses* highlighted the need to theorise the bases for the emergence of ethnic social movements and to address the processes which lead to new public 'voices' breaking through a prior public 'silence'. Before the affair erupted, Pakistanis were virtually invisible as political actors, submerged in hidden networks of kin, friends and work or business partners. These networks were sustained by an elaborate ceremonial gift economy controlled by women, and by agonistic rivalries for status and power among men (see Werbner 1990a). In 1987 Chaudhry Amin was locked in factional battles focused around local political prizes. In 1990 he and his audience had mobilised, along with their opponents, a mass protest rally in London to express their sense of moral outrage and public responsibility towards a global Islamic diaspora, the *umma*.

To understand fully how such a movement emerged we need to go beyond explanations which attribute it to Manichean class, religious and racial oppositions (see Asad 1990). Instead, we need to start by identifying processes of increasing incorporation within the South Asian Muslim community in Britain.

This is because ethnic social movements resemble feminist movements in straddling 'old' and 'new' styles of collective mobilisation (on this aspect of the feminist movement see Habermas 1987: 393–4). Like the 'new' social movements, ethnic social movements are concerned with issues of identity and the defence of the integrity of the lifeworld, and they actualise this sphere of implicit cultural understandings *irrespective* of its political impact upon the public political sphere. At the same time, like earlier nineteenth-century party or trade union movements, members of ethnic minorities are also concerned to gain greater political influence over the state and local government. In Britain, for example, this is evident in the rapid rise in the number of South Asian, Caribbean and African municipal councillors. A survey by the Runnymede Trust found that out of a total of 1,917 elected councillors in London in 1994, 202 (10.5 per cent) were of Asian, Afro-Caribbean or African origin. A full 7.3 per cent were Asians (Muslim, Hindu and Sikh). In seven boroughs of inner London, more than 20 per cent of the councillors originated from these various ethnic groups (*Runnymede Trust Bulletin* No. 276, June 1994: 4).

This inherently complex orientation of ethnic social movements was early on underlined by Castells (1983: 319–20), who argued that urban social movements have three major goals: mobilisation for improved collective consumption; a search for cultural identity and autonomy; and a struggle for local (or sometimes national) power. Seen over time, such movements often lose their impetus, he found, once they achieve some of their aims; they are destroyed by internal dissent or contradiction, while their leaders are continually incorporated in the political machine, so that the initial drive is lost (ibid.: 325). This interpretation of the rise and fall of social movements differs at first glance from Melucci's theory of oscillating visibility. In fact, however, the two theories mesh, since specific campaigns are merely one erratic manifestation, as Melucci suggests, of a far more sustained (but submerged) thrust towards transforming the lifeworld.

But to become a movement, an ethnic collectivity must go through a number of critical stages. It must move from *localised associative empowerment* to *ideological convergence*, and, finally, to *mobilisation* (see Werbner 1991a).

The first stage, *localised associative empowerment*, is marked by the formation of a 'web of filiations and affiliations', to borrow Said's term (1983a: 145), of an associative network focused on distinctive cultural or political issues. In Manchester this associative empowerment took the form of *associational efflorescence*. Pakistanis began early to found a multitude of associations, as we saw in the previous chapter, both formal and informal, concerned with group welfare and collective consumption, cultural and religious activities, or political objectives. Both Chaudhry Amin and his rivals had, of course, founded such organisations.

The second stage of an ethnic social movement, *ideological convergence*, involves the formulation of a common discourse and set of objectives in relation to the state or local government, and with regard to the present circumstances and predicaments of the group. This is a stage in which members of different associations come to be increasingly conscious of common challenges, in which alliances may be formed and new subjectivities articulated through public performance, and emblematically captured by 'new' identities.

The final stage in the formation of a social movement is *mobilisation*, the stage in which the movement emerges as a recognisable, public *protest* movement. Mobilisation occurs in response to a particular issue or event threatening group autonomy or solidarity, or violating the cultural and religious ideals constituting it. The publication of *The Satanic Verses* triggered such mobilisation.

The broad mobilisation in response was made possible by the earlier formation of networks of Pakistani and Muslim associations spanning the whole of Britain. The affair showed that *national* social movements can emerge following the establishment of federated *translocal* associations. Beyond the urban community, links between members of a national diasporic ethnic group are mediated by local cultural and political associations. Such local associations, having specific moral or aesthetic agendas, create over time national and international umbrella associations which foster the organisations' specific shared interests. It is these federated associations which mobilise into cultural or religious social movements. Hence, in the Rushdie affair political mobilisation on a *national* scale was achieved with little difficulty, since several major federated national Islamic religious organisations with local branches existed already. The branches were formed by networks of sectarian mosques and religious institutions following particular Islamic strands and approaches.

The performance: the making of an anti-racist activist

Crucially, the emergence of social movements depends on the second phase, the formulation of widely shared discourses and emblems. The formulation of a common discourse of anti-racism was evident in Chaudhry Amin's transformation into an anti-racist activist during his first year as Community Rep. At the end of the year, he was re-elected for a second year in a negotiated pre-election deal. His election speech in June 1988 concerned participation in municipal committees and meetings, the intricacies of government rules and regulations, and the agendas for combating racial, as well as religious, discrimination. It was a new cultural idiom and Chaudhry Amin was a new man, an expert, a man of knowledge and authority. For one thing, he spoke in English this time. His speech shows how anti-racist narratives are woven into the specific concerns of Pakistanis as Muslims and black people. Ethnic rights, anti-racist battles and communal predicaments are linked together and debated in English, the national political language. But, as in his earlier speech, Chaudhry Amin made no attempt to keep the multiple identities and moral concerns of his audience apart.

After explaining the structure of the Council and listing a whole series of activities in which he had been involved, he first called on the Council to increase the size of the Race Unit through Section 11 funding,[8] to publish the MacDonald Report on the Burnley High School racist murder, and to increase the number of councillors on the Race Sub-Committee. Although much of this left most of his audience bemused and puzzled, it also involved them in the very process of bureaucratic learning he himself had undergone, and this was reflected in the questions asked later. Chaudhry Amin continued his speech, turning to issues of immediate concern to his audience:

> I have worked with various councillors on wide-ranging issues. For example, I have held
> meetings with the councillors from the Market Committee to discuss issues relating to the

---

[8] Section 11 funding was a mode of affirmative action by the state directed towards meeting needs arising out of immigrant language disadvantage (for a discussion see Kalka 1991).

difficulties faced by Pakistani traders in several Manchester markets. I've had discussions with councillors from the Police Monitoring Committee when there have been policing issues affecting our community.... *Halal* meals are now being served in Manchester city schools, and before long they will be available in all schools in the City Council's control. The Council spent a good deal via grants to community groups for the provision of play-schemes during the summer holidays. We can now bury our dead in the traditional Islamic way without any extra cost.

Another problem concerning his audience about which he spoke was the need to keep control of their children and resolve some of the tensions between genera-tions. This is a painful issue for both parents and community leaders. At stake is the ability of the community to reproduce itself socially over time. Chaudhri Amin argued:

Social problems are also on the increase. There is even a growing number of cases where our young people run away from home. In these cases I've worked hard with councillors and also made representations to the police. This issue affects us all. It is our responsibility. We all have to recognise the needs of our youngsters. We have to spend more time with them, and we have to gain their confidence. Our youngsters are our investment. We must be sensitive and compassionate, and we need to take special care bringing them up in a society which has all kinds of distractions.

Most remarkably, by contrast to his speech the previous year, this year Chaudhri Amin explicitly highlighted the problems of racism:

A big concern that I have is the safety of our community. We are subjected to all kinds of racial abuse and racial violence every day. Sometimes it is just taunting and name-calling, but at other times it may be physical violence. I do not have to give you the details because you are all experiencing it all the time. When I've raised these issues with the police on many occasions, it has been clear to me that we are not getting the attention from them to which we are entitled. There is a long way to go but we must be resolute and we must ensure that our youngsters are good and strong in character, and also strong in body. Only then can we ensure the safety of our community, as these young people will be in the frontline, defending themselves against these racist attacks. If the police are helpless to help us, then we have to help ourselves.

He ended his speech by thanking his audience:

During the last year I have had a lot of support from all of you, without which I would not have been able to do any of the things I've tried to put before you today. Thank you all.

In this speech Chaudhri Amin evokes the existential problem facing British Asian as well as Caribbean, African and other ethnic minorities in Britain – the fear of racial violence. The community is imaginatively constructed, in this sense, as a community of suffering.

A community of suffering

Ethnic participation in the wider public sphere concerns two fundamental orien-tations: a demand for ethnic rights, including religious rights, and a demand for protection against racism. Different identities and identifications *empower* these two orientations, pointing to the critical difference between everyday benign ethnicity and racism or cultural xenophobia.

In asserting the difference between ethnicity and racism, I am arguing for a need to distinguish between situational *objectifications* of cultural difference and essentialising *ramifications* that fetishise culture and are inherently violent. This is not to argue that benign 'ethnicity' is apolitical. Ethnic conflict and competition in the public sphere are the very stuff of politics. It is essential, however, to recognise a fundamental divide in the ontology of social relationships implied by cultural xenophobia or racism as against the daily play of ethnic identities and differences.

If there are many racisms (Cohen 1988), historically determined, the *experience* of racism by its victims is always, I argue, an embodied and materially inscribed reality. A racialised, as against an ethnic, relationship is sparked off by violence or violation. From the victims' point of view the historical act of violence becomes the basis for a *politics of moral accountability* (see R. Werbner 1995). For the violaters, the politics is determined by a structure of fear, legitimised by myths and fantasies of an essentialised other.[9]

Pakistani settlers had suffered racial abuse and discrimination since they first arrived in Britain as young male economic migrants, mostly penniless. But they were hard-working and thrifty. Manchester was good to them. Many became successful entrepreneurs, house owners, householders and communal activists. Many also had good, positive relations with their English neighbours and co-workers. Even so, most at one time or another had to endure the shock and humiliation of being branded inferior because of their skin colour or culture. This was particularly demeaning for Muslim Asians of high-caste status, as most Pakistanis in the city were. It was the sense of being marginalised and inferiorised because of an intrinsic, embodied quality beyond their control that generated the kind of anti-racist identity that Chaudhry Amin developed in his work as Community Representative.

Seen from the point of view of Muslim settlers in Britain, racism is more than just a discourse; it is a performance that attacks all that is fundamental to human dignity: the human body, economic property, political authority emblems and, as in the Rushdie affair, a group's sacred symbols. This embodied violence has material force: it opens a social chasm and precipitates schismogenic processes of escalating mutual fear and hatred.

Even when racist violations take more subtle forms, as institutional racism or discrimination, they are still materially inscribed and performed: in exclusion, verbal abuse, or public insults. In Europe, Islamophobia has targeted the *cultural icons* of Muslims, and this has come with demands that they assimilate or 'integrate' (see Werbner and Modood 1997). But there is violence also in the silencing of group voices in the public sphere. Pakistani settlers have had to fight against that violent silencing.

Writing about the Holocaust, Zygmunt Bauman suggests that racism, xenophobia or quasi-nationalism are the very opposite of altruism and moral proximity (Bauman 1990). Racism constitutes an inversion of the moral community: a denial of 'face' in Levinas' terms (see Levinas 1987), an act of violent 'silencing' in Foucaultian terms. Unlike ethnicity, racism tolerates no difference. To mobilise across ethnic differences in order to contend with racism is, however, a difficult challenge. Such mobilisation requires that anti-racist discourses do

---

[9] The literature on such mythologising by the racists is vast. See, for example, Fanon 1963, Moodie 1975, Kapferer 1988, Malkki 1992, 1995.

not simply mirror racist discourses, each racism with its 'own' anti-racism.

Theoretically, the shared experience of being violated creates the ground for mobilising broad alliances of the citizens concerned, as Jurgen Habermas suggests, with the broader defence of the nation-state's civic culture (Habermas 1994). To break through a silence violently imposed, the victims of racism or xenophobia can sometimes generate their own counter-discourses and self-identifications in the political arena; they can forge new moral and aesthetic communities imaginatively that transcend the ethnic differences between them. In Britain black activists created common unities by invoking past anti-colonial struggles and the black civil rights movements (Sivanandan 1990). Communities of suffering thus potentially also become moral and aesthetic communities; they can evolve passionate attachments to newly recovered shared images, symbols and tropes. They can 'own' these symbols collectively. The violation of a basic humanity – of the human body, sacred symbols, property and civil rights – seems to transcend ethnic difference, to create a black/white 'dominant cleavage' (Gluckman 1958; Rex 1986) – a morally paramount division born in violence, which encompasses and subsumes all other cultural and religious differences and claims.

But such a cyborg or transversal politics is a difficult and fragile achievement, as we argue collectively in a recent volume (Werbner and Modood 1997).[10] Paradoxically, racism as violence creates a double act of aggression: against the individual person and against the cultural emblems of whole groups. While attacks against individuals create the basis for uniting members of *different* oppressed ethnic groups into a solidary community of suffering, the attack on communal symbols drives a wedge through this broader alliance. This was the case during the Rushdie affair, which separated Muslims as a community of suffering from the 'Black' community. The rise of Islamophobia in Britain following the affair and the Gulf War, events analysed later in this book, underlined the specificity of racist discourses and violations, and the divisions this specific targeting may generate between racialised ethnic communities, despite their shared experiences of suffering.

Diasporic Muslim ethnicism

In modern, ethnically diverse nation-states there are continuous centrifugal and centripetal pressures: on the one hand, to assert and elaborate particular identities, and, on the other hand, to create broader, more universalistic alliances. While Chaudhry Amin, a democrat, avoided references to divisions between ethnic minorities, these were evident in the speech of his predecessor as Community Representative in 1987, a man who was a member of the Maulana's more militant 'religious nationalist' camp, as he summed up his year in office:

> By electing me you placed a heavy responsibility on my frail shoulders. I had to do my best to solve the problems of my Pakistani brothers. Most of the City Council's policies did not favour the Pakistani nation (i.e. people). We had to change them. In the very first meeting of the Council it emerged that they addressed us as Asians. If so, why did Quaid-i-Azam (Muhammad Ali Jinnah, 'The Great Leader') and all the other founders of the nation establish Pakistan? So even over here [in Britain] Hindus had taken over the City Council.

[10] See especially the contributions by Melucci, Yuval-Davis, Wieviorka, Modood, and Werbner.

... The first thing we told the Council was that we were Pakistani delegates. Hence from now on call us Pakistanis. When skinheads beat our people up they call it 'Paki-bashing' and when it comes to our rights, you make us 'Asians'. Why?

To solve this problem we have created a classification of almost 14 groups and within it Pakistanis are separated, Indians are separated, Afro-Caribbeans are separated from each other. You are all aware of the fact that we have quite a large majority of Pakistanis in this city [compared with other ethnic minority groups].

An example, he explained, of the ludicrous English confusion between Asians and Pakistanis arose in relation to the Pakistani demand for *halal* meat in schools:

The head of Education told me that they 'did not have any cook able to prepare curries'. I answered that 'We only want *halal* food (i.e. ritually slaughtered meat), not all that curry stuff! You simply use vegetable oil [not lard], chips and *halal* meat!'

This thrust towards segmentation and opposition is countered by a parallel movement to recognise greater unities. At a Community Centre meeting on another occasion one of the speakers said:

In this country we are all Paki. They don't distinguish between the one who is a Chaudhri (a village headman and upper-caste landowner) or a Rajput (a member of the ruler-cum-warrior caste, also a landowner) and the one who isn't. We are all black (as only the lowest-caste members in South Asia are).

Multiculturalist approaches which relate victimisation or disadvantage to the cultural definition of collectivities are liable to serious misrepresentations by the media. A *Panorama* TV programme (29 March 1993) singled out 'Muslims' as the 'new underclass', under-achievers by comparison with Hindus, Sikhs and Afro-Caribbeans, deeply implicated in crime, coercively violent to women, lagging in education, inept in business, with high rates of unemployment. If a possible intention of the programme was to stress the greater disadvantages suffered by Muslims and hence their need for special state support, this was not the message which actually came across. Instead, the programme seemed to criminalise not only poverty but religion itself, implying that the continued loyalties Pakistanis felt to their homes and families in Pakistan (which led them to take their children out of school and to send them on long trips back home) were morally wrong, and that the inevitable educational lag still persisting in some sections of the community was somehow attributable to their being Muslims.

Pakistanis reacted to the perceived offence with shame and bitterness, implying a 'Hindu plot' (the presenter of the programme was a Hindu), and denying the validity of the figures cited. Ironically, both the author of the report on which the programme was based (Jones 1993) and the programme-makers and (Muslim) advisers may well have meant it to be a disclosure of the 'problems' facing 'Muslims'.[11] The stigmatising association of Islam as a cultural way of life with crime, poverty and backwardness reveals, however, the pitfalls of displacing class by multicultural politics.

---

[11] The statistical analysis, which was a good deal more cautious than the TV programme, divided South Asians into 'Pakistanis', 'Bangladeshis', Indians and African Asians. These constitute only half the Muslim population of Great Britain, numbering around one million at the time of the 1991 census. It is expected that this figure will have increased sharply by 2001, because of the youthfulness of the population and inter-continental marriages.

Identity politics & the moral economy of the welfare state

Apparent here are the fundamental aporias of the politics of representation. A public identity has ontological connotations; it is constitutive of self and subjectivity through its ethical and aesthetic evocations. It is empowered, empowering and passionately defended. Multiculturalism empowers aesthetic communities, not oppressed class fragments. Hence Modood (1997) opts for alliance politics among equal, culturally constituted, ethnic minority groups, a 'rainbow coalition', American-style.

Yet the immediate thrust of multiculturalism is towards a fragmentation of solidarities, so that the politics of representation becomes the politics of proportional representation, percentage politics. The constant bickering and competition between ethnic groups and internal factions in the public domain generate responses from state and local government bureaucrats ranging from contempt to paternalistic amusement mixed with despair, as policy-makers come to be embroiled in personal conflicts and apparently irrelevant side issues (see Werbner and Anwar 1991; Anthias and Yuval-Davis 1992; Modood and Werbner 1997).

Such cultural fragmentation is impotent to contend with powerful organised racist violence. It is also impotent to contend with media misrepresentations essentialising as 'cultural' disadvantages or traits which really stem from class background or racial victimisation. On the whole, then, effective anti-racist struggles for equal opportunities (in education, employment, housing, policing, etc.) depend on the evolution of common, unitary discourses and the *suppression* of cultural differences between victims of racism. Where racism is fragmentary, haphazard, selective or disorganised, as much of it is in Britain today, there is a tendency for these common discourses to evolve first at the local level, and for struggles to be local and communally based, since they lack the powerful political impulse needed to form larger unities (see the contributions in Werbner and Anwar 1991, and Modood and Werbner 1997).

Ironically, the main block to accelerating cultural and religious fragmentation in the competition for state allocations is the welfare state or local government itself. Rather than being divisive, then, as is usually argued (for example, by Baumann 1996), the welfare state acts as a brake on ethnic fractional demands for resources, by refusing to recognise lower-order cultural, religious and national segments for purposes of state funding or ethnic representation. Fictions of ethnic unity are necessary *administrative* fictions in a welfare state which allocates funds for local communal projects and seeks to consult ethnic minorities on issues relevant to them through multi-ethnic committees. The state is compelled to create such fictions of ethnic unity in order to set limits to centripetal pressures towards increasing ethnic segmentation. The moral economy of state allocations on a tight budget is simple: to support the largest viable group possible in particular domains of voluntary activity (Werbner 1991b).

There is an important paradox to be considered here which stems from the complex relation between the moral community and the welfare state. Left to themselves, moral communities are structured around autonomous unilateral giving and altruistic service for communally defined, self-funded activities. The welfare state, as a provider of state largesse, undermines the 'natural' structures of *khidmat* and unilateral giving, and thus distorts associational leadership selection processes. Yet undeniably, ethnic communities are entitled to receive state largesse as equal tax-payers.

To compensate for the distortive perversion of leadership structures which state intervention sets in motion, it is increasingly necessary for the state to intervene even further, to ensure proper democratic election processes for public office in the organisations it funds. The shift from *khidmat*, selfless service and giving, to voting as a means of leadership selection led, as we have already seen, among British Pakistanis, to internal violence, stemming from the passion driving public competition for the prizes of office and honour. State intervention means, however, that in the long run voluntary activism becomes an 'ethnic' training ground for democratic participation in wider public arenas, and for more encompassing moral dialogues. Chaudhri Amin, an aspiring community leader and ethnic politician, used the platforms set up by the state to contest the power of a religious cleric, himself embroiled in a politics shaped by the British charitable status of the Manchester Central Mosque in which he officiated. The narratives of diasporic and civic identity and the acts of identification each evoked appealed to the moral and aesthetic sensibilities of their potential supporters, while referring to broader anti-racist battles and debates.

Highlighting a particular collective identity in the public domain generates a field of relevant oppositional identities at a particular social scale. This is because collective identities derive their primary 'boundedness' or definition from their placement within a moral and semantic grid of oppositions and resemblances, elicited through political struggle. There is no collective identity in and for itself, as an affirmation without an implied negation. To explain why it is that certain identities within a segmentary series come to be valorised and elaborated at particular historical moments is, however, to shift the focus away from a politics of representation as merely constitutive of self and subjectivity, or as culturally empowering (Friedman 1992), to issues arising from a politics of moral account-ability. For it is felt moral debts, unresolved, historically and materially grounded, which valorise certain group stigmata above all others. These may gain singular ascendency for individuals, obliterating other encompassed or cross-cutting commonalities, and moving these individuals to commit acts of terror and violence, as well as heroism and self-sacrifice, in the name of collective values.

Conclusion

This chapter has highlighted the fact that the politics of representation is a passionate politics, not because people are defending mere economic or political interests (although they do defend these as well) but because such a politics is rooted in the symbolic spaces diasporic communities create for themselves, and which constitute the contexts in which they compete for power and honour. This is so, even when local ethnic politics is also given public expression in arenas created by the state or local government. Migration entails acts of cultural and material *creativity*. Social spaces and symbolic discourses, as well as their material and organisational embodiments, all need to be created from scratch. Within the general conditions of postmodernity the potential exists for an almost infinite creation of new social spaces, given appropriate investment and the existence of receptive audiences made up of cultural or religious consumers. As long as social spaces do not threaten to *displace* or encroach upon the symbolic spaces of others, they remain – at least in Britain – almost invisible, and certainly tolerated. Civil society is by its very nature pluralistic and continuously inventive.

The narratives of identity, whether familial, communal or inter-ethnic, are grounded in these spaces vested with value through continuous material, voluntary and symbolic effort. Identities of religion, nation and language intertwine in the rhetoric of participants as they link their specific predicaments to a shared collective past and to contemporary global events, and debate their moral positions in front of a local audience. The symbolic representations of identity 'overflow' into each other, pointing to the fact that identities as moral and aesthetic allegories contain an excess of meaning.

Personal, individual identities in a world of migrations, exilic diasporas and artificially created postcolonial nation-states constitute, it has been argued, composite 'mosaics' (Fischer 1986; Fischer and Abedi 1990). The metaphor of a mosaic evokes a created, coherent image, composed of bits and pieces taken from larger, absent wholes (see Strathern 1991: 110, on Clifford 1988). Such wholes, it is implied, cannot, by definition, be abstracted or reconstituted merely from the assortment of partial fragments composing the mosaic. If, however, we look not to individuals but to broader collectivities – such as diasporic communities – we need to shift metaphors: larger collectivities may share multiple overlapping identities – moral, aesthetic, political – each of which can be celebrated as a coherent whole, in social spaces created as separate and discrete. In Britain, Islamic piety, South Asian popular culture, Pakistani nationalism and British citizenship are foregrounded by British Pakistanis in separated social spaces they themselves create. Although multiple, these identities do not thus seem, in this sense, to form a 'mosaic'; the play of identities is, like a painting by the Dutch artist Escher, one in which figure and ground alternate, depending on perspective (see Strathern 1991; also R. Werbner 1989, Chap. 5; Rapport 1993; Fischer & Abedi 1990, Chap. 5). To single out or foreground a specific identity, relationship or role means actively *dehybridising* what is essentially complex and multiplex. This is a feature of much symbolic ritual behaviour (Strathern 1991: 79; Gluckman 1962), and it is true of the behaviour of cosmopolitans or circulatory labour migrants, who switch identities when they move from one cultural space to another.

Perhaps the metaphor of 'palimpsest' identities, of 'not-now imaginaries' implicitly backgrounded (R. Werbner 1996: 4), is more appropriate as a depiction of postcolonial and diasporan identity struggles for power and authority. The separations and elaborations of particular dimensions of complex or multiplex relationships and identities must take note, as Fischer and Abedi (1990) recognise, of not only the inter-references but also the interferences between these acts of foregrounding. There is, as it were, a constant 'leakage' between domains and the identities/perspectives constituting them. Moreover, there are contexts in which fusion rather than separation is appropriate. Autobiography may be one of these (Papastergiadis 1993). Political struggles are another.

Although the 'quilting' of a particular ensemble of qualities that defines a 'name', an identity, is an arbitrary construction, it masquerades as an essential, transcendental truth (Zizek 1994: 3–4). It is this sense of ontological unity that endows identities with political force. Rather than being unitary subjects, however, the ethnic activists staging the dramas described in this book articulate, in Chantal Mouffe's words, 'an ensemble of subject positions, constructed within specific discourses and always precariously and temporarily sutured at the intersection of those subject positions' (Mouffe 1993: 71). Such articulations, this chapter has shown, are the product of historically specific battles for honour.

Mosaic identities infuse the political rhetoric of aspiring ethnic leaders performing for audiences of fellow co-ethnics sharing the same constellation of multiple identities. Rather than highlighting singular identities, these leaders combine and fuse their multiple identities in new creative patterns or mosaics in order to move their audiences to passion and fear. In their oratory they shift perspective and scale, referring now to the utterly localised, now to the global, moving between moral and aesthetic arguments, from ethnic nationalism to citizenship, democracy or socialism, from one identity/representation to another.

This public negotiation of identity by members of diasporic communities takes place in a hierarchy of progressively inclusive social spaces, from the domestic and inter-domestic to the mass cultural. At each scale of social inclusiveness different cultural narratives are negotiated. Communal diasporic voluntary public culture lies at the point of greatest ambiguity between the utterly private and exclusive and the fully public and inclusive (see Habermas 1989). This is why diasporic ethnicities and religiosities are formed, celebrated and passionately debated within this diasporic public sphere.

3

Commemorating the Great Leader
Exemplary personhood & myths of nation

A charismatic political mythology[1]

It takes both effort and kudos to catch a big fish. The leaders of one of the two factions dominating Pakistani politics in Manchester in the late 1980s proved their hegemonic ascendancy in the city by being the first to host the new Pakistani Ambassador to Britain (this was before Pakistan returned to the Commonwealth fold and he became the 'High Commissioner'). The Quaid-i-Azam Day memorial celebration he attended was one of many such events celebrated every year in Manchester and throughout Britain to commemorate the birth/death of Muhammad Ali Jinnah, the Great Leader, the founder of Pakistan. The ceremonials were occasions for subaltern leaders to reflect on the state of their nation while throwing barbed darts at the opposition, constructed as an epitome of all that was currently wrong with that nation. The commemorations thus articulated different visions of the past and future – democratic, utopian, millenarian. In each Jinnah was magically transmogrified into another kind of exemplary figure.

Quaid-i-Azam Day is one of the three main Pakistani official national holidays commemorating the creation of Pakistan and its struggle for independence. The second of these official holidays, Pakistan Day, on 23 March, celebrates the Lahore Declaration of 1940, a declaration which set the stage for the battle for a separate Muslim state in the Indian subcontinent. Partition and the independence of Pakistan are celebrated on Independence Day, 14 August, marking the end of British colonial rule. On each of these official holidays rival British Pakistani associations in Manchester invite local and Pakistani dignitaries and convene gatherings of their followers and supporters. The gatherings, part meetings, part public ceremonials, are occasions for displays of rhetoric and oratory as speakers reconstruct the past glories, battles and sacrifices involved in the fight for independence.

To a great extent the three Pakistani national holidays all celebrate a single set of historical events and, indeed, similar themes are invoked on all three occasions. This raises the questions: Why is there a need for a separate event commemorating the life and deeds of a single person? And what can this tell us about the underlying ontological premises Pakistanis as Muslims have about their society?

[1] I use 'political mythology' here, following Thompson (1985), in preference to other terms such as 'mythico-history' used by Liisa Malkki (1995: 54) following Tambiah (1985), but with the same basic assumptions about the moral constructedness and internal coherence of historical narratives.

In addressing these questions we need also to ask what the specific significance of the ceremonials is for immigrants; what are the special connotations the events have for immigrants as exiles, living away from their homeland?

South Asian Muslims conceive of their past in terms of a series of outstanding, exemplary personalities, whether saints, conquerors, or rulers, who appeared from time to time in order to redeem and renew the society. These exemplary men arose at unique historic moments; they not only led the society, they constituted it, and in doing so renewed it in its visionary perfection. Such men are regarded in some sense as having changed the course of history. Yet it must be stressed that they are not conceived of in any simple sense as hereditary leaders, divine rulers by dint of dynastic succession to office. They must both achieve office and have office imposed upon them through the common will of God and the people. Their legitimacy is thus doubly derived and yet proven *post facto*. Their very uniqueness places them above and beyond history as well as within it. Here we may find – perhaps – some justification for an analysis of a 'heroic history' in which the actions and decisions of a dominant ruler, king, chief or exemplary figure are taken as determining the course of a society's history (Sahlins 1985: 35)

In *Islam Observed* Clifford Geertz contrasts two very different forms of Muslim society – the Indonesian and the Moroccan – through historiographies of exemplary persons embodying the 'essence' of their respective societies (Geertz 1968). A parallel comparison is made by Akbar Ahmed in an essay that draws a contrast between two early South Asian Muslim rulers and compares their personalities to those of Zia ul-Haq and Zulfiqar Ali Bhutto, recent Pakistani political leaders. Each pair epitomises in turn, he argues, a contrast between opposed Islamic ways of life and types of Muslim societies (1986: 3–22). Both anthropologists adopt, perhaps unconsciously, a familiar Muslim tradition according to which exemplary historic persons stand for, embody, *are* their societies. National redemption, in these societies, is thus imagined as the dawning of the millennium, signalled by the appearance of a great saviour.

But why is it that history is conceived of in terms of the intermittent ascendancy of such charismatic personalities? Addressing this question in a collection of essays (see Werbner 1990c), contributors show that ideas about the tense opposition between temporal and spiritual power, individual opportunism and self-sacrifice for the community, are prevalent in South Asian Muslim societies. It is a tension which is never, it seems, quite resolved, except through the occasional utopian appearance of a charismatic leader in whom both attributions – temporality and divine spirituality – are encompassed, in the way defined by Dumont (1970; see Figure 3.1 below). For Muslims the 'true' leader is – simultaneously – both divinely chosen and the natural choice of the people themselves; he is both temporal and spiritual, a man of power and office and a religious leader. Democracy under his leadership is thus paradoxically absolute since it allows no room for disagreement. The ultimate paradigmatic example of such a leader is, of course, the Prophet himself. The very duality in the source of legitimation is problematic, but resolved in practice because, as Gellner has pointed out,

> the fact that the voice of God is really the voice of the people is not made manifest and explicit. The voice of the people manifests itself through making feasible the possession or attribution of characteristics which are seen as signs of divine election [such as generosity, influence, prosperity, pacificity and so forth]. (Gellner 1981: 122)

Diasporic Pakistanis' myths commemorating Muhammad Ali Jinnah, the 'Great Leader' and founder of Pakistan, are fashioned in a heroic genre which transforms Jinnah into a divinely chosen leader, the embodiment of the nation in its visionary perfection, above and beyond ordinary time.

A fundamental feature of the legends and myths about Jinnah is the assumption that while secular and spiritual power are usually separate, opposed and complementary, both are encompassed in the case of exceptional, exemplary personalities. This may be set out as a series of ideological oppositions:

Category	Ruler	Saint	Exemplary leader
Power:	Secular	Spiritual	Charismatic
Authority:	Force/impulse	Sacred/controlled	Sacred encompasses force
Time:	Present: corruption/ disunity	Present: cultic fraternity/ morality	Past and future: perfect visionary society (unity/faith/discipline)
Emotion:	Fear	Love	Love encompasses fear
Control:	External (social)	Internal (self)	Internal, exemplary
Self:	Self-glorification	Self-denial	Self-sacrifice for group glory
Person:	Selfishness	Selflessness	Selflessness and social responsibility
Economy:	Greed, generosity	Generosity	Asceticism, generosity
Achievement:	Group honour	Personal mediation with God	Social redemption

Figure 3.1 The encompassment of oppositions in exemplary personhood

In certain respects speeches made in Manchester by local British Pakistanis follow a set, formulaic pattern. The salient qualities of Quaid-i-Azam, founder of the Pakistan nation and sole spokesman for the Muslims of India, are well established. His honesty, persistence and constancy are reiterated by all the speakers. These salient qualities clearly form part of a common lore, a political mythology shared by diaspora Pakistanis and their co-nationals at home in Pakistan. The Quaid's battle for an independent Islamic nation is also part of this lore: ethnic conflict, religious ideals, colonial oppression are all presented as elements within a coherent, common, accepted political mythology.

Beyond this common core mythology are also, however, divergent ideological emphases, and the particular nuances the political mythology itself carries for

Pakistanis as immigrants in Britain – the prior colonial power – and as a Muslim minority, the very status from which Quaid-i-Azam sought to liberate the Muslims of India. In addition, the ceremonials also form the backdrop for local-level factional politics. Just as the state of the nation is measured against the yardstick of its visionary future at the time of independence, so too the state of the local community and the performance of its leaders are scrutinised against such an ideal. The events and the speeches thus have an *indexical* dimension: in part they are only fully intelligible to an informed Mancunian Pakistani audience. Moreover, they contain *unofficial* as well as official messages, directed towards a private as well as a public audience.

Time & narrative

Several questions have come to animate the renewed debate about narrative and collective memory. Building on Halbwachs (1992), more recent writers have stressed the political dimensions of memorialism and commemoration.[2] The question of *why* people narrate themselves needs to be related to several other questions: What *forms* do these narratives assume, and what structure of *time* does the act of narration entail? What *disguised messages* do narratives hide? One particular strand in this debate has focused on the way in which collective subjects – nations or ethnic communities – mythologise and commemorate their pasts.

Narration and commemoration are performative acts (see Turner 1980; Connerton 1989). Through such story telling people recover the past as a meaningful moral world to be desired and reached out to (White 1980). They capture, as Turner argues, the agonistic dimensions of sociality, the evolving development of its social dramas, while at the same time, in telling their stories, they become conscious of and reflective about their own experiences. Commemorative ceremonies may draw their legitimacy, as ritual does, from the sense people have that they are repeating a fixed, authentic tradition. In reality, such events are constantly not only invented (Hobsbawm and Ranger 1983), but *re-invented* as Handelman shows (Handelman 1990; Handelman and Shamgar 1997). Thus against a common view of ritual and ceremonial as fixed and formulaic which Connerton advances (1989, Chap. 2), others have recognised that such structured events need to be seen as creative acts of renewal and improvisation.[3] Indeed, rituals of commemoration and the narratives they embody symbolically may come to be highly contested performances.

Diasporic Pakistanis' rhetorical re-enactments of the events leading to the founding of Pakistan may be interpreted as dramatic acts of reaching out to the past. But they are also, in an important sense, a reaching out to the present and the future. Indeed, the study of narrative reveals that the conflation of time is a general feature of narrative structure: its moral plot *unites* the past with the

[2] In particular Connerton 1989; see also the contributions to Bhabha 1990; Gillis 1994; Ben-Ari and Bilu 1997 and R. Werbner 1998a; Anthias and Yuval-Davis 1992, Chap. 2. On narrative constructions see Mitchell 1980 and Rimmon-Kenan 1983.

[3] That ritual may be seen as creative and improvised, especially through humour and satire, is stressed by many (see, for example, among others, Turner 1980, Kapferer 1983, R. Werbner 1989, and Boddy 1989).

present and the future. Hence Ricoeur talks of the concept of tradition as 'a common destiny' (1980: 186). It is important to stress this point because it denies that our anthropological narrations necessarily distance the peoples we study, for whom tradition legitimates current practice, to an irrecoverably primitive past. Such an argument rests on the assumption that 'our' conception of time is exclusively linear and progressive (Fabian 1983). In reality, the narratives of contemporary nations, ethnic groups or diasporas are equally cyclical: they draw on the past as a moral fable to legitimise the present and to map and anticipate the future. This means that the memory of a past, whether of suffering or of glory, has radical implications for a collectivity's vision of its collective future, and for the real political choices people make. This is a point brilliantly developed by Moodie in his analysis of Afrikaner sacred history and civil theology in Southern Africa as a series of redemptive 'suffering-and-death' cycles (Moodie 1975: 11–18; see also Handelman 1990; Paine 1989).

While all societies commemorate themselves in and through repetitive time, there are recognisable cultural differences in the way different societies construct their moral narratives of community and nation. The question relates to ideas about collective embodiment. Who embodies the nation? Who represents it in its essential, exemplary unity? In many nations, the figure of a woman, often a mother, symbolises the spirit of the collectivity (Yuval-Davis 1997b: 45). But in modern democratic nation-states the symbolic subject sacralised above all others is the nameless, ordinary citizen. The tomb of the unknown soldier, not the Lincoln Memorial, is the ritual epicentre of the United States of America. Citizens who give their lives for their countries are buried with state honours (Werbner 1998; Laqueur 1994). They embody the abstract individual in his or her equality, stripped of all attributes: of ethnicity, class or gender (Turner 1990: 194). They also embody the metonymic continuity between person, body and national territory, forged in the sacrificial act of dying for the sake of one's country (Handelman and Shamgar 1997).

Not all societies, however, recognise the emblematic centrality of anonymity. The present chapter points to the centrality in Muslim society of what may be called a 'charismatic mythology' or historiography.

Contested mythologies

The role of historic legends as charters validating competing group claims is, of course, a familiar one. That such legends and myths assume the form of apparently 'objective', taken-for-granted sacred or historic texts, taught to schoolchildren, stored in libraries, set in formal examinations or invoked in local tourist guide books, does not really 'fix' or reify them as singular and permanent, despite the technologically advanced medium of their production. Such objectifications merely serve to mask the way in which myths are continuously appropriated and reappropriated. The authority of the text is thus to some extent illusory. Even when contemporary historiographies of the nation are objectified in print (Anderson 1991 [1983]), they still need, like prior oral mythologies, to be interpreted in the light of current conflicts and predicaments. Indeed, one might argue that the very nature of myth is that it is generated through argument; we often forget that Malinowski's theory of myth as 'charter' stressed, above all, the competitively passionate style in which the memory of the past was invoked by Trobriand islanders.

Yet the *scale* on which such authoritative published (and increasingly cinematically screened) myths and historic legends come to be politicised is a feature of the modern world. Widely publicised historical accounts, traditions and legends are able to dictate national and even international political agendas and to inspire mass political movements. The anthropological study of people's own perceptions of their past and their societies is therefore today as much a study of a contemporary changing world as it was, in the past, of exotic, remote cultures.

An attempt by Professor Akbar Ahmed, Pakistani scholar and media personality, to make a film of Jinnah's life is an instance of how the politics of commemoration has invaded the media. The filming of Jinnah became almost from the start a highly contested initiative, one in which politicians of all political stripes intervened in an attempt to influence the final aesthetic product. They ranged from Gulf state Shaikhs to the Prime Minister of Pakistan and influential religious leaders (Ahmed, personal communication). As time went by, the film came to be embroiled in public rumours; it was alleged that the script had been written by Salman Rushdie, and there were bitter complaints that the actor taking the part of Jinnah was no other than Christopher Lee, the actor best known for his performance of Dracula (this was true). The Pakistani government reneged on its promise of a subsidy and the producers had to turn to the public for financial support, collecting money in Pakistan's bazaars. The film itself was intended as a counter to *Gandhi*, the multi-million-dollar Hollywood production that portrayed Jinnah in negative terms. Its production coincided with the golden jubilee commemorations of fifty years of Indian and Pakistani Independence in 1997. In the event, it was not screened that year. For Ahmed, Jinnah epitomised all that was tolerant, liberal and enlightened about the visionary state of Pakistan, attributes that had been lost in the mismanagement of the country by corrupt elites and military rulers since Jinnah's untimely death (see Ahmed 1997). This was one possible construction of Jinnah, an enigmatic figure who left no diaries.

Memorialism has thus come to be contested on a global scale. But this mass fascination is also grounded in highly localised, parochial competitions for honour and prestige, conducted through competing visions of the past as present and future celebrated in hidden ceremonials.

Myth as dialogue: contested hegemonies

Myths, legends and traditions are not simply internally consistent or coherent in themselves; they are also dialogical in Bakhtin's terms, for each legend or myth articulated by a people needs to be viewed as 'a *rejoinder* in an unfinalised dialogue.... It lives a tense life on the borders of someone else's thought, someone else's consciousness' (Bakhtin 1979; quoted by Clark and Holquist 1984: 243, their italics). This is especially evident in the contemporary world with its 'heteroglossia of ideological possibilities' (ibid.: 10). It is a marked feature of South Asian nationalist narratives which have long been articulated against the backdrop of a plurality of voices, cultures and ideologies (see Chatterjee 1986).

The narratives of community, nation and exemplary personhood, as presented by the people themselves *for* themselves, are thus fully comprehensible only in relation to implicit, absent *counter* myths, legends, traditions and historical accounts. Tribal leader and holy man, Bhutto and Nurani, two contemporary political figures,[4] Jinnah and Gandhi – each image in a pair, each ideological interpretation its alternative political philosophy, each meaning its potential interpretive opposition. Such intertextuality is not a feature limited to Islamic narratives. Most nations are locked in internal arguments about who they are as collective subjects (on Israeli society, for example, see Dominguez 1989; Paine 1989).

Narratives of past events, imagined or real, confer retrospective meaning upon these events. As such, memories of the past mythologised in the present are reflexive; they commemorate past experiences through a heightened conscious-ness of the present. A corollary of this is that interpretations of the past depend on the narrators' present positioning. Different narrators create generically differ-ent tales of past experiences, glossing those experiences as ideal or threatening, an exercise in nostalgia or a project for the future (on such generic constructions see R. Werbner 1991).

Finally, there is an important point that needs to be kept in mind, which relates to narrative time itself. For diasporic Pakistanis in Britain, the act of dramatic narration of the nation marks a rupture as well as a continuity, since it inscribes a shift in space as well as in time, from there to here. The danger is that spatial disjuncture will stamp the present as a moment beyond the past. To avoid this, the experience of diaspora must be integrated into the national narrative. In telling the past, speakers must relocate themselves within the postcolonial nation and thus revitalise their relationship to an idealised homeland.

Quaid-i-Azam commemorations

On 3 January 1988 a gathering was held in Manchester to celebrate the birthday of Muhammad Ali Jinnah, Quaid-i-Azam, the Great Leader and founder of Paki-stan. This was the second of three public ceremonials held by different local diasporic Pakistani organisations in Manchester over a period of three weeks. Each in turn commemorated and glorified the Quaid-i-Azam, father of the nation. At each of the ceremonies speakers extolled the life and personality of the Quaid, and drew lessons from these for the present state of Pakistani society, its government, its people and its institutions.

In general, Quaid-i-Azam celebrations may be interpreted as an enactment on the *political* plane of an established world vision constituted in its axiomatic principles on the *religious* plane. Just as on the religious plane the Islamic nation, the *umma*, is constituted, above all, in the person of the Prophet, and secondarily in the persons of earlier prophets and latter-day *pirs* (saints), so too the Pakistan nation is constituted in its visionary perfection in the person of Quaid-i-Azam. Quaid-i-Azam is the perfect model of a political national leader, just as the Prophet epitomised the qualities of religious leadership.

---

[4] Nurani was the leader of the Barelvi party in Pakistan who attempted to construct himself as a charismatic saint (see Malik 1990). Zulfiqar Ali Bhutto was the leader of the Pakistan People's Party, who ran on a secular socialist platform. He was executed for treason by General Zia ul-Haq.

Muhammad Ali Jinnah was by all accounts a complex and, in many ways, an enigmatic figure (see Bolitho 1954). His vision of a separate sovereign Muslim nation contained, like all nationalisms, the seeds both of creation and of destruction, universal brotherhood and freedom and inter-communal strife, of constitutional legality and power politics. Not surprisingly, then, he has become, to quote Jallal, a 'monster in the demonology of not very perceptive Indian and British chroniclers, the triumphant hero in Pakistani hagiography' (Jallal 1985: 221).

Seen in personal terms, the contradictions he epitomised – which may be regarded in large measure as a product of colonialism and the struggle against it – are evident: he was himself a non-observant Muslim who fought for the rights of Indian Muslims; his dream was to create a Western-style democracy based on Islamic principles (see Munir n.d.; Mumtaz and Shaheed 1987:8). He thus envisaged a secular democratic state; yet, in founding a state based on a religious identity and intended to protect the rights of a religious minority, he also inadvertently laid the grounds for a potential theocracy (see Alavi 1988). He believed deeply in constitutional reform, yet he (and his opponents) were unable to control the terrible communal violence unleashed by their exclusivist nationalist ideals. He was a British-trained lawyer who, with his monocle, his immaculate, tailor-made suits and his admiration for parliamentary liberal ideas (see Wolpert 1984:12), dressed and spoke like an Englishman; nevertheless, he fought against British domination. He claimed to be the sole spokesman of the united Muslims of India, yet for much of his life the party he headed, the Muslim League, had little influence in Muslim majority provinces (see Jallal 1985). Indeed, he spoke in a language that the majority of Indian Muslims did not understand. He fought in the name of Muslim unity, yet he was continuously confronted by Muslim disunity.

These ambiguities in Jinnah's position and the complexities of the policies and events surrounding India's independence have been extensively discussed by scholars and academics. For Pakistanis celebrating his birthday and the struggle his life symbolised, the vision of those events, however, is necessarily much simpler. The mythic past they evoke is a heroic past, a moment in history when men transcended the mundane and acted as one body for shared ideals. Just as the community, the nation, is sacralised in that moment (see Anderson 1991 [1983]), so too the leader of the nation is sacralised. Purified of all ambiguity and complexity, he embodies the most deeply held values of the society; in his person and 'personality' (as Pakistanis put it) he epitomises the community, the nation, in its transcendent ideal unity. Person and society are juxtaposed and fused ontologically; each not only symbolises the other but *is* the other.

At the same time, the different facets of Jinnah's character and political platform, and the jarring aspects of the events surrounding the battle for independence, are selectively constructed to create somewhat different political myths, each consistent and coherent internally, yet each consonant with opposed current ideological positions. Such mythic interpretations cannot be viewed in isolation, even when the events in which they are articulated remain discrete. They form part of a current, contemporary argument in which different political philosophies and future orientations compete for the moral high ground and thus for hegemonic influence; they are, in other words, *dialogically* related.

Two central themes run like a thread through all the speeches on Quaid-i-Azam Day. The first is the theme of external threat and domination by other nations or religious groups. The second is the theme of the nation as a visionary society. In the following account I separate the two themes for purposes of analysis, although in reality, they were intertwined in the ceremonies I attended, as speakers dwelt on different aspects of the life and personality of the Quaid. The two gatherings in Manchester discussed here were, however, characterised by different ideological stresses. At one of the gatherings, the 'pro-democracy gathering', which I refer to as Function A, speakers put more stress on the visionary aspects of the state and its internal order. At Function B, the 'theocratic gathering', which took place eleven days later, the stress was on issues of national and international conflict, and the religious dimensions of the myth were more consistently evoked.

The religious nationalist ceremonial

An important feature of political mythology, as we have seen, relates to the construction of time implicitly contained in such a mythology. Political myths are not merely charters of present social divisions and current group interests, as has been argued (see Thompson 1985); they are apocalyptic visions of *future potential* dangers and threats. They are also yardsticks, examples of past perfection which are reconstituted as future projects. The present is lacking, the past is a model for the future. This embodiment of cyclical time contains the message that what *was* not only *is* but *will be* again. This conception of time, which is itself ontological, was expressed by Maulana Saheb, one of the speakers in the dominant faction's commemorative ceremony (Function B) and the *maulvi* of the Manchester Central Jami'a Mosque whom Chaudhry Amin was seeking to oust. Maulana Saheb began his speech with the words:

> Our respected guest, Your Excellency the Ambassador, brothers and elders, Asalam-u Aleikum. Those nations which do not keep in touch with their past are wiped out from the arms of civilisation. The development of the future depends upon following examples from the past.

Both the apocalyptic dangers exemplified by past divisions and conflicts, and the failure of the present, were spelt out in the various speeches, and embodied, literally, by the presence of some of those who had personally suffered during the tragic events following the partition of British India. Hence, at Function B the Chairman introduced the first speaker with the following words:

> One of the reasons for choosing Mr S.A. [to speak] is that not only is he a respected elder of the community, but he has also played an important role during the making of Pakistan. He left his home town to come to Pakistan and faced all those hardships which Muslims fleeing from Hindustan had to face.

The opening speaker, having first praised the Ambassador of Pakistan who was guest of honour at the gathering began:

> In the joint movement of the subcontinent, Quaid-i-Azam had a unique position: he saved a deteriorating nation from the slavery and subjugation of foreign rule. This deed of Quaid-i-Azam occupies a unique chapter in history. He partitioned the continent on the strength of his faith and belief. He divided the map of Hindustan and thus achieved a separate independent homeland for the Muslims in which they could practise their faith and belief.

It is a proven truth that no politician greater than Quaid-i-Azam has ever lived. There were the intrigues of our own people and the conspiracies of the British. Not only did he contend with these but he fulfilled all that he promised. He fought and overcame every manner of opposition and founded Pakistan. Thus he proved himself a great statesman and politician. Quaid-i-Azam kept the Hindu and British rulers in their respective places, yet they respected him. I think this is one of the chief reasons why in the end the British and Hindus were forced to bow down before Quaid-i-Azam.

It is another matter that the treachery of some of our own people and the conspiracies of the British and the Hindus stopped Quaid-i-Azam from achieving an even greater victory, and some important regions were not able to become part of Pakistan. There was also a great deal of dishonesty during the demarcation of the boundary line. Even so, it was possible for Quaid-i-Azam with the help of God and the Holy Prophet to achieve such a goal, a goal which will always be written in golden words in the history of the world. May Allah give us the strength to protect and develop our beloved homeland.

Some of the central elements of Pakistani political mythology as a civil religion are evident in this opening speech. Quaid-i-Azam liberated the Muslims of India from slavery and subjugation. He fought against the conspiracies of the British and the Hindus – external enemies – and the treachery of fellow Muslims – internal enemies. His enemies not only bowed down before him, they also respected him for his intelligence and honesty. His strength was that of his faith and his belief in his cause: to liberate his fellow Muslims so that they could practise their own faith and belief freely. In his battle he was aided by God and the Holy Prophet. His achievement, the creation of an independent Muslim state, is of major global historical significance.

The following speaker, a young 'international lawyer', gave an account of some of the events preceding independence, and stressed – as many of the speakers did – the injustice and discrimination against Muslims in India which inspired the battle for a separate state. He added:

Violence erupted between the Hindus, the Sikhs and the Muslims, although Jinnah was a great believer in peace and non-violence, and his wish all the way through was that matters could be resolved peacefully.

It is important, in the construction of the national mythology to stress that violence is imposed by outside enemies. The nation, like its symbolic leader, is fundamentally peace-seeking. It must, however, defend itself and in doing so it has to make terrible sacrifices.

The sufferings of the Muslims at the time of Partition were linked by the Chairman of Function B, Seth Saheb, to Quaid-i-Azam's exceptional qualities as a leader. Thus he recalls an incident at the time of independence. Jinnah

began to eat less as a sort of sacrifice. He used to say to his sister: 'Fatima, my nation is dying of starvation, how can I sit and eat at this lavish table?' One time during the Partition Quaid-i-Azam asked a reporter about news from Bengal. The reporter replied 'Muslims are being slaughtered'. Tears came into Quaid-i-Azam's eyes. He sighed and said: 'Yes, nations have to cross rivers of blood before they reach the banks of freedom.'

In his speech Maulana Saheb described the sufferings of the Muslims of India, incorporating these sufferings, and thus the whole struggle for independence, into the central Judaeo-Qur'anic myth:

The cruelties that the Muslims of the subcontinent endured were much worse than those endured by the Israelites. The Muslims were deprived of their share not only in politics but

Plate 3.1 A factional celebration of Quaid-i-Azam Day
with the Pakistani Ambassador

Plate 3.2 Asian business meeting

socially, economically and in all walks of life. All their lands and inheritances were confiscated. They were given to the Hindus and whatever we earned was given to the Hindus. Now look at the position of [Muslims left behind in India]. Demonstrations are held in Amritsar, Ahmadabad and Bombay, and Muslims are killed mercilessly. I would like to ask you: whenever a Hindu or a Sikh picks up a sword to kill a Muslim, does he stop to ask him whether he is a Shi'a, a Sunni or an Ahl-e-Hadith, or does he just see that he is a Muslim, or hear the *Kalima*, and then kill him? Oh Muslims, look at the Palestinians, they are being killed ruthlessly and here you are, sitting passing resolutions.

The plight of the Muslims of India was thus linked in Function B with the plight of Muslims elsewhere in the world. Pakistan, an Islamic state, was part of a wider nation, the Islamic *umma*, defined (as Pakistan itself is) by its religious observance. Once again, the Chairman raised this theme:

Today we have some news from the Middle East which has deeply grieved us [he is referring here to the news that Israeli soldiers had entered the Al-Aqsa Mosque during Friday prayers and dispersed the congregation at the mosque with tear gas]. The blood-stained hands of the Jews which have murdered many Muslims in the past, and have attacked the Al-Aqsa Mosque, have again committed this deed. What can I say? Whatever I could say would not be enough. We are unlucky. What else can we do? We draft resolutions and pass them. Our rulers pay little attention, for them it is a case of in through one ear and out through the other. For many years the Jews have been playing with the lives and blood of the Palestinians but no Muslim country has raised its voice in protest. I would like my voice, through His Excellency the Ambassador, to reach our government. Our hearts cry. I wish that today we had great personalities such as Salah-al-Din al-Ayyubi, Musa bin Nasir or Muhammad bin Qasim who, in response to the letter of one woman, travelled from Damascus and reached Hindustan at the age of sixteen. Nowadays who knows how many innocent women are raped? But what can I say? Our leaders seem to take no notice at all even if it is pointed out to them.

The Chairman here contrasts the present failings of the Islamic nation as a whole, and its various governments, and their inability to defend Muslims under attack, with Jinnah's heroic fight in defence of the Muslims of India. The vision here is one of a continuously beleaguered Islamic nation. Jews and Hindus are thus variations on a common theme. This is evident in the next part of Seth Saheb's speech:

[The Jewish deportation of Palestinians] reminds me of a similar method adopted by the Hindus. In 1964–5 they sent trains packed with Muslims across the Vagga border. The Government at that time protested strongly but was able to do nothing because it limited itself only to protests. Now let us satisfy our grieved hearts by passing a resolution: the last news was that the Israelis had attacked our most important, respected and sacred Al-Aqsa Mosque.... Today in this function we strongly protest against this atrocious act of the Israelis and we make a request to the United Nations to offer protection not only to our holy places but to the innocent Palestinians.

In the same vein the *maulvi* responded to the Chairman saying:

Mr Chairman, you were saying that nobody listens to your plea. But who is there to hear anyway? Damascus may still be present but regretfully there is no Mohammad Bin Qasim. Madina Munawara [the town of Medina in Saudi Arabia] may be present but there is no Khalid Bin al-walid. Egypt and Cairo may still be present but there is no Nur al-Din bin Zangi who would be moved by the plea of a Muslim and who, for the sake of God, with the strength of faith would jump into the fire. Very few people like these are born into nations nowadays. Our non-cooperation [with each other] and mistrust [of one another] are the reasons for our punishment. So when our nation has been fully punished and when we repent, only then will God have mercy on us, and only then will God find a way for us. God will not forsake us because in this world beneath the sky if there is anyone who believes devotedly in God's oneness, it is the Muslims, and if there is anyone who follows the religion laid down by the Holy Prophet, Peace Be Upon Him, it is the Muslims. It is a fact that Muslims will remain on this earth; they will not die out but will spread throughout the world. Judaism will die out. Christianity will die out. Hinduism will die out, and one day the name of Islam and only Islam *la ilaha illa Allah wa-Muhammad Rasul Allah* [the *Kalima*: God is one and Muhammad is His Prophet] will be left. And when this day occurs – I may or may not be here to see it – it will be a day when the conscience of the Muslims will be fully awakened, and they will be able to differentiate between theirs and others, and will be able to unite, *Inshallah* [God willing].

Once again we see here the stress on present failure as against future and past glories. The values of the past, epitomised in the exemplary lives of great leaders such as Quaid-i-Azam and the Prophet himself, are today replaced by a void, a punishment for communal sins. Once the community is purified of these sins, however, it will regain its lost glory. The Islamic nation will then achieve its deserved global hegemony.

Exemplary personhood: the Great Leader

For Pakistanis, one of the marks of a great leader is his reluctance to lead, his modesty (see Munir n.d.; Mayer 1981; Werbner 1990a). But in their political mythology Jinnah is not merely a reluctant leader who has greatness imposed upon him. He is a man chosen by God at birth, divinely predestined to lead his nation. He is a man *loved* by his people, a love which is itself a sign of his divine nature. This idea of divine predestination was particularly marked in speeches made by the conveners of Function B, many of them devout supporters of Sufi orders. On the whole they went further than most of the speakers at Function A in sacralising Quaid-i-Azam's person in explicitly religious terms. Their speeches express their struggle with the fact that, while Quaid-i-Azam could not be a prophet according to strict Islamic belief, his role and divine inspiration were indeed, as they saw it, prophetic. Seth Saheb, the chairman at Function B, began by telling the audience, composed entirely of fellow Pakistanis, of Quaid-i-Azam's unique character. When Sir Stafford Cripps came to India in 1942,

> He toured the whole of the Subcontinent, he met Gandhi and Nehru and Zeldar. He also heard that there was a leader of the Muslims called Muhammad Ali Jinnah. All these different leaders wanted Sir Stafford Cripps to interview them and write about them in his book, but Quaid-i-Azam did not do that. [Finally Cripps approached him and was reluctantly granted an interview].... So Sir Stafford Cripps did get to meet Quaid-i-Azam and wrote an interview. When he wrote about this interview in his book he started a new chapter and wrote: 'Let me introduce you to the uncrowned king of the Muslims of India.'
> So Quaid-i-Azam was an uncrowned King who ruled our hearts. The people could not understand his speeches [a reference to the fact that his speeches were mainly in English] but they would listen silently to every word he said. It is also true that the Muslims of Hindustan loved him so much that if ever there was a possibility that a new prophet would be sent down by God, then the Muslims of the subcontinent would have accepted Quaid-i-Azam as their prophet. Thus we can sum up the respect for Quaid-i-Azam the Muslims of the subcontinent had in their hearts, and although Quaid-i-Azam was not a prophet, and

Allah forbid there will not be a chance for anyone to become a prophet, but I can say with assurance that Quaid-i-Azam must have been one of God's closest and most beloved friends.

Talking about God reminds me of a certain religious point. There is a *hadith* [traditional saying on the life, deeds and sayings of the Holy Prophet] that if a man works just on one occasion for his religion and his country it is even greater than if he prayed for a hundred years. So I was thinking: let us say, for instance, if a man is a hundred years old and he prays from the day he was born until the day he dies, he will only have been praying for one hundred years. Quaid-i-Azam spent many years of his life working for the Islamic community and thinking about it. Everybody knows how much his health deteriorated during this period. He had TB and his lungs were on the verge of collapse, but he was so determined and persistent that he would stop at nothing to achieve Pakistan. A man who has sacrificed so many years of his life to the cause of Islam, the Muslims and fellow human-beings is surely a great person in the eyes of Allah.

Later on in the function, Maulana Saheb, himself a Barelvi follower and *khalifa* of a Sufi order, took up this theme of prophetic status once more. Once again his aim was to incorporate Quaid-i-Azam's achievements into the central Judaeo-Qur'anic myth. He thus began by recounting the deeds of Moses chosen by God to liberate the Israelites from slavery. From this myth he moved on to describe the sufferings of the Prophet's followers in Mecca. Stressing the cyclical recurrence of suffering and liberation he said:

Now compare Quaid-i-Azam's character with that of the Prophet. Recall our Chairman's words that Quaid-i-Azam was not a prophet. In this there is no room for doubt. Prophet Muhammad (Peace Be Upon Him) was the last prophet. He verified this himself. He said 'I am the last Prophet and no prophet will be sent after me.' [If his immediate disciples could not be prophets] then Quaid-i-Azam too could not be a prophet. Now compare the works of Quaid-i-Azam with those of the prophets. God had appointed him to do the same work in the subcontinent as He had given the prophets in the Middle East, prophets such as David, Moses, Solomon, and finally the Holy Prophet, Peace Be Upon Him. We have heard that the followers of Jinnah regarded Quaid-i-Azam as a saint. There is no doubt that during the time of Quaid-i-Azam all the philosophers, intellectuals and religious scholars believed in him as a leader.

... A philosopher, religious scholar and leader of the *ahl-e-Sunnat Jami'at* [the Barelvi party] of that time, [together with another *pir*] ... asked Pir Mehr Ali Shah [the founding saint of Golra Sharif]: we have heard that you think that Quaid-i-Azam is a saint. He answered: 'if he wasn't one before now, then from this day he is one'. The two scholars asked: 'how can you say that from today he is [a saint]'? Pir Mehr Ali answered: 'in God's eyes a person who has saved another from slavery is most esteemed and respected, so cannot Quaid-i-Azam who saved so many thousands from slavery be a saint?'

From here the Maulana went on to recount the freeing of the Prophet's slave Hazrat Zaid bin Haris and Hazrat Bilal. He concludes:

So when Quaid-i-Azam freed so many thousands of Muslims and gave them an independent country then just think what his position must be in the eyes of God and the Holy Prophet, Peace be Upon Him.

The fact that Quaid-i-Azam was not an observant Muslim, while not denied by the Maulana, is dismissed as insignificant, an exterior reality hiding a much deeper truth:

I studied Quaid-i-Azam's personality in the light of the Holy Qur'an, and the more I studied it in this light the more my respect for him grew. I never bothered to see if he had a beard or not [i.e. if he was a religious man or not], and it is my belief that he is better than a thousand of those bearded persons who sell the nation to fill their own pockets. And today I stand on this stage and say that I do not care to know if he prayed or not, and in which way he prayed, what his beliefs were, and I have never bothered to find out what his opinions were. I only know that if he did not have deep respect and esteem in the eyes of God and the Holy Prophet, Peace be Upon Him, then he would not have been born on this earth.

The civil religion constructed through these political myths by the conveners of Function B is clearly consonant with their ideological orientations. The conveners were relatively wealthy, conservative and religious community leaders, Barelvi followers who believed in the intercessionary or mediatory powers of exemplary persons chosen by God. The civil religion they evoked is one which stresses the external threats to the Islamic nation, its fall from grace expressed in its internal disunity, and its ultimate redemption and achievement of global hegemony. Their message is at once millenarian and deeply pessimistic. The myth of Pakistan and the Indian subcontinent is incorporated into the broader mythology of Islam, which is itself a myth of the struggle of true believers against idolaters (in the subcontinent represented by the Hindus) and people of the Book (Jews and Christians) who deny the message of the Prophet and persecute his followers. In this battle exemplary persons, chosen by God, flawless and ritually pure, hierarchically placed above the community by their very nature, lead in their absolute and enduring faith. Quaid-i-Azam is one of these chosen few. The ideology draws on the central themes of sacrifice and martyrdom in Islam (see Ahmed 1986). In the words of a young speaker at Function B:

> Alone he fought against the treacherous British and the Hindus. He kept his serious illness a secret from everyone so that the nation would not lose hope. He himself accepted martyrdom, and until the day he died he thought only of Pakistan.

The 'pro-democracy' ceremonial

Function A was convened by the factional opponents of Function B. It was organised by Chaudhry Amin and his 'patti' (party), and the invited speakers were either practising barristers or men with strong pro-democratic, socialist and populist leanings. It is thus significant that they too stressed the predestined, divinely chosen status of Quaid-i-Azam. The tone was, however, somewhat different. One of the speakers, a judge and barrister, said:

> On the Indian subcontinent there were many people involved in the Independence of India. I think it would be belittling them if I was to say that Mr Jinnah was the only man who was responsible for getting independence for India. No. There were many, many people who were responsible for that cause. There are people throughout the commonwealth who fought against Britain to get their independence. But Quaid-i-Azam, Muhammad Ali Jinnah, was the only man who created a nation. Nowhere in the world before him or ever since has such a task been performed by any individual, or any party. [He discusses the hurdles Jinnah had to overcome] ... To join [all these] together was not a task for an ordinary being, or an ordinary group of people. But God creates from time to time among nations people who are superhuman beings, people who stand not only head and shoulders above, but *way* above the rest of us, and I think Quaid-i-Azam was one of those people. God had given him a special task, and it was God's task that he performed by joining the Muslim League, by helping the Muslims of India to work towards having a nation, a new nation, created from those various groups.

The speaker, while stressing the chosen and indeed unique status of Quaid-i-Azam, nevertheless stressed a broader humanity: the commonwealth, the plurality of nations, the common global struggle by many against colonialism. God was thus in certain respects a broader God, less exclusively Muslim.

Unlike the speakers at Function B who emphasised the threat from external enemies, those at Function A dwelt on the *transcendence* of religious and cultural divisions as an ideal in itself. Thus the first speaker, a successful local barrister, highlighted the fact that Jinnah worked initially for Muslim–Hindu unity, against British domination. It was the Hindus who undermined this unity, who advocated a dual policy. He reminded his audience of the long period during which Jinnah struggled for this unity.

> He was so disappointed by the Hindu attitude during this period that he decided not to take part in politics, and stayed in England from 1930 to '34.... In 1935 the Government of India Act put forward a scheme for provincial autonomy. One hundred million people [i.e. all the Muslims of India at the time] felt disheartened, disappointed, helpless and bewildered. 'Alama Iqbal [the great poet-philosopher] and other Muslim leaders sent a telegram to Quaid-i-Azam and asked him to come back to lead the nation. So Quaid-i-Azam, answered the call of the nation, and returned to his country. It was after this that the 'two-nation theory' was formulated, and declared in Lahore in 1940.

In order to explain the two nation theory the speaker refers back to the Qur'an.

> ... from an Islamic point of view there is no mention of Iran as a nation, the Arabs as a nation or Unan [Greece] as a nation. Instead the Qur'an mentions the believers and non-believers, the cruel, the liars, the traitors. These can belong to any family or tribe but they are one nation. With this idea those people who belong to one belief are members of one nation.... That is in the Qur'anic Surah which says: 'God created you all, so among you one group who are believers and the other who are non-believers.' This idea has been in existence for a long time. Its first battle started with the Prophet Noah when his son refused to join him in the ark and he was destroyed with the non-believers. [You know that] during the Battle of Badr two people of the same family fought on different sides [here the speaker is referring to the battle between the Prophet and his external opponents during his stay in Madina].

It is evident, then, that even at Function A speakers drew in their definition of the nation on religious mythology. Yet they also allowed for the possibility of cross-communal co-operation. Chaudhri Amin himself, in his speech, listed Jinnah's exceptional personal qualities as a leader without any reference to his God-chosen status. He told his audience that the *Quaid* was a 'brilliant student', a 'great wit', praised even by his adversaries for his 'honesty and intelligence'. He was 'incorruptible'. He had no selfish ends in view. All his efforts were for 'the sake of his nation'. He spoke against 'corruption, bribery, black marketeers, favouritism and nepotism. He was above prejudice and always guided by justice and fair play. He was a man of principle.' He was a 'wise statesman' who won a homeland for Muslims by dint of his wisdom and foresight. He would 'always convince others with his logical and weighed arguments'. The opposition 'felt helpless before his reasoning'. He was a 'good orator'. He 'never pursued false hopes and never prevaricated. He turned down the offer of a knighthood and preferred to be called simply Muhammad Ali Jinnah.' The speaker summed up to loud applause: 'Thus we can say that he was the greatest leader ever born.'

To demonstrate Quaid-i-Azam's greatness further, the speaker continued to list his special qualities. He 'never wavered, even in the face of hardship and difficulties.

His 'strong will and immense strength overcame his bad health and growing sickness'. He disregarded his poor health to continue with his mission. Even after the creation of the state, 'the Quaid overcame all difficulties with courage and patience'. Indeed, the speaker says, there is so much that can be said about Quaid-i-Azam's life, character and work that 'it would not take an hour or two. It might take days and days'. He concludes: 'God give us wisdom and patience to follow his rules. God bless our Great Leader Quaid-i-Azam *zinda* Zindabad [live].'

What is evident in this speech is that Quaid-i-Azam can also be sacralised as a secular nationalist leader. As such he epitomises the values of courage, selflessness, justice and honesty. The civil religion that follows from this construction of his person is one which lays stress not on *external* enemies of the Muslim nation, or even internal betrayals and divisions *within* the Muslim community, but on the treachery and incompetence of leaders, and the various types of internal divisions (class, cultural, ethnic) dividing the nation from within. The vision of the future which the mythic moment of statehood projects is here one of a society as a nation-state created by and for the people. It is a vision not of global Islamic hegemony but of a democratic state, based on Qur'anic principles of justice, equality and honesty, within a family of nations. The present state of the nation is thus open to criticism in the light of the ideal values embodied by Quaid-i-Azam, and the visionary state for which he fought.

A visionary state: unity, faith & discipline

A young speaker at Function B presented an optimistic view of Pakistan, the fulfilment of a vision:

> Today Pakistan is prospering. In international law and relations it has a neutral but fair policy of which I'm sure Jinnah would have approved. The economy is expanding, our internal structure is developing to an extraordinary degree, and there are superb signs of all-round improvement in our homeland, bearing in mind it is only forty years old. Pakistan is now a state which I'm sure Jinnah, if he was alive today, would have been proud of, and my brothers too are proud of it.

He goes on:

> We in this country here, especially the younger people, when we go back to our homeland, I for one cannot feel as if I'm without entity or recognition. I feel very proud when I'm in Pakistan. We have certain problems, certain limits here, but at least we have a homeland to go to, and perhaps we will [go there] one day.

For this young man, living in Britain, Pakistan is already a visionary state, a mythical home, a place of perfection. This optimistic view of the present was not shared, however, by most of the speakers. For them the gathering represented an occasion for listing the failures of the present by comparison with a glorious past and a visionary future. As we saw, one of these failures was the failure of Muslim nations to unite and prevent acts of violence against fellow Muslims. Jinnah's motto 'Unity, Faith and Discipline' was repeatedly evoked by the speakers. Islamic unity, stressed at both functions, is an elusive quality, a mythical moment. Thus, Maulana Saheb said in Function B:

> When you are hit upon the head then you remember Islam. Before this no two Muslims have gathered together to talk about Islamic unity. All the time you are after each other's

chairs and positions. You do not stop to think that in the end you are all Muslims and followers of the Holy Prophet (Peace Be Upon Him). What enmity can you have with one another?

Even when the stress was not simply on Islamic unity, discussions of unity inevitably also emphasised elements of disunity: to create unity Jinnah had to transcend differences of origin (and hence by implication caste), custom, dress, language and even race characterising the Muslim community in the subcontinent. This was clear in the speech of one of the barristers at Function A:

> Despite the differences I have already described which existed between various peoples of Muslim faith in the Indian subcontinent, [Jinnah] thought it was possible – and he proved that it was possible – [to create unity], by joining the people [together], people speaking different languages, wearing different dresses, different clothes, and with differences of culture, different ways of life in many respects – but he said, 'No, we are all Muslims, and the Muslims of India will fight to get an independent homeland, an independent state, in which we shall exist to run our own life together, in a way and in a fashion we choose, in which nobody will dominate any other'.

The two functions both took place in 1988, during the rule of General Zia and before the democratic elections following his assassination, and the electoral victory of Benazir Bhutto and the Pakistan People's Party. Most of the speakers at Function A dwelt on the absence of democracy in Pakistan, and the corruption rife in public life. Jinnah's honesty and incorruptibility were thus set against the present state of the nation. The unity he created was a passing moment:

> The fundamental faith never was followed by the Muslim leadership after Pakistan came into being. Nobody ever kept that promise; Pakistan was supposed to be an Islamic state where you could live by the Islamic rules of life. We didn't do that. There was nothing to keep Bangladesh and West Pakistan together. There was no unity, there was no faith. That is the second element of Quaid-i-Azam's creed in which we failed – faith, have faith in God and faith in your fellow-beings.
>
> ... So what happened? We failed in that aspect as well, we did not have faith in Islam strong enough to stand proudly and say we are Muslims, we want to have an Islamic state and live by the Islamic normal rules. At the same time we did not have the courage to follow the will of the people. How many democratic elections have we had in Pakistan? Not many. When there were elections, did anybody accept them? Those who lose don't accept them, those who win, it goes to their heads. We haven't had those elections, we haven't followed the promise given to the people....

This speaker went on to spell out the third element in Jinnah's creed, that of discipline:

> There are two kind of discipline; discipline imposed on people and discipline voluntarily accepted by people. [These two disciplines are part of] the sacramental requirement of nationhood, a nation like ours. Because we have so many differences, because we have so many distractions which can lead us astray.... Imposed discipline is the discipline of the army.... If a man is told – 'die', he must die, for that is the order given to him.... [Self-discipline means what] people impose upon themselves. It is to say, 'No, I am here wrong in what I am doing, this is the right path and this is the wrong path.... I must take the right path, I must fulfil my obligations in the way God requires of me, in the way the nation requires of me.'
>
> That has not happened. We very clearly lost the imposed discipline of the army.... [The previous speaker] said earlier that you must judge for yourselves how much we have followed that path [set by Quaid-i-Azam]. I for my part don't think we have.... We have lost the will to self-discipline ourselves, because how many times have we seen people acquire

power wrongly? Because either it was by force, or once somebody has acquired power then they won't give it up, because it suits their purpose! In those cases it would have been self-discipline to say, 'No, there is a constitution which obliges me to go now. And I must go.' There is that will in the individual to say, 'No, I must fight against wrong. Because my country suffers from the wrong of its people.' And that self-discipline, my brothers, is the important task before us. I think that is the greatest gift Quaid-i-Azam has left us. Those three words – unity, faith and discipline – if we follow those rules I'm sure we will achieve... [the end of the speech is drowned in applause].

The speaker, having first stressed the vision of an Islamic state following Islamic laws of justice, goes on to criticise the post-Independence politics of Pakistan which brought about the war with Bangladesh, the successive military coups and the absence of democracy. He alludes to contemporary politics without naming anyone specifically, and the general tone is thus a great deal more radical than that of the speakers at Function B. Indeed, at Function B the only criticism of the state's treatment of its citizens came from the Pakistani Ambassador himself, who decried the corruption of the Pakistani bureaucracy and particularly of its petty officials.

This corruption was a central theme in one of the barristers' speeches at Function A.

Isfahani Saheb writes that once Quaid-i-Azam said to me that 'My dear, always remember that in public life honesty is more important than in private life, because by dishonesty in private life you can damage one person, but by dishonesty in public life unlimited numbers of people could be affected' [applause]. 'Because of such dishonesty thousands of people who depend on you could suffer wrong.' Now you see what is happening to Quaid-i-Azam's honest and principled Pakistan. Someone [a poet] said once: 'Since you have turned your back [abandoned us], Spring has turned its back as well' [applause].

Here too we find the kind of radical liberal self-criticism absent at Function B. At that function the radicalism was more religiously orthodox and linked to an embattled nationalism stressing external threats and internal religious divisions.

It is striking nevertheless that some of the speakers at Function A thought it possible to have a democratic state 'according to the canons of Islam': an 'Islamic republic', a 'religious' rather than 'temporal' state (second barrister). The Pakistani Vice-Consul told the audience that

Quaid-i-Azam was a staunch supporter and believer in the tenets of Islam. In a broadcast to the American people in 1948 he said: 'Islam in its idealism has taught us democracy, it has taught us the equality of man, justice and fair play for everybody. We are inheritors of these glorious traditions and are fully alive to our responsibilities and our obligations as framers of the future constitution of Pakistan. We believe in the principle of honesty and fair play in national and international dealing, and we are prepared to make our contribution to the promotion of world peace and prosperity among the nations of the world.'

The seeds of a nationalistic religious radicalism are thus inherent in the very ontology of a state created on the basis of a religiously defined nation. A similar dualism is characteristic of other such states like Israel or Sri Lanka (see Handelman 1990; Kapferer 1988; also Moodie 1975). In these states, state ceremony and political mythology are increasingly imbued with religious images and symbols. The pressure from religious elements within the state is to displace the rule of law as the will of the people by the rule of law sanctioned ultimately by God, and thus controlled by religious experts (see Munir n.d.).

Quaid-i-Azam ceremonials as indexical occasions

Quaid-i-Azam ceremonials have specific connotations in Britain. There are two major themes highlighted in the Manchester context, one implicit, the other explicit. Implicitly, there is the underlying realisation of being, once again, a Muslim minority ruled by the British. Racism, racial harassment and racial abuse are something with which British Pakistanis must increasingly live as a constant factor in their daily lives. Their helplessness in the face of such abuse and their inability to redress the situation are tangible evidence of their lack of influence and lowly status in British society. At the same time, the community has prospered economically and its younger generation is at present entering successfully into business or professional occupations. Even though the ceremonials described here took place before the Rushdie affair and the open confrontation with the state which it caused, it is nevertheless significant that *no direct reference* was made during either function to the current predicament of British Pakistanis as a racial and religious minority. If a sense of threat and impotence existed, it was *displaced* either historically, in mythic terms, or globally, on to the international arena. Indeed, at Function A an attempt was made to minimise the conflict with the British. One of the speakers, who had earlier spoken of the broader fight against colonialism, also pointed out that for an earlier leader, Sir Sayed Ahmed Khan,

> If the choice was between Hindu dominance or the dominance of the British, we should choose the British. Not because he loved the British, not because he loved slavery, but out of frustration that if Hindus are to run the country [we Muslims] would be better off with the British because at least they understand, they have the same God; they worship one God, we worship one God. Christianity is a part of Islam, we understand Christianity and Christianity understands that it is consistent with the tenets of Islam.

Another speaker at Function A stressed that 'we have to see what his enemies say about him [Jinnah]':

> In 1918 Mr Montague, who was Minister for India, came to visit India. He writes in his diary about his tour and about Quaid-i-Azam that 'He was one clean and very smart person whose movements caught my attention and left a deep impression; his speech is logical, he is very forceful in presenting his ideas and will not alter them; if you do not agree wholeheartedly with him he will not accept the half agreed upon. I lost my argument with him and Lord Chelmsford tried to argue with him and he also lost his argument.

The speaker went on to cite praise from two Hindu notables and then continues with Lord Mountbatten's views of Jinnah:

> 'Jinnah's personality was very very forceful. He would stand strong like a rock and at the same time he was a very calm and collected person. It was not possible to know what was in his heart. He was very intelligent and grasped my arguments easily. At the same time I felt that he put a curtain between me and himself. He would put aside my arguments and I failed to sway his opinion. I came to India with the idea of keeping it united; that we were leaving this country after centuries and we wanted to leave it as one country.' And he writes that 'I did not succeed in this. In the end I had to bow to his [Jinnah's] demands.'

The ability to out-talk the British is here coupled with an assumption that there can be a common basis for discussion and mutual persuasion. It is conceded that the British as rulers nevertheless recognised merit; that, although they were the 'enemy', 'oppressor' and 'dictator' (*smarajit*), there were also values shared in common by the two groups. This ambiguity, which now characterises relations between Pakistani immigrant settlers and their British hosts, constitutes an underlying theme running throughout the ceremonials. British enmity and 'dictatorship' on the one hand, and the commonality of values on the other, are open to differential stress depending on the current state of both national and international relations. There remains, however, a basic sense of suspicion and resistance. I never witnessed among Pakistanis, as I did at an India Independence Day celebration in Manchester, a toast to 'The Queen, the Duke of Lancaster'! The Pakistanis I questioned thought that such a toast would be highly unlikely and had themselves also never witnessed it. The other side of this is the deep continuing commitment to, and identification with, Pakistan and, more broadly, the Islamic *umma* which the ceremonials represent.

Backstage rivalries

At a more specific level, Quaid-i-Azam ceremonials are also occasions for mobilising factional support. Function A and Function B were organised by two opposing factions and, as we have seen, the focus of opposition in Function A was Maulana Saheb, the *maulvi* of the Central Mosque. Chaudhry Amin, one of the conveners of Function A, used the occasion to reflect on the need to separate religion and politics. While the major part of his speech on Quaid-i-Azam was in English, this part of his speech was in Urdu, reflecting its localised, more private message:

> Last Friday it was proven that a holy man with his religious duties can also take part in politics [referring to a local incident in the Central Mosque involving the Maulvi] and as an example [of the legitimacy of combining religion and politics] the Prophet Muhammad was cited. Now, we have to see whether there are any objections to a holy man taking part in politics along with his religious duties. He can take part, we do not object to this. But there is a small difference: Maulana Shah Ahmed Nurani[5] also takes part in politics along with his religious duties; Maulana Fazal-ur-Rahman also takes part in politics along with his religious duties; and before this Maulana Mufti Mahmood also took part in politics along with his religious duties [these are all Pakistani religious politicians]. There are eighteen religious parties in Pakistan which take part in politics along with their religious duties. But people we call from Pakistan to teach our children about Islam, for which they are paid – we pay them to teach our children about Islam, so they should only do what they are paid for. If they are interested in politics they should stop taking pay from us and go into politics, we have no objections. But they cannot get paid for teaching Islam, and, while people are waiting in the mosque for the Imam to start the prayers, instead he [the Imam] is elsewhere at a meeting, taking part in politics!
>
> Is this not injustice to religion? Indeed, I would call it a fraud against religion. One day they will die, as everyone will die, and answer to God. Islam teaches us 'A worker must be paid before his sweat dries'. I admit that Maulvi Saheb does not sweat during his religious teaching [laughter]. Even so, he should do his work properly, as is his duty, because he gets paid for it. It is wrong for Maulana Saheb to get paid £150 [a week] while he is only there for Friday prayers, and he does not even put on the notice board which prayers he will be there for. He should be in the mosque for all five prayers a day and teach our children. He

[5] Leader at the time of the Barelvi party, the JUP, in Pakistan; see Malik 1990. For a full account of the event described here the reader is referred to Werbner (1991d).

should always talk about religion and teach religion, as this is what he is paid for. Only then will he be earning his wages honestly. If he is only there [at the mosque] for one or two prayers, and the rest of his time he devotes to [community] politics, and he tries to say that it is permissible to take part in politics as well as religious teachings [he is not fulfilling his duties].

Just half a verse of Alama Iqbal – 'Religion is incomplete without politics'; in other words, politics is mixed with religion. In the time of the Prophet Muhammad there were no divisions [*firqe*, sects, denominations]; there was no Shi'a division, no Barelvi division, no Deobandi division, no Bihari division. Today there are seventy-two divisions in Islam. If there is one Qur'an, one *Kalima*, one Prophet, every Muslim believes in the Qur'an, Allah and the reality of the *Kalima*, and believes in the Prophet Muhammad; then where have these seventy-two divisions come from, who made them? I, you, or these people who say that politics and religion are one? They have made these divisions for their own benefit. They change the religion as it benefits them, and then they mobilise some followers and make a new division. Then they say their division will go to Paradise and the others will not. This is how they confuse us about religion. The best way to solve this confusion is, as I have said before, that *maulanas* should stop taking part in politics and stick to teaching religion which is what they get paid for. Every division should be able to pray by their own beliefs. I hear somebody reminding me about time so I will not take long and I think you must be hungry [the speaker is here referring to reception which will follow the speeches]. But it is important for me to ask the *maulanas*: 'Please stop taking part in politics, and stop pointing a finger at people who they think are wrongdoers.'

We see in this speech how the tension between religion and the state, which dominates Pakistani politics at the *national* level, is here put into the context of *local* communal conflicts; indeed, it needs to be stressed that the passions this tension generates are equally intense at the local level.

An implicit riposte to this attack on him by his opponents was given by the Maulana himself during his speech at Function B. Drawing on the example of Quaid-i-Azam's single-minded leadership he said:

We should forget about the opposition parties. Quaid-i-Azam did not waste his time arguing with them, nor should we. I have seen another side of Quaid-i-Azam's life. He was called different names [i.e. insulted], faced with opposition at every turn and was branded with indecent titles, and even today when we read such books, our heads are bowed down in shame. But Quaid-i-Azam never said a word in favour of himself, not did he attempt to disclaim these epithets. Just look at what a beautiful picture Quaid-i-Azam has shown us of his detractors: you must go straight forward to your destination, do not look to right or left. There are people who will try to waste your time but pay no attention [to them] and concentrate on your mission. And Quaid-i-Azam went on moving forward. If he had wasted his time in answering all the questions people asked of him he would never have been able to reach his goal. He answered the English and the Hindus but never bothered to answer the accusations flung at him by some of the opposing Muslims, and never participated in any argument that was initiated by these Muslims.

From his position (at the time) of relative dominance the Maulana acknowledges the attacks upon him but does not deem it necessary to answer them in specific terms. Both attack and counter-attack are disguised, couched in generalities and innuendo, so that visiting dignitaries (the Pakistani Sub-Consul and the Pakistani Ambassador) and uninformed members of the audience are left with only the general message. For those in the know, however, the unofficial message dominates the official one. Even further, Quaid-i-Azam's life, achievements and political philosophy are interpreted dialogically, as part of an ongoing, contemporary *local* argument between leaders and groups representing different communal power bases and fundamentally distinct political ideologies.

Political mythology & exemplary leadership

According to Akbar Ahmed, 'The importance of a leader in an Islamic community, Shi'a or Sunni, is critical. The group is judged by its leadership' (1986: 59). He cites the Qur'an where this sentiment is expressed (the Holy Qur'an 5:109, and 7:6–7). One may argue that the equation between person and society in Muslim societies is even more fundamental: it is an ontological merging of identities – leader and community, individual and nation. This merging is related, as Dumont has argued in another context (Dumont 1983), to a hierarchical conception of society, one in which persons of exceptional purity, divinely chosen, encompass secular power and mundane, worldly social divisions. Such persons, I suggest, fulfil a redemptive role. Rather than being unique individuals placed *in* time and history, they come to be an embodiment of sacred values, placed *above* time and history. They are thus elevated, immanently and intrinsically, above ordinary mortals, and their purity is evidenced by the qualities of their personality and the values expressed in their actions and achievements. Whereas most mortal men are impure transgressors, and so too their society is caught in a morass of failure, corruption and internal conflicts, such exemplary people are able, because of their redemptive stature, to unify the society and inspire it to acts of great faith and sacrifice. To quote Jinnah's message to the nation, cited by Chaudhry Amin as Chairman of Function A: 'The more you learn to sacrifice and bear hardship, the more faithful, pure and strong you will be, as gold is refined when smelted in fire.'

This equation between the divinely chosen and the nation or community leads to a Muslim political mythology and civil religion constructed around the sacralised qualities and values of exemplary persons such as Quaid-i-Azam. As a central figure in this political mythology Quaid-i-Azam is clearly placed, in Bakhtin's terms, in 'epic' time. Bakhtin argues that

> The time of epic is not chronological; it is rather a world of beginnings and peak times in the national history, a world of firsts and bests. Epics are not simply set in time that has receded, for time is best perceived as value. What was in the past is automatically considered to be better, bigger, stronger or more beautiful. In epic, someone is speaking about a past that is to him inaccessible, and he adopts the reverent point of view of a descendant.... Even though both its singer and its implied listener are located in the same time and value system, the represented world stands in an utterly different and inaccessible time and plane, separated by epic distance. It is impossible to change, to rethink, or to re-evaluate anything in epic time, for it is finished, conclusive, and immutable. (Clark and Holquist 1984: 287).

Quaid-i-Azam celebrations are conducted in a tone of utter solemnity, a tone which befits the epic generic mode of presentation and the sacred nature of the occasion. Reflexivity is confined to a condemnation of the sins and omissions of the present. There is seldom any humorous intrusion of other generic modes to undermine the absolute sanctity of the values celebrated. Yet towards the end of Function A one of the speakers attempted to defuse the criticism directed against the *maulvi* with a joke, introducing it by saying that if *maulanas* are getting involved in politics, he prayed that politicians would turn to religion:

I would like to tell you a story about paradise and hell. It would sound better, I think, if I tell it in Punjabi [note the transition to an informal, 'profane' language]. Between paradise and hell there was a wall. One day the wall fell down. The heat from hell began penetrating into paradise and the cool air of paradise started moving into hell. The people of paradise said: 'We should rebuild the wall.' The people of hell said, 'No, we should leave it as it is.' The people of paradise repeated their demand that the wall must be rebuilt. The people of hell said: 'How are you going to build the wall?' The people of paradise said: 'We will appeal to the court of God.' The people of hell said: 'How are you going to appeal? All the lawyers are here, in hell!'

Although perhaps unintended, this joke reflects not only on the speaker (himself a barrister) and his fellow guest speaker (another barrister), but on Quaid-i-Azam as well, one of the most brilliant Muslim lawyers the subcontinent has known, a man whose 'unique achievement was so inextricably the product of his genius as a barrister, perhaps the greatest "native" advocate in British Indian History ... [and even] the shrewdest barrister in the British Empire' (Wolpert 1984: 4). In introducing an alternative generic mode which reconstructs the epic mode in more ironic terms, the speaker reminds his audience of the fundamental frailties of human beings – politicians, clerics, lawyers, all those who presume to lead. The very introduction of such a joke into a Pakistani ceremonial hints at a possible future movement among some British Pakistanis towards a more ironic form of nationalism. It is not accidental that such irony is introduced by a man who, like Jinnah himself, is a respected member of the British law (now a QC and head of chambers), an equal by virtue of his membership in this exclusive club with his British colleagues, and a man whose professional code requires him to represent clients in court irrespective of their racial or religious origins.

Conclusion: myths of nations from the margins

Pakistani diasporans are located on the margins of two imagined communities: Britain and Pakistan. But whereas their British identity is celebrated and commemorated by the august institutions of the state, parliament, the monarchy, the media and the schools, and through a media-dominated Rembrance Day ceremony dedicated to the dead of two world wars, it is they themselves who must invent both their nation's history and the institutional spaces in which to celebrate it. The diasporic public sphere they create is the space in which Pakistan is reflectively imagined, scrutinised, celebrated and criticised. Some diasporans celebrate their marginality as an 'example, for both the homeland's and hostland's nation-states, of the possibility of living, even thriving in the regimes of multiplicity which are increasingly the global condition' (Tololyan 1996: 7). In this they fit the idealised depiction by Bhabha of diasporas as 'interrupting' official versions of the nation 'from the margins' (Bhabha 1994, Chap. 8). Indeed, during the period in which the ceremonial described here took place, much of the Pakistan People's Party leadership was living in exile, in Britain, and has today been replaced by the Pakistani leadership of another party, the Mohajir Qwami Movement led by post-Partition refugees from India. Pakistan as a nation was first conceived of in Britain. Nations may not only be imagined but actually influenced by such global margins, as van der Veer notes (1995). Pakistanis in Manchester have repeatedly supported Pakistan financially in times of war and disaster.

But the men who shape the rituals of nation described in this chapter are not important players on any national scenes. They are subalterns, largely invisible, whose imaginaries count for very little on the stage of history. The ideological work they are engaged in is one of negotiating a collective identity in a strange land, while asserting their individual honour in a local game of communal politics. They play this game by mobilising alternative visions of their collective subjectivity.

Imaginaries from the margin are liable to be not only progressive but narrowly culturalist. Diasporans may support causes inimical to multiplicity, hybridity and global tolerance. Examples of this are diasporic Jewish support for the extreme Right in Israel and Irish-American support for the Republicans in Northern Ireland (see Anderson 1994). Interpreting the nation is a meroscopic activity which generates partial visions of a national ontology.

In his discussion of myths of nationalism in Sri Lanka, Kapferer distinguishes between three facets of a political mythology: myth which, like Ricoeur (1981), he regards, following Lévi-Strauss, as a self-contained coherently structured symbolic entity; ontology, which is a basic set of existential values implied by the structural analysis of such myths; and ideology, which is a set of more or less coherent prescriptive ideas for current action. Ideology, as a current appropriation, draws on the ontology implicit in national myths to mobilise support and to evoke passion and emotive identification. As such, ideology converts myth via ontology into social charter, a reflection of present, contemporary social divisions. It is thus possible for several different ideologies to be based on a single mythological corpus, with each ideology highlighting different ontological elements in the myths (Kapferer 1988).

Quaid-i-Azam ceremonials in Manchester point to a further dimension of political mythologising highlighted in Sri Lanka's national politics, a feature which stems from the notion of time such myths imply. Time is cyclical. A prior mythic unity will be recaptured in a visionary, utopian future. Prior external and internal enemies (in their current manifestations) are apocalyptically destined to threaten the integrity of the nation once more. Ideologies based on political myth thus draw on both the future hopes and the future fears of people. This is especially true if the enemy threatening the nation has not changed its identity – if it is still the Hindus, the British or the Jews for the Muslims of Pakistan, the Tamils for Sinhalese in Sri Lanka or the Africans for Afrikaners in Southern Africa (Moodie 1975). But even when the enemy is different, fear of a new holocaust repeating an earlier one within a 'cycle of death and suffering' is an important feature of a nation's political mythology. Thus in Zimbabwe Ndebele and Kalanga were seen as surrogates of the prior white enemy by Mugabe's government (see R. Werbner 1991); in Israel the Arabs have displaced the Germans, themselves manifestations of earlier enemies, Romans, Babylonians, Assyrians or ancient Egyptians in the apocalyptic political mythology of Israeli society (see Handelman 1990 and Paine 1989).

In this respect political mythology and the ideologies it both generates and embodies do not simply reflect contemporary group material interests and divisions, but a far more complex set of social *experiences* and dialogically related political philosophies. For those who experience racism and exclusion in their daily lives, fears of expulsion and genocide loom much larger than for those who move easily through more tolerant, cosmopolitan circles. The extent to which both diasporans and their hosts are able and willing in practice to bridge cultural divides between them, to move beyond the confines of their narrow groups, affects their imaginings of the future. The more bound they are by their narrow group's particular symbols and images, and its specific history, the more apocalyptic their vision of this future is likely to be.

Recent political myths, like those about Quaid-i-Azam, based on events taking place at a time for which published records, memoirs, biographies and other documentary evidence are widely available, are necessarily complex and replete with detail. This detail is drawn upon selectively, and thus reconstructed and simplified, in the speeches narrated by Pakistani diasporans in their commemoration ceremonies. Different ideological positions go along in these narratives with different kinds of mythic emphasis. In some, the incorporation of recent national myths into the central religious Islamic and Qur'anic myth, which itself draws on Judaic and Christian myths, is more marked. I have tried to show here, however, that the different ideological positions expressed in the speeches share a fundamental ontology. One feature of this is a cyclical notion of history, the idea that the past forms the precedent for a visionary future unity, a unity which for a brief moment did, and will again, transcend the current threatened or divided present. The other shared idea is that society in its utopian perfection is embodied and personified by exemplary persons, chosen individuals who are divinely endowed with transcendent status. Such individuals are perceived to exist outside ordinary time and their presence not only redeems and unites the society, but revitalises its faith and power through sacrifice. The millennium is the promise of their arrival.

Narrating community, building bridges[6]

On the Sunday following its Quaid-i-Azam memorial celebration, Faction A convened an 'Asian Business Seminar' in the resplendent surroundings of Manchester's City Council Chambers, in the company of the Lady Mayoress and the Pakistani Ambassador (see Plate 3.2). Participants at the meeting presented the classic immigrant script of successful integration and social mobility. The Lady Mayoress summed it all up: 'Manchester has always been a multi-racial and multi-cultural city. We were the first industrial city in the world ... the best in the world came to our city.' She went on to say: 'We are truly encouraged by the initiative and enterprise of our Asian community.... Successful trade brings with it peace and respect, and that respect develops into peace and friendship which is the goal for which we all strive.'

The narrative told at the meeting was of a local immigrant community building bridges to its adopted city. This was also stressed by the Pakistani Ambassador who spoke at length about the incredible advances made by Pakistanis since he was last in Britain, and encouraged his audience to contribute to all walks of life in Britain. Manchester, a city of successful 'Asian' businessmen, should lead the way.

The allegory of community was repeatedly invoked. From an analytical perspective, 'community,' like 'family' or 'lineage', is a *relational* concept: it is invoked situationally *by the same subjects* to refer to quite different collectivities, on a rising social scale. Even global diasporas are communities, according to

---

[6] For a full account of the event described here the reader is referred to Werbner 1991d.

Tololyan (1996: 4), 'the exemplary communities of the transnational moment'.

But 'community' in Britain retains certain emotive connotations. It implies a local sensibility, a we-ness, the sharing of a lived-in world of taken-for-granted assumptions, of moral amity and mutual responsibility. In English 'belonging' means being a recognised member of a 'community'. There is no equivalent word in Urdu and in their speeches Pakistanis invoke community in English. The elasticity and ambiguity of the term can be used to create discursive bridges between ethnic groups and to reach out to the wider society (Eade 1991).

Fables of self and community may be constructed oppositionally, to exclude outsiders, but it is more common for scripts of migration to tell a story of increasing integration, of building bridges to the wider society (Dominguez 1989: 146–52). The allegory told at the Asian Business meeting highlighted successful integration into Manchester and Britain. Like most such allegories, it disguised a darker reality of racism and discrimination, of arson and vandalism perpetrated against Asian businesses, of cut-throat competition at the bottom end of the market, of exorbitant insurance premiums and refusal by insurance companies to grant insurance (see Werbner 1991d).

As an indexical event, the title, the 'Asian Business Seminar', disguised the fact that there were no wealthy Hindu businessmen at the seminar. Since it was a factional event, it was also boycotted by supporters of Faction B. From a political perspective, Faction A had successfully 'captured' the Ambassador, the Mayor, and the services of the Department of Trade and Industry. In reality, the Ambassador had come to Manchester to try to mediate between the warring factions, with little success. Although advertised as 'Asian', the event was quite clearly a Muslim and Pakistani gathering, which opened with a Muslim prayer by Maulana Saheb. It was thus an event in which back-stage differed radically from front-stage (Goffman 1959), hinting at divisions rather than amity within the 'Asian' community. As Kermode has argued, narratives contain 'secrets' which do not fit neatly into an overt, publicly intended narrative structure (Kermode 1980). The play was a good deal 'deeper', the stakes much higher than appeared on the surface (Geertz 1973, Chap. 15).

Nevertheless, there was enough truth in the narrative of successful communal integration to make it believable. Thus the Ambassador concluded: 'Here in Manchester you are ahead of the rest of the community because Manchester perhaps inspires people in this way of being able to reach out.'

This constructed reality was not simply an illusion. Hindu and Sikh businessmen and women in the city have continued to expand their businesses and to progress. But for Muslims, the Rushdie affair marked a radical break. Although they continue to prosper as entrepreneurs in the city (see Werbner 2001), it is questionable whether the force of public statements and protests made during the Rushdie affair can be easily eradicated. The new text of confrontation between Muslims and the state has exposed a truth which the allegory of building bridges had hidden. The bridges have been shattered.

Even as it disguises hidden truths, an event's facade constitutes a currently 'real' public truth. The construction of communal myths and sacred histories captures particular moods and builds historical facts around them. At any one time in a community, multiple realities exist in some tension with each other. Socially exclusive events expose conflicts and disagreements between groups. The meeting held by the same group the previous evening, which also entertained the

Ambassador, was conducted in Urdu rather than English and repeatedly invoked, as we saw, the global failure of Islam. But in more inclusive gatherings such as the Asian Business Seminar, broader, more encompassing mythic realities are expressed before a wider and more differentiated audience.

Public events leave traces, but these are subject to re-visioning. The Business Seminar, which appeared at the time to be so mundane and unremarkable, turned out to be a unique event for Pakistanis in Manchester, a moment in history in which the building of permanent bridges between Muslims and British society seemed to be an innocent matter of hard work and personal effort. Then came the Rushdie affair, the Gulf War and the September 11 bombing of the World Trade Center. During the decades following the seminar, this innocence was lost. Like a palimpsest, it was reinscribed with more recent traumatic public actions and public pronouncements.

II
Global Mobilisation
Contesting Culture & Citizenship

4

The Clash of Aesthetics
& the Religious Imagination

Modernist aesthetics & the Rushdie affair

So far this book has traced the public performance of identities – national, civic and local – enacted in invisible public spaces which diaspora Pakistanis create and through which they contest notions of the common good and public morality. The rise and visibilisation of the social movement that came to be known as the Rushdie affair was, from this perspective, a radical watershed in the history of Muslims in Britain, Europe and the West more generally. It mobilised extensive networks and united various actors and fractions who, as we have already seen, were normally fragmented and often locked in internal conflicts and arguments of identity. This sudden visibilisation accords with Melucci's view that 'Latency and visibility are the two interrelated poles of collective action.' 'Hidden networks', Melucci argues, 'become visible whenever collective actors confront or come into conflict with a public policy' (Melucci 1989: 70).

The opening phrase of St John's Gospel encapsulates the symbolic and representational struggle which constituted the Rushdie affair. 'In the beginning was the Word.' Images and words were centrally at stake in what was, from the start, a global struggle. The opening verbal parry was that of a global writer (Salman Rushdie), written in a global language (English), published by a global publisher (Viking-Penguin) for a global readership. From halfway across the world, separated some 4,000 miles from the global city (London) where the writer, a self-declared migrant, lived, came a death sentence in the voice of a global religious leader (the Ayatollah Khomeini of Iran), addressed to followers of a global religion (Islam) scattered around the globe, through the media of boundary-crossing sound and electronic waves. In response, the nations of the West withdrew into their boundaries and accused the Ayatollah of infringing national sovereignty and meddling in the private affairs of other nation-states. It was in response to these global messages that collective mobilisation took place.

The publication of *The Satanic Verses* was a conjunctural moment in which citizenship and faith were both tested and revalued, an exceptional moment of disruption and crisis which compelled Muslims, intellectuals and policy-makers to reflect consciously about what these terms meant. Historical conjunctures, Marshall Sahlins has argued, 'at once reproduce the traditional cultural categories and give them new values' (Sahlins 1985: 125); all the more so, as Gramsci recognised, when such conjunctures reveal critical contradictions (see Simon

1991: 39). For diaspora Muslims in Britain the redefinition and relocation of values meant also, crucially, a new kind of mobilisation for political action. For the first time they sought to become a public presence in British society. Although visibilisation was not without costs, it opened up a space for diasporic dialogue and legitimate protest, a space for reflection about the possible meanings and limits of a transnational Muslim subjectivity.

This was mirrored in the book itself. *The Satanic Verses* is a book about image and self-image, communication and its breakdown, trust and alienation, loyalty and betrayal, passion and transcendence. But at a different level the book and the crisis it generated, as many have recognised,[1] are about language and words, the meanings of words, the images that these words conjure up. The meaning for whom? That, of course, became a key question. The Rushdie affair was not simply an instance of Giddens' double hermeneutic – interpreting the novel's intended meaning. It was an example of a triple hermeneutic leading towards an infinitely regressing hermeneutic: not simply how the author interpreted Islam, what the book *meant*, but what did his readers, Muslims and non-Muslims, believe about their *counterparts'* interpretations. Such speculations became facts, the reason for action. Readers read the book vicariously, through the eyes of a presumed (and often non-existent) hostile and orientalising other. And so interpretation piled upon interpretation in an infinite hermeneutic spiral.

The result of this intractable aesthetic impasse has been a cascade of interpretive literature which is only now subsiding. The anthropological contribution to this debate has been to address the questions of authorial intention, multiple readerships and cultural translation – issues at the heart of the contemporary anthropological project (Asad 1990a; Fischer and Abedi 1990; van der Veer 1996, 1997).

Almost from the start, the publication of *The Satanic Verses* was a historic 'event', in the Ricoeurian sense. It 'imprinted' its mark on time and history (Ricoeur 1981: 206–7) and went 'beyond' its original situation of aesthetic production, becoming 'detached' from its author's expectations or intentions during the process of its production. It opened up unexpected new 'worlds' of reference (ibid.: 208), and came to be the subject of multiple readings.

In the anthropological debate on the affair, diametrically opposed interpretations, both of the literary and of the social text, were grounded in distinct constructions of time and history as bearing upon aesthetic appreciation. One possible approach to the affair was to interpret the confrontation as a clash between 'expert' knowledge and 'commonsense' understandings, the latter tending to conflate science, morality and art within a single communicative infrastructure, rooted in everyday praxis (Habermas 1985: 9; 1987).

More radically, the clash could be construed as a class struggle between the popular aesthetic appreciation of a Muslim working class, which judged the novel from a moral and religious perspective, and the aristocratic tastes of a Western cultural elite. This was the approach adopted by Talal Asad (1990a).

Asad directs his critique against the 'legitimate' or 'refined' tastes of the dominant classes, the 'aristocrats' of culture and its arbiters: writers, authors, critics and journalists. This dominant group aligned itself, he argues, in response to Muslim protests, with the author against what they perceived to be the

---

[1] None, perhaps, more eloquently than Carlos Fuentes 1989.

'barbaric' tastes of an irrational, semi-literate, set of self-appointed Muslim critics. The latter read fragments out of context and judged the book without possessing the aesthetic sensibility required to appreciate its message.

By aligning himself with this Western intelligentsia and a globally dominant Western media, Rushdie, in Asad's view, perpetrated the dehumanising and humiliating of a beleaguered, vulnerable black Muslim underclass in the name of Western 'Enlightenment' values. Deconstructing the novel, he finds it 'a weapon ... wielded in the presence of a post-Christian audience – indeed with the seduction of that audience as a primary aim – it draws astutely on the long tradition of Christian anti-Muslim polemics' (Asad 1990a: 252).

The theme of symbolic violence, as perpetrated by an intellectual elite on the plebeian masses, is also central to Bourdieu's aesthetic theory. Advocating an 'anti-Kantian aesthetic', he argues for a holistic view of taste as a politics of value and dominance, and hence as simultaneously economic, social, political, moral and sensual (Bourdieu 1984). Kant's stress upon a detached 'pure' judgement, rooted in 'understanding' or 'reason', is, according to Bourdieu, merely an expression of bourgeois ideas about the existence of a 'high cultural', autonomous field of art, associated with the rise of a German middle class and its notions of *kultur* (Elias 1978: 8–16,19).

From the perspective of such a holistic aesthetic, the pro-Rushdie lobbyists were merely defending a powerfully established hegemony:

> What is at stake in aesthetic discourse, and in the attempted imposition of a definition of the genuinely human, is nothing less than the *monopoly of humanity*. Art is called upon to mark the difference between humans and non-humans: artistic experience ... subject only to the laws of creative genius ... is the closest approach to the divine experience....
> (Bourdieu 1984: 491)

Humanity, we are told, is claimed as a monopoly of 'culture', not only against petit bourgeois morality, but also against working-class sensuality:

> The opposition between the tastes of nature and the tastes of freedom introduces a relationship which is that of the body to the soul, between those who are 'only natural' and those whose capacity to dominate their own biological nature affirms their legitimate claim to dominate social nature. (ibid.: 491)

Art, Bourdieu argues, naturalised since the Enlightenment as the new religion, with creative artists as its priests, has been captured by the elite as their sole prerogative. The constantly shifting game of taste and symbolic practices is orchestrated from the top.

Yet this rendition of Kant's work represents, in my view, a basic misunderstanding of his aesthetics of 'the sublime'. Bourdieu fails to recognise that, in his *Critique of Pure Judgement*, Kant's primary interest was not in art. His principal objective was to relegate *religion* from the realm of scientific knowledge to the realm of *powerful aesthetic appreciation*. In Kantian philosophy the aesthetic sublime, like the ethical sublime, is that which is beyond empirical verification yet nevertheless open to reflection and dialogue: an imaginative intuition of infinity or eternity which is powerfully moving, without, however, constituting knowledge in the scientific sense (on the sublime in Kant see Bergman and Rotenstreich 1966: 15–70; Lyotard 1986 [1977]: 77). Kant's aim was not the Nietzschian one of sacralising art and literature – as Bourdieu would have it – or of separating aesthetic appreciation from bodily enjoyment. His primary aim was that of demarcating a space for religious knowledge as a realm of unprovable abstract yet powerfully moving experience.

The central problem with the neo-Marxist aesthetic is thus that, by translating taste into a cultural game of power, it denies the power of the aesthetic religious imagination. Paradoxically, then, such a class-based aesthetic starts by privileging secular cultural elites (as the Kantian aesthetic does not) as the ultimate source of all *positive* culture. Hence Bourdieu, following Bakhtin, argues that 'the popular imagination can *only invert* the relationship which is the basis of the aesthetic sociodicy' (Bourdieu 1984: 491, emphasis added).[2] Popular culture as resistance is compelled to constitute itself out of the bric-à-brac of mass culture (Hebdige 1979).

Yet turning culture into a mere power game fails to explain why the religious or artistic imagination moves people – ordinary people – powerfully. Hence, rather than reinstating the 'high'/'popular' cultural divide, the need is to consider further the passionate commitment and empowering potency of religion as a form of aesthetics which appeals to distinct – and sometimes opposed – aesthetic communities.[3]

Aesthetic communities are constituted through a sharing of both cultural conventions and daily knowledge (see Geertz 1983, Chap. 5). The greater the *social* sharing, the more artistic products will echo and resonate with shared experiences and past associations, and thus what is novel or borrowed in new works of art will be recognised as shocking or revelatory. In the past aesthetic communities were *local* communities with a local aesthetic sensibility. But in its religious manifestations it has been possible, for millennia, for aesthetic communities to continue to share intuitive aesthetic understandings despite their spatial dispersion. Through global media and the translation industry this is now true also of all forms of aesthetic appreciation. That specific aesthetics are now global was highlighted by the Rushdie affair.

Regarded as an aesthetic community, the Muslim response to *The Satanic Verses* was not an instance of an underprivileged underclass confronting the priests of an alien 'high culture'. Nor was it simply a clash between an antiquated morality and an enlightened aesthetic. It was, on the contrary, a clash between two distinct aesthetics, and between two distinct moralities or world views. The confrontation was between *equal* aesthetic communities, each defending its own high culture: not 'popular' versus 'high', or 'low' versus 'high', but 'high' versus 'high'. As Asad himself points out, it was the boldness with which Muslims asserted their passionate commitment which generated some of the antagonism against them (see also Asad 1990b).

A further point needs to be stressed here: Bourdieu's anti-Kantian aesthetic, like Asad's criticism of Rushdie's betrayal, relies upon a peculiar revision of the Enlightenment. Against this revision, it needs to be stressed that the Enlightenment did not represent simply a move from one certainty (religious) to another (modern), as is sometimes claimed. As a set of radical philosophical ideas it was

---

[2] See also Barthes (1957: 139). This elitism of Bourdieu's theory has been stressed by others (see Longhurst and Savage 1997: 295).

[3] Bauman 1992 discusses aesthetic communities by reference to Kant, citing Lyotard 1988, but the reference to Kant remains obscure, and the notion would seem more fitting for a post-Kantian than a Kantian approach with its individualist stress.

grounded, not in certainty but, following Hume, in scepticism and uncertainty. It thus remained throughout in *tension* with *modernity*, seen as an era of administrative and technological expansion, influencing it variably and dialectically (see Featherstone 1991; Habermas 1985 on 'cultural modernity'; Jameson 1991, Chap. 1; also Lyotard 1986: 71–82).[4] As Cassirer has argued (1951: 161):

> Not doubt, but dogma, is the most dreaded foe of knowledge; not ignorance as such, but ignorance which pretends to be truth and wants to pass for truth.

If certainty was attacked, religious faith was reformulated:

> The strongest intellectual forces of the Enlightenment do not lie in its rejection of belief but rather in the new form of faith which it proclaims, and in the new form of religion which it embodies…. All apparent opposition to religion which we meet in this age should not blind us to the fact that all intellectual problems are fused with religious problems, and that the former find their constant deepest inspiration in the latter. The more insufficient one finds previous religious answers to basic questions of knowledge and morality, the more intensive and passionate become these questions themselves. The controversy from now on is no longer concerned with particular religious dogmas and their interpretation, but with the nature of religious certainty; it no longer deals with what is merely believed but with the nature, tendency, and function *of belief as such.* (ibid.: 135–6, my italics)

Seen thus, I shall argue in this chapter, *The Satanic Verses* can be understood as a modernist, *not* a postmodernist, text: it is, above all, an enquiry into the nature of religious belief and religious certainties from a humanist perspective. The novel's ultimate message is one of faith in man as the source of rational creativity. Postmodernism, by contrast, is constituted by absolute uncertainty, a loss of the last remaining cornerstone of modernist faith in progress, a realisation of the irrational consequences of rationality itself (see Bauman 1993).

A further point of Cassirer's is relevant here: the Enlightenment's philosophy was not uniquely novel; it drew on earlier epochs and ages before and beyond the Christian West. Hence too, at the very core of *The Satanic Verses* is the idea of the flawed prophet/hero/great leader, a fundamentally *pre*-Enlightenment idea which has its roots in a wide range of foundational narratives: Hindu mythology, the Old Testament, ancient Greek tragedy and Elizabethan tragedy. It is equally evident that if the West sacralises literature, for Muslims it represents perhaps an even greater value. In similar vein, Fischer and Abedi point to the fundamental place of uncertainty in Islam as a moral trial or crucible.

In attacking Rushdie's betrayal, Asad mistakenly renders the basic moral ideas animating the Enlightenment *too exclusively Western.* From that flows the negative association between 'enlightened', 'assimilated' Indians/Pakistanis who betray their own people/culture/religion by promoting bourgeois liberal ideas. Against this view it may be argued that to identify the *values* of the Enlightenment exclusively with the West is to deny many non-Western cultures their ethical foundational autonomy.

The point I am making is simply this: Rushdie did not intend merely to align himself with a present-day liberal intelligentsia against his own people; if this

---

[4] Bauman (1992) stresses the certainties of modernity. It is important to recognise, however, that it was modernity that institutionalised scientific enquiry, political democracy, religious pluralism and modern capitalism – all institutions founded on the tolerance of doubt and uncertainty. Postmodernity has, of course, gone a step further, casting doubt on the rational consequences of scientific rationality and social planning.

seemed to be the case, it was because he was fighting precisely the same *internal* battles against dogma fought in Europe by the writers and philosophers of the Enlightenment against the power of the church, and doing so by evoking earlier, pre-Enlightenment traditions. *The Satanic Verses* aims, not at a *loss* of faith, but at creating a foundation for a 'religion of freedom' (Cassirer 1951: 160).

A further point needs to be made here: the battles of the Enlightenment did not result everywhere in the forging of a central role for intellectuals. In Britain in particular, intellectuals failed to achieve the influence gained by their continental counterparts (see Turner 1992). The English response to *The Satanic Verses* as an aesthetic work exemplifies this marginality. Outside a minority group of writers and journalists who sprang to the writer's defence at some personal risk, the novel was regarded by almost everyone, including national political and religious representatives, as either offensive or a provocative nuisance.[5] It was widely held to be dull and arcane. Beyond the circle of creative artists and the press, few if any invoked the sanctity of art or creative genius, and the crisis was quickly refocused around practical issues of law and order, national sovereignty and the blasphemy law. The most common response was surprise that a novel could be taken so seriously.

Yet despite British pragmatism, aesthetic works do move people deeply. This brings me to the fundamental antinomy implied by Kant's *Critique*: if aesthetic judgement and a sense of the sublime are both rooted in a subjective sensibility and a culturally constituted imagination, can disagreements in aesthetic judgement *between* aesthetic communities be bridged? Is cultural translation, a transcendence of parochial cultural values, possible?

Fischer and Abedi attempt to bridge the interpretive chasm by arguing that the novel's theme has its roots in traditional Islamic exegetical debate and that satirical representations of Islam have a long history in Persian literature. In a dazzling display of exegetical pyrotechnics, they demonstrate that the issues at the centre of the novel have been a focus of Muslim religious debate between doctrinal and non-doctrinal Islamic scholars for many centuries; they were not Rushdie's invention. The problem of translation, they contend, is

> not merely across languages and cultural borders but among interest groups and discourses competing for hegemony within social arenas, be they local, national or transnational. Rushdie's text and social text make vivid the point that in Muslim worlds the secular intelligentsia and the religious intelligentsia are engaged in cultural class-warfare, each using systematic discourses the other only partially understands. (Fischer and Abedi 1990: 108)

Against this view it can be argued that, even if traditional Islamic literature satirises pompous religious clerics or lesser Muslim historical figures, the Prophet of Islam is rarely attacked. There are good reasons for this, I believe, rooted in the aesthetic/ethic of the sublime. Hence it cannot be claimed that the passionate response of Muslims to the Rushdie novel was due merely to a current religious dogmatism or to their lack of familiarity with the conventions of their own

---

[5] That many British policy-makers decided to abandon the author and condemn the novel in the interests of communal harmony was made clear in a speech by a Chairman of the Commission for Racial Equality. Sir David Lane talks of the 'sense of hurt and anguish suffered by Muslims because of the *obscene attacks on all that they hold sacred*' (emphasis added).

literature. It seems quite clear that their response was one of genuine moral and aesthetic outrage. This is, indeed, precisely the tragic impasse which the Rushdie affair generated: while from an Islamic perspective, the novel in its transgression is offensive, read in terms of modernist literary conventions, it is possible to show that it is not an attack on the Prophet of Islam, or on Islam as a great religion. This is the theme I shall develop in the last part of this chapter.

In interpreting the text from a modernist perspective I shall also be arguing that the Rushdie affair was not merely an instance of class or ethnic struggle for hegemony, even though it increasingly came to be perceived in these terms. Such a construction fails to appreciate the fundamental interpretive conundrum which the novel raised. To analyse this conundrum fully, I attempt here to consider both sides of the interpretive chasm – the Muslim and the modernist/ postmodernist. My exposition of the novel itself is necessarily schematic, given the limitations of space, and is narrowly focused on the problem of aesthetic interpretation and cultural translation as these bear upon the present-day anthropological project.

It is important to recognise in advance of my discussion that British Pakistanis' anger at the book was magnified by the anomalies of religious minority citizenship it revealed: on the one hand, diasporic Muslims were constrained by the laws of their adopted land; on the other hand, the publication of the novel revealed that the law was discriminatory and protected only Christian feelings of offence. These anomalies were explained by a student of computer science, on his way to the demonstration against Rushdie which took place in London in May 1989. He was asked by my research assistant whether the death sentence did not infringe human rights. His reply revealed the complex reflections the affair generated for British Muslims:

Human rights and Islam are not two separate things [i.e. contradictory principles]. What this person [Rushdie] has done has hurt a lot of people. According to Islam this person should be killed but because he is living in a non-Muslim country this makes the job a lot more difficult. So I personally do not call for his killing, since we live in a non-Muslim country. If this was a Muslim country or there was Muslim law here then certainly he should be killed, but the most we can do is persuade this [British] government that there should be an equal law for the Muslims [of Britain] as there is [the blasphemy law] for Christians. So then, in future, no one else can take this action – to write in any form a book against Islam or, in fact, against any other religion in the world. That is what we should aim for – to ban the book, to persuade the country to draw up a law that would restrict any writing of this kind in the future.

Q. What do you think this whole demonstration will achieve?

A. The demonstration is a means of expressing your feelings to the community or the society in which you are living. If we are demonstrating peacefully, within the law, we are right to demonstrate. What will it achieve? It will give an impression to both communities that Muslims are not weak, that they believe in their faith, they do have some rights, they do have some principles, and they stand for those principles, they are willing to demonstrate and fight for those principles; they should be treated as equals of Christians, or Jews, or any other community in this country. What the government is saying is that Rushdie has freedom of expression. What is the point of millions of Muslims living in this country? They too have the right of freedom of expression. This is one way we can express ourselves to counteract what he has written, to show the world that we do care about our religion.

Plate 4.1 Manchester Muslims at an anti-Rushdie demonstration in London

Plate 4.2 *Eid Milad-un-Nabi* procession in Birmingham

Religious & secular aesthetics

Muslims have been accused of extracting offending sentences from *The Satanic Verses* out of context. According to modernist literary theory '[a] text is a whole, a totality' (Ricoeur 1981: 211). Significantly, however, it is precisely this textual *unity* that lies at the root of the irreconcilable clash between a religious and secular aesthetic.

More even than their secular counterparts, religious Muslims have responded to the novel in terms of its wholeness, even if they *seem* to be highlighting fragments and sentences out of context. Islam as a religion stresses the spatial separation of the sacred and the profane. Before entering a mosque or reading the Qur'an a Muslim must bathe his entire body, put on clean clothes and leave his (polluted) shoes at the entrance. The space of the mosque is perfumed with incense, while the Qur'an is treated with particular respect. It is always, for example, placed above the ground. Menstruating women, considered to be in a state of pollution, are not permitted to enter a mosque or to pray. For daily prayers, a Muslim spreads a prayer mat on the floor to demarcate a space of sanctity. The very earth can be powerfully sacralised (see Werbner 1996a).

A Muslim aesthetic is thus an aesthetic of *separations*. The Prophet as a subject of aesthetic delight is the epitome of a sacred Kantian 'sublime'; he is the imaginative locus of platonically real absolutes: goodness, beauty, purity, infinity, power, magnificence, light, generosity. He is *al-insan ul-kamil*, the Perfect Man (see Nicholson 1978, Chap. 2). To contemplate the sublime aesthetically for a Muslim is to contemplate the persona of the Prophet. He *is* the sublime, objectified, personified and made real, the subject of supreme love. His closest companions and consorts, those who occupy the same sacred space as he does, are thus sacralised along with him. To a lesser degree all saints and prophets participate in this aesthetic of the sublime.

A novel is a concrete, unitary physical entity. When Muslims I know read *The Satanic Verses* they are deeply offended, not by the rational questioning of the Qur'an's divine source – they are used to such sceptical critiques – but by the juxtaposed contiguity of profane language and profane acts or persons with the image of the Prophet, his companions and wives. The book is perceived as a single and undivided physical space. Muslim critical response is not simply moral. It is an aesthetic response of disgust. The offence is a gut feeling of shock. All the Muslims with whom I have discussed the book feel certain that Rushdie as a Muslim, albeit a lapsed one, intended this offence. The aesthetic canons they deploy make this conclusion logical and inescapable. What they find difficult to comprehend is the West's incomprehension. Instead, they believe that a West which praises the book does so because it shares the author's desire to offend and ridicule them and their faith.

This explains the religious Muslim intellectual response (see Ahsan and Kidwai 1992). It explains also why even the moderately religious responded so violently. Their reaction was one of aesthetic 'disgust' and shock, a reaction rooted in the imagination, intuitive and emotional rather than self-interested, analytical or jurisprudential.

More difficult to explain is why secular Marxist Muslim intellectuals such as Talal Asad, Rana Kabbani or Ali Mazrui also responded by condemning the author and the novel. In great measure, of course, their response, like that of other moderate British Muslim leaders, can be understood as an attempt to deflect attention from Muslim support – in the moral panic following the publication of the novel – for the Ayatollah's death sentence. As the Western counter-moral panic reached its crescendo, these intellectuals refocused the debate around the media's demonising of Muslims. They blamed the author for releasing the demons, thus reflecting a familiar diasporic attitude which tolerates 'internal' criticism, but rejects the right to criticise publicly before a hostile world. The global reach of Rushdie's 'internal' critique made it unforgivable.

The wide condemnation of the novel by both pious and radical Islamic scholars stemmed also, however, from Rushdie's 'borrowing' of the highly offensive tropes of medieval Christianity to describe the Prophet, in a libellous language which also echoed a twentieth-century 'hate' literature against Islam (for many Pakistanis this compounded the widespread belief that Rushdie was an instrument of an evil Jewish plot to defame Muslims). The present chapter argues that in focusing on these passages Muslim critics failed to place them within the broader narrative structure of the book. The libels against the Prophet and his family are voiced or perpetrated in the novel by fictional characters who are cunning traitors and are part of a whole series of dramatic ordeals that the Prophet undergoes. These move the action forward and underlie the narrative structure of the book and its moral message: the way in which character is tested and shaped by ordeals of treachery and betrayal.

The evident offence felt by Muslim secular readers in response to these passages points to the fact that aesthetic canons can persist long after faith has lapsed. The Prophet and the Qur'an are not merely dogmas and articles of faith but powerful aesthetic images of perfection, even though they are not grounded in physical, sensual pleasure. To attack such images is to attack the grounding of identity in aesthetic experience.

Responses made in the press and academic journals by an articulate Muslim elite are echoed in the sentiments of grass-roots leaders. The Muslim narratives discussed here are those of speakers at a ceremonial luncheon held in Birmingham which followed a very large anti-Rushdie demonstration in London the previous day. The ceremonial feast was convened to commemorate the death/rebirth of a Muslim saint. I was in Birmingham as part of a delegation from Manchester, composed of disciples of the saint's successor, Zindapir, and the order he had founded, which extended from Pakistan into Britain. The commemoration began with a *julus*, a procession, which set off from the headquarters of a local saint, Sufi Abdullah, to reach the Birmingham Central Mosque, some three miles away. Before discussing the speeches at the ceremonial luncheon, it is worth reflecting briefly on the significance of such religious processions in the process of Muslim visibilisation in Britain.

Defending the honour of Islam

The emergence of Muslim processions in British cities during the 1980s, and their symbolic significance, form a backdrop to the Muslim response to the trauma of the Rushdie affair. Such processions, held on *Eid Milad-un-Nabi*, the Prophet's birthday, and on annual memorial celebrations of departed saints, bring together Muslims from a single city, and from many cities throughout the UK, wherever a saint has branches of his Sufi regional cult (see Plate 4.2). The processions are led by saints and their deputies, and are preceded by cars decorated with tinsel which blare out through their loudspeakers traditional Islamic refrains – 'Say Allah is Great, Say Prophethood, Islam Live Forever.'

Historically, the holding of such Muslim public processions in Britain is quite recent, and constitutes a radical shift in the terms in which Muslim immigrants have come to present and represent themselves to the wider society. During the initial phases of migration the only public religious signs of an Islamic presence in Britain were the stores and mosques the immigrants built or purchased. Apart from mosques, ritual and religious activities took place in the inner spaces of homes, which were sacralised through repeated domestic *Eid* and communal Qur'an reading rituals (see Werbner 1990a, Chaps 4 and 5). Sacred Islamic spaces were thus confined within fortresses of privacy, whether mosques or homes, and these fortresses protected immigrants from external hostility, from a dangerous exposure.

Since processing began in the early 1980s on the Prophet's birthday and saints' days, the processions have sometimes been the target of attacks, mainly verbal, from outsiders, but this has never deterred the marchers. The organisers of the processions take pride in the fact that these events have always been peaceful, that they have never become the scene of trouble or violence.

Marching through Britain's city centres and immigrant neighbourhoods, the processions not only inscribe the name of Allah on the very spaces stretching between and connecting immigrant homes or mosques – city centre and immigrant periphery – they also call Muslims back to the faith. The *julus* procession, as one religious official told me, is above all an act of *tabligh*, of saying publicly to other Muslims: 'look at us, we are proud of being Muslims, we are willing to parade our Muslimness openly in the streets, we believe that Islam is the last and best religion, containing the true message of God, the whole message, including even its hidden truths; and we are not afraid to show our pride in our religion openly and publicly. But (he explained) we are also making clear that, if you want to be a good Muslim, you have to choose. You can't "mix" with the English (or be, in other words, a part-time Muslim).'

The *julus*, and the public meetings before or after it, also lend themselves to more overt and specific current political statements about Islam in Britain. A *julus* can become, in other words, a kind of political demonstration. Not all Sufi groups are willing, however, to politicise the procession itself openly in this way. In the Birmingham processions I attended in 1989, the banners carried were in Urdu and Arabic, and were inscribed mainly with verses from the Qur'an. In Manchester a year later, by contrast, the banners were in English. ISLAM MEANS PEACE AND SUBMISSION TO THE ALMIGHTY GOD; ALL MAIN RELIGIONS IN THE UK SHOULD BE GIVEN LEGAL PROTECTION; THE BLASPHEMY LAW SHOULD BE EXTENDED TO ISLAM AND ALL OTHER MAIN RELIGIONS; OUR MESSAGE IS PEACE AND LOVE FOR EVERYONE; MUSLIMS ARE PEACE-LOVING AND LAW-ABIDING CITIZENS; WE LOVE ISLAM AND THE PROPHET OF ISLAM; THE HOLY PROPHET IS MERCY FOR ALL WORLDS. The signs thus made implicit references to the Rushdie affair through the demand for a change in the blasphemy law, while asserting that Islam was a religion of peace, thus rejecting the association of Muslims with the violence which the Rushdie affair had generated in the public mind.

Whatever the nature of the processions, the meetings held either before or after them in both Birmingham and Manchester were attended by invited English dignitaries and officials, and the speeches made during them referred openly to current political concerns of Muslims in Britain. This points to the evolving link between Muslim public arenas and the state and its civic institutions in Britain. Pakistanis use public ceremonials as occasions to host civic dignitaries and air their views and grievances before them. The *julus* in Birmingham in 1989 was one such occasion when speakers attempted to explain the Muslim position in the Rushdie affair to a British audience, comprising on that particular occasion the Lord Mayor of Birmingham, his wife, the Chief Superintendent of Police and several other policemen along with a few others (including myself). The meeting points to the relative ease with which South Asians in Britain, unlike British India, can use public arenas as spaces of interaction with representatives of the state and local government. Public ceremonials are thus opportunities for communicative action and mediation, and hence also, for *averting* communal violence (see Freitag 1989a on Indian public arenas).

Whether explicit or implicit, once people have marched openly in a place they have crossed an ontological barrier. They have shown that they are willing to expose themselves and their bodies to possible outside ridicule for the sake of their faith. Once they have organised a peaceful procession, they know they are capable of organising a peaceful protest. Such processions can thus be seen as precursors to more overt (democratic) political protest.

The banners in English are also part of the missionising activity of Muslims in Britain, the propagation of Islam undertaken by many Muslim organisations. The banners appeal to an English audience of potential converts – people who feel that Christianity or secularism has somehow failed them and who are seeking a new religious truth.

In addition, the processions assert the legitimacy of a particular Islamic approach – that focused on saints and their shrines. Historically, this type of Islamic practice has come under attack from other reformist movements – in South Asia, primarily from the Deobandis, Jama'at-i Islami and the Ahl-e-Hadith. The 'counter-reformation' in South Asia was the Barelvi movement, named after the city of its founder. In Pakistan since Zia ul-Haq's regime, the processions are part of a popular national culture: they are shown on public television, while offices, shops and government buildings are decorated with chains of multi-coloured lights, despite constant complaints by the reformists. In Britain, however, they still represent an act of assertion in a struggle between different Islamic approaches, all competing for local hegemony. Moreover, holding a *julus*, particularly a city-wide one on *Eid Milad-un-Nabi*, also attests to the ascendancy of a particular Sufi regional cult in a city. In Birmingham, Sufi Abdullah is the most prominent saint in the city and he holds the processions to which all the other Sufi orders are invited. In Manchester the procession is dominated by members of the more politicised Qadiri order whose deputy (*khalifa*), Maulana Saheb, the *maulvi* of Manchester's Central Mosque, dominates the procession and public meeting in that city.

Beyond matters of local competition, the composition of the procession is also significant. Whereas central *jami'a* mosques are often built and funded by management committees manned by the wealthy or educated, and sometimes even by external Islamic foundations, the processions are open to anyone. Many of those who march are members of the Muslim underprivileged or working class.

It is they who assert, by marching, their pride in Islam, their self-confidence and power. Marching through the streets of a British city, then, is in many different kinds of ways an assertion of power and confidence. This is why the holding of the processions seems to have a deep subjective experiential significance for those who participate in them.

Finally, and most basically, the *julus* is an expression of the rights of minorities to celebrate their culture and religion in the public domain within a multi-cultural, multi-faith, multi-racial society. Seen thus, Muslim processions do not differ significantly from Chinese New Year lion dances, public Diwali celebrations, St Patrick's Day processions or Caribbean carnivals. They are part of a joyous and yet unambiguous assertion of cultural diversity, of an entitlement to tolerance and mutual respect, in contemporary Britain. Through such public festivals and celebrations immigrants make territorial claims in their adopted cities, and ethnic groups assert their equal cultural claims within the society.

The political meeting held before the procession in Manchester in October 1990 took place in the Council Chambers of the Town Hall, in the shadow of the looming Gulf crisis. On this occasion, groups had come from all over Britain to celebrate the procession organised by a key member of their Sufi order in Manchester. I was – significantly, as I discovered later – the only non-Muslim, and the only European, present, with the exception of a single Muslim convert. None of the usual MPs, councillors and invited dignitaries who regularly honour such gatherings were present.

Their absence was highly emblematic. The year before, in the same Council Chambers, more or less the same group with the same organisers, all opponents of Chaudhry Muhammad Amin and his ramifying faction, had come together to discuss the events of the day. I was absent at the time in Pakistan, but the meeting was described later in the British press. The *Manchester Evening News* of Monday, 23 October 1989, reported:

Police Check Speech On Rushdie Death Threats

Hard-line Muslims could be banned from meeting in Manchester City Council Halls after death chants calling for the killing of Author Salman Rushdie broke out at a weekend gathering in the Town Hall. And Police are examining the text of the speech that sparked off the demo.

Nearly 350 Muslims met in the city council chambers to celebrate the birth of the Prophet Muhammad, but it became an anti-Rushdie rally. The chant, 'Death to Rushdie', started after the Director of the Muslim Institute, Dr Kalim Siddiqui, asked for a show of hands on whether the author should die. Rushdie has been in hiding since the death sentence was imposed by the late Ayatollah Khomeini. But the organiser today condemned the death chant and accused Dr Siddiqui of hijacking the meeting.

'We had an understanding from him before he came that he would only be touching on the issue and would be speaking about the teachings of the Prophet' said Mr Sheikh Abdullah Azad, who is Chairman of the Manchester Council of Mosques.

Mr Azad, who claimed that Dr Siddiqui's London-based Muslim Institute was funded by Iran, said: 'I am of the opinion that the death sentence is wrong.' And Mr Azad said that he regretted that Dr Siddiqui's speech had turned attention away from other issues brought up at the meeting, including a call for the release of Terry Waite and other hostages.

The Bishop of Manchester, the Rt Reverend Stanley Booth-Clibborn, shared the platform with Dr Siddiqui. He sat impassively while the death call was made, but later told the audience he regretted some of the things Dr Siddiqui had just said.

Greater Manchester police were today examining the full text of Dr Siddiqui's speech. A spokesman said: 'The evidence is being looked at and the decision will be made in due course as to whether any action will be taken.'

Today City Council leader Graham Stringer said they would be considering a full report on what happened at the meeting before taking a decision.

In *The Sunday Times*, on the previous day, it was reported that Mr Gerald Kaufman, MP, Labour Shadow Home Secretary, had attended the meeting and made a speech, but had departed before the incidents had occurred. He later condemned the death threat call.

Eid Milad-un-Nabi, the birthday of the Prophet, is a joyous celebration of the Messenger of Islam's uniqueness and perfection. For Muslims, he is the moral exemplar. His life, deeds and sayings, as contained in the Islamic traditions, constitute the model of correct religious, ethical and ritual practice all Muslims should follow. This reverence for the Prophet, shared by all Muslims, whatever their sectarian affiliation, reaches its mystical apogee among the followers of Sufi orders and saints who venerate the Prophet as the embodiment of the light of Allah and believe in his continued spiritual existence and active agency as a guardian of the living, having current powers of intercession with God through chosen saints. According to the teachings of the Barelvi movement, the Prophet is regarded as being present or existent (*hadir wa nazir*) (Malik 1990: 39), whether in Medina where he is buried or, indeed, in Manchester. The Barelvi are often accused of divinising the Prophet (*shirk*), but they deny this charge vehemently, while continuing to venerate and address him directly with prayers and greetings.

In Manchester, in their sermons in the various mosques, members of the Barelvi movement reveal their sense of being an embattled group constantly having to defend their position against, as they see it, scurrilous reformist criticisms of their supposedly unlawful Islamic innovation (*bida*) and polytheism (*shirk*). At the same time they claim that they are the only 'true' Sunni Muslims, *Ahl-e-Sunnat wa-Jama'at*, the people of the Sunna.

Among Pakistani Muslims in Britain Barelvis are in the majority, but are weakly organised except as regional cults focused around holy men. Despite shared ritual ideas and practices, religious leaders of such cults vary a good deal in the level of political and religious activism they espouse and practise. It is important to stress that they are not 'fundamentalist' in any literal sense. The movement is an essentially populist and ethical one, a movement in and about the modern world and its encompassing values (see also Modood 1990).

Global and local subjectivities

To become conscious of one's self as a subject is to become aware both of one's *subjection* to wider collectivities (the 'nation', the 'diaspora') and of one's personal moral responsibility, as a rational, active agent, to these wider collectivities. The performance in public of Muslim processions had already wrought a change in Muslim subjectivities through a public bodily exposure of difference. The Rushdie affair precipitated a further transformation. The outrage that the novel provoked among Muslims worldwide cut across national boundaries to encompass the whole Islamic *umma*. British Muslims responded to the novel not only as British subjects but as global subjects of a transnational diaspora. Yet the affair appeared to place on their shoulders a particularly heavy responsibility towards that diaspora. It also led to a discovery of the real limitations of their power as British subjects. This realisation was gradual and highly traumatic. Initially, the Muslim response in Britain was merely part of a more global Islamic response, imported wholesale, like *haldi*, basmati rice and Indian videos, into Britain.

On 12 February 1989, six people were killed and over 100 injured in riots caused by the book in Pakistan. On 24 February 1989, Indian police shot dead 12 Muslim anti-Rushdie demonstrators in Bombay. The response in Britain seemed thus to be simply part of a global transcontinental social movement. There is little doubt that the ideas inspiring the new radicalism travel widely, part of the intellectual baggage Muslim scholars carry with them and preach on their travels. Yet in Pakistan and India the book was soon forgotten, while in Britain the fight over *The Satanic Verses* has been more persistent, and has left lasting scars.

There were local as well as global reasons, I believe, why British Muslims as localised diasporic subjects responded so passionately to the book. Rushdie was himself a British Muslim, and hence they needed both to dissociate themselves from his views while at the same time feeling immediately responsible to the global Muslim community for controlling and punishing him. Their attempts to do so, however, came up against a wall of public and media indifference. This brought about an escalation in the level of symbolic violence, from mild protests and legal probes to book and effigy burning, and death threats. The Ayatollah's *fatwa* finally broke through the media barrier.

For Pakistanis the book seemed to confirm their innermost fears. As 'black' immigrants they had suffered in the past from abuse and racism; the book seemed to constitute final proof that racism and xenophobia were indeed the underlying true realities of British society. There was a sense also of *déjà-vu*: they were back in the British Raj, subject to English oppression. At the same time there was an expectation that, as a religious minority, they were entitled to protection, as they had been in India under the British Raj. This led to the discovery that there was a blasphemy law in Britain but it was discriminatory, and protected only Christians. Here was a political agenda which evoked populist sentiments around the demand for equality. This agenda – extending the law – has kept the affair alive after it has died out in other countries. It is underpinned by a strong sense of confidence which local Pakistanis feel as citizens who are in Britain to stay, secure in their permanent domicile and in their entitlement to equality before the law.

There were, of course, also local political interests in blowing up the affair, just as there had been in Pakistan, India and Iran. Rushdie was a man without an organisation and a following, against whom all the warring British Islamic sects and factions could unite. This was unique. As one young Muslim, a thirty-year-old civil servant, said on his way to the demonstration in London:

> The issue is big. I mean, if you do not struggle and try to mobilise your community then what you will get is stagnation.... In order to have a successful society you must have this sort of issue arising as well, in response to which you can mobilise the people; and there is no doubt in my mind that this is the best opportunity provided in the last twenty to thirty years for Muslims in the West to unite, and to a certain degree, unity has been achieved. It is for Muslim leaders to shoulder the responsibility, to capitalise on this mobilisation and to organise themselves more strongly, in a more disciplined organisation on a national level, in every town where there are a certain number of Muslims ... to create a national body which can be utilized later for many other issues of concern to us.

The less scrupulous leaders of the political factions, and especially mosque-based leaders and clergy, could evoke axiomatic religious symbols and beliefs to shore up their crumbling associations and mobilise new supporters and followers.

Yet it would be a mistake to see the response as simply the result of manipulation by extremists. There was a universal sense of offence and hurt. There was also, perhaps, an unstated fear in the hearts of the older generation: a fear that Rushdie represented the future, the kind of people their British children and grandchildren might be if their elders did not fight the inexorable tide of history at once. The demonstrations were meant as a display of commitment and pride, in front of this younger generation. They were part of the general effort to build up lasting communal institutions for generations to come.

The radicalism of the Manchester meeting – it was not fortuitous that Siddiqui had made his speech and appeal in that forum – is not matched by all followers of Sufi orders. Indeed, most British Muslims express their feelings in far more moderate tones. Some time earlier as already mentioned, in May 1989, I attended a similar political meeting held in the basement of the Birmingham Central Mosque after the annual *julus* commemorating the order's saint's death in Pakistan. The meeting took place the day following the large anti-Rushdie demonstration in London, and the speakers, most of them Labour councillors in Birmingham's City Council, attempted to put their case in rational terms. They stressed the non-fanaticism of Muslims, their hurt and their sense of rejection; they appealed for justice. They spoke of the terrible offence ordinary Muslims felt. I shall quote extracts from the speeches at this meeting in order to highlight this attempt to rebuild shattered bridges while defending the Muslim point of view.

The speeches followed a sumptuous ceremonial dinner, hosted by the Management Committee of the Sufi order holding the *'urs* (a ritual commemorating the death/rebirth of a Muslim saint). The dinner was attended by the Lord Mayor of Birmingham, all nine local Muslim Labour Councillors, the Superintendent of Police and his officers, who had accompanied the march. Like all other participants at an *'urs*, those attending the dinner had shared in the *langar*, the sacrificial food cooked communally at saints' lodges. The food of the *langar* is said to be very pure. It is cooked voluntarily as an act of *khidmat* by men pure of heart who recite *zikr*, the name of Allah, as they cook. We, the dinner guests of Sufi Abdullah and his Sufi order, had feasted on the *langar* and had partaken of its blessing. The end of the feast was a time of goodwill in which contentious matters could be aired in an atmosphere of tolerance and mutual respect.

The first speaker at the dinner, a Pakistani Labour Councillor, addresses the gathering:

> Lord Mayor, Lady Mayoress, Mr Chairman ... so far [Muslim] religious leaders have played a major role in British history [in consolidating] the solidarity, strength and unity of Islam in this country, which promotes human feelings, goodwill and good relations between different communities in this strange [i.e. foreign] land. When I say Islam, the ideology of Islam gives us a lesson, it teaches us to live in peace, to have good relations between different communities and to try to educate our children in such a way that they should be good citizens of [according to] British history [traditions] and good citizens of Birmingham so that they can play a major role in the human community.

The speaker sets out, first, the broader universal principles of Islam shared with Britain, which stress peaceful co-existence. He goes on to point out that Muslims are also a powerful constituency within the British state:

My brothers and sisters, when I talk of Islam, certain people have got different views, different ideas, but you must not forget, in Britain Muslims are the second largest religion here who have the same rights, who should have the same rights as the other religions which exist [in this country]. At present Muslims in Birmingham, as well as in England, and I should say, the whole world, have got the feeling that being a minority in this country, they have been insulted. When we talk about freedom of speech, freedom of expression, it doesn't mean freedom of insult. I'm not against [i.e. attacking] anybody but it [the affair] teaches us a lesson, there is [can be] talk about freedom of speech and freedom of expression but this doesn't mean that you will ... [allow anyone] to insult our leader [i.e. the Prophet] or his personality.

The speaker makes clear here that the battle is over collective recognition and dignity. As Charles Taylor has pointed out, the politics of multiculturalism are a politics of recognition and misrecognition. For the speaker, it is the size of the collective response to the offence which proves the magnitude of the dishonour:

Yesterday I was in London, I participated in the demonstration, which was [a notable event] in British history. A few days before I was listening to a reporter who said: 'I think this movement has cooled down and the British Muslims have become silent.' My brothers and sisters, we don't want to repeat the history of Brixton, we don't want to repeat the history of Liverpool, we don't want to repeat the history of Handsworth [references to inner city neighbourhoods with large Afro-Caribbean populations in which anti-police riots had occurred]. We are a peace-loving nation, we don't want to take law and order into our own hands, and, if you feel that this is the moment [to do so], I completely reject [the idea]; [we must not] repeat the histories of Liverpool and Brixton. We want to carry on an argument in a peaceful way, so that the British people, the British community, should realise the importance and value of Islam in this country.

The voice here is one of moderation, a seeking of rational, peaceful dialogue. But it contains also an implicit threat of violence: just as West Indians rioted in Brixton or Handsworth, so too Pakistanis, if pushed to the wall, may resort to violence. Yet the speaker takes great pain to stress that violence is not the Islamic way. Islam seeks the unity of all communities:

I should say that every year the Muslims of Birmingham celebrate this honourable day for the unity of different communities in this city. I thank the organisers of this ... day and also the police officers who were there, who gave us support. Thank you very much [applause].

The two central points of this speaker, namely, (i) that Islam is a religion of peace and lawfulness, and (ii) that freedom of expression is not an absolute right, and does not extend to 'freedom of insult', are both repeated by subsequent speakers. It is clear from his response that the Chairman of the celebration was hoping to avoid raising the whole issue of the Rushdie affair during the public meeting at the mosque:

Chairman: Thank you. We were not ready [to discuss] this matter. But, as we can't keep religion and conscience separate, Raja Suleiman has touched on a very delicate matter which we are facing in Great Britain. Though we are a peaceful nation, but in the mean-time [at present] ... we can't allow anybody to attack our Qur'an, to attack our Prophet, to attack his wives, this is a very very very delicate, a very very uncertain condition we are facing at the moment. Yesterday I think there were more or less 100,000 Muslims there, under the sky in Hyde Park – maybe somebody has said 30,000, somebody has said 35,000 – but the number is not what matters, what matters is the fact that people from all over the United Kingdom – I think some people have said from Europe as well – participated in this procession.

> We hope that God should help us in this very delicate matter because we don't want to take the law into our own hands, but everything has some limit. And I'm sure that the situation in the city of Birmingham, that I can take a message back from this gathering that it will do everything possible in its capacity.

The Chairman raised two further points also raised by the first speaker: (iii) Even though they do not want to take the law into their own hands, Muslims in Britain will not tolerate insults against the Prophet and the Qur'an; they are willing to die for their religion. (iv) This sentiment is widely shared in the community – indeed, by Muslims worldwide – and is not limited to a small minority.

Another councillor, with a strong regional English accent, repeated these points and stressed the crisis which the Muslim community was facing.

> My Lord Mayor, it is a pleasure and an honour to have you here. Lord Mayor, as you know, I've served you on your committee for two years. As a Muslim councillor I think you know that I served you very faithfully. I think the issue was raised not so long ago in our Labour Group, the issue was very important, I think there was a lot of misunderstanding and we had to try to make clear that the issue was *The Satanic Verses*. Now, the misunderstanding was that the community here, the non-Muslim community, actually thought that we were trying to execute everybody who spoke against Islam, as though Islam was not strong enough. No, that was not the fact, my Lord Mayor. The fact was that the Muslims and Islam are very very strong. Please take that from me and from many other Muslims. The issue was raised, as I said to you Chief Constable, er ... Superintendent (sorry), of Police. People who work here [for the *tariqa*, the Sufi order] are working voluntarily, they are not paid. This is our Muslim aim, to live and love and be peaceful, not actually to fight and kill. Now, *The Satanic Verses*, the question [point highlighted by] of *The Satanic Verses* [affair] was that we live and die for our religion, Islam, that we can tolerate anything, and it doesn't matter if you kill us, hit us, do what you want, but we will not tolerate [an attack] against Islam; and that was the reason, my Lord Mayor [for our response to the novel].

Struggling for words, this speaker distinguishes between the fact that Islam is strong enough, and does not need to defend itself, and the determination of Muslims not to allow their religion to be attacked. The honour of Islam is assured for the very reason that Muslims are willing to live and die for their religion. Yet once again, it is the non-violence of Islam that the speaker wishes to stress:

> The other thing, my Lord Mayor, was that yesterday I was one of the demonstrators who went to London. Now I think it was on television, as well as radio, and I think it was [broadcast] all over the world, that it wasn't just a few councillors from Birmingham or from other cities [who participated]. We were [there] not in tens, we were not in hundreds but we were in thousands. And, Lord Mayor, I can also assure you that throughout the march from Hyde Park to the House of Commons it was the most peaceful [march] ever actually marched, and I think that the police officer here, or the police officer in London, will verify that. Not a single incident took place. We actually demonstrated outside the House of Commons for many, many hours and, at the end of the day, we got back in the coaches and came back [to Birmingham]. [In actual fact, while the march itself had been peaceful, rocks had been thrown at the police outside the House of Commons, effigies of Rushdie had been burnt and signs calling for his death had been displayed publicly. Not all the marchers, however, saw the clash with the police.]
> The idea was to explain to non-Muslims that we're not as bad as people think – we're not killers and we're not demanding anything [extraordinary] – all we're demanding is equal rights, and I think that it is *The Satanic Verses* that took us apart through a lot of blood and misunderstanding [i.e. divided us from the non-Muslims]. Even today, my Lord Mayor, you can see us here, a march from Small Heath to here, there wasn't a single

incident, there wasn't a single incident when we actually criticised anybody else. We marched peacefully to here. And I think the President here will verify that.

If the spontaneous Muslim response was initially one of violent calls for the death of the author and the burning of the book, it is evident that by the time of this meeting – and in response to a British counter-response – Muslim leaders had begun to evolve a counter-discourse which set out some of the moral and philosophical issues supporting their demands for the banning of the book, downplaying the death threats to the novelist, and explaining why they were not mere 'fanatics':

> Some people say that freedom of expression is so important that whatever is written is sacrosanct and must never be banned. My Lord Mayor, that is a simplistic attitude, that is just as fanatical as these people try to make followers of religion out to be. Religious followers should not be called fanatical just for their beliefs. Deeply held convictions should be respected. It is only if and when they lead someone to harm others that it is reasonable to criticise them. A writer would be offended if anyone were to call him a fanatic, but if he uses his writing to harm someone else he can be justifiably criticised. A writer who has very strong convictions, but [exploits this] freedom of expression to the extent that he will not compromise at all, can be said to have made a religion out of literature. And if he does hold such a strong conviction, he should sympathise with others who have strong convictions – he would expect them to respect his [convictions] and he should respect theirs.
>
> My Lord, we have recognised that there should be freedom of expression, and a large part of it is the freedom to tell the truth without fear or favour. Most people in a free democracy would agree that press censorship is a mistake, such as [the kind that] is practised in some communist countries, it is reprehensible. But there is another very important freedom which is enshrined in human culture and that is freedom of religion. If freedom of religion is to be a real freedom, then it must mean that people should be free to follow their faith without fear of unreasonable attack upon themselves. In the physical sense, obviously, this means that nobody should be imprisoned, beaten, tortured or killed for his religious belief. And this includes being put in a mental asylum. My Lord Mayor, man has a mind as well as a body, and most advanced civilisations have accepted that the mind is at least [as important], if not more important [than the body]. In England and Wales, for example, damages for libel are on average higher than for common assault.
>
> In other words, the courts recognise that hurtful words which hurt the mind are worse than a punch or a kick, and that is the basic thing I was trying to get at, my Lord Mayor. You can kick us, you can hit us, you can kill us, but we cannot tolerate an attack against Islam. This is worse than a punch or a kick to the body. This is partly because bruises from kicks and punches soon heal, but unkind words can fester in the mind for a long time. And if they are written down they can remind a victim of his mental asylum [mental agony] all his life. I'll have to end this here, my Lord Mayor, I thank you for coming here and I thank everybody for listening to me. Thank you very much. *Asalam Aleikum.*

The speaker spells out the various existing legal limitations on freedom of expression and puts in a plea for the protection of religious feelings, adding to the previous points made by earlier speakers that: (v) Words, and not only physical actions, have the power to hurt; (vi) Muslims were not fanatical in their demand to have the book banned. Deeply held religious beliefs should be respected. Indeed, writers can be as fanatical as religious followers. (vii) Muslims demand equality as British citizens before the law – hence the blasphemy law should be extended to protect them as well as Christians.

The next speaker was not a Labour councillor but the Vice-Chairman of the Pakistan Forum – an umbrella organisation of Pakistani associations. His tone was more militant and millenarian, and less conciliatory; it revealed the sense of threat and conspiracy which many Pakistanis felt in relation to *The Satanic Verses*:

> My dear friends, my elders, my brothers, my children. Whenever the personality of the holy Prophet, Peace Be Upon Him, is called into question or disparaged in any way, that very moment, Islam comes to a standstill – unless and until you continue to strive hard for it. The time that you become inattentive all your prayers, your fasting, your recitals, are useless. So this is our job: to continue to strive hard. This is the way to keep ourselves Muslims. We should do whatever we can – the result lies in God's hands. Since I do not have much time to describe [the affair] in detail, I'll quickly tell you why such an issue has arisen.
>
> Islam is a religion which is developing by leaps and bounds, and I am sure that after the next decade or so it will be the first [primary] and largest religion of the world, overtaking Christianity. Wherever you go – America, Africa, Britain or anywhere else – you will see that people are embracing Islam every day. You [i.e. the religious leaders] are to be congratulated for this because you have started producing eaglets who will multiply and bring the message of Islam throughout the world.
>
> As I recited the *kalima* [covenant of Islam] before you in the beginning, it is our duty to present this covenant to every non-Muslim that we meet or come across. This is very important, whether they accept it or not. And also we should organise such meetings or processions whether they appear to us to be successful or unsuccessful – they could be a success in God's eyes.

The speaker starts by reiterating his faith in the millennium when Islam will triumph worldwide. The threat of this is so great, he believes, that the enemies of Islam have conspired to defeat it:

> Now I come to the point. Non-Muslims, especially Jews, when they realised that Islam is growing steadily, they created this evil of Rushdie. But as Iqbal [the great Muslim poet/philosopher] says: 'A little water is enough to make this soil fertile.' So we are hopeful that there will always be people who will eliminate such evils.

The speaker concluded, as many others did, with the call:

> *Pakistan Zindabad* [Pakistan live forever!];
> *Islam Zindabad* [Islam live forever!];
> *Nara-i-Takbir* [Say God is Great!];
> *Allah-hu-Akbar* [God is Great!].
> Thank you very much.

This speaker hinted at the widely held view that *The Satanic Verses* was a political, 'Zionist', conspiracy against Muslims. Ultimately, however, Islam would triumph.

The Birmingham Labour municipal councillors remained, by contrast, consistently mild, stressing their sense of hurt and their rights as citizens in their adopted society. One councillor made the point that defending Islam was important in relation to the next generation of Muslims growing up in Britain:

> In this our second home which we have adopted to be our first home, almost, and have integrated ourselves into this multi-cultural society, I think it's very important for us, for our second generation, to teach it our prayers and traditions and culture, and also our religion, and how to celebrate various occasions in life, so they can, in turn, teach and make the host community understand; and local people who can understand your problems will know that you are not just a fanatic as we have been branded by the various media, and also by some fanatical people. Islam is a very peaceful religion and it is a complete religion in which you can live.

The Muslim community had made a contribution to the city and its economy. This was stressed by the only English councillor to speak at the meeting. One of the other Pakistani Labour councillors referred to this in his speech.

> Councillor Bowen has mentioned the contribution of our Muslims [to the city and its economic regeneration]. I think the irony is that, despite our contribution, still our rights are not being recognised, and frankly, although people do say we have made a large contribution, still when it comes to our religion we are being treated as second-class citizens. For example, about *The Satanic Verses*, we are being lectured about the freedom of the press, but just recently there was an actor who simply said, or was alleged to have said, that [by acting in a film] he [had] made a contribution to the Republican cause in Northern Ireland, and immediately there were a lot of Members of Parliament who said that his film should be banned. Then, a few weeks back, there was a film scandal regarding the Profumo affair and again there was more than one MP who said that the film should be banned because it was not [a fair portrayal of] ... that particular family. But here you are, [in the case of] *The Satanic Verses*, it was well known that the book would upset all the Muslims throughout the world; even according to the *Sunday Times*, when the manuscript was ready, the publishers, as well as the author, were told that by publishing this book they would upset the Muslim community throughout the world. But the author as well as the publisher went ahead and deliberately published this book, knowing very well that it would upset the Muslim community and Muslim feelings. Despite that [knowledge], they published it, in order to make some money, and we are being lectured all the time about the freedom of the press, the freedom of the press.
>
> But what surprises us is why the society should develop two standards – two standards in the sense that on *The Satanic Verses* we should be told about freedom of the press, but when this actor makes a statement then immediately Members of Parliament are saying his film should be banned ... again, people are saying that this film [about the Profumo affair] should be banned, but on *The Satanic Verses* everybody is giving us a lecture – 'don't use the word "ban", don't even use the word "withdrawal" of [in relation to] the book!' I think it's about time that we should be recognised, that our contribution should be recognised, but at the same time our rights and our religion should be recognised so that we should practise freely and no personality should dare to attack our religion or blaspheme [against] it. The law should be changed.... As time is short I must finish – thank you very much. [clapping].

This speaker made the further points that (x) Rushdie was a cultural traitor who had sold his soul for a pot of gold, and (xi) that double standards were used by the authorities and the government in determining when freedom of speech should be limited. Many of the speakers stressed that the Muslim community had to teach its religious traditions to the next generation of young British Muslims. Altogether, the eleven points raised in the speeches form the core of the Muslim case against Rushdie and *The Satanic Verses*. They can be represented as a series of oppositions:

	Muslim self-perceptions	**Non-Muslim response to Muslims**
Society:	Peaceful/law-abiding	Muslims politically aggressive
Individual:	Entitled to rights as citizens	Muslims inferior racially
Feelings:	Respect religious feelings	Islam the target of insults
Community:	Display of unity/pride	Muslims violent/fanatical
Ethic:	Generosity and equality	Selfishness and greed
Future aim:	Islam universal	Aspire to victory over Islam

The meeting concluded with a conciliatory speech by the Lord Mayor, which stressed the English tradition of mutual tolerance and respect, and the common roots of Islam and Christianity.

> Chairman: Now I'd like to request the Lord Mayor to speak once again.

> The Lord Mayor of Birmingham: Lady Mayoress, Chairman, fellow councillors, distinguished guests, ladies and gentlemen. Could I first of all thank you for the lovely bouquet of flowers which you presented to the Lady Mayoress. I am going to talk about religion because that is what the day is about. I mentioned this morning, I think, the Anglican Cathedral, [where I went] for a service. During that service, the Provost mentioned the problems you see and feel, and he said he thought the Muslim community was trying to tell us something about the importance of religion. There is a lot of understanding in this city about being a minority and about religion. We have a great tradition of tolerance in our country and in our city.
> ... I'm not really a religious man in the sense that I go to church all the time. I had a religious teaching from my parents and school, but, as I say, I do not go to church very often. But I like to have a basic understanding of where we are all going, and what we are doing. What does strike me is the basic similarity between these two great religions, the Anglican religion and the Muslim religion, the attitudes of the Muslims and the peace in Islam. There is very much similarity, there is more which unites us than divides us. You can pray in the name of Islam, and there is much similarity between us, we are very very close.
> ... I will say just a few words, if you may give me the honour, that we say when we become officers in the Anglican church: 'May the peace of God which passeth all understanding be with you forever more' [clapping].

Finally, the Chief Superintendent of Police spoke. He commented:

> Against the background of yesterday's event [the anti-Rushdie demonstration in London], it's been a pleasure to take part in your procession today. I think it shows how events can contrast between one event and one place and another [i.e. between the *julus* that day and the anti-Rushdie demonstration the day before], and I hope there will be many more [of the Birmingham processions] that will go off in exactly the same way.

Blasphemy & citizenship

The debate in the basement of Birmingham's Central Mosque reflects the wider debate about *The Satanic Verses* which has become a debate about the limits of freedom of expression, and the language in which religion and religious belief may be criticised. England is a Christian state, the monarch being head of the Church of England. State schools have religious assemblies every morning. The English blasphemy law was upheld successfully as recently as 1977 in British courts in the *Gay News* case, and was confirmed by the House of Lords in 1978, and in the European Court of Human Rights in Strasbourg in 1982. The *Gay News* case clearly revealed that the law as it stood was discriminatory, providing protection in its present form only against blasphemy against the Anglican church. The most significant feature of the British law as it was used has been the stress on the rights of Christians in Britain not to have their *religious feelings* offended by *scurrilous language*. In other words, it is not the expression of religious doubt or scepticism, or the criticism of religion that is at stake, but the use of profane, insulting language in religious matters.[6]

Despite the fact that contemporary Christianity in England tends to be humane, liberal and tolerant, and that most English people are either secularists or non-church-goers, suggestions to abolish the blasphemy law have met with a good deal of resistance. The real question now appears to be how and if the law should be extended, since it is obviously discriminatory.[7]

On the one hand is the Muslim position, perceived by some as an expression of fanaticism and religious 'fundamentalism'. From an Islamic point of view, however, the position is not so much extremist as part of a more general demand for basic citizenship rights and equality before the law. As citizens, British Muslims feel that their religious feelings are not accorded the same value as those of Christians. At the same time, since *The Satanic Verses* constituted an offence on a public international scale, crossing national boundaries and addressing a global audience, they feel that they are justified in responding to the offence globally. Civil society has extended beyond national boundaries. Islam is a universal religion and the Islamic *umma* must be protected against global insults at a correspondingly global level. Hence their support for the Ayatollah's *fatwa*. Such sentiments are shared by all Muslims in Britain, irrespective of sectarian affiliation. For the ecstatic believers of the Barelvi movement, however, less sober and more ardent than the scholastic Reformers, the distinction between *Dar-ul-Islam* and *Dar-ul-Kufr*, the land of Islam and the land of infidels, is of little consequence. Such hair-splitting distinctions, appropriate for the era of the camel, are evidently deemed by this form of radical modernist Islam to be entirely inappropriate in the age of Concorde, neo-colonialism, inter-continental ballistic missiles and the international division of labour. Thus adherents of this movement both accept and reject the bounds of their current legal status, inconsistently appealing to a global identification. Just as their personal emotional network and most valued attachments span continents, so too, ideologically, they identify with the Islamic *umma* as a global community.

Yet, of course, as several commentators have stressed, it is the *security of citizenship in Britain* and legal protection from racism, unequalled until recently throughout most of the European Union, which allow British Muslims to protest and express their moral outrage and to speak out against the injustice they feel has been inflicted upon them.

It is this sense of injustice which is widely shared among local British Pakistanis, even among those who are otherwise moderate, gentle, law-abiding, cheerful and not particularly pious citizens. It has created an insidious doubt, a credibility gap, a fundamental sense of mistrust, a vague fear, counteracted by a fervent belief that the attainment of human fairness, justice and equality is a real possibility.

Against these radicals, the old-style Islamic fundamentalist-reformists have adopted a far more consistent stance. They take Islamic law based on the *sunna*

---

[6] For a discussion of the history of the blasphemy law and its implications for freedom of speech, see the CRE Discussion Papers 1989a, b & c, Lee 1990, Webster 1990 and Ruthven 1990.

[7] The Law Commission, in its 1985 Report on Offences Against Religion and Public Worship, reported that out of 1,800 contributions to the debate, 1,700 supported the retention of the blasphemy law (see CRE 1989a: 67). Despite this, the Law Commission recommended its abolition on legal grounds, and because it was discriminatory. This recommendation was not, however, taken up (see CRE 1989a: 66–79).

of the Prophet very seriously and believe, above all, in a self-help programme of Islamic expansion in Britain.

The leader of the UK Islamic Mission, for example, a trained *maulvi* in the reformist tradition, described the Rushdie affair as getting out of hand 'as too many things have got mixed up together in it': racism, youthful resentments, the ignorance and emotionalism of uneducated people, Muslim politics and the lack of a unified Muslim leadership in Britain. In contrast, he claimed, the Islamic Mission, with its democratically elected leadership and bureaucratic structure, has clear, limited, achievable political targets. At the beginning of the affair this organisation and others like it lobbied the publishers and various Muslim countries in an attempt to have the book banned.

Later, when the affair threatened to erupt into violence, they were the first to recognise the counter-productive impact that the Muslim populist response would have. Although they continued the anti-Rushdie battle, they still felt that lobbying was a more useful strategy to employ, and that confrontation would only backfire. But the influence of such organisations is small. The Muslim 'street', in Manchester as in Algeria, Jordan or Lahore, is with the new Islamic populism and its new assertive populist-democratic consciousness.

This consciousness was articulated by some community leaders and religious clerics in the mosques, appealing directly to local Pakistanis. In contrast to Pakistani Labour councillors responsible to a broader constituency, including non-Muslim voters, these community leaders were more interested in confrontation than in compromise. They were fighting internal power battles *within* the Muslim community and seeking to mobilise support for their particular faction. Theirs was a narrow constituency, hence they unreservedly adopted the new Islamic radicalism. Salman Rushdie epitomised for this movement all that its followers were battling against: like the Kings and Emirs of Saudi Arabia and Kuwait, he had sold his soul and the souls of his people to the West for worldly riches. He had access to the 'Zionist' media with their false depictions of Islam. Indeed, the radicals claimed, he was a stooge and mouthpiece of this Zionism. He cast doubt on the certainty and divinity of the Qur'an – one of the two focal unifying and legitimising symbols of this global movement (the other being the Prophet and the Golden Age of Islam he established). Rushdie was secular, corrupt, 'Western' in his lifestyle. Above all, he had attacked the sacred persona of the Prophet, depicting him in the medieval demonic terms used by the Crusaders. He had desecrated his image with filthy language, in a book written in the profane language of the street. Such a man deserved to die and the Ayatollah's *fatwa* was, indeed, an expression of collective will. Long before it was enunciated, Pakistanis in Manchester hinted to me that this was the fate Rushdie deserved.

Against this Islamic radicalism, once the *fatwa* was proclaimed, was a liberal radicalism, led by writers and the press, espousing the cause of freedom of speech and the rights of authors to express deviant and subversive opinions, if necessary in subversive language. Their position was inspired by the American model which protects freedom of expression in the First Amendment (see Lee 1990: 40), and places religion firmly in the private domain. This group would like to see the blasphemy law abolished, and the disestablishment of the Church of England. (For a brilliant exposition of the current British radical liberal position see Wilson 1991.) The radical liberal defence of Rushdie only served, however, to persuade the Islamic opposition that he was indeed a sell-out, a cultural traitor.[8] Rushdie had openly and publicly attacked Islam, an act comparable, according to some, to declaring war against Islam. It is this offence, apparently, which is punishable by death, whereas a mere private renunciation of the Prophet's teachings is punishable only in the afterlife.[9]

A middle liberal position has emerged which argues that the use of blasphemy is a double-edged sword, which is often employed by religious extremists to control their own followers by demonising the other. These extremists evoke sexual images in order to degrade the other. Blasphemy thus plays into the hands of such religious extremists and should be avoided as a tool of criticism, lest it backfire.[10] Another moderate line argues from a legal position that there are no absolute rights to freedom of speech and that the law must be regarded as essentially a clash between competing values which must be examined contextually in order to judge, case by case, whether the infringement of one set of values is justified in terms of a more fundamental value, in this particular context.[11] Such a view would require careful consideration of the values implicit in the novel itself.

Yet what is the most astounding feature of the debate, and almost everything that has been written about *The Satanic Verses*, is that *no-one has understood the book itself*. They have understood parts of it, its subversive intention, its expression of religious doubt, its attack on religious fundamentalism, its colonisation of language,[12] but no-one seems to have analysed the book as a unified, symbolically coherent totality. Indeed, the assumption appears to be that no such coherence exists, almost by definition, in so postmodern a piece of work.

Conclusion: painful insults

Before going on to analyse the book let me present an image which I have carried with me almost from the start of the Rushdie affair. A little Pakistani boy (or girl) is on his way to school, holding his mother's hand. His face is shining and scrubbed, his clothes clean. As they walk along the pavement some English louts hurl racist epithets at them – 'Dirty Pakis, why don't you go home!' They quicken their steps, ignoring the insults. They do not retaliate. Nor do they report the matter to anyone. The community and its leaders are hardly involved in anti-

---

[8] The most outrageous statement is by Weldon (1989). For various other responses in the press see Apignanesi and Maitland (1989).

[9] See discussions by Ibn Ally (in CRE 1989a, especially pp. 25–7) and Akhtar (1989: 76–8). Rushdie is said by Ibn Ally to be an apostate (*murtadd*), and by Akhtar to have created public disorder (*fasad*) and corruption of the world (p. 77) and 'declared war upon God and his Messenger' (pp. 77–8). For a response to Akhtar see Ruthven (1990: 122), and a further discussion of the reasons behind the *fatwa* (ibid.: 112–28). According to Ruthven, 'In Islamic law, the emphasis was always towards protecting the honour of the Prophet and the Islamic community more than regulating religious belief.' He says that 'According to Ibn Taymiyya anyone defaming the Prophet *must* be executed, whether he is a Muslim or not.' (p. 51). See also his discussion of *Dar-al-Harb* and *Dar-al-Islam*, pp. 51–2.

[10] This position is brilliantly argued and illustrated by Webster 1990.

[11] The most important exposition of this position is by Lee 1990.

[12] For an excellent discussion of this aspect of the book see Fischer and Abedi (1990), who also go some way towards analysing its symbolic unity, as does Ruthven (1990: 11–28). Both, however, fail to clinch their analyses. Closest to the spirit of the book is perhaps van der Veer (1989) in a short article.

racist activities. But, unknown to the English louts, there is an invisible shield protecting the little boy and his mother. That shield is Islam. Despite the insults they feel protected, morally *superior*. They see the attackers as stupid, ignorant, inferior, irrational.

Which is worse? The attack on the little boy or the attack on the Prophet of Islam? I put this question to a Muslim religious scholar and leader. I explained that for me the answer was obvious – the attack on the little boy is worse, and reveals the root cause of immigrants' problems, namely racism. He answered that racism was simply a matter of colour, and that, in any case, there are many people already fighting against racism. For Muslims in Britain, he said, the challenge is to have their religion respected and their rights as a religious minority upheld.

For an ordinary Pakistani the answer to my question is equally obvious – attack me, attack my son, attack my wife, but do not attack my Prophet. I was told that there is a *hadith* according to which the Prophet said: 'You cannot be a Muslim until you recognise that I am more precious to you than your parents, your wealth or your life.' If the morality of the Prophet and his message are cast in doubt that invisible protective shield that allows British Pakistanis to live their lives to the full, optimistically and hopefully, in a spirit of self-help and communal mutual support, will be irretrievably shattered and each individual within the community will be exposed to the stigma of, as they perceive it, their inferiority and powerlessness.

But, one may argue, that invisible shield around the boy is also a cage. It will prevent him from growing up and prospering and becoming a full member of his new society. No, the others answer, the shield is a haven, not a cage. But if the real enemy is racism, sometimes disguised as religious intolerance, you are fighting the wrong enemy, and most important – losing valuable allies in the process. The world seems irrational, you become alienated. You don't need to lean on Islam in order to feel superior. You are equal because you are a human being. We don't care, they reply – you cannot attack our Prophet, this is where we draw the line, where we become fanatics.

The initial response to the perceived offence of *The Satanic Verses* was the furious reaction of a people who regard their honour and dignity as values to be defended at all costs. Hence Ruthven has argued, following Gilsenan (1982), that the Islamic code of honour ties slanders of sexual transgression with crimes against God, 'a fusion of the sexual and the sacred in Islam that is all the more powerful because it reinforces a social code rooted in Mediterranean and Asian values of honour and shame' (Ruthven 1990: 30). The Prophet, deeply enshrined in the realm of the hidden and the sacred, should above all be kept apart from any obscene and blasphemous discourse (ibid.: 31).

This apparently simple correspondence reveals, however, a complex dialectic. It is a dialectic which lies at the core of cultural notions of honour and shame in Punjabi Muslim society, and explains why sexual imagery has come to be merged in it with ideas about the sacred.

In many senses, Pakistanis expect their women to be the guardians of 'Culture'. Men are regarded as naturally 'natural', violent, often irrational, defenders of the family in a world in which the state has only a partial control over the means of violence (see Lindholm 1990). It is because women play such a crucial role as cultural guardians that a 'natural' woman, such as a promiscuous woman, is regarded as such a great danger. She denies her essential role as cultural guardian and in so doing threatens the very foundations of society. Without her, culture is shattered. Women are therefore protected from contexts where violence and violent language may be encountered, or where their underlying 'natural' nature may be aroused. They are shielded from politics, the central arena of 'natural' violence.

It may be possible to argue that for many Muslims, especially in the Sufi tradition, the Prophet presents an anomalous perfection. Kurin (1984), for example, points out that he has female, as well as male qualities, and we find evidence for this in Sufi *na'ats*, the poems in praise of the Prophet. He is the guardian, indeed the creator, of culture, a man who transcended in his being his passionate self, a man of reason and rationality, of love and humanity. Yet he was also a warrior and a ruler, a man of politics. He had knowledge and compassion, power and patience. It is not that his sanctity must be preserved from 'scurrilous language' simply because such language strikes at people's deepest identity; it is that he should be venerated as a *man* and respected and protected as a *woman*.

Izzat can be translated as honour, a man's inner pride in his ability to protect his reputation, his possessions and his womenfolk through his physical power and virility. But it can also be translated as social status or rank, and, finally, as respect, the etiquette and manners due to a person admired or loved. Three separate concepts are here combined in one. The Prophet is the most elevated in status and thus his persona must be treated with extreme respect. His name is never mentioned without an appropriate religious praise ('Peace Be Upon Him'). He is loved like a woman, respected like a man. He must be protected like a woman, in order that he protect his followers as only a powerful man can.

The Satanic Verses seems to be an attack on this image. All of the critics, left, right and centre, have taken this for granted. Everyone except Rushdie. But is it really such an attack? Rushdie has repeatedly argued that the Prophet himself would not be offended by his portrayal in the book. To examine this claim, the literary interpretation in the following chapter analyses the novel as a symbolic unity focused around the image of the Prophet, portrayed as the exemplary, perfect person. Clearly this critical strategy deviates from the ethnographic approach adopted so far in this book. Its aim is, however, ultimately ethnographic and dialogical: to engage directly in a debate with British Pakistani Muslims about the meaning of the book from my position as a Westernised, secular ethnographer.

5
The Satanic Verses
Allegories of sacred imperfection

The Prophet & his counter-selves

The Satanic Verses is constructed around the central figure of the Prophet who stands in opposition to six characters, who are, in fact, three paired characters. Four of the characters are counter-selves of Rushdie himself, and all these four are partially or entirely flawed ethically, negative figures who seem to lampoon and ridicule the author – his unprepossessing appearance, his cowardice in the face of adversity, his betrayal or jealousy of women, his scepticism, his arrogance and vindictiveness.

These four counter-selves stand in profane opposition to the Prophet. The two other figures, also a pair, stand in extreme opposition both to Rushdie himself and to the Prophet. This third pair represents uncompromising religious absolutism. The important point to note, however, is that this is not simply a book about religious belief or about migration and its implications, although these are undoubtedly central political themes in the book. It is, above all, a book about fundamental moral values and the ordeals that human beings face and which test these values. It is, in other words, a book about personal and public ethics.

The book is built around two key space/time settings, Bakhtinian chronotopes, each of which also contains an internal division. One chronotope is that of the modern world split between London and India (or Iran), representing diaspora and home. The other chronotope is set in the Hijaz during the rise of Islam and is split between Mecca and Madinah, representing home and diaspora. In each setting there is a migration and a return (with one minor exception). Of the four counter-selves, one of each pair lives in each of the chronotopes. The final pair appears in the modern chronotope and is opposed to the figure of the Prophet in the early Islamic chronotope (see Figure 5.1).

The two chronotopes mirror, reflect and comment upon each other. This is underlined by a further pair of women, one in each chronotope: Hind, the powerful wife of the ruler of Jahilia, the city of sin and ignorance before its purification by the Prophet and his followers, and Margaret Thatcher, Maggie the Bitch, Mrs Torture, in the crumbling London of corruption and racism, who like Hind is also trying to fight the tide of history and recreate Britain's imperial glory. A third woman, Ayesha, Empress of Desh, counter-person of the Shah of Iran, parallels the other two women in attempting to reverse the tide of history by returning to a Zoroastrian calendar.

Plate 5.1 Anti-Rushdie demonstration in London

The book, in other words, is a structuralist's dream, and the actions in both chronotopes parallel each other and throw light on the meanings implied by the events and actions each chronotope contains. I shall attempt to show, through a structuralist analysis, the basis for Rushdie's persistent claims that the Prophet of Islam would not be offended by his book, before arguing that in a deep sense his project partially fails.

The book is moved along by the known episodes in the life of the Prophet. Let me start, however, by representing the four main counter-selves and the values for which they stand (see Figure 5.2). The first pair is composed of Chamcha, meaning 'stooge', 'yes-man', 'slave' and 'spoon'. He is the anglicised Muslim Indian migrant who leaves home, rejects his father, marries a tweedy Englishwoman, adopts a pukka English accent, lifestyle and mode of dress. He is the background voice in various TV ads and puppet shows, a chameleon actor who can imperson-ate anyone. Chamcha represents denial of self, self-hatred, hatred of his past, religion and people, hence although he is rational, he is without feeling or love, helpless against racism which he does not believe exists. The man without integrity, he is opposed, we shall see, to the Prophet as the man of total integrity.

His reflection in the Meccan chronotope is Salman the Persian, the classic hypocrite (*munafiq*) of the Qur'an, the man who betrays the Prophet, secretly distorting the verses he is supposed to be writing down – and for a while getting away with it. Like Chamcha he is a coward, never confronting the Prophet openly, loveless and emotionless, too clever by half. He is also a slanderer, the man who carries the blasphemous message of the medieval Crusaders and depicts the Prophet maliciously as the anti-Christ, sexually insatiable and promoting sexual perversion and homosexuality, inventing rules for his own convenience.

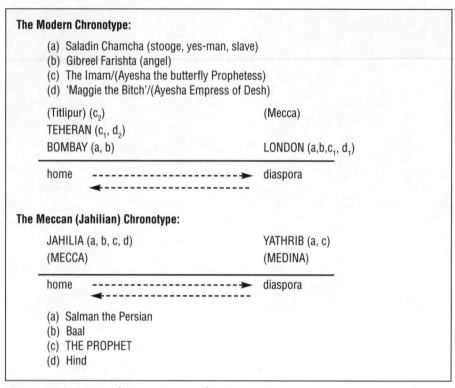

Figure 5.1 Major chronotypes in *The Satanic Verses*

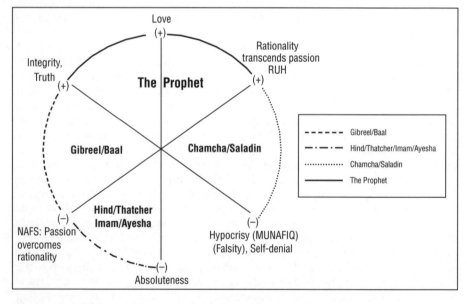

Figure 5.2 The juxtaposition of values in *The Satanic Verses*

To understand these figures one must go back to Fanon's theory of colonial subordination and the effect it has on the colonised, according to which the oppressed (and especially their elites) become pale copies of their masters, and, in so doing, inevitably take on the demonic stereotypes in which their masters cast them. Hence Chamcha, the perfect Indo-Englishman, falls from the sky in a Gramscian rebirth, and becomes the devil – horns, tail, hairy body and enlarged penis – arrested and beaten up by the British police. As the self-hating migrant he lacks integrity and thus assumes the image imposed on him by his racist hosts. Similarly Salman the Persian, the hypocrite, adopts the libels and slanders of the medieval Crusaders. Both act in their demonic capacity as Satanic testers, in both cases of the more positive and yet still flawed other pair of counter-selves. Both are forgiven. Chamcha is the luckier: he rediscovers himself when he feels hate for his oppressors and love for his own people. At this point he loses his demonic appearance. In the end, he returns home, rediscovers his love for his father, and his love for his Indian childhood sweetheart who has become a crusading secular Muslim fighting in India against communalism and sectarianism. For Rushdie she is the image of the true, organic hybrid: a liberal who yet retains her integrity and love for her country while fighting against archaic authenticities and the violence these unleash. Chamcha is forgiven and spared. His life is saved by the man he tempted and finally ruined. Salman the Persian is also forgiven by the Prophet, his life is spared and he too returns home to Persia. A far worse character than bumbling Chamcha, however, he never feels emotion and hence never finds love.

The second pair – which is also one – represents true creativity and the artistic imagination, flawed by a passion which cannot transcend itself and ultimately ruins each of the characters. If the first pair represents the Islamic battle against hypocrites, the second represents the Islamic battle between *nafs* (the vital, passionate soul) and *ruh* (the reflective eternal soul): the internal *jihad*. Here the central myth is that of Shakespeare's Othello, the noble Moor who, tempted by the Satanic Iago, loses his soul in jealousy, and destroys his beloved and himself. Gibreel, the first of these characters, is in many senses Othello's double. Like Rushdie himself, he is a celebrity, an Indian film star who acts in theological films, in the roles of various gods, both Hindu and Muslim. Hence a tolerant man. He has great talent, integrity and vision (*Satanic Verses*: 427), and yet he betrays himself and everyone around him. Indeed, his life is a catalogue of betrayals. It is juxtaposed alongside the Prophet's life, the life of a man who is tempted only once and repents in time, and who overcomes all the ordeals with which Satan and his fellow-men test him.

The juxtaposition of Gibreel with the Prophet can be set out as a series of parallel and opposed events. Both are, or become, orphans, and are adopted by loving 'uncles'. Whereas the Prophet sees a slave being flogged, stands up to his oppressor and pays for the slave only to free him, Gibreel sees Chamcha his friend being carried off by the police and does nothing about it. For his act of courage and generosity the Prophet is rewarded by the loyalty of the freed slave, who becomes one of his most devoted companions. For his disloyalty, Gibreel is later the target of revenge by Chamcha who slanders his beloved, Alleluia Cone (Gibreel's crucible as Cone mountain in the novel is the Prophet's crucible). Chamcha, playing Iago to Gibreel's Othello, drives Gibreel to murder and suicide. Whereas Gibreel betrays his first mistress, Rekha Merchant, going off with another woman, the Prophet is totally loyal to his first wife, also a merchant and trader, and only remarries after her death. Rekha Merchant takes her ghostly revenge on Gibreel for the rest of the book. The Prophet's wife provides him with support throughout his life, especially at the start of his career as a prophet, when he is fearful no-one will believe him.

In the third event, Gibreel believes the slander that his young mistress has betrayed him and goes mad with hatred. By contrast, the Prophet trusts his beloved young wife Aisha, when she is left behind in the desert for several hours and brought back by a young shepherd. He refuses to believe the slander about her. Historically, this wife later became one of the pillars of Islam, an important person in her own right. Finally, Gibreel, driven mad by his passion and jealousy, becomes an agent of revenge and death, sparking off a race riot in London which leads to bloodshed and destruction. He finally kills his beloved and her supposed lover, and then commits suicide. A redeeming feature of this otherwise negative character is that he saves Chamcha's life, repaying revenge with kindness, and later does not kill him. The Prophet in his power, when he returns triumphant to Mecca, is compassionate and forgives all his adversaries with the exception of the poet Baal. One character uses his power for destruction, the other for purification and reconstruction.

The central episode in the book, that of the Satanic verses, parallels Gibreel's temptation by Chamcha. The Prophet is tempted by an offer made by the ruler of Jahilia and thinks he hears the voice of the angel Gabriel telling him that he should compromise and recognise the three female idols of Jahilia as angelic daughters of God. Significant here, I think, is the role of his truly loyal companions who believe in his message, feel betrayed by him, and who ultimately enable, perhaps compel, him to come to the realisation that he has erred. He goes back to the mountain and receives the true message – overcoming this one and only temptation to which he had succumbed. Rushdie implies that it is this temptation which makes him human and thus ultimately compassionate and forgiving of the sins of others. He has, as it were, encountered the true reality of the devil, and he continues to recognise 'his' power of temptation even to his death-bed.

Gibreel (who is also the Prophet's tempter, travelling in his nightmares through space and time), succumbs, by contrast, to the Satanic voice and never fully repents. He thus becomes, as already mentioned, an agent of destruction.

Gibreel's counterpart in the Jahilia chronotope is the poet Baal. He too is opposed to the Prophet. Here Rushdie creates a second dualism between the antithetical worlds of the harem and the brothel, mosque and anti-mosque. Rushdie explains, in an essay which initially appeared in the *Independent on Sunday*, that 'the presence in the harem of the Prophet, the receiver of a sacred text, is likewise contrasted with the presence in the brothel of the clapped-up poet Baal, the creator of profane texts. The two struggling worlds, pure and impure, chaste and coarse, are juxtaposed, by making them echoes of one another; and *finally the pure eradicates the impure*' (Rushdie 1991a: 19, emphasis added).

More generally, the Jahilian chronotope divides internally into two sub-chronotopes, juxtaposing the pure and the impure in *time, Jahilia-before* and *Jahilia-after* (see Figure 5.3). Jahilia-before is a city of sand that hates water and perversely celebrates the Prophet Abraham's betrayal of his wife (i.e. the Biblical version of the myth). Jahilia-after is a city that worships water, and the sufferings

Jahilia-before	Jahilia-after
Den of iniquity and sin	City of purity
Worships sand	Worships water
Women denigrated*	Women respected**
Impure	Pure
Brothel	Harem
Prostitutes	Prophet's wives
Baal	The Prophet

*Hence Abraham 'the bastard' worshipped perversely in Jahilia-before for sending his wife into the desert

** Hence Hajra (Hagar) ritually remembered on the *hajj* and Abraham as a loving husband tested by God

Figure 5.3 The Meccan chronotopes

of Hajra, Hagar, Abraham's wife, an ordeal set by God, are no longer forgotten. In both the *hajj* and *umra* pilgrimages to Mecca, Hagar's suffering and heroism are commemorated by all pilgrims who run between the two hills, Saf and Marwa, seven times, as she was said to have done before the holy spring, the *zamzam*, miraculously appeared and saved her baby son's life. According to Islamic traditions, she was later rejoined by Abraham who rebuilt the *ka'ba* with his son Ismail.

The brothel is part of Jahilia-before. While the first Jahilia chapter, 'Mahound', portrays the ordeal of the Prophet in which he overcomes temptation and achieves his singular divine vision, the second Jahilia chapter, 'Return to Jahilia', portrays the ordeal of Mahound's true challenger, Baal, the secular poet-genius, who transcends his cowardice and selfishness to find true feeling. The transformation is a gradual one, and like that of the Prophet in the earlier chapter, it involves an initial failure. It begins with a transformation in the brothel itself: as the whores take on the names of the Prophet's wives and adopt Baal as their 'husband', they also assume some of the qualities and values of those wives, and expect Baal to behave accordingly, as a loyal 'husband'. As he changes he begins to understand and empathise with the Prophet and even defends him to Salman the Persian, when the latter slanders him. Baal, however, like Gibreel his counterpart, betrays his 'wives' in his cowardice, watching them passively as they are bundled off by the police, desperately appealing to him for manly protection. To redeem this act of cowardice and achieve final integrity he performs a deed of supreme courage: sought for by Mahound's men, he nevertheless turns up at the jail now bursting with pimps and prostitutes, an absurd figure of fun, to recite magical, beautiful love poetry for his jailed 'wives'. His poetry is so marvellous that the guards, their eyes running with tears, do not prevent him from nailing the text of the poems to the prison wall. This he does for twelve consecutive evenings, serenading the prostitute-namesakes of the Prophet's wives, while at the same time publicly dishonouring the Prophet and his family. Nor does he repent this act of public irreverence: '"I am Baal" he announce[s]. "I recognise no jurisdiction except that of my Muse; or, to be exact, my dozen Muses"' (*Satanic Verses*: 391).

Is this apparent dishonouring of the Prophet and his family intended as such? Is the equation Baal draws between prostitutes and loyal wives really the offence it is taken to be? For a religion which stresses family loyalty and sexual purity, a challenge to these values is deeply insulting. For a secular religion of the individual, the celebration of love cannot be construed as offensive, because it glorifies human values *despite* human frailties. Against this one may ask: is pluralism without offence of singularity possible? And is the infliction of offence on those holding other values, however irrational these may seem, permissible in the name of this pluralism? The Prophet's answer is a resounding 'no': promiscuous poet and prostitutes must both be executed. And in this act lies the unresolved contradiction in the book

The confrontation between true, sincere religious vision, and equally genuine secular inspiration, drawing upon a promiscuity of sources, many muses, high and low, rather than a divine singularity, is at the heart of the book. The religion of submission, Islam, cannot tolerate, Rushdie implies, non-submissive, yet ethical, inspiration. Baal is executed by Mahound not simply because of the blasphemy and dishonour he is perceived to have inflicted upon the Prophet and his wives, but because he speaks in the name of an alternative moral order. In executing him the Prophet signals the limits of his compassion and magnanimity in victory. He must use brute force to eliminate what essentially cannot be suppressed: a morality which constitutes an attack against rule-bound love, through a genuine, selfless celebration of earthly love. Yet the Prophet knows, as his followers do not, that, while his own religious message is powerfully singular, what inspired not only his miraculous Qur'anic poetry, but the passion and feeling of his message, was the part-devilish goddess he had publicly renounced, Al-Lat, the Muse. On his death-bed he faces this truth and, while choosing the singular ethical God once again, acknowledges his debt: 'Still, I thank Thee, Al-Lat, for this gift' (*Satanic Verses*: 394). This final moment of self-truth and humility is, Rushdie implies, what makes the Prophet a great human being, *imperfect and hence not a God*, and Aisha, his beloved wife, is the first to recognise this truth about her husband (ibid.).

The central chronotopes, Jahilia-before and Jahilia-after, contain the organising metaphors of the book, and its key ideas which link agency with moral transformation (on these concepts see Fernandez 1982 and Richard Werbner 1989). By implication, there are also three further sub-chrontopes: London-before, the London of English imperial domination; Iran-before, the Iran of the Shah with its murderous secret service and religious revisionism; and India-before, a place of peaceful villages. None of these has a redemptive 'after': the London-after of migration and ethnic diversity, the Iran-after of the Ayatollah, and the India-after of communal and sectarian hatred are all places in which chaos and violence are constantly close to the surface.

Hence, against the four characters of the central chronotopes, counter-selves of the author, and against the Prophet himself, are set two other characters – a man and a woman. The 'imam', who is the counter-self of the Ayatollah Khomeini, a man of absolute faith and no compassion, implacably opposed to change; like the Prophet he is a man of integrity and purity, an absolute lover of water, but unlike him he lacks love. He rejects all that is not water; hence for the imam wine becomes blood, fun and levity turn to violence and death (*Satanic Verses*: 209). In a sense one may say that he has never encountered the reality of the devil and this makes him unforgiving and thus an agent of destruction. His counterpart in India is Ayesha, the butterfly prophetess, who leads a village on a pilgrimage to Mecca by walking through the sea, taking them to their death by drowning with her unbending faith. She too has integrity and will power, while lacking compassion. (A third character in London, Dr Uhuru Simba, counter-self of Malcolm X, represents perhaps uncompromising black power which unleashes terrible violence.) Together the six counter-selves (Gibreel and Baal, Chamcha and Saladin, the Imam and Ayesha) represent three key negative values, both in Islam and in the secular liberal ethos Rushdie espouses. They are opposed to the Prophet who represents in all cases the opposed positive values (see Fig. 5.2). As the Prophet is transformed by his ordeal, so too Chamcha, Baal and to some extent Gibreel, are transformed by theirs. Only Baal, the poetic counter-self of the Prophet, achieves a fleeting greatness.

Set against these six figures, the Prophet is the almost perfect man: he is a creative genius who transforms the world; he overcomes temptation, transcends passion, is always a man of integrity. He is courageous in weakness, magnanimous in power. He teaches love and respect for women. Yet this perfection too has its limits. The Prophet can never be a total victor. There will always be those who rebel against his rules or slander him and his followers. And in demanding submission to his ethical view, he must deny, if need be by force, the legitimacy of alternative 'gods', especially those celebrating the primacy of emotion over rule, although these may represent equally valid moral and ethical orders. This essential limitation renders him human, not divine, but his humanity is that of a great man.

What's in a name? Rushdie makes names work for him. They disguise identities, demonise and divinise inversely. They are external impositions or self-disguises: Saladin Chamcha is not the heroic Saladin, the historic Islamic conqueror, victor over the Crusader armies; Gibreel Farishta is no angel; Ayesha, the counter-self of the Shah of Iran as well as the butterfly prophetess, is nothing like the original namesake who understood the true message of the Prophet (*Satanic Verses*: 393); Salman the Persian is entirely unlike the Prophet's wise companion. Baal is not the false Canaanite idol his name implies. So too Mahound is not the anti-Christ monster medieval Crusaders made him out to be.[1] By implication, real identities are hidden, while character and action give meanings to names, whether positive or negative, not the other way round. Why use names in this way? Why call prostitutes, whether in Jahilia or London, by the names of the Prophet's wives (*Satanic Verses*: 460)? 'Our names meet, separate, and meet again', Baal thought, 'but the people going by the names do not remain the same' (ibid.: 359).

This play on names is, I believe, linked to the central project of the book: to reclaim Islam for secular Muslims, a new breed, as an *ethical* religion.[2] Rushdie does this by exploring the central values of Islam as he understands them, but

---

[1] See Armstrong 1988: 160; Ahmed 1991b: 3; also the *Shorter Oxford English Dictionary* under the entry for 'Mahound'.

[2] That Rushdie is part of a modern literary movement in the Muslim world, with its roots going back to Muslim satirical writing, is demonstrated by Fischer and Abedi 1990 and Ruthven 1990. For an excellent discussion of the complex relationship between Asian diaspora writers and the homeland see Ghosh 1989.

also by rejecting reformist Islam's current stress on female seclusion or purity and on ritual praxis at the expense of ethics. Thus it is that in the end the book stakes a claim for the sacredness of the profane, of the whores in the brothel who are victims of exploitation. Even prostitutes constitute the battleground of angelic and Satanic forces. To condemn them outright is to deny their sacred humanity. The liberal credo desacralises the sacred in order to sacralise the profane – above all the individual, portrayed as the locus of the cosmic battle between good and evil. By mixing the profane and the sacred, good and evil, the author asserts that all human beings are in some sense sacred – the liberal message – and yet we are all the product of our ability to overcome trials and ordeals – a central Islamic message. What differentiates us as human beings is not our names, the external labels/identities we assume or others impose upon us, but how we meet the various crucibles we face. It is these trials and ordeals, the mountains we climb (Everest, Cone) that reveal the angelic or Satanic within us. Muhammad the Prophet, call him Mahound, call him Paki, call him black bastard, was the perfect man because he stood up to abuse, and transcended his frailties, his inner desires and greed. This entitled him to become the agent of a supreme ethical revelation. The move from a religion of purity to a religion of ethics stressing the value of the individual is clearly an aim of the book, whether it is achieved or not.

In order to understand the book's message it is essential to recognise the central paradigmatic myths and intellectual writings upon which Rushdie draws. These are (i) the religious traditions, the *sunna* of the Prophet; (ii) Shakespeare's tragedy *Othello*; (iii) the Hindu *Mahabarata*, with its tales of transformative gods and avatars (see Shulman 1985; also Kapferer 1983, for discussions); (iv) Gramsci's notion of death and rebirth, as well as cultural hegemony; (v) accounts of libels against Muslims and the Prophet as the anti-Christ in medieval Christianity (see Armstrong 1988); (vi) Muslim, especially Persian, traditions of satirical poetry (see Fischer and Abedi 1990); (vii) Fanon's view on racism and colonialism; (viii) William Blake's *Marriage of Heaven and Hell*. Indeed, Blake's deep religious faith, conjoined with a total rejection of the established Christian clergy of his day, is a key unlocking Rushdie's own vision of the poet/prophet Muhammad in *The Satanic Verses*:

> The reason Milton wrote in fetters when he wrote of Angels and God, and at liberty when of Devils and Hell, is because *he was a true Poet and of the Devil's party without knowing it*. (Blake 1946: 250, emphasis added)

This is a heavy witches' brew and one cannot blame ordinary Muslims, deeply familiar only with the first of these sources, if they fail to crack the code and thus inevitably get the message topsy-turvy. One cannot, by the same token, expect English intellectuals who are unfamiliar with the life of the Prophet to get the message either. Muslim secular intellectuals who should know better, since they are obviously familiar with the works of Gramsci and Fanon, have almost universally condemned the book.[3] From conversations with some of them, I believe that

[3] See the articles by Asad 1990a, b who, like others, attacks the tendency of liberal 'fundamentalists' to sacralise literature as the new sanctified religious text; also Mazrui 1989, Kabbani 1989, Akhtar 1989 and Jussawala 1989. Bikhu Parekh, a British Asian of Hindu origins, while appreciating the brilliance of the language and imagery in the novel, fails to follow its central message 1989; see also his discussions in the CRE Discussion Papers 1989a, 1989b, 1989c. Fischer and Abedi 1990 defend some of the alleged misrepresentations in the novel by a brilliantly authentic use of Talmudic/

these intellectuals cannot forgive the author for *deliberately* writing a book which he *knew* (or had no excuse *not* to know) would provoke violent religious passions, riots and possible deaths, and would inevitably strengthen the hands of the religious establishment. No symbolic schema, no humanist agenda, justifies this provocation in their eyes. On the whole they make little attempt to plumb the structurally coded message of the book.

In addition to its central mythological sources, the book contains a wealth of other literary references, from Melville and Marquez to T.S. Eliot. As many have recognised, the novel is a veritable minefield of unacknowledged literary allusions, which may well throw further light on its symbolic significance. Rushdie has attempted to create a true hybrid, an integral unity of Islamic and Western myths, a new organic whole. Most Muslims, however, do not see this as a valid aim for which to aspire. They wish to retain their sacred traditions in their compartmentalised purity. Hybridism, the response to change, novelty and other cultures, and fundamentalism, a return to a past complete, whole and unchangeable, stand in implacable opposition. Most Muslims choose the middle ground, keeping the pure and the impure separated in discrete social domains. In their daily lives they switch between the sacred and the secular with apparently consummate ease. Postcolonial critics such as Homi Bhabha, in celebrating Rushdie's hybrid creativity (Bhabha 1994, Chap. 11), fail to recognise that the popular response to the book reacted not simply to its hybrid mixings, but to its conflation of what are guarded as normatively discrete, symbolic domains (see also van der Veer 1997).

Aesthetic debate & the problem of postmodernity

Of the four chronotope-narratives intertwined in the book (London/Bombay, Titlipur, Mecca, London/Teheran), which embody the six key actors, the London/Bombay narrative is the most accessible to a Western audience. Its tropes are recognisable, its intellectual spoofing of postmodernist simulations delightfully funny, and its fantastical storyline decodable as a serious attempt to grapple with the issues of uncertainty, migration and 'divided selves', to use the author's phrase. It is also this narrative which allows us to consider the possibility of real aesthetic communication and *debate* about the 'sense' of a text, and hence also its potential 'meaning'.

In his deconstructive criticism of the novel, Asad brings as an example of Rushdie's hidden agenda his liberal elevation of literature as the new religion, conveyed in the novel through the 'sympathetic portrayal' of the figure of Abu Sufyan, eclectic reader of world literature. In a deconstructive re-analysis he argues further that the *un*sympathetic portrayal of Pamela, the do-gooder white woman who marries Chamcha, is related, not to the fact that she betrays her brown husband by continuously hobnobbing with blacks, but to her interracial marriage which undermined white supremacy assumptions. Rushdie, the assimilated Muslim Asian, adopts here, in Asad's view, the 'core values' of the English upper classes to which he aspires to belong.

Yet a closer examination reveals that this type of ad hoc representational and fragmentary analysis which takes bits of the book from here and there, out of context, is simply inadequate as an interpretive tool. Asad fails to recognise that these two characters, Abu Sufyan and Pamela, are neither good nor bad, but symbolically *one and the same*, part of a pantheon of misalliances and hybrid eclectic figures (six in all), who remain passive, uncreative, unable 'to change the world'. Rushdie mocks all these figures gently, rather than passing judgement upon them. The activities of well-meaning white liberals or the tolerance of Sufi world renouncers are commendable but fruitless, just as the various misalliances remain sterile. Such figures are opposed in the text to true hybrids, who are the only figures able to create, procreate and act positively. Hence, Part V of the novel, 'A City Visible but Unseen', takes up the novel's central theme of multiplicity versus unity (hybridity), disintegration versus integration, impotence/destructiveness versus creativity, from a postmodernist perspective.

By imaging tolerance (a multiplicity of muses) as sexual promiscuity, Rushdie draws, however, on powerfully dangerous Pakistani ethical-cum-aesthetic stock images: conjugal 'arranged' marriage in a moral orderly world; romantic love in a world of dreams and the cinema; and sexual promiscuity in a world of fantasies/nightmares of social anomie. If for Rushdie dogmatic singularity is the cause of communal terror and intolerance, for many Muslims it is Western sexual promiscuity which unleashes uncontrollable social violence. Their knowledge of the West, gleaned from films and television, and from personal observations and experiences in deprived inner city areas, is one of moral, social and aesthetic chaos (see Ahmed 1992). Rushdie's novel contains the message that love and compassion can transcend the dangers of cultural/sexual 'promiscuity' and create a basis for real tolerance; purity encompasses impurity. Most British Muslims have concluded, by contrast, that liberal secularism inevitably leads to sexual promiscuity which is the cause of social disintegration and uncontained violence.

The ethical-cum-aesthetic impasse is thus rooted in the core imagery of the novel. The *same* key terms and organising metaphors evoke opposed emotional associations and fears in different readerships, and lead to opposed processes of ethical reasoning. Common ethical values held by both Muslims and liberals (love, compassion, loyalty, integrity, truth, faith) are embodied in polysemic aesthetic images which underline the social contradictions and dilemmas surrounding these values. A semiotic analysis of the text cannot resolve this cultural opposition between two worldviews, the aporia at the heart of the novel; all it can hope to do is illuminate its specificities for both readerships. The 'explanation' of the text opens up two contradictory 'worlds'.

Rushdie's aim of creating a liberal-secular-Islamic unity is, given the opposition to it, a political agenda. And, in addition to the personal level at which fundamental values are explored, the book also operates on the political plane. For example, it images the demonisation of immigrants, whether or not they attempt to assimilate. It attacks false anti-racist battles, witch-hunting by the police, false representations by the media. These are all, ironically, central concerns of British Muslims. In another way too Rushdie is a conventional Sunni Muslim – namely, in his disapproval of Shi'ite martyrdom. Both the imam and the butterfly prophetess seem to be Shi'ites. He thus objects to the purely authentic, the timeless, the eternal, the totalising, the uncompromising; this is *not*, the book shows, what the Prophet of Islam represents.

At the political level the book is – as so many, following Rushdie himself, have noted – also a book about migration. Migrants too face an ordeal: the confrontation with another culture which stereotypes and demonises them, just as the people of Jahilia and medieval Christianity demonised the Prophet. How to overcome this culturally destructive construction of self by the other? How to do so by remaking the world with love rather than violence, while remaining true to oneself, retaining one's own integrity? This indeed was the Prophet's greatest achievement. This is the question raised by *The Satanic Verses*. Oddly enough, however, here too Rushdie reveals himself as a typical Pakistani immigrant. All the characters in the novel either die or return home. Chamcha and Salman both return home. So do the imam, Gibreel, Baal and the Prophet himself. A migrant can only find himself, and love, by returning to his origins.

Nevertheless, the book *is* blasphemous. Why? Because juxtaposition of opposites necessarily implies comparison. Metaphor becomes metonymy. Metaphors of obscenity and libel are contagious, they pollute the pure. A book full of profanities dealing with the Prophet, however much it depicts him as fundamentally almost perfect, is necessarily blasphemous, even if one does understand its symbolic structure – which of course few people even attempt to do.[4]

Profanation is magical; it unites what is contrasted. Profanation also stands above analytic schema as a series of performative utterances. Obscenities do not only mean; they are *acts*. If the English blasphemy law as it now stands was applied to Islam, the book would undoubtedly be banned. There is no mention in that law of literature and its merits. Indeed, the intention of the writer is deemed to be irrelevant! The law in England (not the whole UK) does *not* sacralise literature, irrespective of the views of writers and intellectuals, including Rushdie himself. On the contrary, the law in England sacralises religious *feelings* and these have been offended.

But why mock the Prophet's wives, even indirectly, at all? And why use obscene or indecent language in a book about the sacred? Here, I believe, we need to refer to Rushdie's hidden guru, Bakhtin, and his theory of carnival (Bakhtin 1984). According to Bakhtin,

> in grotesque realism, ... the bodily element is deeply positive. It is presented not in a private, egotistic form, severed from the other spheres of life, but as something universal, representing all the people. As such it is opposed to severance from the material and bodily roots of the world; it makes no pretence to renunciation of the earthy, or independence of the earth and body.... The material bodily principle is contained not in the biological individual, not in the bourgeois ego, but in the people, a people who are continually growing and renewed. (ibid: 19)

As one secular Muslim commented, Rushdie is praising the Prophet, not for being pure, but precisely *because* he was a lover of women and sexuality. According to Bakhtin, degradation and profanation are humanising and revitalising acts (1984: 21), and Rushdie's intention is thus to renew and humanise Islam. Whether he can achieve a similar symbolic transformation in our bourgeois world, detached from its body/earth sources, remains, however, an open question.

My uncertainty stems also from what seems to me to be a tragic flaw in the book, which is not, it must be stressed, a symbolic or structural flaw. The novel's central chapter, 'Return to Jahilia', while symbolically valid, is *emotionally* hollow.

Islamic logical argumentation. A less virtuoso but equally scholarly discussion is Ruthven 1990.

[4] Especially since structuralism as an approach has been widely criticised (partly, in my view, because it has been misrepresented and misunderstood), while the intertextual references in the novel require knowledge of quite different religious mythologies and literatures which few individuals

Structurally, it is the story of Baal and his moral transformation from selfish coward to true lover. The Prophet himself remains a background figure; we do not know him from the *inside* as conqueror, forgiver, purifier, husband, executioner, rule-maker and victim of slander and dishonour. The identification generated in the first Jahilia chapter with his agonies and doubts, his suffering from slander and mockery, is entirely absent in the second Jahilia chapter, with the exception of its key last two pages. Instead, the libellous voice of Salman the Persian is paramount. The absence of Mahound's authentic counter-voice undermines the dialogical meaning of the Jahilia narrative, so that the brothel episode seems simply to confirm and augment the Persian's libellous accusations, rather than constituting – as intended – an act of earthly revitalisation.

Is this a failure of the artistic imagination at the very core of the book, or was it intended? Is it, as it seems, a hollowness at the heart of the novel which is also, possibly, a hollowness of the heart? Does Rushdie, while asserting that the Prophet (and thus Islam) is magnanimous, compassionate and humble, really see him in the final analysis as a religious tyrant? This much is clear: the Prophet remains true to himself. According his own lights he cannot tolerate the dishonour brought upon his wives, or the unsubmissive challenge by unregularised emotion to his divine vision. Poet and Prophet respect and fear one another yet, apparently, they cannot co-exist. This is the central unresolved and irreducible paradox at the heart of the novel: just as a singular, rule-bound, divine vision tolerates no pluralistic alternatives, so too tolerant pluralism, especially one grounded in unbounded emotion alone, cannot encompass singular visions, thus contradicting its claims to universal tolerance. The poet who asserts earthly love must do so by publicly insulting the most deeply held values and the loved ones of the Prophet and his followers. The Prophet asserting the love of God must destroy the creator of beautiful love poetry, and punish some of society's most wretched victims. Rushdie recognises the paradox without resolving it, or allowing for the possibility of a truly tolerant Islam (or secular vision of it). And so we are faced with the renewed dilemma of what attitude to take towards the novel as a whole, given the enormous offence and humiliation it has caused.

From a literary modernist perspective, *The Satanic Verses* is, I believe, a great novel; brilliantly constructed, breathtakingly broad, an epic of modernity, of personal values in the context of disjunction and change. It brings Islam, as a great ethical religion, into the literary universe we share globally. But it is also a novel which has knowingly offended hundreds of thousands of people. In Britain the debate favours either the total abolition of the blasphemy law or the creation of a law protecting all major religions from religious incitement or hatred. It is not clear, however, whether anything at all will be done. The legal problems are so complex, the emotional underpinnings so sensitive.

The dialogical nature of the novel is profoundly prophetic. *The Satanic Verses* has raised questions regarding the limits of freedom of speech in the context of globalising communication systems and increasingly privatised censorship. What are the limits of religious pluralism, multiculturalism, citizenship rights, equality before the law, race relations? How do we interpret, define and judge great literature, and what value does it have in an increasingly secular world? If we deny protection to religious feelings, are we not guilty of 'medicalising' such feelings as deviant or abnormal (see Asad 1990), and in so doing, denying the fact that such feelings are widely and genuinely held? Yet legitimised and harnessed politically, those same passionately held feelings have in the past inspired terrible atrocities in the name of the very ethical ideas they claimed to defend. At the same time, are we able to say with certainty that extreme liberal ideas cannot also be intolerant and dangerous? As some, like Asad and more recently Modood, imply, can liberals also be 'fundamentalist', imposing anti-religious views on others coercively? In Britain, the debate on these issues continues (see Werbner 2000b).

Violence breeds violence, but also new mediating structures (see Miles 1994). In Britain, there have been protests and demonstrations, and a good deal of vilification of Muslims by the popular press, but not a single death or serious injury. Only one person, a proven arsonist, has been imprisoned. Rushdie has recently been able to move around more freely and, at the time of writing, has moved from London to New York. In attempting to submit by becoming a Muslim, and thus to create bridges to his community (see Ahmed 1991b), he has encountered the face of compassionate Islam, willing to forgive and accept him, and the face of vengeful Islam, vindictive to the bitter end, finally leading to his renunciation of his conversion and to renewed confrontation (see Rushdie 1991b). Imam and Prophet continue to battle over his soul.

If this is so, however, it is partly because the book has caused a deep sense of alienation among British Muslims; a hurt that will not easily go away, a resentment, a sense of suspicion and fear. These events and emotions cannot be obliterated. They resurfaced during the Gulf crisis. If there is a positive dimension to this tragic confrontation in Britain, it has been that, on the one hand, the author has been unambiguously and vigorously protected by the state, his rights as an individual upheld; at the same time the citizenship rights of British Muslims have been, somewhat belatedly, acknowledged, and with this has come a recognition – although it has emerged more gradually – of their rights to equality before the law in matters of faith. British Muslims have concluded from the affair that they should get more seriously involved in national politics so that they can influence Parliament more directly. But political involvement in the wider arena brings with it a measure of social responsibility and, at the very least, a moderation of rhetoric.

The questions remain, however. Where do we draw the line between freedom of speech, the value of great literature, on the one hand, and rights of religious minorities, on the other hand? How will these rights be determined? Above all, the Rushdie affair has revealed the complexity of living in a modern, multiethnic, multi-faith world.

Aesthetics & cultural translation

A detailed structural analysis of *The Satanic Verses* reveals shared polysemic images which 'open up' different and opposing 'worlds'. By evoking images and values significant to both worlds, Rushdie has created the possibility of cultural translation – but also of radical miscommunication. This raises the question posed at the outset: can cultural translation form the basis for aesthetic persuasion? The Rushdie affair suggests that cultural translation cannot in itself alter aesthetic canons or deeply held ethical convictions. What cultural translation can do, however, is to enhance *self*-awareness along with the consciousness of alternative aesthetic and ethical discourses.[5]

The anthropological project is usually construed as one of explaining the rationality of the people we study to a Western audience at 'home'. In doing so anthropology, it is argued, renders the bizarre normal, the exotic sensible and fitting, and the violent structurally logical (Asad 1986; Strathern 1987a). This chapter, perhaps unusually, goes beyond this project, for it aims also to expose a Western rationality to a *Muslim* audience, reversing the directionality of dialogical engagement. The chapter, in other words, is not only an anthropological work representing an other; it is also a work by an anthropologist (myself) addressed, in a persuasive mode, to that other.

My deviation from the usual practice arises from a personal predicament: as an anthropologist doing research on British Pakistanis, I found that my role as participant observer came to be literalised during the Rushdie affair. I was, literally, both an observer and a participant; my research took place in a globalised world/nation state to which I, as a citizen, also felt a moral responsibility. I was also committed, as a member of a broader diaspora, to fighting *against* another fundamentalism for the sake of peace with Muslims and Christians in another part of the world. If, as I believe, social anthropology is not merely a mode of accumulating knowledge but a critical project, then I could not deny my views as a participant in this wider moral field. My critical role entailed, among other things, a right to speak out publicly as a concerned citizen.

The Rushdie affair challenged this taken-for-granted right. On the one hand, British Muslims, who were the subject of my research, clearly felt themselves to be victims of a racist conspiracy. There was no doubt about the sincerity of their passion or the depth of their felt offence. These were evident in my daily interactions with them during the height of the affair. They have been highlighted in the speeches reported here. At the same time, I felt strongly not only that the author of the novel should not be condemned to death but, more radically, that his book had been misunderstood. *The Satanic Verses*, as I have argued here, is a serious book written from a humanist perspective about Islam as a great religion; it is not a superficial postmodernist text satirising and debunking Islam (for a similar view see Berman 1992). If the book was only that, it would matter rather little if it were censored or banned.

Yet even suggesting the possibility that the book was respectful to Islam to Pakistani friends and acquaintances elicited an extreme emotional response. My mildest comments were greeted with dramatic gestures; telephones were banged down by normally moderate, gentle friends in mid-conversation; an acquaintance threatened to punch me in the face, and I was warned not to attend political meetings by friends concerned about my personal safety. I found myself silenced also by the fact that the people I had studied trusted me not to misrepresent their community to a hostile world. In addition, there was my enormous debt of gratitude to Pakistanis for the help and generosity they had extended to me over the years.

I had never experienced this kind of silencing before during the entire course of my research, even though fieldwork is a practice which depends in large

possess.
[5] The intertextual complexity of the novel is so great, and so dependent on a knowledge of Islam and Prophetic traditions, that English readers have often failed to grasp its positive message (for an

measure upon self-disciplined silence. In addition to the usual need for tact and discretion, the study of another culture entails a suspension of belief. To explore the logic of ideas about sorcery, kinship, ritual or religion requires an empathetic identification with these ideas. Along with such empathetic silences, however, the ethics of anthropological fieldwork demand that personal identity and political commitments be made public. This ethic had been, in my own case, the basis for building up relations of trust across an all too real religious and political divide.

The Rushdie affair, in silencing me, challenged this ethic, producing a sense of extreme dissonance. The same dissonance is increasingly experienced by contemporary anthropologists studying Third World societies divided by violent ethnic or religious conflicts. The question inevitably faced in such contexts is how to fulfil a critical role, while acknowledging both the hospitality received and the historical roots of the present social malaise which almost everywhere has its origins in Western colonialist and postcolonialist policies (for works confronting this dilemma see Kapferer 1988, Dominguez 1989, Fischer and Abedi 1990, R. Werbner 1991).

Initially the experience of dissonance was so great that I determined, as I mentioned in the Introduction, never to study Muslims again. As time went by, however, my sympathy and understanding of the Muslim position grew, leading me to seek a way out of the impasse. One way, I thought, was to engage in a critical aesthetic argument *with* British Muslims about the meaning of the novel and its intention. That nobody had undertaken this project appeared to be mainly due to the fact that the majority of Western readers believed along with most Muslims that the novel was, indeed, intended as an attack on Islam, especially once its offending passages were pointed out and explained to them (on this process of 'revelation' see Parekh 1989a & b).

It has become evident, however, that the perceived futility of such a project is also grounded in current literary theory which privileges the individual reader as the ultimate arbiter of interpretation. Deconstructionist, neo-Marxist and neo-pragmatist approaches, while differing in important respects, are united in denying the possibility of universalist yardsticks of truth and hence also of texts as bearers of 'objective' meanings, just as earlier structuralist and poststructuralist approaches had rejected the relevance of authorial intention to a disclosure of 'correct' textual interpretation.

The question of whether it is possible to establish commonly agreed upon interpretive parameters is of more than passing interest to anthropology as a discipline. The current postmodernist critique has questioned the very grounds for evaluating anthropological analyses or re-analyses. It casts doubt on whether it is possible to judge some interpretations to be superior to others, or to agree on grounds for evaluation. By the same token, cross-cultural analyses, it has been argued, are merely a matter of perspective and selection, so that there are potentially an infinite number of such comparisons, each equally valid (see Strathern 1991; Rorty 1992b). Theoretically, then, we confront the possibility that we cannot, as experts, either challenge cultural interpretations or approaches, or judge between them.

The tragic dimensions of this theoretical thrust were highlighted by the Rushdie affair. Exceptionally in this instance, the establishment of textual meaning, and hence indirectly also of authorial intention, was not merely a matter of abstract theorising but, quite literally, a matter of life and death. If neo-pragmatists, postmodernists and deconstructionists were right, there was no ultimate, objective 'true' textual interpretation of the novel to be considered intersubjectively. In other words, the novelist could not be saved through an analysis of the novel, since it was theoretically unsound to assume a universalist rational discourse which might bridge the evident interpretive chasm between Muslims and secular Westerners. Instead, each group was doomed to remain locked in its own language games, based on opposed premises and rules of interpretation. There was no code hidden in the text to be uncovered which might 'explain' it, no mode of cross-cultural communication which would allow for a rational debate about the meaning of the novel.

What remained, then, was to regard the novel merely as an extraordinary political 'event'. At the same time – quite inconsistently – the opposed protagonists continued to cite passages from it selectively, in order to 'prove' their particular positions.[6] This was true even of anthropological discussions of the affair and the novel, as we have seen. Recently, in a growing critique of postmodernist approaches, some philosophers and literary theorists have begun to explore the centrality of argument or dialogue in re-establishing – in a modified form – Kantian ideas of universal truth and rationality. Habermas's work on the public sphere is central to this counter-critique (Habermas 1985, 1989 [1962]; Holub 1991), and it has been followed by others attempting to formulate theoretical positions which would allow for the possibility of constructive dialogue across interpretive communities. Hence, McIntyre (1988) argues that rational debate is necessarily conducted from *within* a specific culture or 'tradition of enquiry'. It is the moral convictions of one's own tradition of enquiry which enable one, through empathetic acts of conceptual imagination, to reach an understanding of other traditions of enquiry, and make it possible to engage in logically grounded dialogue across traditions. Against postmodernists he argues that

> the person who finds him or herself an alien to every tradition of enquiry ... because he or she brings to the encounter with some traditions standards of rational justification which the beliefs of no tradition could justify ... views the social and cultural order, the world of traditions, as a series of falsifying masquerades. (McIntyre 1988: 395)

It is, in other words, only from a condition of *non*-alienation that genuine dialogue between members of two unlike traditions can be initiated. By implication, only by arguing from the conviction of a modernist aesthetic tradition, can one both recognise the nature of religious Muslim aesthetic convictions and enter into a genuine dialogue with British Pakistanis about the meaning of *The Satanic Verses* as a text, and hence also about the intentionality of the author.

In similar vein, Christopher Norris argues against Rorty's view that 'truth is what's good in the way of belief' (Norris 1989: 113) and against the Foucaultian notion that

> 'truth' is merely a localised effect of knowledge/power, of the will-to-truth that gives certain hegemonic discourses the power to impose their perspective on other, more marginal languages. (Norris 1989: 102)

He warns further against the

> relativist trap of assuming that translation must be in some sense a radically impossible enterprise. [The relativists'] mistake is to suppose that these localised problems of linguistic

example of such a misreading see Brooke-Rose 1992).

and cultural grasp cannot in principle be sorted out by reference to the *much wider areas of agreement that must exist between all communities of language use.* (ibid.: 111, emphasis added)

In short, he concludes that

translation is a feasible project – whatever the distance of cultural horizons – because there exists this large central core of necessary presuppositions. (ibid.: 112)

The view taken is a neo-Kantian one which stresses the ultimate reliance within any language on epistemic evidence and logical rules of validation, argument and enquiry. Citing Apel, Norris goes on to endorse a transcendental pragmatics that allows for the possibility of truth across languages through self-critical reflection and dialogue, despite the fact that all truths are ultimately framed within specific languages or language-games. Such an approach, he argues,

maintains the necessity of criticising false ideas and beliefs, no matter how widely accepted these may be in some given cultural context. (ibid.: 117)

In his work on hermeneutics, Paul Ricoeur stressed that the ultimate objective of interpretive appropriation is one of self-interpretation, on the one hand, and a struggle to understand alien values, on the other (Ricoeur 1981: 158–9). Echoing this view, Umberto Eco went on to attack the anti-essentialist, postmodernist 'hermetic approach to texts'. Eco reiterates his semiotic position which, like Ricoeur's, distinguishes the 'intention' of the text (i.e. its structuralist 'explanation' in Ricoeur's terms) from its multiple readings (Eco 1992). It is by reference to this decoded intention that a 'model author' (in contrast to an empirical author) can be uncovered. Modernist works, Eco has argued (Eco 1989), are deliberately 'open', allowing for multiple readings (just as cultural forms such as rituals may be said to be open), but at the same time such texts are not infinitely malleable: they contain a hidden code which, as it is progressively uncovered, reveals the coherence of more and more symbolic elements in the text. The text thus has an objective (if ultimately polyvalent) meaning ('intention', 'explanation') which transcends its individual readers. From this it follows, he argues, that rival interpretations are subject to objective evaluation. Hence, in addition to an implicit model author, the text also posits a 'model reader', a reader who has decoded and grasped the text in its full complexity.

The 'opening up' of the text to the world implies, then, also a parallel opening up of authorial intention. A text which has a positive ethical meaning in the world renders its producer, personified by the text, a moral person, or, more precisely, a person grappling with ethical-cum-aesthetic issues. In the final analysis, then, ethics and aesthetics, author, text and the worlds opened up by the text, cannot be kept apart.

In this chapter I have tried to disclose why from a modernist perspective *The Satanic Verses* did not intend to defame Islam and mock Muslims or their Prophet. Nor is the novel, I have shown, merely an exercise in pastiche. Instead, it has to be read as a re-mythologising of myths, a secondary myth in Barthes' terms, a re-vision of a past which is also a future. That future – hybrid, uncertain, impure – is as nightmarishly monstrous and threatening for many Muslim immigrants of the older generation as were Gibreel's nightmares or Chamcha's devilish horns, tail and giant penis. For the younger generation of South Asians depicted by Rushdie, the Mishals and Zeenas of this world, that future is the lived-in world they know, to look forward to with anticipation, to enjoy. Two pasts, two futures.

Conclusion: the politics of interpretation

It may seem naive to argue that the interpretation of a novel 'matters' politically. In denying the political utility of such an interpretation, however, Western intellectuals (and, indeed, politicians) have failed to recognise the political price which *non*-interpretation exacts. Only by using modernist tools of analysis – coherence, unity, exhaustive explanation – can we arrive at an alternative interpretation of the vision of Islam intended by the novelist and the novel. In abandoning our own ethical and aesthetic canons, we have, by default, endorsed the Islamic interpretation of the novel. From that vantage point, it seems self-evident that *The Satanic Verses* abuses all that is holy to Islam – the Qur'an, the Prophet, the laws of proper moral conduct. Hence the Western defence of the novel and the novelist has been interpreted by British Pakistanis quite logically as an attack upon their virtue, dignity and honour.

No appeal to freedom of speech can disguise the fact that words, as Stanley Fish argues, are actions, which can cause real damage (Fish 1992). By preaching freedom of speech we merely exercise our superior political power to coerce and humiliate Muslim believers into a resentful silence.

However serious our disagreements over the interpretation of the novel may be, an argument *about* interpretation *shifts the terms of the debate* to ethical and aesthetic issues. This is a critical shift away from paternalistic coercion towards a politics of recognition and cultural dignity (Taylor 1992). Pakistanis in Britain, and many Muslims worldwide, responded to the novel in a politically violent manner out of a sense of deep offence, a conviction that the novel was enjoyed by Westerners because it was an attack on Islam and its values. It is therefore *politically* necessary and expedient to demonstrate that, from a Western perspective, the novel can be read quite differently – as a serious attempt to explore the possibility of a liberal, more 'open' Islam rather than a mockery of it, *The Satanic Verses* compels Westerners to engage seriously with Islam as a great, global, monotheistic contemporary religion.

6
Invoking the *Umma*

Fabulating the Gulf crisis

The Rushdie affair highlighted the way global media images are reworked as locally significant narratives. At the same time, we have also seen repeatedly that diasporas fabulate their local experiences in a global idiom. The experience and imagining of Pakistanis in the diaspora are thus mediated, above all, by internationally *shared* images. This was evident in the Pakistani response to the Gulf crisis which emerged as a global Islamic fable. Through this fable Pakistanis constructed a powerful, ideologically grounded, allegory of their predicament as an enclaved Muslim community in the West, while simultaneously asserting their membership in a global diaspora.

From the start, the Gulf crisis, in pitching Muslim brother against Muslim brother, was the stuff of tragedy. Given also the historical and contemporary political complexity of the events leading to the crisis, and the debatable moral reputations of some of the protagonists, the construction of villains and heroes in the dispute necessarily involved a process of selection and reworking of phenomenal 'facts'. Saddam Hussein, the ruler of Iraq, the Gulf state kings and princes, George Bush, the American President – all could be constructed in moral terms from different perspectives.

Of course, the television images beamed into British Pakistani homes in Manchester already constituted, for the most part, a moral fable, seen from a Western perspective. The fable cast Saddam as a vicious, tyrannical, insane villain. In Britain, support for the international alliance built up by President Bush was very high, among the highest in the Western world. Against this interpretation, Pakistanis created a counter-narrative, a 'resistive reading', an alternative fable, which cast Saddam Hussein in the role of hero. This same fabulation of the events and cast of characters was repeated by different ideological constituencies throughout the Muslim world, from Algeria to Pakistan (see Piscatori 1991). Like its Western counterpart, it was a global fable, globally fabulated.

The Muslim 'street' from Karachi to Manchester backed Saddam Hussein. As the crisis developed a global segmentary opposition between popular or radical Islam and the West emerged. In the face of this global narrativising, how are we to interpret the remaking of this narrative in each locality? If we start from an assumption that global events are necessarily filtered through local experiences, we need to ask why British Pakistanis, a small, socially vulnerable and relatively new ethnic minority, chose to cast Saddam Hussein in a hero's role *against* the overwhelming British interpretive consensus. Since the conflict pitted Muslim against Muslim, while the international alliance included many Muslim regimes, the local Pakistani minority could, theoretically, make one of several choices:

(i) it could have accepted the British media's construction of Saddam as a villain;

(ii) it could have remained neutral;

(iii) it could have recast Saddam in the role of hero through a local remythologising.

It made the third choice. Either of the first two choices would have served British Pakistanis' *local* interests and, indeed, allowed them to express solidarity with their adopted country. That they chose the third alternative necessarily raises questions about the complex nature of the relation between enclaved diasporas and their adopted countries.

In order to explain why the appropriation was, in effect, *anti*-local, we need to consider two central questions:

(i) What purpose do global current affairs, such as the Gulf crisis, serve in the revitalisation of communal self-consciousness, and what reflexive images of community did this global raw material enable local leaders to construct?

(ii) In what respect does the construction or appropriation of myths or fables of current affairs reflect a response to a common global predicament of urban Muslims everywhere, to what extent was it a feature of the spread of a new social movement, and to what extent was it a *tool* of localised agonistic action?

The problem of identity and identification is critically implied by both questions. It could be argued, for example, that a peripheral Muslim community such as that of the Manchester Pakistanis, in fabulating the tragedy of the Gulf crisis from an anti-Western perspective, was merely toeing a 'party line', created and legitimised elsewhere. But even if this was the case, in so doing, leaders were undoubtedly also seeking to assert their identification with this global Islamic movement. And, moreover, the question of *why* this particular global fabulation emerged still remains to be answered.

Many of the early commentaries about the Gulf War stressed the central role of the media and of video technology in its representation (see, for example, Mumtaz Ahmad 1992; Taylor 1992; Norris 1991; Heikal 1992, to mention but a few). Since media coverage in the age of CNN was virtually non-stop, and bombing forays were imaged as video games, both the crisis and the war assumed a surrealist, flickering, two-dimensional sense of unreality. Despite accusations of Western 'propaganda', however, Saddam Hussein's achievement in the crisis was to have his own speeches beamed on prime time to a global audience who also witnessed the carnage in Kuwait and Iraq caused by Allied bombardments and advancing Allied troops. Given the almost infinite multiplicity of images and information that the war generated, it was ultimately left to politicians and viewers to try to make sense of the unfolding drama.

A narrative construction of reality is not so much a factual distortion (since facts only gain their facticity within narratives) but a perspectival shaping of a morally meaningful 'plot' (on plot see also Becker 1979). According to Aristotle, the plot (Greek *mythos*, *fablos* in Latin) is 'the first essential, the life and soul, so to speak, of Tragedy' (Aristotle 1941: 1461). The plot consists of the action, with the characters being subordinated to it as personified moral agents (on this subordination see the discussion by Rimmon-Kenan 1983: 34–42). Action is '...what makes us ascribe certain moral qualities to the agents' (Aristotle 1941: 1460). Hence for Aristotle:

> /Tragedy is essentially an imitation not of persons but of action and life, of happiness and misery.... Characters [are included] for the sake of the action./So that it is the action in it, i.e. its Fable or Plot, that is the end and purpose of the tragedy ... the Characters come second. (ibid.: 1461)

Although 'plot' is the English translation of the Greek *mythos* and Latin *fablos*, the meanings of 'myth' and 'fable' evoke alternative modes of moral emplotment. If we regard the 'detachment' of a discourse, following Ricoeur, as an essential phase in its construction as a meaningful text (Ricoeur 1981), then the contrast becomes evident: a 'myth' is a narrative of the past which gains its transcendent significance from its detachment in time (it denotes a lost, earlier 'world'); a 'fable' is a narrative about personified creatures, usually animals, which gains its transcendent significance from its detachment in space or domain (the space of nature, the animal world). The legends of the Prophet and his life are myths of origin, shared by a contemporary Islamic global community, a mythic charter of the global 'spread' of Islam; globally significant current affairs have the potential to become fables shared in *space* by a contemporary Islamic global community as 'simultaneous consumers' in calendrical time. A global image beamed into millions of individual homes at a particular moment of the day conjures up an 'historically clocked' co-present but spatially dispersed imagined community (see Anderson 1991: 32–4). Through such images, as Anderson argues, the 'imagined world comes to be rooted in everyday life' (ibid.: 35–6). For the anonymous dispersed individuals who share a simultaneously produced set of global media images to form a 'community', however, they must also share a singular perspective or 'focalisation' on these events (see Rimmon-Kenan 1983, Chap. 6), transforming themselves thus into an interpretive community.

Contemporary fables of current affairs thus arguably revitalise the great myths of the past and root them in everyday reality, renewing individual identities of the 'consumers' of current affairs through space-time identifications. The particularities of the story told (e.g. the Gulf crisis) achieve their emblematic status through being embedded in some kind of generic tale (Bruner 1991: 7), a fairy tale of good and evil, David and Goliath, Jack and the Giant, a canonical script which through innovative breach, draws a moral lesson anew (ibid.: 11). The power of the fable is thus partly the power of individual identification with the moral hero.

A further important distinction which needs to be set in advance of my main discussion is that between narrative as fable or myth and narrative as allegory. The fable, we have seen, is a transcendent, globalised narrative. To the extent that it makes an oblique ideological critique it can also be regarded as an allegory which comments on a local set of events, values and power relations (for anthropological approaches to allegory as oblique ideological critique see Boddy 1989; Lavie 1990). In this sense the local and global are mutually constitutive. Allegories work by analogy (see G. Clifford 1974). They move from pretext to text, from the birth of Islam and the persecutions of the Prophet, to the battle of Karbala and the martyrdom of Hussein, to the Gulf crisis and the challenge to the

West, and finally, to British Muslims' battle to change the British blasphemy law and have *The Satanic Verses* banned, and the battle of black people in Britain against racial violence and discrimination. This reliance on sacred pretexts and intertextuality is a fundamental feature of allegory (see Quilligan 1979, Chap. 2).

With these distinctions in mind, it is possible now to turn to an exposition of the British Pakistani Muslim interpretation of the Gulf crisis.

Dialogics ✳

My family and I spent the academic year 1989–90 in Washington, DC. In September 1990 we returned to Manchester to find Saddam Hussein, the President of Iraq, firmly established as a public hero among Mancunian Pakistanis. The more Western politicians denounced his bestial monstrosity, the more British Pakistanis extolled his courage, his strength and the justice of his cause. 'But,' I asked, 'don't you care about the Kuwaitis?' 'Not really,' even my most moderate friends replied. 'They are Muslims. What difference does it make who their ruler is?' 'But,' I wondered, 'are you not concerned that Saddam might invade Saudi Arabia, take over Mecca Sharif and the Holy Ka'ba?' They merely shrugged their shoulders: 'He won't do it,' they said. 'And anyway,' they implied, 'even if he did, he's still a Muslim.'

Talk of violating international law and defying the UN Charter by gobbling up a member state was regarded with the utmost cynicism. What about Kashmir? And Palestine? Where has UN justice been in relation to *those* countries?

'But,' I ventured, 'he is a tyrant. There is no democracy in Iraq.' 'Yes,' they conceded, 'democracy is a good thing. There should be democracy. But tell me this,' they added, 'which is the greater evil, America or Saddam Hussein?'

Above all, these Mancunian Pakistanis stressed that the dispute was a private Muslim conflict which should be settled by the Muslim nations without outside interference. They valorised religious identity beyond the national divisions within the Arab world, regarding the latter as superficial and insignificant by comparison with the need to achieve a common front against the outside, Christian and Jewish, world.

What struck me most forcefully, however, even in these early conversations with moderate non-activists, was that once again, as in the Rushdie affair, British Pakistanis seemed to be setting themselves morally apart from British society, denying categorically what their fellow British nationals regarded as axiomatic moral imperatives. 'Our boys' were in the Gulf, risking their lives, threatened by chemical warfare, poised to fight the fourth largest army in the world, to defend the values of international law and justice against a ruthless dictator who had invaded and taken over another country.

Admittedly, there were arguments in the wider society too about the tactical advisability of going to war and the heavy costs this would entail. Many thought sanctions should be given a chance. Many doubted the sincerity of the West and saw the war as being really concerned with oil resources, not morality. There was an underlying isolationist tendency: why go to war with possible disastrous environmental consequences and terrible loss of life about a matter not 'our' direct responsibility? The strong but small British peace movement was quite vocal. Had local Pakistanis merely supported this movement (which they did passively), the English would have understood their reasoning. If they had just asserted that the conflict should be settled by Muslims internally, without outside intervention, their desire to see such a peaceful solution to the dispute would have appeared defensible.

But British Pakistanis were not simply talking of tactics, the environment or the potential loss of life. They expressed no horror at Saddam Hussein's tyranny and no sorrow or concern for 'our boys', at risk in the Gulf. Instead, they spoke of Christian soldiers desecrating the holy ground of the Hijaz, of Western aggression, of a Western medieval Crusader revival, of the need for *jihad*. Thus they placed themselves almost entirely outside the broad moral consensus which encompassed both war and peace movements.

On the face of it, British Pakistanis' political stance struck against their own most basic interests as a minority in Britain. What was surprising was their almost naive lack of awareness that this was the case. Later, after suggestions appeared in the press about British Muslims being a fifth column, mosques were daubed with graffiti, and racist attacks on Asians (irrespective of whether they were Muslims) increased, some of the more moderate local Pakistani community leaders tried to suppress the most vocal expressions of support for Saddam Hussein. Yet, at an all-Muslim conference in Bradford to which the national press were invited, participants almost unanimously voted in support of the Iraqi leader (see Ahmed 1992: 198).

Strangely, perhaps, Pakistan itself, like other Muslim countries, was a member of the international Alliance, so British Pakistanis might have been expected to support that alliance. Alternatively, they could simply have kept their heads down and remained entirely neutral. Both strategies would have suited their interests as a local ethnic-cum-religious group. Instead, those I spoke to chose to take a publicly pro-Iraqi stance. Seen from the outside, even the most liberal members of the wider society could only interpret this stance (as the media and personal acquaintances did) as further evidence of British Pakistanis' fundamental irrationality. The less charitable non-Pakistani Britishers claimed that the stance bordered on treason.

It is worth pointing out, however, that there was nothing *illegal* in the British Muslim stand on the Gulf crisis; members of the community were perfectly entitled to hold deviant political views. But these views seemed completely out of touch with the social environment in which they were articulated.

To seek the roots of this British Pakistani political dissent, I begin my account with an analysis of speeches made at a political meeting held in Manchester in October 1990 as part of the the Birthday of the Prophet's Memorial Day celebrations, *Eid milad-un-Nabi*, a meeting which took place in the shadow of the Gulf crisis. The meeting, mentioned briefly in Chapter 4, was organised by Maulana Saheb, the *maulvi* of the Central Jami'a Mosque, and Khaddam Saheb, his ally, both leaders of Faction A, the dominant faction among Manchester Pakistanis at that time.

The meeting

In the corridors of Manchester Town Hall, an ornate, pseudo-Gothic Victorian edifice, Granada Television was shooting an episode of 'Coronation Street', the

Plate 6.1 *Eid Milad-un-Nabi* procession in Manchester
on the eve of the Gulf War

local working-class soap opera. Bearded men and young boys dressed in black,
white and green who had come to attend the meeting, added to the melange of
these incongruously juxtaposed cultural worlds.

I arrived as Muslim leaders and their supporters began to gather in the City
Council Chambers for their annual *Eid milad-un-Nabi* meeting. The Maulana was
there already, a charismatic figure with his flowing black beard and piercing
eyes, smartly dressed in black, a fur hat on his head and a green shawl draping
his shoulders. We were back in the Council Chambers where the Asian Business
Seminar had been held.

Beside Maulana Saheb on the podium was an English Muslim convert, a large
red-headed man, a lecturer at the local polytechnic, his huge bulk ensconced in a
grey *shalwar-qamiz*. Also present was the Maulana's trusted ally and right-hand
man, Khaddam Saheb, the local old-timer and radical community spokesman,
neat and dapper, his sharp goatee beard an outer expression, perhaps, of its
owner's political acumen. Among the invited guest speakers was a Muslim ex-
academic from a northern city, and the proceedings were chaired by a relatively
nondescript member of the current Jami'a Management Committee, still entirely
dominated by the Maulana and his radical ally.

Around the hall were large banners in English bearing a series of religious and
political messages (see Chapter 4). The banners were held aloft by young boys.
The meeting had been convened to mark the Prophet's birthday and preceded a
procession from the city centre to the Central Manchester Jami'a Mosque. The
banners made implicit references to the Rushdie affair through their demand for

a change in the blasphemy law, while asserting that Islam was a religion of peace, and thus rejecting the image of Muslims being associated with violence which the Rushdie affair had generated in the public mind. This message was particularly significant here, of course, since, as we saw in Chapter 4, the year before, on *Eid milad-un-Nabi*, the same congregation had supported a public call for the death of the author, made in front of MPs, the Bishop of Manchester and the national media.

The Council Chambers filled slowly. The Town Hall, ornate, pompous and resplendent, struck me once again as an incongruous setting for the gatherings of pious Muslims who use it regularly for their meetings. Built by prosperous Victorian burghers, it was once a symbol of Manchester's manufacturing and commercial wealth. Currently, however, it is dominated by a left-wing Labour Council. The history of the city echoes through these incongruities, but the irony was lost on the present congregation. They used the chambers, as we have seen, in order to enhance their prestige and that of their group within the Muslim community in the city. Nevertheless, the speakers' rhetoric at the meeting was perhaps not so out of place as it seemed to be on the surface. As we shall see, they were there to challenge the established political order in Britain and the Muslim world, and in doing so they were in fact following a long tradition of radical dissent in the city.

On this occasion, groups had come from all over Britain to celebrate the procession organised by Maulana Saheb who is a key member of their Sufi order – the most prominent deputy or *khalifa*, vicegerent, of the saintly head of the order, Pir Abdul Qadr Gilani, based in Walthamstow, London.[1] Significantly as I later discovered, I was the only non-Muslim present – and the only European, apart from the Muslim convert. None of the MPs, municipal councillors and invited public notables who regularly grace such Muslim gatherings with their presence was there. Nevertheless, most of the speeches were in English, and addressed the major issues of the day.

That gap, the gaping absence of non-Pakistanis, the emptiness on the podium, the vacuum addressed in English, signified the sharp rupture which had occurred between the community and the wider society. Unlike the saint's day memorial meeting in Birmingham discussed in a previous chapter, local Muslim leaders in Manchester appeared to have overstepped a moral boundary the previous year, and this had rendered their public arena politically useless. They could no longer use ceremonial occasions as pretexts to air grievances and debate sensitive issues with state and municipal representatives. Nevertheless, the speakers acted as though those representatives were still present as they developed their narratives of dissent.

---

[1] This particular order is in large measure a British 'invention', although the *pir* of Walthamstow, who has taken on the namesake of the founder of the Qadiri order, Abdul Qadr Gilani, is a minor living saint who originates from a poor neighbourhood of Rawalpindi where a shrine to one of his ancestors is located on the main road leading to Golra Sharif. The *pir* was, at the time of writing, engaged in fund-raising among his disciples in Britain to rebuild a *Dar-ul-Uloom* near the tomb. A sign over the threshold of the building states that the cornerstone was laid by one of the *pirs* of Golra Sharif. Most of the Sufi orders in South Asia are represented in Britain. As we have seen, Birmingham is dominated by Sufi Abdullah, a Naqshbandi, professing allegiance to a living saint near Kohat, in the North West Frontier Province, who also has a *khalifa* and branch in Manchester.

Purity & dissent

The foundation texts of English working-class dissent, it has been argued, are taken as much from Bunyan's *Pilgrim's Progress* as from Paine's *The Rights of Man* (see Hobsbawm 1959: 145; Thompson 1963).

> Here is the inner landscape of the poor man's Dissent ... – Vanity Fair, the Enchanted Ground; a way 'full of snares, pits, traps and gins'. Here are Christian's aristocratic enemies – 'the Lord Carnal Delight, the Lord Luxurious, the Lord Desire of Vain Glory, my old Lord Lechery, Sir Having Greedy, with the rest of our nobility'.... The world of the spirit – of righteousness and spiritual liberty – is constantly under threat by the other world. First it is threatened by the powers of the State: when we encounter APOLLYON we seem to be in a world of [monstrous] fantasy. (Thompson 1963: 35)

One of the striking aspects of the October 1990 meeting was the speech of the English convert to Islam who spoke directly after the opening prayer and sermon by the Maulana. His language echoed with the familiar cadences of traditional English dissent, although he began with a prayer in Arabic and a general introduction about *Eid milad-un-Nabi*. From the start of his speech, the speaker stressed that Islam is a religion of *change*, i.e. of reform. He went on to explain the kind of change he had in mind:

> And this world, Islam says, must be changed to end all oppression. All men and women, Islam says, must be treated with respect and dignity. There must be no inequality, no injustice, no exploitation, no brutality, but all men and women must be brothers and sisters, part of a Muslim nation and part of a Muslim state. Islam is the belief in Allah *subhan-at'allah* but it is also a belief in a unique type of society, a unique social structure. The Prophet *sa'lat-u-wa'salaam* was sinless and perfect, he was Allah's instrument to transform mankind [the audience murmurs its approval] and change the world.

Here then was the visionary depiction of an Islamic Utopia translated into the everyday language of human rights and social equality. Now the speaker turned to a recurrent theme among Muslim public speakers – the need for Islamic revival.

> Now to win people to Islam – and it is a pity there aren't many non-Muslims here today – this is the reason we're going to go into the streets, because in the streets you'll meet lots of people who aren't Muslims, in the street, they're not in here, but they're out there. To win people to Islam it is absolutely necessary to win their hearts over to a love of Muhammad *sala 'alaihi wa-salam*. He must be seen by them as the light of the world, as the most wonderful and lovely person. Islam has become weak because Muslims have lost this direct love for the Prophet *salat wa-salem*. Instead of loving him and modelling themselves on his *sunna* (way of life), Muslims retreated, they often became no more than make-believers in a creator. The real life of mankind they left to something other than Allah *subhan-at'allah*, to something other than the *sunna* of Muhammad *sala 'alaihi wa-salam*.
>
> Life for them was dominated by money, or greed, or power, or success. They believed in a creator but they did not integrate the wisdom of the creator into their everyday lives. The way to do that, and the way to do it now, is to revive and stick to the *sunna* of the Prophet *salat wa-salem*. But they forgot or neglected that and ran after the lifestyles of other religions and other nations.

The speaker evoked the assimilative pressures of the West which threaten Muslim integrity and purity:

Now today the Muslims have largely forgotten the *sunna*. Most Muslims dress in a way that pleases the West, most Muslims eat in a way that pleases the West, most Muslims marry in a way that pleases the West, most Muslims earn their living and do their business in a way that pleases the West. They will tell you that they believe in a creator but they will not model themselves on the final and most perfect messenger from that creator. In place of the *sunna* is Westernization and the pursuit of the empty dream known as 'being up-to-date'. We're not going to follow the *sunna* of the Prophet *salat wa-salem* but we're going to be up-to-date, whatever the hell that is.

Some may think that the birth of the Prophet *salat wa-salem* should not become a vulgar commercial event like Christmas which is mainly an excuse for advertising alcohol on the television. But it must be our intention to show the Christians how properly to commemorate the person who for us is the most close and lovable friend we have.

... On *milad un Nabi*, the 12th of Rabi'ul Awwal, we must celebrate, as the best way of showing our love of the Prophet *salat wa-salem*. It should be an event of enormous spiritual significance. There should be no materialism like Christmas. A huge celebration as well, a huge celebration. If only our procession today had every Muslim in Manchester – that's the kind of celebration we want. A huge celebration would win over the unbelievers, would win over the enemies of Islam, would soften their hearts, would soften their hatred against Islam. [the audience shouts its approval with calls of 'Say he is Great, Say Allah is Great,' etc.].

... and this [Christmas nativity tale] is on the television for weeks and weeks and weeks before Christmas, and we all get sick and tired of hearing endless stories, stories, stories. You know, imagine if the details of the life of our Prophet *salat wa-salem* were as widely broadcast this time of year as is the Christmas story. Imagine what that would be like. But the message that we would bring on *milad un Nabi* would be far greater than the sentimentality of a television Christmas. The sentimentality of a Christmas television – it's silly nonsense and mostly boozing and drinking.

Alcohol, greed, materialism were set in the speaker's speech against spirituality, love, purity. Finally, he returned to his central theme: Islam's message is one of liberation.

We would be showing how the Prophet *salat wa-salem* brought real liberation to mankind. Islam is real liberation ... ending all oppression. Providing the ideal model for our family and country in his *sunna*. We would show the Prophet *salat wa-salem* as the liberator above all others, as the friend of the poor and downtrodden everywhere. *Milad un Nabi* would also be the beginning of economic and political campaigning to rid the world of racism. *Milad un Nabi* should be a celebration against racism. To rid the world of class oppression. To rid the world of exploitation, to rid the world of maltreatment of women, and all the other evils that the Prophet ... set out to end.

We see here the fusing of global discourses of liberation, anti-racism and even feminism with a discourse of Muslim religious love for the Prophet, much as early Methodism fused love and dissent, according to Thompson. Moreover, just as English radical movements had their demons and demonology (Thompson 1963: 832), so too Islamic radicalism has its Satans, of which America and the West are perceived as the external sources of corruption and evil (Beeman 1983). On the whole, however, despite mild references to the triviality of English television (all silly stories, drinking and boozing), the first speaker drew his inspiration more from Paine than Bunyan. The demonology of the West and the media was a far darker theme in the speeches that followed.

Western demons & the media

Like the first speaker, Professor Q., the visiting scholar, adopted the rhetoric and style of a lay preacher. He was a verbose man whose speeches usually lasted at least an hour, often a lot longer, as he threaded his way from theme to theme, reaching periodic crescendos before launching once more, usually by association, into a new subject.

His brief was to comment on the Gulf crisis. He started by stressing the immutability and centrality of the Islamic identity – 'Islam is not like a scarf on the head; it is like the colour of the blood running through all the parts of the body' – the supremacy of the Prophet, and the importance of parading one's Islamic identity publicly.

Finally he turned to his main subject matter. He began by discussing the distortions perpetrated on the public by the media:

> Now I go over to the subject assigned [to me]: the Gulf crisis. Every time you turn the television on, it may be nine o'clock, it may be one o'clock in the middle of the day, it may be six o'clock, it may be ten o'clock, it may be Newsnight, seven o'clock on a Saturday, the World News programme [these are all times and titles of regular news programmes on British television], or anything, the Gulf crisis is on the agenda. It is on the menu. I am very sad and very displeased and angry that the sole information British television is providing us with is most poisonous, most biased and most prejudiced information. It is something which they cook up and then they present it to the people; and because we are television, newspaper, radio [addicts], they have become part of our life, our style, when we have nothing else to do we make a cup of tea, sit down and turn the box on, and we keep on accepting whatever comes from it as if this is something which is authentic – it is not. It is a method of passing on ready-made information. We go to Marks and Spencer, buy clothes and put them on – we get ideas from television, we look upon [watch] them and then we accept them. [But these opinions and images are] ... not true.

The speaker stressed a recurrent theme: the media present distorted images of the Islamic world, lies and propaganda, concocted for a Western audience. This complete lack of trust in the veracity and independence of the media means that even the most public 'facts', such as the plight of the Kurdish refugees, are taken by Pakistanis to represent something other than their obvious meaning for a Western audience. The fundamental rejection of Western news coverage goes along with alternative interpretations of the same events, mobilising a different set of facts. The speaker now promises to provide an independent and objective explanation of the present crisis:

> So what I'm going to do is to take you along, briefly, through the ideas [about the Gulf crisis], so that our young Muslims in particular, and our Muslim brothers whose mother-tongue is English, they and other people may be able to join me and see what the true Muslim perspective is. What is it? [i.e. what is the Gulf crisis?] Why is it? Who created it? How will it end?
>
> As a Muslim, Mr Chairman, I believe that the whole thing will be resolved by Allah Almighty. The superpowers may do anything [they like], but at the end of the day things in the past have always happened and Allah *subhan allah* ultimately has pulled the strings, and things have happened ... they are surprised and their mouths are half shut or even fully open [in astonishment]. They are surprised, amazed, God, how did this happen [that Muslims emerged victorious]? God is God [here the speaker repeats a verse in Arabic]. 'God has the sovereignty, the suzerainty and the absolute power to control things at any time he likes.' After all, He is the creator, He is – in *Sura el hasham* you find how many

beautiful names there are, ninety-nine names of Allah *subhan allah.*

So God is God, man proposes, God disposes, and in this case I think Bush proposes and God disposes [of him]. These people [Bush and the Western powers] are in for a big shock, those who are thinking that they will control the destiny of the Gulf. They look upon the [crisis] as an Arab question, an oil question, a Middle Eastern question – I say to them: No! This is a Muslim question. This is a question of the followers of Allah *subhan allah* all the world over, and the followers of the *sunna,* and it will be *Ahl-e-Sunnat wa-jama'at* [the followers of the Sunna, a reference to members of the Barelvi movement which includes the present congregation] who are the greatest overwhelming majority of the [Islamic] world population who ultimately will be expressing their will.

In this part of his speech, the speaker expressed an almost millennial faith that God will protect His followers from diabolical conspiracies. Implicit in this expressed optimism was, however, a real fear that the West was too powerful, and that only God could help the Muslim world to overcome its Satanic opponents. The speaker himself may not have spoken from a sense of *personal* failure.[2] Similarly, Mancunian Pakistanis as a community have, on the whole, prospered. But relative economic success has not brought with it political power and here lies a deep source of frustration. By reflecting on global events, the speaker displaced this local sense of political powerlessness on to an international arena.

Global injustice

Next the speaker went on to condemn the sham and hypocrisy of Western claims to be protecting 'international law'. Like others at the meeting, he evoked the problems of Kashmir and Palestine. But he also denounced the whole international system, the very structure of the United Nations, which he regarded as biased, and based on unjustifiable inequality.

What do we hear? Usually we hear – it is a question of international law. It may be Margaret Thatcher, it may be the United Nations, it may be Bush – they say, because Saddam Hussein has committed an aggression, he has gone into Kuwait, therefore it is a question of international law. The United Nations was created so that small nations should be protected, and big nations and small nations should all have justice according to international law – this is what they say. Saddam should go back, should pull out of Kuwait and everything will be fine. I am a graduate of law, I am a law graduate myself, although I have always taught English literature because I have two degrees, but in law there was always the danger of telling lies in the courts and in literature I could speak my mind honestly, so I chose to use this degree, but still, the knowledge about law which *subhan allah* has given me is with me. International law is for all people, for all nations – or is it only for bigger people to enforce international law?

Now, the United Nations, the United Nations is a very respectable word these days. How does it work? There are five members. If they say no to anything the whole thing falls. Where is your equality? Where is your equality before the law? USA, USSR, Britain, France and China – these five nations have the power of veto; if anything comes on the table and one of these five says, 'No, I am not satisfied with this thing', the whole thing is to be thrown into the dustbin.

This international law that you talk about, this United Nations that you talk about, is just like an angel which is beating its golden wings but is producing nothing. Where was

---

[2] In fact, I was told that he had suffered tragic personal loss and had not achieved a status commensurate with his education.

the United Nations in Kashmir, when, in 1948, we were stopped by India from following the will of the people there? From 1948 until today we have been going to the United Nations. What do we get? Pieces of paper. Have these forces of America and France and Britain and all the world over – the multinationals and the French and the Germans – did they go to Kashmir to enforce those resolutions? They never did – you know it, I know it, the world knows it, that Kashmir – when India advanced in Kashmir – India was what Iraq is today and Kashmir was what Kuwait is today, and what happened? Nothing happened. This is a mockery of international law.

You come and tell us that we must try to respect the law. We respect God's law, we respect the law of the land where we go [migrate to], we respect the law of the land where we are born, we are law-respecting people. You preach, you teach, you do not practise. These Bushes, the sooner they are burnt, the better; these Thatchers, the sooner the thatched roof goes, the better it will be, change will come. You can fool people for a short time but you cannot fool them all the time.

Now Kashmir is a question, right? Now Palestine. The Palestinian question. And I think I am happy that Saddam Hussein, Saddam Hussein [is] a very good Muslim [and] a brave man, he at least told them. What did the United Nations do when Israel occupied the West Bank and became an aggressor? So Israel is what Iraq is today and the West Bank and Gaza what Kuwait is today – what did you do then? In 1949 Israel came into being. Pakistan came into being in 1947, Israel came into being in 1949, and ever since then into all the chests of the Muslim world, the West has planted a little carbuncle, a poisoned arrow, Israel – they have put it there and are giving it all the arms and support of international law. Yes, if Israel does something, it is justified, if Iraq does something, it is unjustified. What is this double standard? How do you dare talk about international law? I tell you – international law is only a little juggler's trick, it is only a magician's trick, just as on television a magician says: 'Well, look here, this is a paper, I will change this into a pigeon in a minute.' This sort of jugglery is absolutely rubbish and I was impressed when our brother [the Chairman] said – 'Kashmir, Palestine, Afghanistan – that is a different story'. When a superpower is involved things are – not only here, in many small pockets throughout the Muslim world where Muslims are trying to raise their heads and seek equality they say – international law, international law is ...

Here the speaker was interrupted as the congregation rose to welcome an incoming, well-respected Holy Man. As at other points during the speeches, the men shouted out the familiar refrains: *Nara-i-Takbir* (Say! He is Great!); *Nara-i-Risalat* (Say! Prophethood!); *Islam Zindabad* (Islam! Live Forever!),' etc. As they shouted they repeatedly raised their arms in fist salutes, in a show of collective power.

In speaking of Palestine, Kashmir and Afghanistan, the speaker expressed the direct identification of the present congregation with Muslims in different parts of the world. Islam is a universal, transnational ideology, and Muslims are concerned with the affairs of Muslims living beyond the narrow limits of their immediate community. What the Gulf crisis had underlined, according to this speaker, was global injustice. And the reason for this was not hard to seek – sheer economic greed. Thus the speaker continued:

The real question is not international law – the real question is oil, it is economic considerations, it is the access they want in order to ensure that their own interests are protected – the West wants to protect its own interests.

But worse still, American greed is matched by the greed of the leaders of the Gulf states. These autocratic corrupt Muslim regimes created by colonialism had allegedly made a pact with the American President.

Right – so the point that I have made – that the international law plea is a hoax, it is a mockery, it is a trick, so I reject it. And I have now gone on to the second point – why America? The American economy is itself in the doldrums and it is in the dustbin. Bush does not care for his own country but he has all the sympathy for the Saudi Arabian kings who are corrupt and useless anyway – we do not care how things happen. We believe in Allah, we are God-conscious people, we are Prophet Muhammad *sala 'alaihi wa-salam* conscious people, we are not Emir-conscious people. The Prophet never became a king. How can you become a king? You are planted there by the West to save their own interests. The oil companies which are in Saudi Arabia or in the Middle East, they have shares, there are people from America, from Britain, from France, from other places who are working there.

The external, corrupting evil influence (Beeman 1983) had made a deal with the internally corrupt. The West, however, had failed and was crumbling from within (see also Voll 1987):

So what I am saying to you today is that international law is [only] a word in the mouth, it does not stand anywhere. The real cause of their going there is because of the corrupt, indecent, immoral, hollow kings – these kings today are just like crowns on the head and inside there is nothing – you touch them and they fall to the ground because they have no character. Ordinary Muslims in the world have great character. I have hope in the ordinary people of the Muslim world but I have no hope whatsoever in any Emirs or any sheikhs or any kings – whatever name they may take.

Here the configuration of the new populist Islamic radicalism takes shape. The 'ordinary people' are extolled. They form a world-wide community. The corrupt, spineless regimes of the oil-rich Gulf states are merely Western creations; Islam accords them no legitimacy. Was the Prophet a king? And if he, the most supreme of all human beings, was not a king, is anyone else entitled to claim kingship? The target of all the speeches is a single target: inequality. Inequality *between* nations and inequality *within* nations. Oddly enough, however, this advocacy of equality goes along with membership in a movement which recognises an essential inequality: just as the Prophet was the most supreme of all prophets, so too among the living and dead there are saints (*awliya*) who are intrinsically superior to run-of-the-mill, 'ordinary' human beings. (Thus for Sufi followers, saintly authority substitutes for scriptural authority, see Gellner 1992.)

To understand this apparent contradiction we need to recognise that at stake is not merely Paine's liberalism and the radicalism of the Enlightenment, but an Islamic version of Bunyan's internal quest for purification as well. Kings are intrinsically inferior to pure men of God. Hence God's message of equality is the supreme message and its carriers, saints and holy men, are superior to any Emir or Sheikh, however powerful and wealthy the latter may be. The places of these holy men, the shrines where they are buried, are for the congregation gathered at the meeting – all followers of Muslim saints – places of supreme sanctity. Like the first speaker, this sanctity is combined with a modernist perspective. There is no room for autocratic kings and rulers in this vision. Hence the speaker continued:

And these American armies are not in there to protect the holy shrines... uneasy lies the head that wears the crown, you know. The British queen is a very wise lady, she does not interfere with the government here and fits into the picture, and she will carry on well, but those kings and those dictators and those people who are the crown-holders, they are uneasy anyway but they have to protect, call their supporters, their police, those who have planted them [i.e. the Americans and the British], but now they ... realise – Muslim civilisation, Muslim lifestyle, Muslim economic ideas, rejecting interest [usury], the Muslim contribution to medicine, the Muslim view of life, is challenging the Western view of life. The West believes in enlightened self-interest – working your way in an enlightened way. They believe in interest, protecting your own interest. We believe in selfless devotion to God, we believe in loving....

Islamic Utopias & myths of heroes

Why did Saddam Hussein, himself a corrupt, ruthless dictator, escape the infamy of the Gulf state rulers? Is not Iraq also a Western creation? Partly, the opposition to the Gulf state rulers is a sectarian opposition to the Wahabi movement. But the main reason Saddam was praised was because he dared to challenge the West directly, and to question the old colonial divisions forced upon the Arab world. This was evident in the replay of the crisis in 1998. For the battle was not perceived to be only a battle about power, oil and money; it was, above all, a cultural confrontation – a battle for cultural supremacy; almost, even, a battle between the idols of Western materialism and the Muslim all-powerful God. It was a battle for the 'control of historicity' (Touraine 1991: 16). Touraine argues that a social movement

> produces an ideology, i.e. a representation of its social relations; it also produces a Utopia, by means of which it becomes identified with the states of the struggle and with historicity itself. (ibid.: 98)

Transcendent values and local adversaries are juxtaposed.

Thus, the speaker moves from the international scene to the local, British scene:

> Now Western culture feels threatened. Look here, these Muslims in Britain, we thought they would slowly dissolve into British society just as sugar mixes with milk, and then they would all be gone. But look at them – they talk like Muslims, they look like Muslims, they behave like Muslims, they respect their parents, they respect their family, they work for longer hours, they are not behaving [like others]; they don't taste alcohol, they do not go gambling, they do not go....

Once again we come back to familiar non-conformist, puritanical values: respect for authority, family norms, hard work, abstinence, frugality.

> So they find that these Muslims are a strange sort of people – that we [i.e. the English] had been thinking that they would all be mixed up [assimilated]. We [Muslims] will not disrespect our faith, our culture.
>
> I work alongside English people. I respect them. But I do not allow them to interfere in those areas which are the areas defined by the Qur'an and by the *sunna* of the Prophet Muhammad *sala 'alaihi wa-salam*. My daughters, my sons, my wife, my family, my neighbours, my town, all these people I regulate with the light which comes to me from studying the life of Muhammad *Rasul Allah*.

The battle is first a media battle:

> So the real crux of the Gulf situation is that there is a cultural conflict between the West and the Muslim world today. They think through their media. The media are playing a tremendous role. But I think, Mr Chairman, that Saddam met them on their own ground through Sky Television – he started broadcasting information which was picked up by Amman, Amman telecast it to London, London telecast it to America, so whenever anything happens – he says I am going to release this, I am going to do that, we hear him say it.

But Muslims have the right to have their culture recognised and respected:

> The processing [domination] of people of the Muslim world will go on and this we are not going to accept. They [claim that] all the cultures in England are equal, all the religions are equal, all the – now we will have to say Europe in 1992 – all the languages are equal. But this is not true. We live in a multicultural society [hence] British culture cannot be accepted as superior to Muslim culture. All cultures are equal. We have every right, and in the Gulf situation the whole world is watching how all these idols, these images of the cultures of the West are cracking. These *lat* and *manat* and *hubel* [pre-Islamic female idols worshipped in Mecca which are mentioned in *The Satanic Verses*] of the West, the United Nations is coming up. They were thinking that by dividing up the Muslim nations into small states, Muslims would fight with Muslims, Iran and Iraq – oh, they have experimented with all that, but how God changes things! I wonder [how] the nation-state is gradually now exposing itself – Islam – they talk about international law – Islam is a universal frame.... This universe is a Muslim universe – God has said that Islam is a universal religion – you cannot cut Muslims into small pieces – we are not a cake on the table of the West, that you may make small slices and give them to people.
>
> But in the end I would like to say that it is most unfair that in the name of international law you should stop food, you should stop medicine [for the Iraqi people], you should try to class people as – I am against the Saudi rulers and all the rulers who are planted, who do not believe.

Historicity and culture are now global landscapes, as are the political and ideo-logical landscapes which shape them (see Appadurai 1990):

> ...We look towards the Ka'ba and *Masjid el nabwi* [the mosque where the Prophet is buried in Medina], Mecca *muazma* (the great) and Madinah *munarwa* (the light) with respect, the people who rule over those parts should not look towards Washington and New York with the same sort of loyalty. Loyalty ultimately belongs to God, and I say that there should be justice, there should be equality, there should be understanding, there should be humanity, and the Gulf crisis will undergo changes, God always keeps on making changes, we have also to change ourselves. [Here the speaker quotes a verse from the Qur'an and translates it into English:] 'God does not change any nation or people unless that nation changes itself.'

This powerful speech showed once again how closely British Muslims identify their particular cause – the promotion of Islam in Britain in order to preserve an Islamic identity for future generations – with the global cause of Muslims. Similarly, the fight against religious legal discrimination in Britain was seen as an extension of a broader, international fight against Western domination. To over-come this domination and internal decadence the community must first change itself, a central tenet of Islamic modernists (see Ahmad 1967: 262).

This is not a straightforward fundamentalist view: on the contrary, it expresses an approach which stresses a potentially *changing* rather than immutable, divinely predetermined, world. In the fight against Western domination, the national divisions within the Arab world are regarded as a major weakness exploited by the West. The divisions are artificial, colonial inventions; the rulers of these Arab nations are mere colonial puppets. By implication, the solution would be to create a new, unified Islamic empire which would be powerful enough to meet the West on its own ground. At the time of the meeting, in October 1990, British Paki-stanis were still hoping that Saddam Hussein was the man to achieve this strength and unity, with his powerful army and intransigent stance against the West.

There are obvious parallels to be drawn here with the Khilafat movement in India, which mobilised to defend the 'universal' Caliph of the dying Ottoman

Empire in millennial spirit, almost entirely misreading both the secularism of Ataturk and the complicity of the Khalifa with British colonial hegemony (Alavi 1997). The movement, however misconceived, nevertheless points to the fact that South Asian Muslims have long fostered a diasporic consciousness tinged with religious millennialism, even before their postwar migration to Britain.

'Why are we such dead people?'

The final speaker at the meeting, Khaddam Saheb, a veteran of many radical meetings, was asked to speak specifically on British issues affecting the Muslim community. He could not, however, resist commenting on the Gulf crisis as well. Like the previous speaker, he spoke in English:

> Allahbad, fellow Muslims, *buzurgan* (respected elders, holy men), *bhaion aur beton* (brothers and sons). Today the world of Islam is going through a deep crisis. So is the Muslim community in this country. We are going through a deep crisis because the world of Islam is divided. We see time and again on the television Muslim leaders coming to the microphone, and to please the West they start by saying, 'Although we condemn Saddam Hussein', they start with the sentence but they go on, 'We also condemn the double standards adopted by the West'. I say to you here today – I do not condemn Saddam Hussein! I regret the timing and the method used at this moment to unite Kuwait with its own real territory of Iraq, but I congratulate him [Saddam Hussein] for putting some of the important issues that the Muslim world faces today on the agenda of international debate. I have got today's paper [in front of me] and I will read you two lines from it. It says: 'Anyone with a sense of sympathy, a sense of humanity, must sympathise with the Palestinians. Their lands are occupied, they have no political rights and they are daily the victims of a misguided policy which believes that the security of Israel must rest on the closure of schools, illegal settlement and even collective punishment.'
>
> These are not the words of Palestinian leaders. These are not the words of those Muslim leaders who are condemning Saddam Hussein. These are the words of Douglas Hurd, the Foreign Secretary of this country. He did not utter these words for 21 years, for 22 years, for 23 years of the occupation of Palestine. He has uttered these words to justify the Western action in the occupied lands of *Hijaz* and *Najr*. Today Kuwait is not occupied. Kuwait is in the hands of Muslims and Arabs. Maybe the rulers may be disputed. But the occupied lands are the lands of Palestine. The lands of Kashmir. And the lands of Hijaz and Najr which are today called by the name of its family, Saudi Arabia.
>
> There is only one country in this world – there is only one country in this world which is known by the name of a family. We do not call this country 'Winston's Britain', or 'Queen's Britain'. We do not call America 'Bush's America'. But today the lands of Hijaz and Najr (i.e. the Arabic Peninsula) are known by the name of a family which was put there, which was imposed on those people about 70 years ago by the Western imperialists.
>
> So I congratulate Saddam Hussein for taking the action he has taken. Probably the timing is not right, but it has definitely brought the attention of the rest of the world to an important issue, the important issue that faces the Muslim world. Now we say that the world is divided. The Islamic world is divided. It is divided only in one respect. The Muslims of the world today are not divided. They are with the action taken by Iraq. They are with the people of Palestine, they are with the people of Kashmir. It is the ruling families, a small handful of people, maybe a hundred, maybe two hundred, whose own security depends on the Western imperialism, whose own security depends on the Bushes and the Thatchers today. They are the people who are on one side and the Islamic world is on the other side.

Only action, protest and resistance can sway Western regimes and compel them to recognise the value of Islam. And the bearers of the banners of protest are 'ordinary' Muslims, including the Muslims of Britain; they are the true Muslims, pitched against their false leaders. The speaker attacked attempts by the press to describe the internal divisions among British Muslims:

> Therefore, today I have been given the topic to talk about the Muslims in this country. I don't know if any of you have this morning read the article in *The Observer*. Julie Flint has written about British Muslims and the crisis through which they are going. And she has defined at the present moment the loyalties of the Muslims, those with Saudi Arabia, and those with the West. And she has described the Muslim world of this country, the Muslim world of Britain, as divided among Wahabis and Barelvis. I say to you 'No!' 'Barelvis' is not the right word to use. Because Hazrat Imam (the founder of the Barelvi movement in India) was a Barelvi only two hundred, a hundred years ago, highlighting a special philosophy which has existed since the day [of the Prophet]. We are *ahl-e-sunnat wa-jama'at* – [people of] the true faith of Islam. And these Wahabis, Deobandis as well [fundamentalist and reformist Muslims], they are distractions, they are descriptions of small sects who have migrated, who have moved away from the real thing. So when we describe ourselves, describe yourself not as 'Barelvi' but as 'the true Muslim'.
>
> British Muslims are facing a crisis – a crisis because British Islam to some extent is dependent on the money which is coming from foreign countries [i.e. Iran and Arab oil-rich countries], to build the mosques here, to pay the wages, to pay the salaries of some of the *imams* [clerics] who occupy the *mimbars* [pulpits].
>
> I don't know whether you know this but about a few weeks ago, a conference was called – 120 *imams* of mosques from the United Kingdom were called to Mecca and they were told to toe the Saudi line or their wages would be stopped, their salaries would be stopped, and they came back here and started preaching the Saudi line. (Here the speaker refers to an actual event reported in the press.)
>
> And that is where the division has come within our community. I sincerely hope and sincerely believe that those *imams*, who are occupying the *mimbars* will have enough faith in Allah and his Prophet, not to depend on the Saudi money for their salaries and their wages, and that they will be prepared to tell the truth to the people as to what is happening today in the occupied Hijaz and the occupied Najr.

The speaker called on these *imams* to resist Saudi political pressure and attacked the collaboration between a religious establishment and the quietist tendencies of certain religious streams. At this point Khaddam Saheb, like those before him, went on to attack the media. More clearly than the others, however, he expressed a widely held view of a conspiracy:

> As regards the problems that are facing the Muslim community in this country, we are a growing community and we are continuously being misrepresented in the British media. We are being misrepresented in the British media because, Number One, the effects of the Crusades, although hundreds of years ago, are still persisting in the Christian psyche. [This theme has emerged since the Rushdie affair.] We are misrepresented because, by and large, the media in this country are being controlled by Jewish and 'Zionist' forces. Therefore we will not get a fair hearing. That is why we need meetings of this nature up and down the country to be able to present the true Muslim perspective on the issues that are facing us.

Revealed here are some of the fundamental elements characterising social movements: the raising of consciousness; the struggle for autonomy, for the control of a cultural field; a grass-roots oppositional politics; the stress on identity; the imagining, in Castell's words, of 'reactive Utopias' (see Castells 1983). A genuine movement has to transcend a sense of localism and a narrow concern with a single

issue (see Hannigan 1985: 449). The speeches reported here reveal this transcendence as well as the application of the wider allegory to local predicaments.

While social movements transform a local sense of injustice into 'a wider ideological critique', to be effective they must also transform this critique 'into a programme for action' (Hannigan 1985: 442). As we saw in Chapters 1 and 2,
effective mobilisation hinges on the creation of broader alliances and requires
internal fund-raising (see Werbner and Anwar 1991). The political reputations of
the speaker and his factional allies, and their image as cunning wheeler-dealers,
make such mobilisation impossible. The troubled finances of the mosque continue
to rankle and raise questions. Not surprisingly, Khaddam Saheb, above all an
activist, evoked his own personal, as well as collective, frustration and sense of
impotence: if for others rhetorical identification sufficed, for him words without
action were hollow. What was lacking, he lamented, was proper *political
organisation and mobilisation*. Judging from his behaviour in committees, he was a
man who believes in practical, tangible achievements. Yet because he lacked
local kudos and trust, his personal power to fund-raise or mobilise support
beyond his narrow constituency was highly limited. So he expressed his sense of
frustration with the basic political passivity of Muslims in Britain:

> But we also need something more. There are only just a quarter of a million Jewish people
> living here. But whenever a minister, a foreign secretary or a prime minister makes a
> speech about the issues of the Middle East or about the issues of Israel, he looks back to the
> Jewish community. We are one-and-a-half million Muslims in Britain today. [Official
> estimates report just under one million British Muslims.] Perhaps more, but, when they [the
> politicians] issue statements about the Middle East, about Israel, they do not look at the
> Muslim lobby. Because it does not exist. It is the duty of the leadership of the Muslim
> community to create that lobby, to create that influence, and it is today, this year and last
> year, that has seen the Islamic, British Muslims going through a crisis. [He is referring to
> the Rushdie affair.] I hope that the positive side of it will be the creation of a strong, a
> powerful Muslim influence in the affairs of this country. *Inshallah*, within ten years we
> should have fifty members of parliament, hundreds of councillors up and down the country
> sitting in the town halls.
>
> What we need is for the people of my generation to give way to the younger generation
> which is coming up, to take the torch of leadership from our hands, and to go forward as
> the leaders of future British Muslims, Islam. We are the past. Let the younger generation
> take over and take it [carry the torch] forward so that the voice of Muslims here is truly
> representative of the British Muslims who were born or grew up here in this country.

Once again, continuity, the reproduction of culture, and its revitalisation from
one generation to the next emerge as major concerns. The speaker then went on
to list some of the problems and achievements of the local British Muslim community. First was the problem of immigration laws which divided families and
prevented the community from recruiting overseas Muslim clerics for the growing
number of mosques. Once again he called despairingly for more activism.

> We have got to mobilise opinion so that the Muslims look at the Immigration Act in a
> different light. It threatens our religious life in this country. We need to mobilise, we need
> to march up and down Downing Street demanding that these rules [laws and regulations]
> be changed.

He went on to complain that in the field of education there was 'total discrimination, and open discrimination.' While Church of England, Catholic and Jewish
schools had all been granted state-aided status, Muslims were denied this right,

'some phony reason is found by the Minister of Education to deny state-aided status to Muslim schools'.[3] Once again the call was for self-help and activism:

> But we cannot depend on Muslim or state charity. We have within the Muslim community, especially in Manchester, people who have been, with the grace of God, given a lot of wealth. We will not take this wealth to our graves with us – what God has given us must be spent for the benefit of Muslims here. So I'm asking, and I'm appealing, to the rich people – and not all rich people are alike – that Manchester needs Muslim schools, and there are people rich enough to be able to contribute so that we can run that school for a year, for two, for three till we are able to force the British Government to provide state-aided status for that school. So from this meeting today a call should go [forth] that within a year or two we should have a Muslim school for girls. In the first place, a Muslim school for girls, a primary school perhaps, then a secondary school for girls, established for two years. Let us put [make] September 1992 our target [date].[4]

Despite this clarion call, however, this leader – like Maulana Saheb himself – had been involved in too many past fund-raising fiascos to have much hope of mobilising the substantial funding from members of the community needed for such a major enterprise. His primary skills lay in his ability to manipulate statutory bodies, and he liked to take credit for Council grants to the community. Thus, in his next statement, he announced the good news that the City Council had allocated half a million pounds to build 16 apartments for young Muslim couples. He argued that young Muslims who have grown up in Britain needed to live outside the extended family, and said that at present community representatives ('we') were looking for land on which to build the apartments. A grant for five-bedroom houses for large Muslim families had also been negotiated. The speaker told the audience that the names for the two schemes had

> *Inshallah* ... been given. One has been given the name of 'Fatima Jinnah Gardens' for the extensions, which will have gardens along with the extended family homes, and the second will be called 'Jinnah House'. This will be for the young generation, sixteen flats for the young generation.

In this choice of a name we get a sudden flash of insight into the indexical dimensions of the occasion. The meeting, which seemed to be addressing global issues, was in reality representative of only a fraction of the local Muslim community. The group organising the event had accumulated over the years a wide array of enemies and opponents. None of these were represented at the meeting.

The most tangible fiasco for which this faction could be said to have been responsible was the loss of a major building designated as a community centre which was bought by the previous mosque committee. That building, which was lost by default, was to be named 'Jinnah House' and members of the community had donated £50,000 towards a down payment for its purchase (on this case see Werbner 1991d). Now Khaddam Saheb suggested that a council scheme, *funded by the Council*, which he claimed to have negotiated, should be given that name. The implicit message was that this new building would replace the one that had been lost. Yet the very fact that the new scheme was to stand or fall on

---

[3] In January 1998, eight years after this meeting, the first Muslim school in Britain was awarded grant-maintained status, after a concerted campaign of lobbying. There were never any demonstrations on this issue.

[4] In fact, a very successful *private*, fee-paying primary and secondary school for Muslim girls was subsequently established in Manchester, although not through the efforts of this speaker.

municipal grants reflected the limits of Khaddam Saheb's leadership within the community.

The sense of impotence is displaced in his calls for activism:

We are a million Muslims. We are not able to get 5,000 people to go to Downing Street to be able to protest about this basic inhuman injustice! Mrs Thatcher was there, at the United Nations' Conference for Children. There are a number of Muslim children, British-born, British children, whose fathers are not able to join them because of the immigration rules, [and others] whose fathers are being deported, day and night, because of immigration rules. Why are we such dead people who are not able to stand up for our rights and be able to fight? I don't say break windows, but fight, fight for your rights by joining the political process in this country, by joining the demonstrations which are taking place, and by organising demonstrations up and down the country to ask for your rights, because even when a child doesn't cry, the mother [who] doesn't give the milk [fails]. We are an Asian society and to preserve our rights, to preserve our identity, to preserve our integrity we need to fight, and fight hard. So be prepared from now on to lead that fight. Manchester started it, twelve years ago – the first procession in this country took place in Manchester twelve years ago to celebrate the birthday of the Prophet Muhammad. [In fact, processions prior to the one referred to had been held in Birmingham.] And I say now that on other issues Manchester should give the lead.... The Celebration is not just to describe *Eid milad-un-Nabi* but it is also about fighting for the rights of our people.

We get a hint in this speech of the reason why British Pakistanis fabulated Saddam Hussein, despite his record of tyranny and aggression, as a potential hero and saviour rather than a villain. The answer lies in the subordination of character to action in tragic fables. As a culturally enclaved minority in the West, British Pakistanis are having to come to terms with a loss of autonomy and cultural self-control which the experience of permanent settlement in Britain has generated. Hence settlement is associated with a growing fear of an impending 'structural paralysis' (Gearing 1970), a lack of communal autonomy. The threat of this paralytic malaise is a nightmarish potentiality for the speakers at the meeting, a hidden, buried intelligentsia of local preachers and lay activists. The implicit danger of their impotence to overcome such a threat exceeded even the reality of everyday racism.

A magical Islamic radicalism

'Why are we such dead people?' We hear in these words the heartfelt call of the layman, the political activist, who evokes in his populist rhetoric concrete images laced with calls for action. I turn now, therefore, to these forgotten preachers of Islam,[5] the local civic dignitaries and men of honour like Khaddam Saheb, Chaudhry Amin or Seth Saheb who are honoured to deliver a sermon and speak at public ceremonials by virtue of their work or *khidmat* for the community.

[5] 'Forgotten', that is, by the scholarly Islamic studies literature on mosques, saints and clerics. There has been, however, a good deal of discussion of 'lay' leaders of established Islamist movements such as, for example, the *Jama'at-i Islami* (Maududi, the leader of this early 'fundamentalist' movement, was himself a journalist, see Binder 1961; so too was 'Ali Shari'ati, see Abrahamian 1988), as well as more recent organisations and 'new' religious intellectuals in Egypt and elsewhere (see Kepel 1985; Eickelman and Piscatori 1996: 13; Lindholm 1997: 206–9), and of the preaching activities of laymen of the Tablighi Jama'at (Kepel 1994; Eickelman and Piscatori 1996: 156; Metcalf 1996). My stress here is on the role of *civic* leaders who are only part-time religious activists at best.

The meeting in Manchester was organised by Maulana Saheb, the *maulvi* of the Central Mosque, who was also the most important deputy (*khalifa*) of a British-based Sufi Qadiri order. The majority of those attending were members or supporters of the order. All were also potential supporters of the Barelvi movement. In Manchester, it was some of the Barelvi followers focused around the Maulana who were the most radicalised. In their processions on the Prophet's birthday members of the order asserted the legitimacy of the movement in general, while attesting also to the ascendancy of their particular Sufi regional cult in the city. The radical rhetoric represented an attempt to mobilise support for this group by evoking powerfully emotive images of a beleaguered Muslim world and asserting the determination of its leaders to confront this external persecution fearlessly and directly. The fact that this 'courageous' stand involved no personal cost for the speakers themselves was, of course, glossed over. Unlike the councillors who spoke in Birmingham, none of the religious or lay leaders at this meeting were active in mainstream politics where the votes of the majority group or other ethnic minorities could determine their electoral success. The political battle for power in which they were involved was a purely internal one, within the Pakistani community.

Their radicalism could also be explained in terms of felt threats to sectarian beliefs (see Modood 1990; Ahmed 1991b). In the Rushdie affair they were enraged by the attack on the Prophet Muhammad, who is the subject of supreme adoration for Barelvis as for all Sufis. In the Gulf crisis, support for Saddam Hussein stemmed from their continuous opposition to the Wahabi movement and its Saudi rulers, regarded as the desecrators of saints' shrines throughout Arabia, including that of the Prophet himself (see Ahmad 1992).

Nevertheless, this political radicalisation of saintly followers remains surprising because Sufi saints and their cults have been regarded as politically dead for some time by Middle East scholars. Their very existence as a contemporary political force is denied. In the case of the Maghreb, for example, it has been argued that, while the early fight against the colonial invasion was conducted by saintly tribal leaders, once that battle was lost, the struggle shifted to the cities and was led by scholar/reformers, who engaged in a class-cum-symbolic battle for cultural supremacy (Colonna 1984). As a result of this anti-colonial struggle, and the institutionalisation of religion in modern Algeria, the Reformers emerged as the only viable politicised religious force. Sufism, the religion of ecstatic love, lost its political influence.[6]

In South Asia, by contrast, the Reform movement met with powerful scholarly opposition in defence of Sufi saints and the cultic beliefs and practices surrounding saints' tombs. As a result of this confrontation, what emerged was a religious movement which united saints *and* scholars, *pirs and maulvis*, the charismatic elect *and* the knowledgeable doctors, within a single organisation (see Metcalf 1982). The scholars have their own Islamic schools, usually known as *Dar-ul-Ulooms*, their own religious networks, their mosques, their religious establishment and their political party.

The reformer jurists' and saintly jurists' organisations mirror each other while their members are locked in continuous religious controversy. The saints, who

---

[6] There is evidence that in modern Algeria descendants of saintly families are important leaders in the current Islamicist revival. What is less clear is whether they espouse Sufi politico-religious ideas of the kind enunciated by Pakistani Barelvi supporters. On the face of it, this seems very unlikely.

tend to favour political pragmatism, rarely participate in these scholarly disputations. They use the *'ulama* to provide religious services, preach sermons and organise religious institutions, while they themselves concentrate on the organisation of their orders, recruitment of disciples, and dispensing of divine blessing and healing to their devotees. Sometimes *pirs* are also learned men, while doctors sometimes become saints (see Malik 1990). On the whole, however, the saints disdain the *maulvis* while relying heavily upon their services.[7]

Hence, in Pakistan the battle for religious ecstasy was never lost, despite the institutionalisation of Reform Islam. It is a battle conducted on both sides by Sunni, *Shari'a*-trained, learned doctors. As articulated intellectually by the Barelvis, it is a battle between the heart and the mind, love and pedantic scholarship, ecstatic devotion and mere religious observance, mystical symbolism and lifeless literalism. It is, importantly, a *modern*, contemporary battle about definitions of personhood, citizenship and sources of authority. In the course of this apparently purely religious dialogue, broader political issues are debated, and it is to these that I now wish to turn.

Since Islam has never had a centralised, established church, it has never had religious dissent in the specifically Christian sense. The real issue is when and why a rhetoric of civil rights, democracy, equality and socialism expanded beyond narrow elitist Muslim Modernist circles, to become part of a broad-based, popular South Asian religious ideology.

It seems clear that these new discourses did not originate either with the sober and determined puritanical Reform scholars or with the pacifist saints and fiery, populist scholars aligned against them. The interests of both religious establishments remain, as before, mainly to increase their political influence in the state or local community; they are not interested in civil liberties, economic equality or democratic rights. These have always been associated in Pakistani politics with secular or 'modernist' groups. But on both sides there is also a third element: lay preachers who are usually community leaders involved in mosque politics. It is they who, in the present Islamic revival, articulate grass-roots sentiments and help explain the processes which have given rise to the current movement of Islamic radicalism.

To understand this, we need to recognise that modern politics in South Asia generally, and Pakistan in particular, has never been entirely secular. Irrespective of ideology, it has always seemed impossible for political parties to conduct their politics in a purely secular idiom. Religious groups early on formed their own political movements, and the pendulum of religious politics has tended to swing from a scramble for colonial or postcolonial state patronage to a more radical demand for the Islamicisation of the state. But even the People's Party, which won the elections in West Pakistan on a socialist ticket, utilised an Islamic idiom and appeared to have increasingly relied upon saintly patronage to mobilise

---

[7] There are, of course, celebrated exceptions to the quiescent tendency of Sufi *'ulama*: the 1857 uprising against the British did, apparently, involve at least some *'ulama* (Metcalf 1982: 82–4). It was followed by Sayyid Ahmad of Rae Bareli's nineteenth-century *jihad* against the British in the North West Frontier (ibid.: 52–63). Charismatic *mullahs* have now and then led iridescent movements in the Frontier (see Barth 1985; Ahmed 1991a, b & c). Later, in the early twentieth century, the Khilafat movement arose to save the Sultanate, in response to the collapse of the Ottoman Empire (Ahmad 1967). Both the latter movements shared a millenarian misperception of the contemporary realities of power relationships.

political support (see Sherani 1991). Nationalism in Pakistan is inextricably intertwined with Islam, the *raison d'être* for the very existence of the state, and it has hitherto proved impossible to separate the two.[8]

Mosque, community and lay preachers

'Loyalty ultimately belongs to God, and I say there should be justice, there should be equality, there should be understanding, there should be humanity.' So proclaimed one of the speakers at the meeting discussed here. The move from God to liberty and equality is not deductive; it is intuitive and emotional. We love God and the Prophet, hence we detest autocratic, greedy leaders. Like lay Methodist preachers, the men involved in mosque affairs speak for the ordinary man, not necessarily for the religious establishment of their particular brand of Islam (on a parallel feature of Methodism, see Hobsbawm 1959: 126–49; Thompson 1963: 430–40). Indeed, it is my impression that they speak with the *same* political voice irrespective of whatever Muslim religious movement or sect they happen to be affiliated to.

These lay preachers have introduced a radical change of rhetoric: not Islamic authoritarianism but Islamic love, equality and individual liberties. Yet the underlying tension between love and authoritarianism *within* the movement itself is also evident (as it was in Methodism). Barelvis do not need to be rich, learned, educated or prominent to qualify as good Muslims. All they need is to love the

---

[8] A vast scholarly literature documents the relation between Islam and politics in South Asia. During the Mughal period the Islamic clerical establishment was, in general, fragmented and decentralised, relying on the powerful patronage of rulers and royal courts (Metcalf 1982: 16–45). As in the Ottoman Empire, the religious experts acted as advisers, jurists, scribes and administrators to the Mughals. The Reform movements, which arose in the context of the erosion of Muslim power in India, tended towards isolationism and separatism, seeking religious and communal autonomy rather than confrontation (ibid.: 147–53). The British colonial regime fostered its patronage relations with powerful saints (*pirs*), relying upon their political influence in rural areas. These saints tended for a lengthy period towards accommodation with the authorities rather than confrontation (Gilmartin 1979, 1984).

It was after the emergence of modern anti-colonial politics, however, that religious involvement in the politics of South Asia became more sustained and broadly based. Here it needs to be said that no purely secular Muslim politics has ever existed in the Indian subcontinent. Even the Muslim League's fight for Pakistan was conducted in a religious idiom. Moreover, the League relied on alliances with religious organisations. Hence, in mobilising support in the Punjab, the League appealed to powerful saints who weighed heavily with the electorate (Gilmartin 1979). It also made common cause with some of the Indian religious movements (including the Barelvis) which supported the Pakistan movement. Other Reform groups were against the movement, while still being anti-colonial; they chose to support Congress and the unity of India (see Ahmad 1972: 258–9; Hardy 1972). Of the latter, some revised their political stance after Partition, as in the well-known case of the Jama'at-i Islam headed by Maududi, which had taken an anti-nationalist, and particularly anti-Muslim League, stand (see Binder 1961: 70–97). In general, however, it can be said that, as the anti-colonial movement gathered pace, and as independence seemed imminent, virtually all the various religious groups, from landed charismatic saints to urban puritanical scholars, supported the cause of liberty against repressive, *external* domination. The problems of civil rights and democratic freedoms remained, however, the domain of the League and the Modernists.

After Partition 'liberty' came to be buried in conservative religious politics. Whereas major rural saints engaged in quietist patronage power politics (see Sherani 1991), the '*ulama*, many of whom became once more employees of the state, also founded political parties which fought alongside and against each other for greater say and influence in the state apparatus (see Binder 1961; Ahmad 1972; Malik 1989, 1990; Iqbal n.d.).

Prophet of Islam and his *awliya* (his chosen 'friends', i.e. Sufi saints). The movement is an essentially egalitarian one. At the same time, cult leaders – Sufi Shaikhs – are highly authoritarian. Imbued with charismatic power, they head an organisational hierarchy based on strict discipline and unquestioning obedience. Their power over their followers, including the *'ulama* under them, is immense. Nor do they deny the inequalities of wealth and power prevalent in their society. Indeed, they acknowledge these in practice by honouring politicians, civil servants and moneyed elites with privileged treatment at their lodges. Paradoxically, however, it is precisely *because* they are spiritually superior, by birth and ascetic practice, to secular, powerful, wealthy monarchs and rulers, that their disciples feel able to challenge the legitimacy of those leaders, and to make demands for equal political and economic rights.

The *'ulama*, the learned doctors, are, by contrast, disdained by saints and followers alike. *'Ilm*, 'external' knowledge of the Qur'an, *sunna* and *Shari'a* law, is rated in Sufism as inferior to *ma'arifa*, gnostic knowledge, and thus the practitioners of *ilm* are regarded as either pedants or ignorant fools. In the past, many village *mullahs* were indeed relatively uneducated, even in Islamic studies. The *mullahs* tended, moreover, to originate from castes inferior to those of saints who usually claimed to be Sayyid, Siddiqui or Qureshi, as well as to landowning *zamindari* castes (see, for example, Barth 1960; Malik 1989). Contemporary urban Barelvi *'ulama* at major mosques, however, are far better educated than their predecessors were (Malik 1998), and in Manchester, Maulana Saheb, the radical *'alim* of the Central Mosque was a Mughal by caste origin, and was clearly fighting in his radicalism a personal battle to assert his equality with members of the wealthy business and professional elite of the community, most of whom originated from landowning castes and shared the universal disdain for *'ulama* in general, and Barelvi *'ulama* in particular, prevalent in South Asia.

There is thus a tension within the Barelvi movement itself between the realities of strict organisational hierarchy, the ambiguous position of the more educated *'ulama* who run large urban mosques, and the 'pir-brothers' – ordinary followers of a single saint who see themselves as equal, as all Muslims are equal, irrespective of wealth or family and caste origin. The populist rhetoric of the *maulvis*, caught in the middle, is thus explicable partly in terms of their rather precarious status.

Missing is the familiar neat Middle Eastern logical, dualistic alternation model based on a series of corresponding opposites – saints and scholars, tribe and city, syncretism and reform, kinship and decadence, purity and literacy, pluralism and monism, hierarchical intercession and egalitarianism, tolerance and fundamentalism (see, for example, Gellner 1981: 1–84; Keddie 1972; also Eickelman 1976). In the South Asian case, the continued co-operation among three interdependent interacting social categories – saints, scholars and laymen – creates an internal oscillation between quietism or conservatism and sudden eruptions of radical populism. Such moments of Islamic radicalism tend to be immediate responses to political events as these are perceived to impinge on the actors, either as direct participants or as members of broader Muslim communities, national and transnational.

The speeches at the meeting in Manchester, especially those in English, drew, in large measure unself-consciously, on a repertoire of familiar English political rhetorical tropes: exploitation, racism, class oppression, injustice, liberation, civil rights, identity, integrity, as well as on more clearly Islamic notions and rhetorical tropes. This rhetoric of modernity is familiar to local Muslims from the Urdu, as well as from the British, press and media which immigrants read or view regularly, in what has probably become a global set of political calls for 'justice' (see Ahmed 1992: 195–6).

The narratives of oppression had a peculiarly 'British' ring: they denounced racism and media distortions, and called for equality for women, multiculturalism and ethnic rights. In Pakistan, Reform scholars tend to attack caste practices, ostentatious weddings, the worship of the Prophet, the adoration of saints' tombs, the laxity of women, economic usury and interest, and political corruption, and to stress female modesty, public honesty and the payment of the charitable *zakat*. These themes are taken up by some of the Young Muslim associations associated with the Jama‘at-i Islami and other Islamist tendencies in Britain. They were only secondary, however, in public speeches made by Sufi lay preachers.

The speakers at the Manchester meeting were undoubtedly appealing to a *British* sensibility. The conjunction between an Islamic rhetoric of love and a radical socialist rhetoric – which would not have been out of place at a Labour Party Conference – raises, however, the question of whether this conjunction does not, perhaps, represent a step towards the future *secularisation* of Muslims in Britain. At present, the values articulated draw their legitimacy from religious imperatives, but, at the same time, they are also regarded as self-evident truths which need no specific scriptural references for their validation.

As long as political confrontations in the Middle East, Kashmir or Bosnia continue, and as long as anti-Muslim or immigrant sentiments and practices persist in Britain, the conjunction between Islam and socialist-liberal values is unlikely to be ideologically severed. Religion and ethics are conjoined within a single discursive formation by the *ethnic* and *class* dimensions of these confrontations. The relative autonomy of each set of arguments, the Islamic and the dissenting, does, however, point to a potential line of severance between religion and ethical values of modernity and civil society. For a younger generation of Pakistanis growing up in Britain, the definition of what Islam is and means may well come to be increasingly constituted, not by the Qur'an and *Hadith*, but by dissenting political ideologies. Just as the foundation texts of English working-class dissent combined Bunyan's *Pilgrim's Progress* with Paine's *Rights of Man* (Hobsbawm 1959: 145; Thompson 1980 [1963]: 35), so too for British Muslims, their foundation texts increasingly fuse a multicultural rhetoric of anti-racism and equal opportunities with the ethical edicts of the Qur'an and *Hadith*.

The speeches at the Town Hall in Manchester combined theology, especially the adoration of the Prophet and his exemplary life, with a stress on the pride of bearing an Islamic identity and the uniqueness of being Muslim. At the same time, the radical challenge to the established order was unmistakable. The attack was three-pronged: against the injustice of international law and global decision-making, both of which ignored Muslim *national* interests; against the corrupt illegitimate regimes of the Gulf states, denying the *economic* rights of 'ordinary Muslims'; and against British legal discrimination which denied local Muslims their basic *citizenship* rights. If the latter referred to immediate local interests, speakers clearly felt that their specific predicaments could only be fabulated in a broader, more global allegory of dissent. Hence the unmitigated radicalism of participants. Yet to label these lay preachers as 'the Muslim street' is, as Thompson argued in relation to the English bread 'rioters', to misread the level of urban organisation and moral political rationality of urban Muslims (Thompson 1971).

The popular sentiments expressed by lay preachers responsive to media and anti-racist discourses necessarily in the course of time come to motivate the religious rhetoric of their *'ulama*, the mosque clerics, as well, always concerned to defend their vulnerable status. The result is a rising crescendo of rhetorical dissent. As public arenas allowing for the formulation of these innovative dissenting ideologies, the place of urban mosques is critical.

In this respect a further instructive parallel may be drawn between the eighteenth- and early nineteenth-century Methodist 'labour sects' in Britain and current Barelvi Islamic dissent. Like the Methodist chapels, urban mosques in Britain are centres of communal affairs, drawing labour migrants into communal activities. The mosque is the base for teaching collective discipline, organisation and internal fund-raising, a springboard for regional and national political alliances, a training ground in polemics and adversary politics.

The link between saints and doctors among Barelvis means that the movement is a powerful *urban*, as well as rural, organisation. Indeed, it creates organic links between town and village, and its lodges and mosques provide welcoming havens and communal centres for migrant travellers.

Mosques – in the plural, for they have proliferated in British cities – are supported not only by Pakistani factory workers but also by small shopkeepers, market traders, petty manufacturers, artisans, professionals and a few larger businessmen (see Werbner 1990a, Chap. 10). These supporters are all men with a sense of individual pride, a measure of personal autonomy, who hold strong ideas about the rights due to them as citizens and productive workers. They are not people to be pushed around. Yet they lack real political power and influence in Britain and this powerlessness has been underlined in recent years by the Rushdie affair, the Gulf War, Bosnia, Kashmir, Palestine and the general increase in racial harassment.[9]

This points also to the limitations of any approach that explains current responses by privileging differences in South Asian theological positions over emergent ideologies in Britain. Any purely culturalist approach, which stresses specific 'beliefs' (such as the adoration of the Prophet) without considering the social organisational conditions for the production of discursive practices, is in danger of reifying the past (see Ruthven 1990; for an alternative pragmatic analysis see Samad 1992).

In Britain, the intercalary position of urban *'ulama* makes them responsive to the views of their congregations, even when their salaries come from external sources. This became evident during the Gulf crisis. Attempts by the Saudi government to muzzle Saudi-funded *'ulama*, the majority of whom were expressing public support for Saddam Hussein during the crisis, completely failed, and the Saudi government subsequently decided to withdraw its funding from British mosques. The episode highlighted the extent to which it is local agendas, set by

---

[9] Parallels may be drawn with the Iranian revolution in which the urban *bazaaris* played, it has been argued, an important role. There too, analysts have shown, Shi'a Islam shifted from a quiescent symbolic interpretation of martyrdom as suffering, to an activist view of martyrdom as personal sacrifice for the sake of a cause (see Hegland 1987: 242–3). The radicalisation of urban Iranians arose in response to a sense of direct attack by the state on the clergy and the urban lower middle and working classes who had been relatively autonomous and mobile socially (Beeman 1983).

lay preachers in Britain fighting local battles for power and influence, that shape the rhetoric of religious clerics.

British Muslim immigrants are caught in structural contradictions generated by their position as sojourner-strangers wishing to advance themselves economically while sustaining their autonomous culture and religion. The predicament experienced cuts across class and religious divisions and encompasses a wide range of communal leaders, following different Muslim sectarian groups. Their rhetoric, conjoined with *'ulama* interests in extending their local influence, generates, in effect, a *convergence* in the public rhetoric of the different Islamic sects.

It is important, however, to recognise the 'magical' aspects of the 'subversive bricolage' characterising the dissenting rhetoric of Sufi followers. I mean this in a dual sense. First, in many respects vocal protest is perceived to be powerfully effective in its own right, without necessitating further, more practical, organisation for action. This valorisation of a posture and rhetoric of courageous resistance appears to be well understood by Saddam Hussein himself, who celebrated his 'victory' over the US in 1998 precisely on the grounds that he verbally withstood a threatened attack, even if, in practical terms, he succumbed to international pressure. In this respect Barelvi followers differ in their political and material agenda from the Islamist movements. Second, the dissenting rhetoric globalises current predicaments, rooted in racist exclusions and economic deprivation, by reconstituting them as a cosmic battle between Islam and the West. This displacement can be regarded as a 'magical' resolution of 'contradictions which remain hidden and unresolved' (see Cohen 1981: 82, on working-class 'magical' displacements).

Without doubt, the intention of lay Muslim preachers in their simultaneous incorporation and critique of Western discourses is to '... disrupt paradigmatic associations and therefore to undermine the very coherence of the system contested' (Comaroff 1985: 189). However, as Comaroff perceptively recognises, these 'purposive reconstructions invariably work with images which already bear meaning; ... as a result, subversive bricolages always perpetuate as they change' (ibid. See also Hebdige's original discussion (1979).)

Both this oratory of Barelvi followers and the symbolic gestures they dramatically deploy, from the raising of fists in shows of power to high-pitched shouts of 'Allah-hu Akbar', gloss over the multiple contradictions experienced by them as stranger-citizen-workers or economically mobile but marginalised intellectuals. Despite such apparently 'fanatical' demonstrations, the pragmatic commitment to establish themselves economically and politically in Britain is evidently a paramount consideration, one endorsed also by the saints who head the various orders. Radical public orations, such as those following the publication of *The Satanic Verses* or preceding the Gulf War, are, like the Khilafat movement in India, passing 'magical' moments, reflexively symbolic performances rather than sustained political programmes or new modes of social praxis. To say this is not, however, to deny the passionate commitments they express. Triggered by periodic moral panics, ethnic mobilisation occurs whenever the aporias of being a stranger-immigrant are exposed beneath the opaque surface of daily life. In the subsequent crescendo of dramatic rhetoric, ideas of religious redemption and millennium are merged with clarion calls for equality and democracy; the moral panic then gradually fades away, leaving only traces of these rhetorical tropes, as the vast majority of Sufi followers return to their everyday concerns and activities, and concentrate on the education of their children and the expansion of their businesses.

The speeches create an imaginative identification between the particular cause of British Muslims – the promotion of Islam in Britain in order to preserve an Islamic identity for future generations – and the global cause of Muslims everywhere. Similarly, the fight against religious legal discrimination in Britain is represented as an extension of a broader, international fight against Western global domination. To overcome this domination and internal decadence, the community must first change itself, a central tenet of the Islamic Modernists (see Ahmad 1967: 262). Here the close connections between South Asian Sufi, Modernist and Islamist approaches become apparent: all three groups regard the world as potentially *transformable* rather than immutable and divinely predetermined. The need is for hard work, adjustment and self-reform. Globally, the national divisions within the Arab world are artificial colonial inventions, exploited by the West in order to extend its domination. The rulers of these Arab nations are mere colonial puppets. But redemption can be achieved through individual and communal commitment to the forging of a new, unified Islamic empire which will be powerful enough to meet the West on its own ground.

We see here how apparent oppositions can only be comprehended within a single field of action and signification. Indeed, it is increasingly evident that new religious and nationalist movements in the context of modernity emerge reactively, in contrast to and in competition with each other. What is required is a symbolic transformational analysis of the relations of power and ideological opposition within and between movements, as these are played out in a single semantic field. Ethical notions of redemption, personhood, sacred space, power and morality cannot be understood as existing autonomously, in and for themselves, but only relationally, in creative opposition. Moreover, within world religions a semiotics of individual or communal redemption is likely to be appropriated differently in different contexts and historical moments: in Christian separatist movements in Zimbabwe or Ghana (see R. Werbner 1989, Chaps 6–8), in the totemic nationalisms of Zionism in Israel (Paine 1989) or, as the present analysis has attempted to show, in the interaction between Islam and British society. In all these, creative visions of millennia constitute arguments of identity between social groups which both mirror and oppose each other.

For some of the Islamist groups, both in Britain and throughout the Muslim world, the rejection of capitalism and other dimensions of modernity is a sustained, long-term project. Not so for British Sufi followers. For them, economic progress, equality and the rights of citizenship are just as important a dream as that of re-establishing the true Muslim state. As a result, the swings between temporary utopian hopes for Islamic dominance and a sense of communal failure and total powerlessness, are as yet more evident in their attitudes than in any determination to engage in sustained practical political action. During these swings, what is continuously elaborated is a politically constituted religious rhetoric, a rhetoric of dissent which, above all, narrates the particular place of British Pakistani immigrants, as 'ordinary Muslims' within Britain and the broader, international Muslim world.

Mosques are central foci of communal activity for local British Muslim communities. They bring together religious experts and local community activists, and the dialogue between these two groups, enacted publicly during public ceremonials or religious meetings, has generated greater political awareness, even in groups normally opportunistic and quiescent, such as those of Barelvi followers. Until recently, however, most mosques in Britain, and most religious leaders, remained politically introverted, engaged mainly in internecine religious conflicts and factional rivalries. The publication of *The Satanic Verses* marked a watershed in this state of affairs. It revealed the need for broader organisational frameworks, as well as setting new agendas for common action, required in order to challenge the state and its current laws. It politicised the British Muslim identity, and linked it to broader processes of Islamic politicisation occurring globally. It added a new political urgency to earlier demands for Muslim burial-grounds, *halal* meals in schools, state-funded voluntary-aided Muslim schools, mosque planning permits and so forth (see Nielsen 1988). It also increased pressure on Muslim political aspirants (local councillors or parliamentary candidates) to articulate specifically 'Islamic' demands or points of view within the mainstream political arena.

The Gulf crisis sharpened the need for political protest and added further complexity to the emergent political philosophy articulated from mosque pulpits and communal podiums.

Conclusion: competing global fables, agonistic local allegories

The response of Pakistani Muslims in Britain to the Gulf crisis resembled, and was part of, a transnational Muslim response throughout the Muslim world (see Piscatori 1991). In this sense it reflected a global 'ideoscape' (Appadurai 1990) and it was legitimised by leaders of major sectarian divisions and by a Muslim press and media reporting or reflecting their opinions. The fable was a global fable. But its local production also clearly reflected and embodied local rivalries for hegemony between the extensions of these global Islamic movements in Britain, and between different Sufi orders vying for dominance in a particular city. To articulate an allegory of resistance and to interpret the allegory in local terms was to stress a commitment to local action. If the pretext was Islamic and global, the text was British.

To move beyond narrative and fully comprehend a social movement, we need to go beyond its ideological expressions and discover where structural contradictions and thus agency are to be found. How does political mobilisation take place empirically? The fact that calls to action by lay preachers rarely went beyond radical rhetoric was likely to be a source of disillusionment for their audiences in the long run, but, as a spontaneous response to current affairs, these fabulations of world current affairs revitalised local Islamic identities and sense of empowerment. They were 'good to think' and 'good to say' or to narrate.

In a critical *tour de force*, Christopher Norris attacked Jean Baudrillard's *Guardian* article which appeared two days before the Gulf War broke out. In his article, Baudrillard argued that the war would never happen since it was merely a 'figment of mass-media simulation'; that in a nuclear age 'war had become strictly unthinkable except as a rhetorical phenomenon' (Norris 1991: 11). Norris takes the article as an extreme example of postmodernist (neo-pragmatist, deconstructionist) thinking which textualises reality *ad absurdum*, denying the validity of any distinction between fact and fiction. The consequence of such a tendency, Norris argues, is to deny even the possibility of rational argument over facts between opposed views held by different interpretive communities. Instead, if truth is what is 'good to think', there can be no bridge across the interpretive chasm between language communities.

Against this view, he demonstrates that all narratives, even fictional ones, are at least partly anchored in experience and thus subject to logical yardsticks of judgement and evaluation. It is obvious, he says, that the fables and narratives of the Gulf War, mostly generated by Western media propaganda, could not disguise the loss of Iraqi life and some of the more blatant atrocities committed by the international alliance. Hence, he disagrees not only with Baudrillard but with Michael Ignatieff who argued in *The Observer*, citing Edgar Morin in *Le Monde*, that all the revelations and developments of the war merely served to confirm for people the moral positions they already held. The war was thus 'an encounter between "blind moralities"'' (Norris 1991: 62).

Although Norris makes a convincing case for the rootedness of narrative in experience, he fails to locate (and hence to address theoretically) the reasons for the multiple fabulations of the Gulf crisis. The sheer facts of the crisis were never really in dispute and few startling revelations have emerged since to challenge these facts. All along, the problem has been one of interpretation, a refraction of visions and worldviews, contrasting political moralities and differing definitions of what is sacred or profane, permissible or inadmissible, villainous or courageous. At stake in the Gulf crisis were ethical issues of 'historicity': of past, present and future. The facts, viewed differently from different vantage-points, led to differing predictions of the course the unfolding drama would take. The reading by different political constituencies of motive, intention and character as signposts of future action differed radically. Ultimately it was character, as read on the basis of past action, which was seen to determine the threat of apocalyptic disaster or Islamic utopia. The anticipation of casualties was itself subject to this subtextual reading of character and motive. In addition, the dangers and breaches perceived were also ranked differently – environmental disaster, loss of human life, unsupervised nuclear proliferation, global economic collapse, the threat to national territorial integrity, to the international global order, of Islamic hegemony, of Western desecration – all these were *moral* facts to be configured into a coherent and meaningful plot. To this must be added the problem of real history – the significance attributed to colonial and postcolonial pretexts – and the problem of *disguise*. In matters of ethics and politics, it is often not facts which are disputed or contested, but the ranking of facts in terms of the *hidden* motives they obscure and disguise. The dramatic plot, the fable, is ultimately one of revealed human passion – of greed, cruelty, nobility, humanity, justice, insanity, evil, caring, responsibility.

Any narration of morally grounded facts thus depends on perspective or focalisation (Rimmon-Kenan 1983). In explaining a narrative we need to 're-imagine the moral assumptions of another social configuration' (Thompson 1971: 131). This is not to deny the existence of hard realities (images) to be argued over rationally: the Gulf War did take place and human life, the environment, cities and military hardware were destroyed. Palestinians were evicted from Kuwait, Kurds and Shi'ites subjected to genocide, atomic reactors destroyed, missiles dismantled, oil wells set on fire and capped, sanctions imposed with little effect, and in the upshot, President Bush lost an election while Saddam Hussein survived to tell the tale.[10] All these are facts; none of the fabulators (Muslims, Americans, environmentalists, internationalists, socialists, capitalists) could have predicted them all. They were merely possible scenarios, potentialities to fear or desire. As Aristotle argues in the *Poetics*:

> ... the poet's function is to describe, not the thing that has happened, but a kind of thing that might happen.... Hence poetry is something more philosophic and of graver import than history, since its statements are of the nature rather of universals ... what convinces is the possible.

Persuasive rhetoric constructs a fable of the possible out of reality's raw material, from the vantage-point of a particular political morality. The plot is generic, global and universal. The allegory is local and reflects local predicaments, fears and aspirations. But the fable must tell a tale worth telling. Once the war was fought and ambiguously lost, there was no point in continuing to narrate this particular fable. Goliath had crushed David – a non-event not worth the candle. The lay preachers who fabulated their hopes of victory turned their imaginations to other global matters – Bosnia, Kashmir, Palestine.

At the height of the crisis preceding the Gulf War, however, there was a moment in which the imagining of a fable of triumph, a fairy tale of heroism, seemed to depict the possible. Under these circumstances it is perhaps not surprising that the clerics and lay preachers of the Barelvi movement in Britain paid little heed to the price they might pay for their dissenting support for Saddam Hussein. Although their statements were only semi-official, and they often retracted the most radical statements when questioned publicly by the media, it seems quite clear that they wanted the wider society to be aware of their disaffection. Theirs was a confrontational posture, as yet not fully worked out, more protest than actual action. The swings between temporary utopian hopes for Islamic dominance and a sense of communal failure and total powerlessness were more evident in their speeches than any determination to engage in sustained practical political action. During these swings, what was continually elaborated was a politically constituted religious rhetoric, a rhetoric of dissent which, above all, narrated the particular place of British Pakistani immigrants, as 'ordinary Muslims' within Britain and the broader, international Muslim world.

---

[10] As this book goes to press, sanctions against Iraq are crumbling fast, but there is talk in the USA of a possible further attack on the Iraqi regime.

III
Creating New Spaces

7
Being South Asian
Fun spaces, cricket & other celebrations

The state of effervescence in which the assembled worshippers find themselves must be translated outwardly by exuberant movements ... religion would not be itself if it did not give some place to the free combinations of thought and activity, to play, to art, to all that recreates the spirit. (Durkheim 1915: 381–2)

Effervescence, aesthetics & morality

In the corroboree, Durkheim tells us, an emotional aesthetics of play and sensuality, of song, music, movement and merry-making, goes beyond mere play, to release and revitalise the moral forces of society, stripped of any quotidian 'fatigue'. The pulsating oscillation between the 'slavishness of daily work' and the exuberance of religious effervescence marks the continuous renewal of society as a moral reality beyond the individual.

Durkheim's insights provided, of course, the ground for Turner's analysis of liminality (Turner 1974) as communitas and for Douglas's interpretation of humour as anti-rite (Douglas 1968). Both recognise the emotional camaraderie and fellow feeling released by humour and licensed behaviour, and the levelling of difference, structure and hierarchy these imply. Similar themes seem also to echo through Bakhtin's analysis of the medieval carnival. He too identifies the pulsating rhythm of a 'two world condition' (Bakhtin 1984: 6) in which the carnival spirit of fun, laughter and bodily sensuality surfaces periodically in relation to the natural cosmic cycle (ibid.: 9). During carnival, hierarchy is suspended along with all privileges, norms and prohibitions as people are 'reborn for new, purely human relations' (ibid.: 10).

Yet the Bakhtinian affirmation of grotesque realism disguises also a darker allegory – of repression, of the 'prohibition of laughter' (Pomorska 1984: ix), even if the laughter of carnival is 'indestructible' (Bakhtin 1984: 33). Durkheimian morality is here transmuted into a semiotic struggle over the definition of morality, waged between an elitist, official, unchanging aesthetic and the unofficial parodic freedom of folk culture. The shift is to a focus on a politicised aesthetic, empowering different class segments. The present chapter discloses the way in which such a morally grounded, semiotic struggle has developed among diasporic Pakistanis in Britain.

So far the picture of British Pakistanis that has emerged from this book is of a very sober and serious (if loquacious) group of people. This is very misleading.

Pakistani postcolonial identities are forged by the intersection of three trans-national lived-in cultural 'worlds': the world of a pan-South Asian aesthetic, encompassing music, dance, poetry and humour, grounded in shared social and sensual experiences; an anglicised postcolonial Western 'Commonwealth' culture; and an Islamic reformist culture which denies the legitimacy of the other worlds, and strives to recreate a pristine purity. Reform Islam in South Asia, rather than being dominant, however, is constantly vying for hegemony against the pervasive impact of mass South Asian popular culture.[1] In this sense the familiar Bakhtinian semiotic of popular or folk versus elite cultures needs to be reconceptualised: untenable is a simplistic Marxist view which posits a direct correspondence between cultures of resistance and subordinate status. Islamists feel themselves to be a beleaguered group in the face of the inexorable invasion of both Western and 'Hindu' consumerism and commodified popular culture.

The worlds impinging on Pakistani society, both at home and in the diaspora, are more than the ideological *'présences'* which Hall sees impinging on Caribbean identities: *présence Africain, présence Européenne and présence Américaine* (Hall 1990: 230). Hall focuses on the way these cultural influences create a hybridised Afro-Caribbean subject dialogically (ibid.: 230–5). The aim of the present chapter, by contrast, is to show how lived-in 'worlds' become the grounds for real struggle in *internal* Muslim and Pakistani symbolic battles, fought over the definition of moral value and the practices embodying it. The 'hybridised' Muslim subject is a person occupying multiple symbolic spaces.

An important question permeating discussions in and of contemporary Muslim society surrounds the conflict between religion and secularism (see Lewis 1994). As Lewis points out perceptively, it is common for religious Muslims to conceive of the domain of 'non-religion' as a space of 'anti-religion' (*la-dini*, 'without' religion), so that secularism is interpreted as equivalent to atheism (ibid.: 134, 127).

It is significant for the argument made here that the majority of diaspora Pakistanis in Britain embrace both the world of Islamic asceticism and sobriety and the (secular) world of South Asian ('Indian') popular culture with its laughter and sensual gaiety. Many also partially embrace the world of Western secularism and play. Yet while the vast majority – men and women, young and old – participate as *spectators* in these worlds, their participation as creative and inventive *actors* varies: Pakistani women, who are the creative celebrants of pre-wedding rituals, and young Pakistani men who actively participate in sport, dominate the unofficial worlds of sensuality and play. Older Pakistani men, by contrast, as we have seen, are actors on the stage of local-level ethnic and religious politics where they display their oratorical skills in passionate power struggles. At stake in these struggles, as we shall see in Chapter 9, is the control of public arenas, such as the Central Mosque, as well as the privilege of hosting British and Pakistani politicians and dignitaries, as we saw in Chapter 1.

Symbolic practices are embedded in social situations. If we ask ourselves, not what is Islam in Europe, but who are the *Muslims* of Europe, then we shift from talking about disembodied systems of meaning, religious approaches or social organisations to talking about the symbolic practitioners themselves – men and

---

[1] This popular culture, although shared by Hindus, Sikhs and Muslims in North India, is often labelled by Muslim reformists or Islamists as 'Hindu' and hence unIslamic and non-legitimate.

women engaged in specific discourses in particular settings. These symbolic practitioners are not *only* Muslims, as Al-Azmeh has trenchantly argued (Al-Azmeh 1993, Chap. 1) and the social situations they create or in which they take part are not only, or even primarily, religious. The spaces they occupy are as varied – and sometimes conflictual – as are the audiences at whom their narratives and fables are directed. Social identity, in other words, is *indexical* and positioned. It is constituted situationally, within a particular social and historical context, both as practical knowledge and as purposeful action. It is publicly negotiated and objectified by social actors in relation to their imagined audiences.

In their passionate fabulations, Pakistanis, we have seen, reveal the sentimental roots of their identities, anchored in a moral lived-in world and its imaginative extensions and attachments. It is within this moral world that speakers articulate their sense of worth and value (see also Epstein 1978). In this respect identity can be conceived of as a subjective expression of *moral virtue*. But identities are also grounded in aesthetic pleasure, collectively celebrated (see Geertz 1993). At stake, then, in the management of multiphrenic identities are moral and sentimental questions of attachment. To sustain their sense of personal integrity, diaspora Pakistanis must order their social identities hierarchically by value and saliency in relation to a series of encompassing symbolic domains and social spaces.[2] Seen together, these define the diasporic public sphere.

The diasporic public sphere

If space and identity interact, then clearly the spread of world religions, colonialism and empire, migration and displacement, nationalism and pan-nationalism, has generated a world of individuals bearing multiple, contradictory, multi-phrenic subjectivities. British Pakistanis are, simultaneously, Muslims, South Asians, mostly Punjabis, more or less Westernised. They manage these identities by creating different symbolic domains of activity and keeping these domains separate. In particular, the purely sacred, formal and serious activities of 'high' Islam and the profane, asyncretic, hybrid amalgam of Islamic and Asian/Western cultural and symbolic practices, are compartmentalised, or, to use Clifford Geertz's apt term, kept in 'disjunction' (Geertz 1968: 17–18, 105–7).

If to have fun is to sin, then being sinful is fun. In the present chapter a semiotic of contested moralities and aesthetic modes of celebration is examined as it illuminates the development of a diasporic Pakistani communal public sphere. The struggles documented here occurred, we need to remind ourselves, in Manchester, a city with a relatively affluent Pakistani population of about 20,000, set within a wider conurbation settled by some 100,000 Pakistani immigrants and their descendants, virtually all Punjabi and Urdu speakers. The vast majority of Pakistanis both in the city and in the wider conurbation are pious Muslims, and many are extremely religious.

[2] I use 'social space' here in the triadic sense defined by Lefebvre 1991: 33. On inconsistent identifications see Clifford 1988: 338; Werbner 1991a; Fischer 1986: 195. On the multiple identities of British Pakistanis see Werbner 1991b.

I define the diasporic public sphere, following Habermas, as a place where private citizens come together to deliberate on issues of public or national significance (Habermas, 1989). Although highly restricted in scope and almost invisible to non-Pakistanis, the British Pakistani diasporic public sphere is nevertheless, as we have seen in this book, a space for debate and voluntary action in response to national and global issues (see also Freitag 1989a & b). It is in such ethnic public arenas, moreover, that communal narratives are first fabulated, formulated and reformulated in front of a local ethnic audience. Ethnic empowerment is therefore as much about the creation and reproduction of *autonomous* ethnic spaces as it is about the penetration into the *wider* public sphere controlled by the state or media.

Until recently the diasporic Pakistani public sphere was entirely voluntary and personal. As such, it bears historical resemblance to the nascent European public sphere analysed by Habermas, before this sphere came to be dominated by the culture industry. For Habermas, like others in the Frankfurt School, the expansion of the culture industry spelled a fragmentation of authority and of rational discourse in the public sphere, since mass culture, they felt, constituted desire in inauthentic and contrived terms, and exploited the hedonistic instincts of the masses. Against this critique, however, I want to highlight the relation between Pakistani grass-roots popular culture/political activism and the South Asian culture industry. Ideologically, 'Bollywood' (Bombay's answer to Hollywood) and the South Asian music industry, while manufacturing an endless supply of flamboyant kitsch, nevertheless tap indigenous North Indian and Pakistani roots of humour, sensuality and satire which serve, I argue, to empower marginally positioned Pakistani social categories, such as women or youth.

The remarkable development in Britain during the 1990s has been the emergence of a South Asian, media-dominated public sphere of South Asian satire, song and humour. It is marked by iconoclastic satirical novels, films and TV programmes, from 'East is East', or 'Bhaji on the Beach' to 'Goodness Gracious Me', which spoof the migrant generation, its conservatism, bigotry and eccentricities. Through humour and music it has captured mainstream TV, culminating in an annual BBC celebrity evening recognising South Asian talent and distinction. The South Asian public sphere in the UK includes a range of South Asian newspapers and journals such as *Eastern Eye*, devoted to South Asian news and current affairs encompassing the four nations and religions of South Asia (India, Pakistan, Bangladesh and Sri Lanka; Hinduism, Islam, Sikhism, Buddhism). Cable and satellite TV from the subcontinent is watched by Pakistanis in their homes in a taken-for-granted way. It includes several Pakistani stations, and Indian stations such as Zee TV, which transmit globally to South Asia and across the world. Several simultaneous film screenings of Indian movies are shown at one of the major new cinemas in Manchester, attracting a young South Asian audience, while emporiums of South Asian 'fun', nightclubs and cinemas, are being opened or purpose-built in all the regions of major South Asian concentration such as London, Leicester and Birmingham.

This emergent South Asian public sphere has been captured not by nationalists or religious experts, but by the South Asian 'chattering classes', and by the children of migrant settlers who dominate the South Asian culture industries. Against the rigid identity divisions stressed by their parents, they stress fun and tolerance.[3]

This highlights a critical dimension of the present discussion. At stake in the evolution of the public sphere is the question of ownership: who owns the public sphere? Who controls the discourses allowed to be made 'public'? Who dictates what is 'official', that is, legitimate, as representative of the group or its 'culture', or 'unofficial', illegitimate, and hence denied public voice? Control of the public sphere as a contested arena is constitutive of authority, just as authority constitutes the public sphere.

The question of ownership is particularly germane to discussions of contemporary Muslim societies where Islamic radicals vie with feminists and conservative modernists for control over public spaces. In Manchester, the Pakistani ethnic public sphere, as a contested arena, went through a radical transformation in the 1990s during which the authority of Pakistani male elders and their monopoly of communal public space were contested. The challenge came from Pakistani women, on the one hand, and young Pakistani men, on the other, two groups currently carving a space for themselves in the public sphere.

Very roughly, three historical phases mark this transformation. The first phase, between about 1950 and the mid-1980s, was a period of communal reconstruction and consolidation dominated by first-generation immigrant Pakistani men. It was followed by a brief period outlined here, from the mid-1980s onwards, which was one of intense political contestation between male elders, women and youth. This was also, as we have seen, a time of male protest against *The Satanic Verses*. Since then there has been a partial capitulation of exclusive control by men, and with it the emergence of a gendered and familial Pakistani space of voluntary action which is also a space of 'fun', that is, one marked by gaiety, humour, music and dance.

Moments of effervescence are performative moments: they occur periodically as 'highs' which punctuate everyday life. Each Pakistani lived-in world (Muslim, South Asian, Western) potentially has such moments of public renewal and revitalisation. Yet each celebrates discrete and even contradictory and competing moralities. Both in Pakistan and in Britain, Pakistanis avoid conflict (and continue to have 'fun') by 'framing' these spaces (see Bateson 1973: 150–67) and celebrating them situationally. The framing separates the profane from the sacred, the pure from the impure: music, dance, humour and sensuality are distanced from the religious activities focused upon the mosque or the sobriety of Pakistani national commemorations. The ideological challenge posed to this pragmatic *modus vivendi* has come, however, from a more strident Islamic meta-message which claims for the sacred and for the guardians of the sacred (pious Pakistani male elders) a total monopoly over public space, to the absolute denial of the legitimacy of all other forms of Pakistani public celebration.

[3] The new media and popular culture have also had an emergent impact on the opening of the public sphere in the Muslim world more generally (see Armbrust 1996; Eickelman and Anderson 1999).

Contested spaces

In the face of attacks by Muslim puritanical ('fundamentalist') movements, the space of fun has come to be for diasporic Pakistanis, as indeed for Muslims worldwide, a highly contested space. The mosque and official Islamic events are framed consensually by strict taboos and exclusions. More controversially, however, outside the mosque a sensual Punjabi aesthetic of music, dance and verbal licence has been defined by the Muslim reformist groups as unIslamic and sinful, particularly so with regard to the conduct of women, their sexuality and their right to be visible in public. In this sense, fun has been delegitimised and marginalised by South Asian Islamic reform movements, a fact highlighted most often in relation to veiling (see Mumtaz and Shaheed 1987 esp. 29–31, 77–98; Kandiyoti 1991; Najmabadi 1989: 65–8). But an equally prohibitive definition in reformist discourses has been of instrumental music, dance and masquerade (and hence also ritual celebrations, Hindi films and musical concerts) as sinful. Islamic Reform aims to restrict bodily expressions of emotion and desire. This is often constructed by South Asian Muslims in oppositional terms, vis-à-vis the Hindu majority in India. Hence Barbara Metcalf reports that the nineteenth-century Deobandi reformists in India

> objected to customs such as *sama'* (musical sessions to induce ecstasy) ... and elaborate weddings and funerals on the basis of their similarity to Hindu festivals. (Metcalf 1982: 153)

A reformist tract, *Heavenly Ornaments*, became a standard gift for Muslim brides in India. The very same book, in its English translation, is now required reading for *British* Pakistani women who are members of Tablighi Jama'at, one of the most influential Islamic reform movements in the West (Metcalf 1990: 5). In the late twentieth and early twenty-first century it is not, of course, only Hindus who are targeted but, by analogy, the permissive West. Hence Chapter 6 of the book depicts the sinful pleasures associated with customary celebrations:

> Everyone knows what sin and evil the dancing of harlots [professional singers and dancers in India who were regarded as prostitutes] entails. All the men look at unrelated women. That is adultery of the eyes. They hear the sound of the women singing and talking. That is adultery of the ears. They talk with these women. That is adultery of the tongue.... If dancing is this evil, just think how sinful the people must be who arrange for dances.... Moreover, the musicians play various instruments ... that too is sin. Hazrat Apostle of God ... declared: 'My Provider ordered me to destroy these instruments'. (Metcalf 1990: 95)

Women, the guardians of (allegedly Hinduised) 'sinful custom' (as against purified Islamic law) are particularly prone to sin:

> Now, as for the dancing arranged for the women [in exclusive female celebrations], you should consider it equally illegitimate, whether there are drums and other instruments or not. Books forbid the performance of monkeys – isn't it much worse to have people dance? Moreover, the men of the house sometimes catch a glimpse of the dancing, with all the evils described above as a result. Sometimes the [women] dancers sing, and their voices reach the men outside. The men who hear women sing are committing a sin, as are the women responsible for the singing. (ibid.)

Masquerade too is prohibited:

> Some women put a man's hat on the head of the dancer. It is sin for a woman to look

or act like a man.... In short, all the dancing and music that goes on today is a sin (ibid.)

Along with singing, dancing and masquerade, ostentatious dress and jewelry are also sinful ('the noble *hadis* forbids jingling jewelry, because Satan is present in every sound', ibid.: 109).

Just as the English Puritans attacked the permissive excesses of Elizabethan England, so too 'fun' in the form of music, dance and customary celebration has come under attack by Muslim reform movements (see also Werbner 2001). Their scripturalist zeal is not limited to South Asia. Patrick Gaffney describes how, in Upper Egypt, a student musical comedy performance was interrupted:

> [B]earded militants entered forcibly and took over the stage, expelling the actors. They declared that the production was not in keeping with Islam and they demanded that it be cancelled completely. In its place, they announced that they would conduct an Islamic programme. (Gaffney 1994: 100)

In similar vein the Islamists prevented the establishment of a café on campus because it would encourage 'idleness and mixing of the sexes' (ibid.: 103). In revolutionary Iran, too, dancing, music and especially the cinemas were, Beeman tells us, 'singled out for harsh attacks from the mosque and religious schools', and were defined as instruments of Satan, the great tempter (Beeman 1983: 196, 210).

In Manchester, Muslim religiosity is not only austere but also contentious and politicised. The city's Central Mosque has been, since the 1980s, the focus of religious sectarian conflicts and struggles for power and dominance and, as we shall see in Chapter 9, these often involve public arguments and fights, which are sometimes quite violent. Until relatively recently, there were no 'legitimate' cultural modes of celebration in the city which were Islamic and yet not mosque-based or religiously focused; no official cultural spaces Pakistani parents in Britain shared with their children and which constituted a publicly sanctioned substitute for Western popular culture.

The cricket team's visit & other celebrations

1987: The hybrid Eid celebration

On 31 May 1987, an *eid* party for children was held in the newly built Pakistani Community Centre in Manchester. This was the first of a whole series of public *eid* parties held that year. It revealed some of the underlying cultural dilemmas faced by Pakistani migrant settlers, as Muslims, in Britain. The *eid* party took place in the afternoon, and was organised by the all-male Management Committee of the Community Centre. The walls of the Community Centre were bare. The children and their mothers, dressed in their best, faces shining and expectant, were seated in rows facing the stage. The children were looking forward to an afternoon of entertainment and fun, as appropriate for *eid*.

The first part of the celebration, compèred by an Urdu male teacher, was devoted to reciting the Qur'an. Children were called to the stage to recite their chosen passage, in inaudible voices as it turned out (since the sound system was not yet working). The young audience grew restive. The organisers kept glancing at their watches. A lady, her head wrapped in a thick scarf, rose and gave a lecture on ritual ablutions and on the religious reasons for performing *eid*. The children by now looked thoroughly depressed. Finally, the entertainers arrived. Two Englishmen, dressed as clowns, with heavy Lancashire accents. They sang music-hall songs and nursery rhymes in English. The children cheered up. The expressions on the adults' faces shifted from boredom to puzzlement. The entertainers brought in some monkey puppets and one of them tried a bit of ventriloquism. Things became a little noisy and chaotic, but the children entered into the spirit of it all.

The contrast between the lugubrious religiosity of the first half of the party and the English triviality of its second half was quite startling. At 4.30 pm the compère signalled to the entertainers, who departed as suddenly as they had arrived, and the food was distributed. Each child received a paper plate with a samosa meat pastry, Asian salty savouries, sweets and a drink. The committee of male elders helped to distribute the food. Each child was also given a party bag with a balloon, a small rubber prehistoric monster and a packet of crisps (potato chips). Everyone seemed very happy and the party was voted a great success. The organisers were a little apologetic, especially about the sound system, and explained that this had been the first time they had organised such an event.

1987: The transgressive Eid celebration

That evening, two other *eid* parties took place in Manchester. Each in its way pointed to further cultural dilemmas. One party was held at the *Indian Cottage* restaurant in Rusholme, the Asian retail shopping centre of Manchester, an area of delicatessens, jewelry and sari shops, and 'Indian' restaurants serving mainly Punjabi and North Indian food of the highest quality. The party was organised by the owner of the building in which the restaurant was housed, an extremely wealthy Pakistani wholesaler who was on the verge of becoming a household name in Britain with his 'Joe Bloggs' designer label. The wholesaler, according to a view shared by many, was a rather arrogant man, disliked by some, and especially so by the more pious. Flagrantly non-observant, he took little part in local-level Pakistani and mosque politics and remained somewhat peripheral to communal affairs in this area. As a major buyer from local Asian manufacturers, however, his business reputation was excellent, and he had extensive trading connections with Asians, both Muslims and Hindus, in the local clothing trade.

Dinner at the *eid* party cost £10 a head. My friends, mildly religious, middle-class urban Pakistanis, who were invited by an ex-college acquaintance from Lahore, were reluctant to go after they were informed that 'there would be drinking' at the party. 'How can we go?' my friend asked me, 'when *eid* is the time when we explain to our children that they should be good Muslims?' I persuaded them to accompany me to the party, much against their better judgement, for the sake of 'the research'.

The party, which was by invitation only, included some of the more anglicised elite Pakistanis in Manchester – bank managers, Pakistan International Airline officials, businessmen, professionals, accountants. Most came from Pakistan's urban educated middle classes; at least one person to whom I was introduced was closely related to one of Pakistan's top business families.

Altogether about 100 people were gathered by about 8 pm. There was a young Asian (Hindu) *bhangra* band from Bolton, *Zankar*, entertaining the assembled guests with live *bhangra* music.

Even before the dinner started the wholesaler made some attempt to get people dancing. His wife, a buxom attractive woman, danced in the empty space at the centre of the restaurant along with some of the girls. Dinner was served buffet style and was both abundant and delicious. During all this time there was no sign of any drinking. If the endless glasses of Coca-Cola drunk by the gathering were laced with rum or whisky, this was not publicly evident.

At around 10.15 pm about half the guests departed. At this point the party warmed up. The wholesaler was on his second whisky, as was his accountant friend. Acting as impresario, he summoned various women to sing. They sang Asian *ghazals* in lovely voices, cheered on by the remaining guests. One of the singers was the owner of a sari shop in the area; a young male singer was the son of a local jewelry shop owner; another singer, from the wholesaler's own party, had a deep, husky voice.

At 10.30 pm a waiter carried out a giant magnum bottle of champagne. The wholesaler announced that free champagne was being served and suggested that all those who were drinkers should sit on the left, all the non-drinkers on the right. The middle was left for the undecided. My companion, a rather conservative middle-class man, complained about the speaker's faulty Urdu (thus imputing that he was probably uneducated). I asked a waiter who the wholesaler was. 'A millionaire', he whispered to me.

While the singers sang, the wholesaler circled £10 notes over their heads and threw the money, £10 at a time, to the band. In all, I watched him throw about £100 at them. Another wholesaler joined him, circling £5 notes in similar fashion before throwing them to the band. By this time the first wholesaler, a little tipsy, was dancing with his equally tipsy accountant friend in a joky manner, lifting him up and spinning him around. The women joined them, dancing Asian, sensual dances. It was all very enjoyable and full of fun. We left at about 11 pm. The party was still in full swing.

The Islamic prohibition on drinking is one often breached by Muslim men. But there are degrees of transgression. This was a semi-private party, yet it was clear that not all the participants were drinkers. The party's ostentatious flouting of Islamic rules in public thus broke not only religious edicts but customary Pakistani conventions of polite behaviour. Drinking, like smoking, follows certain rules of etiquette. Men do not drink or smoke in front of elders or women. Women, in most circles, do not drink in public. Our millionaire wholesaler was not simply drinking. He was making a point of drinking, and of drinking on a Muslim festival. He was, as it were, throwing down the gauntlet, openly challenging the local Pakistani mosque 'establishment' to a symbolic duel, in the sure knowledge that his financial prominence would protect him from real damage. It was not just good fun; it was doubly enjoyable because it was openly sinful and because it broke all the rules.

1987: The political Eid celebration

While this revelry was going on, another very different *eid* party was being held not far away. This party was organised by the community association in

Longsight, the central residential Pakistani enclave in the city, to which Chaudhry Amin and some of his rivals were attached. The association members were deeply involved, as we saw in previous chapters, in the local politics of the Central Mosque. I heard about this 'party' later from various people, and the following description is based on their combined accounts.

Of course, there was no drinking at the party. Nor were there any women, music or dancing. Instead, a *halagula* (quarrel, scene) irrupted during the evening concerning a power struggle at the mosque. The background to the confrontation was the forthcoming elections for a community representative to serve on the Council Race Sub-Committee, discussed in Chapters 1 and 2. One local community leader told me that he had stood up in public and accused Maulana Saheb, the highly controversial and powerful *maulvi* of the Central Jami'a Mosque, of being a liar in the presence of the several hundred men gathered for the party. He was, apparently, followed by another leader who told the Maulana: 'This is our association. You shouldn't be here, you are interfering. Go back to the mosque!' According to one witness, someone had then stood up and said: 'You should be ashamed of yourselves! All this fighting is giving Manchester a bad name. No-one wants to come here.' Another witness told me: 'There were two groups. The A. group and the R. group. They started to shout and scuffle. I left in disgust.'

1987: The Hindu–Muslim celebration

Some time later, in September 1987, I was invited by a Gujerati Jain friend to accompany her to an evening of entertainment at the *Katmandu*, a restaurant in the centre of Manchester. She had been asked by a friend to sing Gujerati folk songs during the evening.

We arrived at the restaurant at 9.30 pm to find the party in full swing. One room of the restaurant had a large buffet dinner laid out. In the other room a musical group from Bombay were providing entertainment. They included a tabla and dholki player, a harmonium player, a female singer and four dancers, all youngish women, almost girls. The women dancers, who were plastered with make-up, were remarkably unattractive, the singer had a high-pitched screechy voice, and the only accomplished performer appeared to me to be the young tabla player. In short, a sleazy musical group direct from Bombay's night club district.

Many of the men were drinking, the Pakistani men seated along one side of the room or standing against the wall, the Gujeratis, who had come with their wives, sisters and daughters, sitting on the other side. I recognised a Pakistani manufacturer and a local wholesaler and community 'leader' who had brought along the Deputy Agricultural Director of Jhelum District, visiting after a brief course in the USA. 'Isn't this all very different from Jhelum?' I asked the visitor. 'On no,' he replied, 'it's just the same there.' The two men were both drinking and seemed pretty drunk. Two Pakistani accountant partners were eating in the other room. One was the current treasurer of the Central Mosque. It was a mixed Asian party – there were Gujeratis, Punjabis, Hindus, Muslims, Jains, etc. Many were prosperous businessmen.

The women danced a mixture of belly-dancing Asian-style and disco shake, repetitive and unimaginative. One of the guests circled £5 notes over a dancer's head, first circling the notes over his friend's head. The friend, a rather un-attractive, large plump man, rose to his feet and danced with the least unattrac-tive of the four dancers. Men were throwing £5 notes at the dancers now, but I found it hard to believe that the dancing excited them. Perhaps it was the combination of drink, very loud music, drumming and dancing, I thought to myself, which they found stimulating.

It did not seem quite the setting for Gujerati folk-singing; or so I thought. But after some time my companion was called to the microphone to sing. At this, the Gujerati families all stood up decorously, traditional dance 'sticks' in hand, and danced Ras and Garba folk dances in a circle, men and women, while the Pakistani men lined themselves against the walls watching them. The dancers were clearly enjoying themselves, dancing in traditional Gujerati style. After they had danced for a while, the Bombay band took over again. My friend and I chatted with some of the men and women before leaving.

The drinking at the *Katmandu* was clearly quite different from that at the *Indian Cottage*. As far as the Pakistani men were concerned, it was illicit, discreet, even surreptitious, and all-male. This contrasted with the more relaxed drinking and dancing of the Gujeratis who had come in family groups, having long abandoned any taboos against drinking in public.

Considered together at this particular historical conjuncture, the four events seemed to me to reveal a cultural 'gap' in the lives of Pakistanis: an absence of a domain of popular culture which could bridge the gulf between the austere public religiosity of the mosque and official occasions, and a transgressive breaking of religious taboos; a lack of a cultural middle ground for families and children, of the kind Gujeratis had apparently evolved, a popular cultural social space for entertainment, fun and laughter which could be said to be at once 'Pakistani' and yet acceptable from an Islamic religious point of view.

If religious, male-dominated celebrations were an utter disaster, elite celebra-tions were 'fun' in that they openly transgressed the Islamic moral prohibition against drinking alcohol and against public displays of female sensuality in dance and song. These celebrations drew on Western or South Asian forms of entertainment to infringe Islamic reformist ritual prohibitions, without challeng-ing either Western or South Asian hegemonic values. As morally transgressive, the events were marginalised, defined as deviant by the majority of Pakistanis. They constructed a Pakistani diasporic ethnicity which was unofficial and delegitimised, a space of 'sinful fun'; set apart was a class fraction (Westernised elite and wealthy Pakistanis/Asians) whose members were willing to shed, at least temporarily, one facet (Islam) of a multi-faceted ethnicity, while continuing to celebrate their national and regional cultural attachments. This fraction, being wealthy and politically powerful, could not be ignored or entirely marginalised. Yet these elite Pakistanis remained peripheral to the central arena of diasporic politics since they were perceived to promote an ideological capitula-tion to Western dominance. They were 'brown sahibs', *'ghora*-minded' ('white'-oriented, with a 'white' mentality). Moral transgression was thus primarily a means of defining an exclusive, elitist social status in a social context in which the Pakistani ethnic majority in the city remained deeply religious. The transgression created a conjuncture between normatively separate cultures (Western and South Asian Muslim) which empowered a fraction of an already powerful group – wealthy, high-caste male elders – without fully challenging structures of dominance within the local Pakistani community.

That such celebrations should move into a semi-public arena points, never-theless, to the fact that this Westernised Pakistani elite was now making a hidden political bid for *communal* dominance against the more religiously conservative elite fractions. During the late 1980s and early 1990s, however, the appeal of Westernised genres of cultural transgression was limited to a small minority, and the Westernised Pakistanis who promoted these celebrations were unable to mobilise broad constituencies. Their empowerment has been one of wealth and of connections to the wider society. Few of the organisers even pretend at present to assume ethnic leadership roles. Hence, this form of cultural transgression may be said to be syncretic without being innovative.

On the face of it, then, the 1980s revealed a hiatus: an absence of cultural traditions which were Islamic (in the sense of being consonant with the values of Islam) and yet not mosque-based or religiously focused; of a cultural space Pakistani parents in Britain could share with their children and which consti-tuted a publicly legitimate substitute for British popular culture. Although the next event I attended pointed to a potential social space of this type, it too seemed to imply a denial of a specifically *Muslim* South Asian form of popular culture.

1987: The cultural evening

On 5 December 1987, I attended a Cultural Evening sponsored by the Pakistani Women's Association at a local high school hall. The evening was organised by a woman who had recently arrived in Manchester from Karachi and was currently teaching Urdu at a local high school for girls, as well as Arabic at afternoon Qur'anic schools. She had mobilised all her students to put on an amateur performance. The audience was a mixed one: the girls were seated facing the stage, dressed in their best *shalwar qamiz*, giggling and chatting, surrounded by their families. Young teenage boys lounged about at the edge of the hall, drinking cokes, swapping jokes and inspecting the girls who pretended not to notice them. The stage glittered with tinsel while an incongruous paper Father Christmas hung bemusedly from the hall ceiling.

The performance consisted primarily of 'playback' mimes of Indian film songs and scenes. A young couple dressed in shining satin enacted a film scene of romance and desire. They mouthed the words of the song blasting from the loudspeakers with dramatic gestures. The girl was a graceful dancer. Their act was followed by an energetic *bhangra* dance performed by a rather large, clumsy woman, the bells on her ankles ringing as she stamped the floor and was twirled around by her lively, athletic companion. Next was a live show, a rather beauti-ful young woman singer accompanied by an Asian (Hindu) band.

The stress in the evening was on a kind of generic pan-Asian culture, highly commercialised and conventionalised, which highlights romantic love, expressed through song and dance and hinted at through sensual gestures and movements, rather than through explicit acts. It is the kind of familiar genre found in Indian and Pakistani films and watched endlessly at home by Pakistani families, men, women and children, on their VCRs. There was no sense of shock or unease in the audience. The performance was clearly accepted as natural and proper by those present.

There was little that was specifically Islamic about the evening, apart from the songs of praise to the Prophet in the opening act. It was Indian rather than Pakistani, Asian rather than Muslim. This public domain of dance, song, satire and romance was very much a creation of women. As we shall see, it can have a more uniquely and distinctively Islamic flavour.

If diaspora Pakistani women threaten to take over the control of public culture from men by providing amateur family entertainment, they must not only create this social space and its symbolic contents, but also protect it from external attack. Young men too must fight to create their own spaces, because male elders, who currently control the symbolically prestigious public space of community activities, are unlikely, it seems, to relinquish their hold over this domain without a struggle. This was made evident in a series of events which occurred between 1987 and 1992, the first of which concerned a passionate attachment universally shared by Pakistanis and English males, which was not religious or Islamic but had its roots in the British Empire.

1987: The cricket team's visit

About a week after the *eid* party at the *Indian Cottage*, in June 1987, the Pakistan national cricket team, captained by the revered and legendary Imran Khan, came to Manchester. The team had come to play at Old Trafford, the world-famous Manchester cricket ground, on the first leg of its English World Series, consisting of three five-day Test matches and two one-day matches. The match in Manchester lasted five days and thus members of the team spent almost a week in the city. Their visit generated wild excitement among Manchester's Pakistanis. In particular, the competition to host the team was intense. Anyone who knew anyone who knew someone who was related to a member of the team activated his links in an attempt to gain the privileged chance to entertain or throw a party for Imran Khan and his illustrious team-mates.

The result of this competition was that three parties were held for the visiting cricketers. By far the largest of these was organised by three young businessmen friends, one of whom had a link to the team captain. They held a public Benefit Dinner for Imran Khan, 'Prince of Pakistan, Crowned King of All-Rounders', as their poster declared. The dinner was held at Stockport Town Hall; tickets were £25 a person (or couple). The Benefit Dinner was intended to honour Imran Khan's announced retirement with a financial contribution (later, he was prevailed upon by the Prime Minister of Pakistan to withdraw his resignation and delayed it until 1992).

The Benefit Dinner took place in the Town Hall's spacious Great Hall, with its domed ceiling, elaborately decorated with white Baroque-style plaster friezes, and marble-faced staircase, complete with lush foliage iron balustrade. The Town Hall, built at the turn of the twentieth century, is hired out, when not in use by the Council, for anything from political rallies to weddings. On this occasion, in honour of Imran Khan, the walls were hung with transparent plastic banners edged in green with the inscription in Urdu and English 'Imran Khan Benefit Dinner'. Guests were seated at tables covered with red plastic moulded tablecloths and laid with real china. Each table was lined down the middle with the same plastic green banners as hung from the walls, to create a colourful celebration of red, green and white. The atmosphere was festive. The organisers had clearly invested thought, hard work and a considerable amount of money in the preparations.

We arrived to find the speeches already in progress. The hall was quite full. There were some 500–700 people present, the vast majority young men. I recognised some acquaintances – market traders, workers in Pakistani-owned factories, a few manufacturers. We sat at one of the few tables where women too were sitting, alongside two successful clothing manufacturers and their wives.

On the stage was a long table facing the hall and decorated with flowers. Each member of the Pakistani cricket team was summoned on to the stage in turn and was applauded rapturously by the crowd. A rousing cheer greeted Javed Miandad, the great batsman, and the crowd stood up to acclaim him as he entered. Finally, Imran Khan himself emerged. The speeches, mainly in Urdu, praised his achievements. An Englishman made a speech which, although witty, seemed to make the crowd restless. They began to chat and lose interest. M., one of the young organisers, then made a speech in English. He thanked the various people who had helped to organise the event. The money collected, he explained, would go to Imran Khan to use as he pleased.

It was now the turn of Imran Khan himself to stand up and thank the crowd who had congregated to honour him. Tall, young and good-looking, he spoke fluent English, with barely the trace of an accent. He assured the audience that he had not solicited the Benefit Dinner. It seems strange, he said, that a cricketer should need money, but he has many expenses. His tone was a little apologetic. Clearly, the idea of a Benefit Dinner was not culturally familiar and required some explanation. After his speech, it was announced that some poster-size signed pictures of him would be auctioned. The players then sat down at a large table just below the stage where members of the audience crowded around them, seeking their autographs. After some ten minutes, they were instructed by the team manager not to sign any more autographs.

The food was delayed a little. It was 9 pm. Suddenly, there was a commotion, a fight. A young man from the audience, it emerged later, had gone up to Imran Khan and wiped a £5 note across his face, saying (I was told) 'Here is some money if you want it!' The incident zipped through the crowd like an electric shock. Everyone stood up, many on their chairs. One of the organisers intervened. I saw my market trader acquaintance rush to the stage. It was all over in seconds. The offender was removed from the hall by his collar and everyone sat down again. The meal was served, rather slowly. While people ate, the pictures were auctioned. One went for £250, two for £100, the final picture for £150.

I joined the autograph-seekers to see if I could get Imran Khan's autograph. He was nowhere to be seen. Some young girls who had come with their brothers were crowding around the stage door, hoping to get his autograph, giggling and laughing. There was a little commotion. The broadcaster of the Asian programme on BBC Radio Manchester, a long-time acquaintance, told me that Imran Khan 'is completely dazed, he doesn't know what is happening to him, he is so depressed'. I asked why and he said, 'Because of "everything" – the misbehaviour of the crowd, the fight. You can't hold an event in the Asian community without trouble!' Eventually Imran Khan emerged to sign some more autographs.

My companions at the table complained about the organisation. What do you expect, they said, of such an 'open' event? I was struck by the difference between their perceptions of the evening and mine. By comparison with the many public ceremonial events organised by male elders, the function, in my view, had been a great success. The assembled audience was gigantic by the standards of most communal functions. The decoration of the hall, the layout of the tables, and the speeches, had all been prepared in good taste with an eye to detail. The food was tasty. Above all, the event was unique in mobilising a very large number of *young* men. It was a celebration by them and for them. It was they, after all, who were the keen cricketers and cricket fans, and they were clearly enjoying themselves. Surely, respectable elders must realise that this is the 'future' of the community, while they, at best, were its past?

As for Imran Khan's 'depression', it could equally well be attributed to the team's performance on the cricket field. They were losing at the time, playing rather badly. The incident during the evening seemed to me to have been a minor affair, certainly not the fault of the organisers. I told myself that the cricket team should be used to being mobbed far more vigorously for autographs. This was surely not the first time this had happened to them.

Two days later, the English rain saved the Pakistani team from certain defeat. The first Test match ended in a draw, and the team went on to play brilliantly in their next matches and to win the series. Imran Khan himself played outstandingly. He had nothing to be depressed about.

Word of the incident during the Benefit Dinner spread like wildfire through the community. Although this was never confirmed, the incident appeared to have been politically motivated. The perpetrator was sitting at a table with some members of the faction involved in the trouble at the Longsight *eid* party during the previous week. M., the young organiser, told me later that the young man himself had just come out of jail for drug offences, and that he had caused trouble in the past. 'Anyway', M. said, 'Imran Khan himself didn't take the incident seriously. He knows his people better than I do. He is used to the way they behave. He told me it didn't matter.'

The Benefit Dinner raised £6,000 which was presented to Imran Khan by the organisers. Their pictures appeared in the *Daily Jang*. But the event left a bitter taste. It revealed something about relations of status and hierarchy in the Pakistani community in Manchester. The young organisers' efforts were continuously sabotaged by older men. M. told me:

> I feel completely disillusioned with Pakistanis. I would never lift a finger for them again. I thought they would appreciate what I was doing, but I found that all kinds of people whom I considered my friends started to sabotage the event, to tell people not to go. I mean other shopkeepers in Rusholme. If you listened to my speech you would have realised that I was hinting at all the obstacles in the way of the event.

To understand why such attempts were made to undermine the dinner, it has to be considered in a broader context. Both religious institutions and Pakistani national communal associations are controlled by older men, the majority of them first-generation immigrants from Pakistan. Although they are engaged in bitter factional disputes with one another, they recognise the legitimate right of their rivals as male elders to compete to represent the 'community' in the public realm. This is the realm of prestige, where cultural capital is created through fund-raising and visible public organisation. This is the social space in which male elders acquire honour and status. There is no room in this space for young upstarts, political unknowns, and, as we shall see, there is no room in it for women either.

Two other parties were held by members of the community for the cricket team that week. One was organised by the almost defunct North West Manufacturers' Clothing Association, attempting to revive its declining membership. This was a small exclusive event, a dinner party at a smart hotel, which cost £200 a head. Clothing wholesalers were excluded. The second event was a party held by our millionaire wholesaler and his accountant friend, once again at the *Indian Cottage* restaurant. This event was equally exclusive, the participants being friends of the two men. If the previous week's *eid* party was anything to go by, champagne and whisky must have flowed that evening as abundantly as the waters of the river Indus.

M., the young organiser of the Benefit Dinner, was bitter about these parties:

> The Manufacturers' dinner was organised just in order to undermine our event. It was organised at the last minute, while we had announced our dinner six weeks beforehand. Those people are all millionaires. They were supposed to raise money for the whole team but they only raised £2,400. They may not tell you that they are millionaires. You are a woman, and not a Pakistani. But you should see their houses. And they have property in Pakistan, 20-, 30-room houses there. You wouldn't know about that. No, I don't want to have anything more to do with Pakistanis. I just don't care about them any more.
>
> If I saw a Pakistani hurt in the street, I would not help him. You know, there is a joke: On the Day of Judgement God called all the People of the Book to him to pass judgement. First he sent all the Jews to hell. He told the angels: 'Put them all in this first hole and shut it tight with cement.' Then he sent some Christians to hell and some to heaven. Those who went to hell were put in the second hole and once again, God instructed the angels to shut the hole tight with cement. Finally, he came to the Muslims who were mostly Pakistanis. He instructed the angels to put them in the third hole and just leave them there. The angels protested: 'But God, they will climb on each others' shoulders and get out.' God said: 'You don't know these people. They will pull each other down.' So too with the Benefit Dinner. People I thought were my friends were going around discouraging everyone from buying tickets, even telling them the event was cancelled.
>
> It was not just my competitors. One of my friends organising the dinner with me is a jeans manufacturer. Another is a wholesaler and manufacturer. We went around to the wholesalers in town trying to sell tickets and their response was: 'Why are *you* the organiser? And who is he (Imran Khan)? What good has he done for Pakistan? He just chases women!' (They [the wholesalers], who have all their women on the side and go out to bet on the cricket game at the bookies!) I think Imran Khan has done more for Pakistan than anyone else. He has given Pakistan a good name. A man at the top of his profession, whatever he is, a chemist or anything, has the responsibility of representing his country. Yes, he has done more for Pakistan than anyone else.

One of the most vocal opponents of the dinner, he told me, was a knitwear manufacturer. (He refused to reveal the man's name.) 'He actually 'phoned people to tell them the event was cancelled.' 'Why did you decide to organise the event?' 'We're just very keen cricket supporters, we follow the team and Imran Khan wherever they go. You know, after the Headingly match which Pakistan won, the same manufacturer rang me up and wanted his video repaired. I gave him a real lecture on the phone.'

He explained that Glamorgan, Imran Khan's county, had declared the whole year to be a Benefit Year for Imran Khan. Clive Lloyd, the great West Indian cricket player, had had two Benefit years because he was so popular.

> Many of the complaints were: 'Why should we have a benefit dinner for him, he doesn't need the money!' But this is irrelevant. What he does with the money will only be decided at the end of the year. He may set up a special cricket charity, or donate the money to a charity, or he may keep it. It is for him to decide.

Some time later Imran Khan set up his charity trust to establish a cancer hospital in Pakistan. Indeed, as we shall see, he returned to Manchester three years later as a conquering saint. M. told me:

> I personally wrote out the cheque for £6,000. There were only about 40 people at the Manufacturers' event, and all they raised was £2,400. Imran Khan wasn't there. He was unwell. But the rest of the team came. The wholesalers held a dinner at *Indian Cottage*, but it was just a party. They didn't raise any money for charity.

The attack on M. clearly struck deep at his sense of personal honour and he was passionately unforgiving. British Pakistani local-level community politics is, above all, a *passionate* politics. At stake are honour and reputation, and the struggles for power reflect the emotions vested in this domain.

Whether or not there were political motives behind the opposition to the Benefit Dinner – all three young men were known, or their fathers were known – it seems clear that it was their youth and lack of status which most provoked the opposition of the established community leadership. These unknown young men had *no right* to organise a public event for such a public hero, or to raise funds on this scale. The open sale of tickets with the open access which it provided for anyone and everyone to meet members of the cricket team, the egalitarian atmosphere, the youthfulness of the crowd – all these usurped the elders' monopoly of one of the most prestigious public spaces and public personalities. This was their symbolic domain. Hence there was general condemnation of the way the dinner was organised and glee at its apparent failure.

When a women's organisation in Manchester attempted to raise funds for a charitable cause, they too encountered the same kind of response from the business community, and similar attempts were made to sabotage their voluntary efforts.

1992–5: Finding a voice for women in the diasporic public sphere

The Al Masoom Foundation ('Of the Innocent' – a term often used to describe young children) was formed in Manchester in the late 1980s by a Mrs Kafait Khan and her husband. Mrs Khan had moved to Manchester from Oxford where she had been involved for many years in voluntary activities, serving as the Vice-Chair of the Oxford CRC and Chair of APWA, the All Pakistan Women's Association, which she had co-founded with the Pakistani ambassador's wife. During her years in Oxford she was involved in various campaigns, first to set up Qur'anic schools and mother-tongue classes in Oxford, then to bring pressure to bear on a local girls' grammar school to accept Pakistani pupils, and later to collect clothing and donations for disaster victims in Pakistan and Bangladesh.

Her voluntary activities came up against political opposition both within the community and in the wider society.

By the time she arrived in Manchester Mrs Khan was a seasoned campaigner with a good deal of voluntary work experience. She established the Al Masoom Foundation Trust, initially to raise money to build a cancer hospital for children in Rawalpindi, the first of its kind in Pakistan. The Foundation also collected clothing to be distributed to the poor in Pakistan. These were sent in containers and distributed there personally by Mrs Khan or the voluntary workers of the Burni Trust in Rawalpindi. She explained:

> Our ambition is to help the truly poor, the street boys and girls left behind, abandoned. We collect money and clothes to give to people who have never been given anything, dowries for girls whom no-one knows are there. We have an organisation in Rawalpindi. I myself go there – I sit in villages with the very poor, I live with them. We collect clothing from various parts of Britain through our networks of friends.

Mrs Khan's home was virtually a warehouse for all the clothing that streamed in. The corridors and garage were piled high with bags of clothing. Her cupboards were bursting with electrical appliances donated to the Foundation for distribution in Pakistan. She told me:

> We are sending a container to Pakistan in the next fortnight. I've put together dowries for twenty girls. Each receives 15 suits, 2 sets of bedding, 3 pieces of small jewelry (earrings, a ring and a necklace) and £400 in cash (collected as a donation). One suit is a wedding outfit in red. We also give a watch, a small clock, a dinner set, a tea set and an electrical appliance. We send a container every six months, and each container holds goods worth £600,000. I myself have given away almost all my jewelry.

In the 1990s Mrs Khan built up a circle of devoted women voluntary workers in Manchester. Most of them came from urban middle-class backgrounds in Pakistan in which *noblesse oblige*, and its associated philanthropic work for the poor, is an established tradition (see Caplan 1978). In 1992 the charity mounted a mercy appeal in a bid to raise cash to save an eight-year-old Pakistani boy suffering from a fatal blood disease, aplastic anaemia. The boy, who had arrived in England from Jhelum, had only a few months to live unless £37,000 could be raised to pay for a life-saving bone marrow transplant. His sister, who lives in Manchester, was willing to donate her own bone marrow which was compatible with his, in order to save her brother's life.

The voluntary workers set about raising money through a series of amateur shows and *mina bazaars* (fairs), held in school halls in the various neighbourhoods where Pakistanis are residentially concentrated. The very first event they held raised £3,000. Mrs Khan is a pious Muslim who has worked as a volunteer Urdu and Qur'an teacher. Virtually all the shows held by the group at the time were exclusively for women and their children. Men did not attend, except as technical assistants and cameramen. The women were careful not to be accused of unIslamic conduct. Nevertheless, the shows were focused around South Asian music, dance and dramatic performance. Mrs Khan explained: 'I believe that music is not religiously acceptable in front of men, but it is fine when only women are present. It is for happiness and our religion does not prohibit us from being happy. Otherwise the events would be far too boring,' she commented. 'Some religious people', she added, 'are too extreme.' To get a flavour of the

Plate 7.1 The 'groom'

cultural performances staged by the women, let me describe one of the events I attended, which took place in a school hall on a Sunday afternoon.

We arrived to find the hall filling with women and children. Samosa, rice, curry and drinks were on sale. There were stalls for toys, crafts, jewelry and clothes at the back of the hall, but the highlight of the event was undoubtedly the drama put on by the women volunteer workers of Al Masoom. All the parts, both male and female, were acted by young women and teenage girls from the local high school, who dressed up as men for the male roles. This in itself created a sense of fun and humour, reminiscent of the transvestite masquerading and joking at the *mehndi* celebrations at Pakistani weddings which I have described elsewhere (see Werbner 1990a, Chap. 9). The drama this time enacted a morality tale of a young Muslim Raja seeking a bride. He wants, he says, an *intelligent* woman, but where can such a woman be found? He seeks the advice of his *wazir* (adviser). The *wazir*'s wife suggests a test: the bride will be the woman who can answer the riddle – how can a live chick be born of a cooked egg? It is rumoured that the daughter of a *pir*, a saint, living in a remote area is very intelligent, and the *wazir* is sent to speak to her father. The riddle is put to him and he turns in despair to his daughter.

His daughter, however, who is indeed extremely intelligent, is not fazed by the riddle. She tells her father: 'Take me to a place where the Raja goes every

Plate 7.2 Al Masoom women and Gerald Kaufman, MP, outside Manchester Town Hall at the end of a 'Women in Black' march

Plate 7.3 Women from Manchester organising men from Bradford at a Pakistan People's Party demonstration in London in support of Kashmiri independence

day.' The father takes her to the Shalimar Gardens in Lahore. She sits on the ground with a bowl of cooked rice in her hand. When the Raja passes by with his entourage of courtiers she pretends to sow the rice in the ground. The Raja is puzzled by her behaviour and asks: 'What are you doing?' The girl replies: 'I am sowing cooked rice.' 'But how can rice grow from cooked rice?' the Raja asks. 'The same way a live chicken can be born out of a cooked egg' is the triumphant answer. The Raja recognises that his riddle has been answered and asks the girl's father for her hand in marriage. There is a traditional *mehndi* ceremony. The girl is brought into the midst of the celebrating women and this is the pretext for a large number of dancing, singing and musical performances, with the girls around the bride forming an audience within an audience. The drama ends, of course, with a wedding.

The drama was followed by a fashion show of very expensive *shalwar qamiz* outfits, lent by a local sari shop, 'Eastern Collection' advertised in the programme as 'featuring the latest designs from Asia'. Young girls, the daughters and sisters of the Al Masoom volunteers, displayed the clothes in a delightful parade, imitating professional fashion models. The cost of the outfits varied from £150 to £300 and there were, apparently, no buyers. But the women in the audience were invited to come and inspect the clothes backstage and many of them were sold later. After the fashion show there was an auction of gold jewelry donated by women from the community. At this point Mrs Khan presented a giant cheque for £20,000 to the hospital surgeon who was to treat the boy. The surgeon had agreed to start the treatment once the women had raised this initial sum. Finally, there was a raffle (I won a clock). The event had raised several thousand pounds and had provided entertainment for the women and children.

Mrs Khan writes all the dramas herself, in Urdu, and her daughter directs them. She is guided, she explains, by several simple considerations:

> When I write the plays I keep in mind that they should have culture and art, but also everyday life. They should also be a little bit funny. And they should have some kind of a message, a moral message. In this play, for example, the question was: who is more intelligent? The king or the poor man's daughter? Because the play should have some music and dancing, I usually include in it a ceremony such as a *mehndi* to provide an excuse for a celebration. The women dress up as men, so of course we do make the men look slightly ridiculous.

In another drama staged by the women at another of the charity shows, the plot involved the marriage negotiations between an English Pakistani family and a family living in Pakistan. The dramas are thus based on well-known Islamic fables but also on the everyday experiences of the audience. They touch on one of the most important social transitions for Pakistanis – marriage – a transition which involves a family's status and honour and reflects on power relations between men and women, between parents and children, and between different classes and castes. The moral message is an Islamic message and the entertainment is at once Muslim *and* South Asian. The two are inseparable for the audience, and this is reflected in the popular culture objectified on the stage. Mrs Khan explains:

> We always start with a Qur'an portion and then a *na't* for the Prophet. Then we have a little speech. We make sure there is a little play with music and dance for entertainment.

We use 'playback' (in which the singers mime the words of popular songs played on tape and pretend to sing them).

This was only one event of many the women staged over a period of several weeks. During this period they raised £27,700, virtually all of it from ordinary members of the community. Their appeal was directed at the less affluent Pakistani families and they themselves were astonished at the fund of goodwill which they uncovered. They had tried to approach the business community, the wholesalers and manufacturers, the big retailers and restaurant owners, but, with one exception, their appeal had failed. It was greeted with the words: 'Have all the men died in the community?' (i.e. why are women fund-raising?) There were attempts to discredit the organisers and to demand that they hold public elections for office, a thing most male-dominated associations assiduously avoid doing themselves.

On the face of it, one would expect the women's efforts for such an obviously worthy humanitarian cause to be greeted with praise by community leaders, and to be supported by the Pakistan High Commissioner. But instead of support, the established community leaders and organisations actively boycotted the events held by the women and harassed them severely, in an attempt to sabotage their association. The High Commissioner told the women that he would only attend such events if half the money was donated to charities supported by the High Commission. Mrs Khan herself received a number of threatening telephone calls. One caller threatened that if she involved herself in this bloody show, they would kidnap her son from school. It was a man pretending to be an Englishman but she could tell he had an Asian accent. Before one of the shows, she told me, 'Somebody rang up and said: "We are sick of you, we are going to kill you." I said: "Go ahead and do it! You are a chicken! How can you kill me when you have no guts to come forward and sit in front of me? You are just a coward (*buzdil*)."' Mrs Khan had not bothered to call the police. These people, she said, are 'just crackers'. In an even more severe attack in 1995, a black man threatened her with a knife, telling her to stop her activities. This time she did report the incident to the police.

She and her workers were determined to continue despite the attempts at intimidation. Being middle class, all the women had their husbands' full backing for their work. Mrs Khan herself was a battle-hardened soldier in the field of ethnic politics and was not easily discouraged. Moreover, the group had succeeded in enlisting the support of the local press. A picture of the workers handing over the giant cheque to the surgeon had appeared along with two articles about their appeal. The women of the community were clearly behind them. At Burnage High School, which had suffered a terrible racial murder some years before, the school raised £7,700 for the appeal benefit in a day of sports activities and fairs. This was the highest sum ever raised by the school.

Mrs Khan told me: 'I will not go after the businessmen. I am not interested in them. We are succeeding without them. When our success is clear, they will come to us.'

During the 1990s, Al Masoom generated an entirely new public sphere in Manchester, one in which the presence of women's organisations became a routine taken-for-granted matter. Among the more spectacular achievements of the organisation were its philanthropic fund-raising for Bosnian Muslim refugees and trips overland to Bosnia to distribute in person the donations made by Manchester Pakistanis. The women were the first to stage a 'women in black' march to protest against the violent raping and torture of women and children in Bosnia and Kashmir. The march, an all-women affair, moved through the central Asian shopping centre to the Town Hall in Manchester where it was addressed by Gerald Kaufman, a local senior Labour Member of Parliament. The women held communal Qur'an readings gatherings to pray for a cessation of ethnic violence in Karachi, and also a giant women's festival, *chandrat*, the 'night of the moon', to celebrate the end of the month of fasting, Ramadan, with dance, *mehndi* (henna painting), singing and feasting.

Conclusion: a feminine public sphere

In South Asia and in the Muslim world, particularly in Egypt, a feminine public sphere of voluntarism and dissenting discourse emerged in the nineteenth century, in tandem with the growth of public voluntary activity by women in the West (Badran 1995; Jayawardena 1986; Werbner 1999; Werbner and Yuval-Davis 1999). This subaltern counterpublic, as Frazer (1992: 124) calls it, expanded the discursive space of the official public sphere as well. In Manchester, the emergence of a female public arena was marked by a radical transformation of the micropolitical topography of the local diasporic public sphere. It challenged established hierarchies. Because of their autonomy and ability to raise funds and reach out directly to British Members of Parliament, the women faced continuous opposition. For more than five years, the solidarity of local Pakistani women in the face of this sustained attack was quite remarkable, with many of them ignoring their husbands' criticisms in their determination to join and participate in the organisation's activities. In the end, the Al Masoom Foundation collapsed, as many such organisations do, following an ambitious and expensive concert initiated by the director which brought over artists from Pakistan, and allegations in its aftermath that funds had been mishandled or appropriated by her as she tried to recover her losses. The very success of the organisation sowed the seeds of its ultimate failure as it moved from raising funds through amateur dramatics, performed in school halls, to hiring well-known artists to perform in expensive concert halls.

Al Masoom had long-term plans to build a children's hospital in Rawalpindi (the original idea of a specialist cancer hospital was dropped following Imran Khan's campaign). The Trust had already acquired a plot of land set aside for the hospital. Another hospital appeal for Pakistan was currently under way in Britain. This appeal, for a cancer hospital in Lahore, was launched by Imran Khan himself, the 'Sun King of Pakistani Cricket', 'Mr World Cricket' as *The Guardian* described him.

Some time before the Al Masoom Bone Marrow Appeal was launched, Imran Khan returned to Manchester once again, this time to appeal for money for his project. Like the Al Masoom charity events, this one combined Muslim and Asian popular culture in a blend which was uniquely Pakistani and Muslim South Asian. The appeal took place in December 1990, on the eve of the Gulf War, a year after the Rushdie affair had exploded into British politics. What was remarkable about the event was, among other things, the fact that no mention was made of either of these political time-bombs.

If the Imran Khan Benefit Dinner had clearly been regarded as a threat to elder male domination, young Pakistani men, unlike women, can gradually be incorporated into elders' associations as they mature. The line between 'youth' and 'elderhood' is highly ambiguous and depends on the achievement of further status attributes (wealth, professional or political standing, etc.) Young men are often recruited to meetings requiring factional shows of physical strength or voting power, as we shall see in Chapter 9. Their exclusion from leadership in the prestige public domain is thus only temporary, yet it remains particularly significant in the British context. For it is in the field of sport that young British Pakistanis express their love of both cricket and the home country, along with their sense of alienation and disaffection with British society, through support of their national team.

It is at the level of Pakistani mass cultural stardom that the publicly 'official' and 'unofficial' were merged in the city for the first time, so that the feminised domestic sphere of popular entertainment, music and humour, and the young Pakistani male cult of masculinity received the seal of Pakistani male elder legitimacy as an expression of Pakistani nationalism. At this point, however, the organisation was taken over once again by male elders who dominated throughout. Nevertheless, the other social categories – women and youth – were not excluded, hence the new space created was defined as simultaneously *public and familial, Islamic and culturally open*. This was a truly creative innovation, a revolution rather than a rebellion. Yet it did not appear revolutionary. On the contrary, once created, it seemed so natural and responsive to Pakistani (middle-class) cultural sensibilities that it was as though this had always been the shape of local public action.

8
Multiple Diasporas, Imran Khan & Humanitarian Islam

1990–5: Imran Khan & humanitarian Islam

The Imran Khan Cancer Hospital charitable appeal, the first of a series, was without doubt the most prestigious event ever held by Manchester Pakistanis in their short history in the city. It represented a first of its kind in the official diasporic public sphere: not fund-raising for the building of a mosque or an emergency appeal following a war or natural disaster in Pakistan, but a sustained appeal for a humanitarian institutional cause in the home country, the country of origin, the fountain of sentiment, love and nationalist loyalty. It brought together all the Pakistani 'Who's Who' of the region and a star-studded cast of international celebrities.

The Benefit Dinner took place in the Alexander Suite of the *Midland Holiday Inn*, the most exclusive hotel in the city. Tickets were £50 a head, and most parties consisted of family groups of about 10 members, seated at round tables, each representing a donation of £500 for the cause. It was organised by some of the major businessmen in the city and it included familiar faces: the accountant who had thrown the party at *Indian Cottage* for the cricket team some years before, along with his millionaire wholesaler friend; one of the young men, the jeans manufacturer, who had organised the Imran Khan Benefit Dinner at Stockport Town Hall. Present were businessmen not only from Manchester, but from other towns in the region – Sheffield, Liverpool, Blackburn, Rochdale.

The performers were international stars: Dilip Kumar, the beloved Muslim Indian film star, King of the Bombay screen; Mohin Akhtar, a well known actor and comedian from Pakistan; Tina Sani, a well known singer; a famous musical group; and, of course, Imran Khan himself, the lion of Lahore, the sun in the celestial firmament, adored and adulated by young and old alike. The evening raised £115,000 for the appeal, the highest sum raised in one evening in the whole of Britain, topping Birmingham's £100,000.

In the audience were men and women, all dressed in their best. Anyone who was anyone in Manchester was there. The audience was an exclusive one – no place here for the factory workers of Longsight. The menu was sumptuous. At some of the tables people were drinking wine discreetly, but this passed without comment. It was a sophisticated gathering, such as could be found in elite circles in Delhi, Lahore, Karachi or Bombay. It was not a place for religious bigots or narrow-minded *maulvis*. The evening was set apart as a moment of universal harmony and humanitarian brotherhood.

211

Plate 8.1 Imran Khan (centre) in Manchester

Plate 8.2 Fund-raising

Yet it was an evening of fun, laughter, singing and music. Like the celebrations staged by the Al Masoom Foundation, it was Islamic and Asian combined. It embodied, naturally, as a taken-for-granted, what the world could be like if there were no wars, no racial and religious bigotry and no ethnic intolerance or violence.

In order to capture the atmosphere of the evening, I quote from the speeches, which were mostly in Urdu. Mohin Akhtar, the actor, described as 'Stage Secretary', was the compère of the 'show', and delivered the opening speech, introducing Imran Khan:

Mr President, respectable chief guests, His Excellency the Sub-Consul, ladies and gentlemen.

All his life Imran Khan Sahib has been hitting fours and sixes, and making centuries, and ... during this time his *karavan* [caravan, convoy] has kept increasing all the time, as have his companions. You can see his companions – they are not like ordinary people, they are shining like *minar* [towers] of light in the sky, and in the bargain, I too am shining, *hamja se zare* [particles of grain like us are also shining in the reflected light]. They have been ruling over the sky of films for over 50 years (as stars), and these people are blessed from Allah, gifted [*inam*], very close to Him [*qarib*], His friends [*wali*].

Now you can see: since Imran Khan has taken this step of working for Allah and for humanity, what kind of personalities have joined him. We are very happy about this. The century I mentioned earlier is the century he made when the generous people of Birmingham donated £100,000. Now we have to see ... how much compassion there is in the breast of Manchester, how much pain they have (in their hearts). We shall feel it today, tonight [laughter].

Now this is for us to consider: whether the steps (i.e. the rungs of the ladder of philanthropy) will rise [laughter and clapping] or not, and whether we can overtake Birmingham or not.

You are not doing anyone, or Imran Khan, a favour (by donating). It is wholly for God. Allah's law is very clear: you will get 10 per cent in this world and 70 per cent in the hereafter. This is God's promise.

We see in this speech how Islamic themes are interwoven into the public domain of charitable giving. The celebrities are likened to Muslim Sufi saints, *awliya*, friends of God, close to God. And giving is giving to God, a sacrifice which will increase a person's merit. Whether or not these sportsmen and entertainers flout Islamic rules in their private lives – whether they drink, chase women, etc. – is suppressed during the evening, because in the official public domain they behave as exemplary Muslims, and are seen to be working for the public good of the whole community, performing *khidmat*, public service.

A cabaret act is followed by another speech in which the first donations, £3,000 each, were announced. The speaker then goes on:

There is nothing much to say about Imran's life. People from Pakistan and India, and even those who are not of us (i.e. foreigners) have one complaint about him – that he doesn't get married. His marriage has become a puzzle and whenever such a question is raised in the press or TV he wears a very strange smile on his face. I am going to sing a song which depicts his whole life, why he didn't marry and if he doesn't, what will happen to him. (He sings a verse): 'I'm still young (*jawan*) and that is why I'm a *badnam*' (have a bad name).

This reference to quite another domain of Imran Khan's activities is also a deliberately humorous intervention, going against the heroic/sacred praises of the cricketer and thus literally humanising him and bringing him down to earth: Imran Khan's love life was at the time, before his marriage to Jemima Goldsmith, a constant source of media gossip and banter, but it was all done in the best of humour. The king has only one flaw.

> Imran Khan: Thank you for coming, even if you've come only for the excitement.
>
> Since we started this project last year we have raised 5 million dollars and have been granted 15 acres of land [applause] at Johopak in Lahore [applause]. This is our aim – to try to start the construction of the hospital in March. But there is a problem – the equipment alone will cost 5–6 million dollars. We shall try to get some aid from the Government, or matching funds from aid agencies, so that the project will start treating people by the end of the year. This is our desire – that our community abroad should provide us with foreign exchange. Even today (December 1990) the value of the rupee is about 15 rupees to the pound and it's very difficult for us to build this construction with Pakistani rupees.
>
> The money we have in Pakistani currency will go towards the construction and running costs. I'm not urging you to give lavishly. Just give 50p or one pound, depending on your ability. But you should keep this in mind – that in Pakistan there is not a single institution ['organisation' – *idara*] where people can be treated for cancer. The average person cannot do a thing about this illness, and by the time he or she realises it is cancer, it is too late. Only the rich can afford to go abroad for treatment, about 3–4 per cent of the population.
>
> The person who suffers from cancer suffers pain and the people who are left behind, his family, suffer a great deal more than him. [He thanks the organisers] This is my top priority commitment: to see this hospital through. It is more important than my cricket; and I would like to see you next year too. I'd like to thank Dilip Kumar, Sarra Banu (Kumar's wife), Mohin Akhtar (the comedian), Tina Sanni, and all the others.

The compère then introduced an Irishwoman in a wheelchair, explaining that she fell from a horse in her youth:

> She has had eight operations, hours of pain, and devoted her life to help others. She received an MBE in 1989 for raising £150,000 for the Manchester Royal Infirmary Cancer Appeal. She is a symbol of faith and courage. Helen Larkin MBE.

Helen Larkin took the stage and appealed in moving tones for people to give generously. The compère then announced a large number of donations, most of them of £1,000, from various businessmen and firms. One donor, Ashraf of the *Shezan* restaurant, donated £5,000. The compère urged people to donate publicly:

> There may be people who don't want their names mentioned, but 'You light a candle from another candle' [i.e. one donor encourages another].

He then went on to introduce the next speaker:

> The greatest man in the world, who has achieved greatness through his art, famous that when he acts, the character descends upon him [i.e. he enters under the character's skin], which is the evidence of a great actor. People find substitutes for their desires: if it's hot, they use an air conditioner, if cold, a heater. In the past people used to walk, then they invented bicycles and then supersonic (Concorde) aeroplanes, but why is it that no-one has found a substitute for Dilip Kumar? An institute of acting, a school of acting, a college of acting, a university of acting. What is Dilip Kumar? D I L I P – five letters. Dedicated, incomparable, long-lasting, international, performer. I request Pakistanis and Indians to welcome him with enthusiasm. In spite of being busy, he could find time to come here. Dilip Kumar! [Music, applause].

> Dilip Kumar: Ladies and Gentlemen. I have been thinking about the title of this beautiful evening. Compassion, the beauty of love, hyperbole; in the background of this beautiful

evening is a dot – this dot is the sole centre of all this. And that blot is pain.... Pain is seen when someone else is suffering from it. But feeling pain is totally different, and it is this which the words of our sister (Helen) have enabled us to experience.

[In English] My dear Helen. I was at a loss to name the evening at first. It was (initiated by) a great person, a great humanist, and a gentleman we all know and have come to love over the years, Imran. When you spoke, something sparked within me. You talked about pain and pain can be talked about, pain can be heard of, pain can be observed, perhaps, but to experience pain, to experience the agony of those operations – that has given you the ability today to address and talk about it, and to communicate it to all those friends that are here. And that reminded me of those silent people who cannot talk, and have no new names to convey the pain and the anguish of their terrible disease that you say is a killer – cancer kills. And to think that there are more than 120 million people in that country, in Pakistan, who have no recourse if they are afflicted with this pain, then it becomes a moral obligation for all conscientious members of that society, and conscientious members of human society as well, irrespective of their nationality, irrespective of their creeds and their ethnic identities (to help).

As Dilip Kumar speaks, we hear the voice of the cosmopolitan, a man who explicitly comes to warn of the dangers of religious communalism and ethnic hatred and strives to transcend them:[1]

We realise that the world today is a global village and we, all human beings, have got to learn to live with one another, and you can't live with one another in a state of isolation of mind or spirit, you can live with one another only if you begin to love and care – that's mutual living, that's mutual coexistence, which is gracious. And in this twentieth century when man has stepped on the moon and outer planets and come back, when never before in the annals of human history was so much achieved by science and technology, it is really a shame that we in our subcontinent, and I refer not only to Pakistan but to my own country, of which I happen to be a citizen, I was born in Pakistan, I am a citizen of Bombay, India [he is a Muslim Indian]. Which is itself an irony, when the world is growing towards not just internationalism but towards universalness, that we are talking about nationalities, we are talking about ethnic identities; we, the people and some of the leaders of human society talking about religion, practising irreligiousness, practically in every step of their thinking and actions.

(The speaker probably has in mind here religious communalism in India, but perhaps also the Rushdie affair and the response to it. This is the only hint about the affair during the whole evening.)

Yes, we've had too much of this religion. There is but only one religion that is preached by all the gospels, by all the sacred books, and that is of the decency of man towards fellow human beings [applause]. And I stand here with that stamp of Indian nationality to support the cause of my brother (Imran Khan) in this exercise in humanism, universal humanism, irrespective of the fact that the hospital is coming (will be built) in Pakistan. It could be built in Timbuctoo, in China. We all owe it to one another as members of the great fellowship of human society. We have to reverse the terms, we have to think and feel in terms of developing a scientific temper and a universal heart, to feel the pain and anguish of others. And when my sister Helen talked, I knew that it came from the core of her heart, and there was all the passion of sincerity in whatever she said today.

Imran Khan, his extraordinary gifts and elevation to a new spiritual plane is the next theme of the film star:

---

[1] On the cosmopolitan appeal of the Imran Khan roadshow see also the description of his appeal in Akbar Ahmed's book, *Postmodernism and Islam* (1992: 263). Ahmed notes the shared enjoyment of a mixed audience of the performance by the great Qawwali singer, Nusrat Fateh Ali Khan.

I am standing here not saying anything of my own, but only echoing the sentiments that have been expressed by others before me [applause]. The reason why I journeyed from Bombay to this place was because of my sense of respect and care for this great sportsman. First, a great gentleman who had reached the zenith of his career, the optimum of his physical capabilities, and has now transcended into yet another sphere, a greater altitude. I know that any man of great merit, whether it be in sports or in any other field, and you will allow me, Imran, if I say that you and I belong to the community of the performing arts [applause]. As you perform on the field, I perform in front of the cameras, but the actual exercise – drilling, mental and otherwise – is the same. I came here to pay my respects ... and to do whatever little I could to express that I am at one with you, and that we are humanists who are trying to evolve a new dimension in thinking and feeling of human problems, of human anguish.

You've turned a golden page in your already illustrious and golden career; and I know that when you reach the zenith as a cricketer and a skipper, signs I see in all your activities, when a man reaches a certain altitude, a certain degree of excellence, it is only because of an obsession for his work, an obsession for what he wants to do; it is only this obsession which has brought him to this high degree of excellence in his sports, this historical ... (distinction) in his field of sports, and it is the same obsession which moves him to build this hospital, to go ahead and do things for other people and alleviate the pain and suffering which are, at present, without attention.

It was because of this obsession which you have that these people are sitting here, and it is this obsession itself which carries you and your message to the four corners of this globe, and will make you succeed and achieve what you want to achieve [applause].

Now the film star turns to re-emphasise the central thread running through his speech: the universal humanism of Islam, implicitly pitched against narrow sectarian interests.

And you, ladies and gentlemen, if I am here then let me be a little useful. Let me say a few home truths. We've all come from great distances, from thousands of miles, for a cause which is not personal, it is impersonal. It's an issue of human decency, it's a cause of humanism for which this young man has been striving day in and day out. I have been watching him for the past four days (during their appeal tour). Reciprocate in a fitting manner, in a manner which makes him feel, makes us all feel that it was rewarding to have come to Manchester.

I will not ask for funds. Whatever you can, you give. I will not ask you to respond to this small petit talk, but appeal to your higher self. Do the best you can today. Because after this night is over and everybody has gone home, the cause will still remain. This night will not remain, there will be another day tomorrow, but the cause will be there, the pain will still remain, the need will continue, so let us do the best we can for that need today, tonight, tomorrow and in the days that will come. Thank you [applause].

Compère: How can I thank Dilip Kumar? The pain he was hiding for many years, he revealed today.

The evening continued with joking, singing and music interspersed with announcements of the names of donors and the current tally of donations. The total now was £43,000. The compère acted out an amusing skit on matrimonial relationships and then drew a little girl on to the stage and asked her name.

Compère: Tell me, in your school they must have told you not to tell a lie?
Little girl: Yes.
Compère; Do your mother and father never fight?
Little girl: They do.
Compère: Tell me, who starts the fight?
Little girl: Mummy. [General laughter]

The evening continued, as the dinner was served, with cabaret acts, joking, some teasing of the compère by the audience and little comedy acts. After the tally reached £70,000 the donations slowed down. The compère tried his best to keep the ball rolling:

> We have reached £81,500. We are going to publish the brochure which gives the name of the city and how much it donated to the cause.

It was late, after midnight. Mr Ashraf, a knitwear manufacturer, announced that he would pay for the extra hire of the hotel suite for as long as the evening continued. But the going was tough. Imran Khan was looking depressed again. Playing cricket must be a lot easier. The problem is that none of the truly wealthy Manchester businessmen were coughing up large sums. Our millionaire whole-saler sitting on the podium, as expressionless as a bloated toad, had donated a mere £2,000 (I was told later), and that anonymously. He left when the pressure increased. Some of the wealthy businessmen had donated a mere £1,000 each, mostly anonymously. There was an economic recession. Interest rates were high. Businessmen were struggling. It was yet to be seen whether the Christmas sales would provide a bonanza. The very wealthy were not forthcoming, the rest had given all they could afford. We were stuck at £80,000 and the evening was dragging on and on. It was like squeezing blood out of a stone. But the compère persisted. Eventually, at 1.30 am, the fund-raisers had almost touched the £100,000 watershed mark. It was then that Mr Ashraf, the little knitwear manufacturer, stepped in to save the 'honour' of Manchester. He donated £15,000 in a lump sum, on top of his earlier donations, and the evening was over. Imran Khan was too exhausted even to grant an interview to my friend from the local Asian radio station. Tomorrow he was off to Bradford, then Glasgow.

The scale of the sum raised needs to be seen in perspective. At a mosque cornerstone-laying ceremony in Birmingham, which I attended in April 1992, £160,000 was donated for the new mosque building in less than an hour! This sum was collected, not for the Central Mosque of the city, but for the more narrowly based mosque of the Sufi order headed by Sufi Abdullah, the local Naqshbandi *pir* who convened the meeting described in Chapter 4. Altogether the order had raised £500,000 over the previous two years. Pakistani disaster and war appeals, sponsored by the High Commission, have, over the years, raised millions of pounds (see Werbner 1990a, Chap. 10). Clearly, religion and mosque-building are still seen by Pakistanis as the most elevated causes for voluntary donations. Nevertheless, the Imran Khan Hospital Benefit Appeal was a first of its kind in Manchester – the first publicly legitimate event to be devoted to fund-raising for a welfare cause in Pakistan, using the appeal of media stars, music and song in order to mobilise an elite mixed audience of men, women and young people in an atmosphere of mutual tolerance – the first serious event for a serious cause celebrated by serious people in a non-serious manner.

South Asian popular culture: gender, generation, identity

The celebration of South Asian popular culture as 'fun' is not merely a pastime or a moment of licence, peripheral to an understanding of British Pakistani society's 'culture'. If this was the case it would be difficult to explain why excessive shows of force by Pakistani elders, guardians of a 'pure Islam', are needed to suppress such celebrations of fun. Nor can popular culture, whether in the form of cricket, music or drama, be reduced to singular identities – nationalist, ethnic or religious – to be entirely 'captured' and manipulated by political leaders (see Abner Cohen 1991 and 1993).

Part of the reason for this unsuppressible, irreducible quality of fun lies in its symbolic elaboration of emotion and passion, and its 'democratic' accessibility to all social strata. Fun creates powerful counter-discourses and it is these which cannot be rooted out. Where one cultural identity ('Muslim') encloses the group in a purified fortress of difference and otherness, other Pakistani identities played out through fun constantly breach the barricades, appealing to groups beyond the boundary and to human sentiments which incorporate this otherness in parodic self-mockery or humanitarian love and caring.

Popular culture is not merely celebrated by socially marginalised groups such as women. As Bourdieu has insightfully recognised (Bourdieu 1984), popular culture empowers not only subordinate classes but also *superordinate* groups, often those concerned with the innovative production of high culture, or elites wishing to set themselves apart from the conservative middle strata. Specific modes of popular culture valorise different class fractions and social categories.

Both identity and status are necessarily expressed symbolically in interactive contexts. Hence, if 'fun' is the special prerogative of subordinate and elite groups, these groups – as social agents – must create the 'spaces' or social contexts in which fun is culturally produced. It is in this sense that 'space' must be tangibly objectified. Distinctively, immigrants from Pakistan to Britain have had to create not only fun spaces but the sacralised spaces of high Islamic and nationalist culture as well. A focus on these immigrants as social agents creating their own spaces for cultural and political expression thus entails a shift in theoretical perspective, from an analysis of 'culture' or 'religion' as essentialised, disembodied systems of meanings and *prescribed* practices to a focus on cultural *performance* as indexical and historically constituted through practical knowledge and purposeful action.[2] Collective identities, in being continuously negotiated and objectified publicly by social actors in relation to their imagined audiences, are never permanently fixed.

What produces and sustains the social spaces in which particular Pakistani symbolic discourses and practices are created, negotiated and elaborated? Remarkable in the case of Pakistani settlement in Britain have been the resources of time, wealth, effort and symbolic imagination Pakistanis have been willing to *invest* in their alternative public arenas. Equally marked has been the extent to which they are willing to *mobilise to defend* and protect these domains of public performance when and if they are threatened 'externally'. *Investment* is an act of creation; *defence* is an act of preserving that which has been created.

Migration thus entails more than cultural transplantation. It entails acts of cultural and material *creativity*. Social spaces and symbolic discourses, as well as their material and organisational embodiments, all need to be created from

---

[2] I use the notion of 'knowledge practices' to refer to an explicit discourse and its associated prescriptive practices, in the sense discussed by Foucault (e.g. Foucault 1977). This contrasts with the taken-for-granted, common-sense assumptions embedded in the quotidian, Bourdieu's 'practical knowledge' (Bourdieu 1977).

Plate 8.3 'The bridegroom gets the bride'

Plate 8.4 Young British Pakistani cricket supporters

scratch. These creations may meet resistance from the receiving society since migrants are not creating their social spaces entirely in a void (see the contributions to Metcalf 1996a). Yet not all new ethnic and religious creations meet such resistance or are perceived to threaten existing social arrangements. Within the general conditions of postmodernity the potential exists for an almost infinite creation of new social spaces, given appropriate investment and the existence of receptive audiences made up of cultural or religious consumers. Hence, as long as Pakistani social spaces have not threatened to *displace* or encroach upon the symbolic spaces of others, they have remained – at least in Britain – almost invisible, and certainly tolerated. Civil society is by its very nature pluralistic and continuously inventive. The 'war of positions' I thus describe is an 'internal' one, within the diasporic community itself.

To appreciate further the struggle for the definition and control of a collective 'voice' in the public sphere, the need is to consider more general transformations arising out of the commodification of South Asian culture. Popular culture in South Asia has its traditional spaces sited in two major domains: a feminised youthful domain I shall call wedding popular culture, and a youthful male domain of sport. The first domain, that of wedding popular culture, draws its symbolic inspiration from female pre-wedding ritual celebrations, and especially the *mehndi* rite (see Werbner 1990a), a ritual initiation of the bride and groom which licenses fun, music, dancing and transvestite masquerade (see Plate 8.3). *Mehndis* are traditionally held in purdah, behind the 'veil', in the secret enclosure of the women's quarters, by an intimate circle of kinswomen and friends of the bride and/or groom.

While the customary pre-wedding practices of Muslim South Asian men are also marked by licensed behaviour, lewd joking and transvestite dancing, these are less elaborate, arguably because the tension between the illicit and the permissible is not so great. Reform Islam expects young women to hide their sensuality and exhibit extreme modesty and bodily control. Music and dance are usually prohibited, and the only permissible expression of sexuality is in marriage. Men, especially young men, are by contrast allowed to be more 'natural' and wild since they must engage with the outside world of danger and honour. Men and women are segregated in public, and women must cover their bodies and heads in front of male elders and strangers.

From this space of absolute segregation and female enclosure popular wedding culture has been projected in contemporary South Asia on to the widest space of mass media commercialised popular culture – films, television, live entertainment, music, dance, singing – in which love, sensuality, comedy, parody, romance and passion are literalised and objectified in commodified aesthetic forms for the widest possible consumer market. What was feminised, restricted, hidden and marginal has become inclusive and dominant. What was sexually segregated is now publicly mixed. What was unofficially licensed as satire in hidden female celebrations is now licensed in public. Popular cultural stars – male and female – are adored and hero-worshipped. Women stars appear in public as sensual beings who sing, dance and openly fall in love.

While wedding popular culture is the space of romantic love, sport – especially cricket – is an expression of controlled masculine aggression and competitiveness. The intense enthusiasm for cricket as spectacle in South Asia amounts to a cult glorifying the human body, not as a denied vessel to be transcended by ascetic practices, but as an active, valorised vehicle to be nurtured and cultivated in order to enhance human physical capacity *in* the world. Hence sport is the masculinised domain of popular culture. Cricket – the game of the 'Other', the former imperial oppressor – which has become a national and international sport, has also become a popular cultural expression of modern Pakistani nationalism and of friendly competition in the international arena. It is the sport of the Commonwealth, a medium of communication, along with the English language, between prior colonies. It is a sub-culture with its own values of *noblesse oblige*, fair play, upright conduct, sportsmanship, correct public behaviour, team spirit, and so forth. The national cricket team is an emblem of the modern nation-state, Pakistan, as a 'Western' invention.

Since cricket has become a part of professionalised mass media entertainment, its stars have become national heroes. The huge financial stakes involved in the international game make it more exciting, competitive and contentious than its imperial predecessor. Today it is subject to highly controversial public disputes, it is screened live on satellite television, it provokes bitter public disputes between national teams, or between team captains and umpires, and allegations of corruption and bribery involving hundreds of thousands of pounds. Imran Khan's wedding to Jemima Goldsmith became a media event not only for Pakistanis, who remain bemused at the rapid turnabouts of their hero while continuing to adulate him, but for mainstream broadsheets in Britain: four-column pictures of Khan in colour (sometimes with his bride) have repeatedly dominated the front page of *The Guardian* and other 'respectable' newspapers as columnists pontificate over the Islamic future of Jemima and the Pakistani prime-ministerial prospects of Imran. The libel case brought against him by Ian Botham and Alan Lamb, two English cricketers, and which Imran Khan won, highlighted the way race, gender, class and Empire are explosively conjoined in contemporary cricket (see Werbner 1997c). All this is a reflection of the masculine glamour and politicisation of the game.

The events in Manchester recorded here highlight two popular cultural domains which Pakistanis, both at home and abroad, all share and which are not specifically Islamic, although they mesh with Islamic traditions as domestic manifestations: a feminised domain of 'marriage' popular culture and a masculinised domain of male 'honour', power and aggression. Both are transgressive of Reform Islamic precepts which stress purity, bodily containment, spirituality and intellect (*ilm*). Both also transcend and hence transgress (from the Islamist viewpoint) the boundaries of the Muslim community or *umma*. Wedding popular culture encompasses a pan-Asian Urdu- and Hindi-speaking population, including Muslims, Hindus and Sikhs, who share common aesthetic traditions, similar wedding songs and dances, musical instrumental genres, as well as comic and satirical tropes which cut across religious and even regional linguistic boundaries (see Raheja and Gold 1994). Cricket too transgresses the boundaries of the *umma*, creating links between nations having different religious persuasions, while at the same time it poses an alternative to the religious community in its glorification of the modern nation-state, a Western invention which promotes a very different definition of order, law and morality from that of Islam. Pakistani transnational subjectivities thus draw on three intersecting transnational cultural spaces (Islamic, South Asian and Pakistani) *none of which coincide with the nation-state*.

Performative space & identity

As performative spaces, each cultural domain also represents a source of personal gendered and generational identity empowerment, and dramatises a powerful aesthetic tradition through voluntary activities enacted by opposed social categories: Islam – by male elders; wedding popular culture – by women and young people; and cricket – by men, especially young men. The divisions can be summed up as follows.

A paradoxical situation has thus emerged in which South Asian wedding popular culture is both the highest and the lowest, the most exclusive, restricted and segregated, and the most inclusive, universal and tolerant, having the broadest appeal in terms of generation, gender and religious divisions. While Reform Islam is inclusive in its transcendence of linguistic and hence regional, national and ethnic boundaries, and tolerant in its transcendence of class and race, it remains intolerant in its rejection of alternative aesthetic and ethical expressions (see Metcalf 1982, 1987). Muslim religiosity attacks virtually all forms of popular culture and hence the relationship between these cultural domains is one of powerful contestation. The status of the 'owners' of the religious domain – clerics, saints and male elder community leaders or spokesmen – has been rendered ambiguous by the mass commercialisation of both South Asian popular culture and cricket in India and Pakistan. As on the subcontinent, so too among diasporic Pakistanis in Britain, film and cricket stars compete for popular

Table 8.1 Imagined diasporas of British Pakistanis

Cultural domain	Gender/ age	Aesthetic/ morality	Boundaries	Empowerment
Islam	Male elders	Purity, spirituality, self-denial, solemnity	Religious community/ *umma*	Dominant male elders
Wedding popular culture	Young women (Women)	Sensuality, love, comedy, satire, sexual expressiveness	Pan-Asian	Women and non-orthodox elite families; youth
Cricket	Young men (Men)	Physical power/ aggression, individual responsibility, team spirit	Commonwealth nation-state	Young men and non-observant elite men

supremacy with saints, '*ulama* (legal experts) and politicians. Although Muslim religious and political leaders utilise the press and media to gain publicity, they cannot, on the whole, compete with the sheer seductiveness and glamour of Indian and Pakistani film or TV stars and cricket heroes.

In Britain, Pakistani settlers have had to create the domain of official Islamic national high culture and its spaces, and these, as mentioned before, have been entirely controlled until recently by male elders. It was this reconstruction and control which marked the first phase of migration. During this phase, domestic wedding *mehndi* rituals, held by women in the confines of their homes, were early on revitalised by immigrants as young girls and boys reached marriageable age (see Werbner 1990a). Sports and mass South Asian 'canned' popular culture were enjoyed during this period by diasporic Pakistanis as imported commodities, packaged in South Asia. This left a diasporic public sphere in which men, whatever their political and religious persuasion, predominated. The contours of the space of official high culture and politics they created was sober, earnest and intellectual, while being also, as we have seen, a domain of passionate political argumentation and poetic rhetorical creativity; a testing ground of individual leadership qualities in an endless game of factional power alignments.

Implied here was a certain communal *closure*. Despite the fact that the Pakistani religious-cum-political domain had come to be increasingly fractured and factionalised since the mid-1970s, it nevertheless remained socially encapsulated, with religiosity, wealth, elderhood and leadership conjoined. Non-observant Pakistanis remained marginal in the community.

Sporadic attempts by women to form their own organisations had all failed. Young Pakistani men's organisations were conspicuous by their absence. The empowerment of these two subordinate groups – Pakistani women and young men – relates to the maturation of second-generation immigrants and the cultural dilemmas generated for their parents by permanent settlement. Dispersed urban living and the need to provide alternative forms of entertainment for young people and children, to compete with the magnetising attractions of Western popular culture, have underlined a growing Pakistani parental predicament: how to preserve and reproduce community not merely as a domain of religious observance but as a site of fun, leisure and celebration into which young Pakistani men and women can be socialised? It is worth pointing out here that the large Asian youth 'raves', *bhangra* discos or clubs which surfaced in Britain in the late 1980s (and which were forbidden pleasures for most young Pakistanis) served only to exacerbate Pakistani parental dilemmas.

It is this growing need for a public space of legitimate 'fun' which has entailed the movement of a locally constructed 'wedding' popular culture from the interiority of the domestic domain into the diasporic public sphere. The reconfiguration of the public arena of communal politics as *gendered*, and the capturing by women in particular of the moral high ground, embodied in performances which are patriotic and pro-Islamic yet anti-fundamentalist, has undermined established male hierarchies in the city.

What is this public arena? The problem is one of theorising the nexus between popular and political cultures, between mass media images and simulations and local-level voluntary communal public culture as praxis. It is through voluntary action that public ethnic spaces are created and it is in public that ethnic ideologies are negotiated by local-level leaders and activists in front of a local audience. The public culture produced through cultural praxis is, by its very nature, pluralistic since it evokes a variety of aesthetic, moral or religious sentiments in order to mobilise audiences or congregations for a range of communal ends, whether for the common celebration of religious and national festivals or for philanthropic and charitable causes.

Pakistani public arenas of communal voluntary action can be located at a particular point in a hierarchy of progressively inclusive social spaces, from restricted inter-domestic spaces of celebration (weddings, funerals) which mobilise friendship and extended family networks, to mass culture directed at mass audiences. At each scale of social inclusiveness different cultural narratives are negotiated. The most inclusive – that of mass culture – reaches into the other cultural spaces and is thus all-pervasive. It also travels across national boundaries and ethnic or religious communities, and enhances both the awareness of alternative cultural forms and the direct access of individuals to these alternative forms of cultural expression.

I have argued elsewhere that the domestic *mehndi* ritual has an incorporative capacity to comment and absorb alterity and to image alternative realities, such as the pervasive sexual promiscuity of British society. This capacity stems from its liminal deployment of parody, pastiche and satire (see Werbner 1990a, Chap. 9). The same is true on a vastly greater scale of South Asian mass popular culture more generally, which borrows themes and consumer goods selectively from Western popular genres without losing its distinctive South Asian flavour. This incorporative capacity is enhanced by the shared stress in Western and South Asian – and indeed, Islamic – popular cultures on bodily expressiveness and enjoyment. Quite unlike Islamic reformist 'high' culture, South Asian popular culture is 'fun': it celebrates the body and bodily expressiveness or sensuality through sport, music, dance and laughter. If Islamic morality is rule-bound and cerebral, stressing self-control and enclosure, South Asian popular culture is transgressive, openly alluding to uncontrollable feelings, sex and other bodily functions. It glorifies physical strength, beauty and prowess. It mobilises satire, parody, masquerade or pastiche to comment on current affairs, to lampoon the powerful and venerable, to incorporate the foreign and the Other beyond the boundaries.[3] Reflecting this incorporative capacity of popular culture, new Pakistani professional pop groups have begun to emerge in Britain which celebrate hybridity through an amalgam of South Asian, Western and black hip hop genres. These groups often satirise familial themes such as arranged marriages and they also attack racism, while glorifying Asian and Muslim masculinities.[4]

Since South Asian mass culture is openly for sale, its reach is fundamentally indiscriminate, especially in its packaged forms as TV programmes, films and audio-video cassettes, books, newspapers and periodicals. It thus attacks the dominance of exclusively Muslim discourses in the public sphere. In seeking mass consumer markets, the South Asian culture industry not only celebrates collective values but revises, channels and reshapes these values.

[3] On the incorporation of otherness beyond the boundary through grotesque realism, satire and ritual masquerade see Handelman 1981; 1990, Chap. 10; R. Werbner 1989, Chap. 3; Boddy 1989; Werbner 1990a, Chap. 9.

[4] Research on this subject was conducted by John Hutnyk at the International Centre for Contemporary Cultural Research as part of a project supported by the Economic and Social Research Council, UK. See Sharma et al. 1996.

At the other end of the scale, Pakistani domestic and inter-domestic celebrations objectify the specific culturally shared images and symbols negotiated in intimate familial circles. *Communal* voluntary public culture lies at the point of greatest ambiguity between the utterly private and exclusive and the fully public and inclusive. This is why diasporic ethnicities and religiosities are formed, celebrated and transgressed within this sphere.

The revolutionary nature of the Imran Khan hospital appeal and its populist style was to become more apparent as the Imran Khan roadshow gathered momentum and donations for the hospital began to pour in from Pakistanis at home as well as abroad. In December 1994 the hospital opened in Lahore amid widespread expressions of adulation for the cricketer-turned-philanthropist and mass shows of popular support from ordinary citizens. At the same time the press alleged that Imran Khan had assumed the mantle of sainthood and was plotting to overthrow the Pakistani government, while a court case against him was pending for failing to register his charity with the proper authorities.[5] In a televised interview in February 1995, Imran Khan defended his actions. He made clear that in his view the Pakistani elite had betrayed its position by abandoning Islam and the masses in Pakistan: 'Islam plays a very important part in my life because Islam means humanity for me,' he told a BBC 2 Newsnight reporter. 'There is nothing anyone can give me. I give people,' he added, underlining the Islamic stress on *khidmat*, selfless giving and devotion to the community which had earned him his current saintly accolades. The saint in Islam is always a giver, never a receiver.

From a sociological point of view, the achievement of Pakistani nationalists such as Imran Khan or Mrs Kaifat Khan, the leader of Al Masoom, has been their capacity to legitimise an alternative 'humanitarian hybridity': by celebrating Islam through humour and music, they invoke a vision of a less defensive, more open society, one which contrasts sharply with the current Islamist stress on closure and external threat.

Ironically, many (but significantly, not all) of the donors in the audience attending Imran Khan's Manchester appeal had also attended, during the *same* period, public communal events, such as that described in Chapter 6, in which speakers declared their support for Saddam Hussein's invasion of Kuwait. The framed spaces of ultra-nationalist religious rhetoric and patriotic charitable pop, however, were kept totally separate, and remained in disjunction.

---

[5] Articles on Imran Khan appeared in *Q News*, a British Muslim weekly in English, 20 January (Malik 1995), and in *The Guardian*, 7 February (Chaudhary 1995). A series of financial scandals involving the Pakistani national cricket team also erupted about this time and was reported in the press. Khan's surprise marriage to Jemima Goldsmith was frontline news in all the broadsheets and tabloids. For a while Pakistanis in Britain wavered about how to construct the marriage in moral terms, but in the upshot it appeared that Khan's charisma had not faded. By 1996 the Cancer Hospital in Lahore was a reality but was marred by hostility directed against Khan by the then Prime Minister, Benazir Bhutto. A bomb which exploded at the hospital appeared to be aimed at the cricketer. In 1996, Khan was sued by Ian Botham and Alan Lamb for allegedly referring to their uncouth working-class origins and this too made national headlines (for an analysis see Werbner 1997c). Both lawyers and articles saw the dispute as entangled in emotive issues of race, class and empire. Khan also set up his own 'Justice' party which failed, however, to win a single seat in the Pakistani elections in 1997. He appeared to be moving increasingly towards a reformist Islamic lifestyle, and away from his earlier nightclubbing mode of existence. One way or another, however, Khan has seldom been out of the headlines, and his charisma, as I have argued elsewhere (ibid.), calls for analysis.

Islam, nationalism & popular culture

To consider further the implications of the polarised opposition between sinful fun and moral sobriety, we need to examine the relationship between Pakistani nationalism and the other two sources of identification: South Asian popular culture and Islam. Historically, Pakistan as a modern nation-state was created by a separatist Muslim national movement in British India. Despite the conjuncture of Islam and nationalism which fuelled the Pakistan movement, there has been a growing tendency for Pakistani immigrants in Britain to suppress their 'Pakistani' identity in the wider, national public sphere; instead, Pakistani ethnic leaders and elders evoke a singular identity, that of being 'Muslims'. Increasingly, they have distanced themselves from the broader 'Asian' identification, and they also reject an activist 'black' self-representation, espoused by some anti-racist left-wing groups. On most occasions they insist on being labelled 'British Muslims', the only exception to this being when they bid against other ethnic groups for municipal funding or local representative positions.

Yet this marking of a singular, *Islamic*, identity disguises, in reality, a continuing valorisation of *different* dimensions of a complex cluster of personal identities. Perhaps because Islam is perceived as 'high culture', it is, for diasporan Pakistanis, a primary source of public identity, to be defended at all costs. Nevertheless being a Muslim continues to be for the vast majority integrally grounded not only, as the present chapter has highlighted, in an apparently unsuppressible Punjabi popular cultural tradition, rooted even more broadly in a pan-South Asian aesthetic, but, as we have seen throughout this book, in Pakistani nationalist sentiment. The round of celebrations of 50 years of Pakistani Independence in 1997 affirmed this loyalty, like the Quaid-i-Azam Day celebrations reported here.

1992: when blood flows green

To return to cricket. In April 1992 the Pakistan national cricket team, captained by Imran Khan, won the World Cup Limited Overs Cricket Competition in Sydney, Australia, beating England in the final. The cliffhanger between Pakistan and England revealed a hidden but obvious truth: that when it comes to sport, there is no such thing as 'being British'.

Two years previously, in a controversial speech in the House of Commons in April 1990, on the eve of a Test series between England and India, Norman Tebbit, the extreme right-wing Tory MP, castigated British Asians and declared that they should demonstrate their loyalty by supporting England. 'If you come to live in a country and take up the passport of that country, and you see your future and your family's future in that country, it seems to me that it is your country. You can't just keep harking back.'

Tebbit's remark, greeted by a storm of protest at the time, was clearly absurd in a country which regularly fields four national teams for any sporting contest (English, Scottish, Welsh and Irish). Nevertheless, his words underline the concern of the Right in the face of the apparent unwillingness of Asians, and especially Pakistanis, to 'integrate'.

While the English mourned their defeat, British Pakistanis all over the United Kingdom were celebrating their team's victory. When it comes to sport, it seems, blood is thicker than the English rain. I asked a few Pakistani friends whether they supported Pakistan or England. 'Obviously', they responded, 'we support Pakistan. It's natural, isn't it?' (see Plate 8.4)

This taken-for-grantedness needed no additional explanations. For local Pakistanis, including those born and bred in Britain, loyalty to the Pakistani team appears to be natural and instinctive, something, they seem to feel, they have imbibed with their mother's milk, or inherited along with their father's blood. As one celebrating young man told a *Guardian* reporter: 'If you cut my wrists, green blood will come out' (the Pakistani flag is green).

A 17-year-old teenager, Suhail Choudry, told me:

> We don't have Sky satellite TV and I knew nothing about the match until I heard about it from the (English) boys at school. They were curious to know whether I supported England. I told them: 'I'm proud to be British, but when it comes down to the hard core, I'm really a Pakistani.'

In Bradford, a Pakistani swore that he would cut off his magnificent moustache if the English team lost. The face-shaving ceremony took place in front of the TV cameras.

Mr Shadoo, a local Manchester Pakistani businessman with a large electronics shop in the Asian retail centre, is a keen amateur player and sponsor of two local Pakistani cricket teams. Altogether, he estimates, there are some 40 Pakistani amateur cricket teams playing in various amateur leagues in Greater Manchester, about ten of them in Manchester itself. His own team won both the cup and the league in one of the amateur leagues one year, and was runner-up in the other. The first team has now been promoted from the third to the second division. The average age of the team is about 30, he thought. The vast majority of the players were either born or grew up, as he did, in Britain.

He told me they had celebrated the World Cup victory by sending each other boxes of sweets (*mithai*). Those who had satellite TV got up at 5 am to watch the match broadcast live from Australia. Amid the general jubilation, Mr Shadoo was magnanimous in victory: 'It was a very good game, an entertaining game. Both teams played very well.'

Pakistani cricketers, like other players from the Commonwealth, play professional cricket in Britain and abroad all year round. In Britain they play for teams such as Glamorgan or Lancashire. Cricket is an almost exclusively Commonwealth game, fanatically loved by both the English and their former colonial subjects. It thus seems hardly surprising that 'multi-ethnic' Britain has become a microcosm of Commonwealth divisions and loyalties in the field of sport. Sporting contests objectify both social divisions and nationalist sentiments, while attesting to an alliance between contestants. Members of the Pakistan team like Imran Khan or Wasim Akram are, after all, much admired by supporters of their English county teams. There is a sense of friendship and fun in the competing loyalties. Sporting contests are, it would seem, like *moka* in Melanesia, a *substitute* for war, a token not of hatred or disloyalty but of friendly rivalry in the midst of peace.

Mosques or cricket teams?

Even before the Rushdie affair exploded into the public political arena in Britain, self-declared diaspora leaders of the British Pakistani community in Manchester were stressing that they were 'British Muslims' rather than 'Pakistanis'. They had faced the facts, they said: they were in Britain for good, and they expected that their children would not retain their own deep sentimental bond to Pakistan.

There were good reasons for Pakistani Muslim community leaders to highlight their *religious* identity. Their rights as a racial and ethnic minority had been established under various Race Relations Acts, and were not in dispute. Yet Muslims were still battling for the same legal rights achieved in Britain historically by religious minorities such as Catholics and Jews. Local struggles for mosque planning permits, for special Muslim cemetery areas, for *halal* meals in schools, for special uniform concessions for girls, and so forth, were being conducted in many localities (see Nielsen 1988). In particular, the battle for voluntary state-aided Muslim schools has met with implacable government resistance, despite the existence of many such Catholic, Jewish and Anglican schools (see Nielsen 1992). These battles were potentially *winnable*, and victories were likely to bring communal leaders honour and glory.

There were other reasons for the stress on Islam. For Pakistanis Islam and nationalism are closely identified. Pakistan, after all, is a Muslim nation carved out of India. While the Pakistan movement was primarily secular, the creation of Pakistan also reflected a rejection of both British colonialism (and hence Christianity) and Hinduism, and everything culturally associated with these alien creeds. In the public official arena Islam is dominant: in Manchester the Central Mosque is the focus of communal politics, the locus of highest value in the Pakistani community. Moreover, in their efforts to build permanent communal institutions, the community has established a vast network of afternoon Qur'an schools in *Arabic*, which leaves little time for Urdu teaching. Children are mostly bilingual, speaking Urdu or Punjabi at home, but few can read or write in their mother tongue.

In the pre-*Satanic Verses* days, nationalism and religion did not *seem* to clash. Fighting for Muslim rights did not appear to be subject to the accusation of dual loyalties. The same was not true of cricket, as Norman Tebbit made quite clear.

There was, in addition, also a hidden negative reason for leaders to play down the 'Pakistani' identity. 'Paki' had become a term of abuse in the English lexicon, a racist slur. By contrast, 'Islam' had retained a certain respectability in public discourse – until the Rushdie affair, that is.

The publication of *The Satanic Verses* revealed, however, a deep clash between Islam and British nationalism. 'Islam' now became a term to be defended at all costs, a matter of personal and communal honour. British Pakistanis 'became', officially in the media, 'Muslims'.

Yet publicly paraded identities conceal deeply felt communal sentiments. If cricket reveals the sentimental depths of nationalism, having 'fun' reveals Pakistanis' deep South Asian cultural roots and identity. Outside times of prayer or politics, British Pakistanis love having fun. They watch Indian movies, hero-worship Indian film stars, listen avidly to modern *bhangra* music, dance and sing, celebrate and enjoy life like all other South Asians. Hence Al Masoom could challenge male authority and raise money by providing amusement and fun for other Pakistani women and children, drawing on genres of entertainment developed in traditional women's wedding celebrations. The women lampooned men, sang and danced.

If official religion, nationalism and economic production are the domain of male elders, then sport, entertainment and consumption are the domain of young people, women and families. The sacred which is elevated above the profane is thus elevated as a *compartmentalised* preserve of male elder honour. To challenge this ranking of values by controlling fund-raising or by hosting dignitaries is to provoke the hostility of male elders. It is only an international celebrity such as Imran Khan who can challenge this hierarchy successfully, and reach out to a broader humanism *with* male elder approval. Yet daily life, the quotidian, which is profane, is dominated by women and young people. As diaspora Pakistanis sink roots in Britain and come increasingly to resemble their English neighbours in matters of fund-raising and celebration, so too women and young men are likely increasingly to claim their share of the prestige public domain.

Just as male elders create the cultural genres and social spaces where Pakistani nationalism is celebrated officially, or where religious worship is conducted in the utmost seriousness, so too young men and women create the cultural agendas and social spaces for fun and amusement, for consumption and imaginative artistic expression, which also celebrate nationalism and religiosity, but through unofficial genres of parody or sport. Women create public spaces for the family, and especially for children and teenage girls, to enjoy themselves in a distinctive cultural milieu they can share with their parents. The children come to all the wedding *mehndi* celebrations, and they are also brought into the dancing, singing, music and masquerade of the women's public performances. Popular culture, the aestheticisation of everyday life (see Featherstone 1991), draws families together and creates a counter-culture to the pervasive English popular culture and music, something distinctively Asian and Muslim which can be enjoyed nevertheless as sheer fun.

Through situational disjunctions, blendings and juxtapositions, British Pakistanis (who are Muslims-Asians-Punjabis-more-or-less-Westernised) create internally coherent spaces of symbolic practices which are set apart and 'disjuncted'. As we have seen, however, the separation between spaces is never complete. There is constant inter-situational 'commentary' and 'leakage' between spaces and domains. Different symbolic discourses, produced in particular situational contexts, cross-refer to one another, while the symbolic spaces in which they are produced are also subject to internal local-level ethnic political contestations. As the next chapter shows, these have sometimes involved in Manchester not only symbolic but more serious attacks on the cultural premises and autonomy of both associational leaders and the specific symbolic domains they control. In other words, 'situational inter-reference' may become *interference*, a clash, implicit or explicit, between discrete symbolic spaces, a semiotic struggle over the very definition of what is moral (see Fischer 1986; Fischer and Abedi 1990: xxiv, xxxi–ii on the shift from interference to inter-reference).

Because each symbolic domain is constituted, however, by a 'lived-in' world of meanings and connotations, of primordial sentiments, of material objects, of interests and power struggles, of 'natural', quotidian, taken-for-granted personal identities, these attacks seem basically doomed. Sometimes one symbolic domain, such as the 'purified' religious space of knowledge practices, may gain ground temporarily at the expense of another, within a particular community, at a particular historical moment.

The extent to which 'fun' and the spaces of fun are constitutive of identity and subjectivity – whether ethnic, gendered or generational – remains to be fully theorised, although discussions of youth subcultures and popular culture have highlighted certain dimensions of this conjuncture. By juxtaposing a variety of 'social situations', all of them equally typical and pervasive among British Muslims (who are also Pakistanis, mostly Punjabis and more-or-less Westernised), the previous and present chapters have examined not only how identities shift in their situational salience, but also the ways in which they are differentially imaged and constituted in internal ethnic contestations for power and influence. Rather than a pure, unchanging vision of Islam, we see how Islam is differentially objectified or denied, in a context which incorporates both South Asian and English postcolonial themes, comments on them and plays upon them.

One thing is evident. Diaspora Pakistanis do not deny their national roots. Their loyalty and sentimental attachment to the home country are as deep as ever. Indeed, charity shows for welfare in the home country appear to be establishing the grounds for lasting attachments between diasporan British Pakistanis and Pakistan. At the same time, there is still a real void in place of a communal space in which young diasporan Pakistanis can celebrate.

In mid-March 1992 an acquaintance was returning home late at night from a party, and happened to drive through Manchester's main Asian (primarily Pakistani) shopping and restaurant centre. Unexpectedly, without warning, she found herself in a gigantic traffic jam, with cars honking all around her, drivers driving down the wrong lanes, green flags flying from windows and sun roofs, and shouts of 'Long Live Pakistan' amid the general pandemonium. The pavements were packed with policemen. The drivers were all young Pakistanis. Terrified her car would be damaged, she sent her husband to enquire what was happening. The young people told him: 'We are celebrating *eid*. It is our Christmas.'

Two years previously, young men like these had gathered in Manchester from many towns in the greater conurbation and had run amok, breaking Asian-owned shop-windows in their enthusiastic 'celebrations'. The violent confrontation shocked parents. Who were these young people? And why were they attacking members of their 'own' ethnic group? Since then there has been growing talk of the need to provide an appropriate social space where these young Pakistani teenagers can celebrate *eid* and enjoy themselves without causing damage or public disturbances. In the meanwhile, for several years in a row hundreds of policemen have been mobilised each *eid* in full battle gear to 'protect' the predominantly Pakistani Asian commercial centre from 'its' own children! Inevitably, this resulted in tragedy as a young student working as a waiter was picked up by police and seriously injured during the short trip to the police station, losing an eye. Yet the policing of the area at *eid* continues, amid accusations that the young invaders come from beyond the city, and even that they include non-Muslims.

The amalgam of Islam and Pakistani culture, religion and nationalism, is objectified in the green flags the young men wave, and in their continued loyalty to the home country. But these loyalties are also objectified in popular cultural practices, sport and *bhangra* music, and these are *forcing* their way into the official public arena, despite the resistance of male elders and religious officials. Serious politics, like puritanical Islam, must necessarily give way to the need to create public spaces in which the young can celebrate in Britain, as well as to the universal humanism of public Pakistani celebrities such as Imran Khan.

Conclusion: space, voice & identity

The present chapter elaborates a major theme of this book: the development and elaboration, not of global or national public spaces of identity, but of autonomous spaces which urban diasporic ethnic groups create for themselves. It is in these spaces that 'culture' becomes a contested terrain as social classes and categories, positioned differentially *vis-à-vis* each other, struggle to define the cultural shape of their shared collective identities.

Why have the spaces and 'voices' of Pakistani fun, whether in Pakistan or in Britain, been so difficult to suppress by Muslim reformists? In interrogating the link between 'space', 'voice' and 'identity', anthropologists have tended to stress the quality of 'place' as a source of identity which is culturally *constructed* (see Appadurai 1988; Ferguson and Gupta 1992). Reversing the directionality of this equation, the present argument has taken space as a metaphor for voice and identity; as designating an opening which enables a privileged mode of moral knowledge, cultural practice or discourse, semiotically marked and framed as distinct both by the actors who 'own' the space and by others excluded from it (see especially Bourdieu 1985). In this sense space has to be conceived of as representational. The spaces of diaspora are created by the social events which in their totality constitute the diasporic public sphere: the places in which communal narratives are first fabulated, formulated and reformulated in front of a local ethnic audience. Ethnic empowerment is therefore as much about the creation and reproduction of *autonomous* ethnic spaces as it is about the penetration into the *wider* public sphere controlled by the state or the media. The implications of this concern with ethnic autonomy will be developed in the following chapter.

Representational spaces must, however, *be produced* both materially and symbolically (in being 'represented'); they thus require investment, public mobilisation and co-ordinated action (see Lefevbre 1991: 33). In other words, social space, both as a metaphor for empowered identity (or 'voice') and as a public site of performance, cannot be detached from collective mobilisation, agency, social practice or audience.

Reflecting on contemporary Islam, Gellner suggested, echoing Bakhtin, that

> Societies and men need both religion and profanity. It is quite often said that man cannot do without religion, but it may be even more pertinent that men cannot do without profanity. (Gellner 1994: xiii)

The strength of Islam, he argues, is that 'though it firmly regulates daily life, it does not sacralise it' (ibid.). Of course, this is precisely what the Islamists have tried to do: to create a pervasive holistic utopia by aggressively invading public secular spaces (universities, lecture halls, cafés, theatrical performances) and transforming them into Islamic spaces (see Gaffney 1994: 94–112). What they want to do is to totalise space as all vitally and intrinsically Islamic (Al-Azmeh 1993, Chap. 5). What is remarkable is how resilient 'fun' is to such attacks.

On the one hand is the question of separations and disjunctions versus hybridities and heterotopias. The sacred, by definition, epitomises all that is valued, and hence it must be policed and protected. There are clear limits set to satire and fun. Rushdie, of course, ignored those limits when he utilised the Islamic South Asian space of fun and satire to create a radical commentary on puritanical Islam. In apparently attacking the persona of the Prophet he transgressed the boundaries between symbolic spaces, to incur the wrath not only of the puritans but of the vast majority of ordinary Muslims. He went beyond the acceptable amalgams or hybrids of Islam and South Asian satirical creativity. In radically subverting the hierarchy of values between the sacred and the profane publicly, in front of a Western audience, he violated the prescribed disjunctions between symbolic spaces and domains.

On the other hand is the question of ownership and authority: who controls the moral high ground? Who has the right to represent the community? This dual problem of sacred disjunction and public authority is linked, because different subject positions afford access to different cultural resources: in the argument of identity women and young people utilise popular culture not to transgress but to reconfigure morality from their perspective. They draw on prior experiences to create new mythologies played out in front of contemporary British Pakistani audiences. A 'space' includes both actors and audience. In challenging the hegemonic dominance of Pakistani male elders, Pakistani women and young men, positioned differently yet sharing dual or even multiple worlds of lived-in realities, are currently transforming the imagining of their ethnic group's shared collective identities in Britain.

9
Factionalism & Violence
Connecting social spaces

The politics of violence

In Britain in 1992–3 there were 8,000 officially recorded incidents of racial violence, a statistic which disguises the extent of the violence, thought to have been a multiple of this number (*Runnymede Trust Bulletin*, September 1993). For example, Modood et al. estimate that between 1993 and 1994, 20,000 ethnic minority people were physically attacked, 40,000 had their property damaged and 230,000 were racially abused or insulted (Modood et al. 1997: 267). By 1997, Britain was said to have one of the highest rates of racially motivated crime in Europe (Runnymede Trust 1997). In Greater Manchester, reported racial incidents rose from 28 in 1988 to 577 in 1993 (*Runnymede Trust Bulletin*, June 1994). In September 1993, a candidate from the British National Party, the neo-Nazi fascist party, was for the first time elected as a municipal councillor in a London borough. Following the elections, an anti-racist demonstration against the BNP, which demanded the banning of explicitly racist political parties, ended in violence with a large number of policemen and demonstrators injured. About the same time Stephen Lawrence, a young black teenager, was murdered but the police failed to apprehend the offenders, largely, as a Commission of Inquiry into the affair found, because of their own institutionalized racist prejudices against black teenagers. Such processes of escalating violence appear to generate contradictory social trajectories. On the one hand, the pathways of mediation and cross-cutting ties between white and black communities which might counter the growing cycle of violence become increasingly fragile. In Gregory Bateson's terms, violence generates counter-violence in a schismogenetic process of communal polarisation (on schismogenesis see Bateson 1958). On the other hand, opposing this trend, anti-racist movements mobilise an increasingly broader and more committed spectrum of ethnic groups for joint action against this escalating violence (see Miles 1994).

The Runnymede Report (1997) distinguishes between four aspects of Islamaphobia: exclusion (from employment, politics, leadership), discrimination (in employment and services), prejudice (in the media and everyday conversation) and violence (including physical assaults, vandalism and verbal abuse) (Runnymede Trust 1997: 11). In this chapter I will consider these different aspects of racism, not from a historical or anthropological perspective, but in terms of the felt experience which racism, however minor, engenders, and the processes that it precipitates. With few exceptions, cultural difference generates stereotyping and in-group preference. This is almost a truism of culture, seen as a living ethical and aesthetic set of assumptions and practices. This in itself is not racism. Racism arises in contexts of inequality when such prejudices spill into the public domain as a violation of person and group integrity and equal worth. In such cases violence tells a story which is both exemplary and symbolic. It is an extreme act of symbolic communication which generates a transformation in human relationships. Its aim is to essentialise or absolutise ethnic identities.

Throughout this book we have seen that it is not only Western representations of the other which essentialise. In their performative rhetoric the people we study essentialise their imagined communities in order to mobilise for action. Within the spaces of civil society, the politics of ethnicity in Britain is not so much imposed, as grounded in essentialist self-imaginings of community. Ethnic leaders essentialise communal identities in their competition for state grants and formal leadership positions. But it is equally important that leaders narrate these identities in the social spaces which they themselves have created, far from the public eye. Hence, we have seen, much of the imagining that goes towards mobilising ethnic or religious communities in Britain occurs in *invisible* public arenas, before purely ethnic audiences (on the significance of such popular cultural public arenas in India and more generally, see Freitag 1989a).

Self-essentialising is, in other words, a rhetorical performance in which an imagined community is invoked. In this regard, the politics of ethnicity is a positive politics: it serves to construct moral and aesthetic subjectivities imaginatively. The moral and aesthetic communities implied by these subjectivities are not fixed: they overlap and vary in scale. They emerge situationally, in opposition to other moral and aesthetic communities.

The politics of race, quasi-nationalism or xenophobia, by contrast, is a violent politics. The communal identities essentialised by the perpetrators of violent acts of aggression are not imagined situationally, but defined as fixed, immoral and dangerous. In other words, they are reified.

Inter-ethnic violence is an act which demands retribution. It creates, as Kapferer has argued, its own 'meaning' and 'order', in which ethnic identities 'flash off' each other (Kapferer 1997). It is performative, a 'display' of self-sufficient autonomy and rejection of otherness which becomes in the course of time routine practice, grounded in common-sense social constructions. Thus, for example, the signifying practices of racial violence come to be constitutive of self and identity for white working-class adolescents (see Hewitt 1986). Unless checked, violence generates an escalating cycle of fear and counter-violation which creates over time an unbreachable moral chasm.

It was such a cycle which led to the racialisation of British Muslims in the course of the Rushdie affair. The agonistic development of the *Satanic Verses* affair can thus serve to illuminate the schismogenetic nature of essentialising discourses as social processes grounded in violence.

Agonistic moral panics: *The Satanic Verses*

The Satanic Verses was a politically polemical novel inserted into an already charged political field. The field was marked by a cycle of agonistic moral panics,

Plate 9.1 Demonstrations against alleged police racial violence in Manchester

Plate 9.2 Factional show of reconciliation after the elections to the Jami'a Mosque in Manchester pass peacefully

which generated a chain of essentialisms and counter-essentialisms.

Moral panics demonise tangible surface targets through a process of 'displace-ment' (see Cohen 1972: 9). In a moral panic, underlying social contradictions converge on apparently concrete causes. As moral panics overlap, as the 'demons proliferate', the sense of threat reaches a point of crisis at which ordinary people begin to fear 'the breakdown of social life itself, the coming of chaos, the onset of anarchy' (Hall et al. 1978: 322–3), in short, apocalypse, which only an 'exceptional' response can forestall.

The historical roots of the Rushdie affair in Britain can be traced to British and American imperialism in Iran, an intervention which violated Iranian national integrity. Supported by the West, the Shah of Iran's modernisation drive attacked not only political freedoms but Islam as the national religion, evoking instead a pre-Islamic Persian history, dating back 2,500 years to Cyrus the Great (see Lewis 1975).

The Shah's deliberate attack on Islam generated the first moral panic, led by the Islamic clergy, which ultimately sparked the Iranian revolution. This revolu-tion led to the second moral panic, this time in the West, which was fuelled by a fear of a violent, fanatical 'Islamic fundamentalism'. Rushdie, and secular Muslim intellectuals like him, shared that fear, as other Islamic countries like Pakistan began, following the Iranian revolution, to abolish hard-won civil liber-ties, and especially the rights of women (see Mumtaz and Shaheed 1987; also Al-Azmeh 1993).

Both moral panics generated essentialist definitions of opponents. Iranians, in their fear and experience of violence, demonised the Shah and essentialised the United States as 'The Great Satan'. The West, and urbanised liberal Muslims in Islamic countries, demonised the Ayatollah Khomeini and essentialised the Muslim hordes. *The Satanic Verses* can be seen as a cultural response to this real sense of fear experienced by a Muslim cosmopolitan elite.

The publication of the novel sparked a new moral panic. Muslims globally perceived the novel as a public symbolic violation, a Western conspiracy to defame and mock Islam and its sacred symbols. In Britain the moral panic was a tangible symptom of the contradictions Pakistani immigrants were experi-encing between their aspirations as economic migrants and the cultural aliena-tion which permanent settlement implied. *The Satanic Verses* and its author became the displaced, demonised targets of the felt threat to Islamic culture and moral values. The Muslim moral panic expressed a hidden fear that English decadence and sexual promiscuity would engulf the community, that Rushdie represented the future – the kind of people British-born Pakistani children and grandchildren might become if parents and communal leaders did not fight the inexorable tide of history now. The fact that the book seemed to mock and deride Islamic culture and values made it a symbol of racism, of the humi-liation Pakistanis experience daily as black victims of racial abuse and discrimination.

Hence a novel which might at another time have passed unnoticed came to be displaced as the devilish locus of a moral panic. The author was literally demonised in the Islamic press and cinema, his slanted eyes and long ears lending themselves to the creative imagination of Muslim cartoonists. A literature defending Muslim interpretations of the book emerged (for one such anthology see Ahsan and Kidwai 1992). A deep sense of hurt pride and offence generated demands for the author's death among local immigrants, even before the Ayatollah's *fatwa*.

The violent response of Muslims to the author and the book (the burning of the novel and effigies, calls for the author's death) triggered a British and Western counter moral panic. This last in the cycle of agonistic moral panics displaced and essentialised local British Muslims as folk devils. It papered over the contradiction in Britain between nationalism as an expression of a shared culture and history, and the multicultural, multi-racial nature of contemporary British society. British Muslims came to epitomise the danger to the nation as a moral community, to freedom of expression, to physical safety, to universal cultural *communication* between all citizens.

Muslim and English moderates attempted to dissipate the panic by refocusing attention on the blasphemy law and its bias in favour of Christianity. Indeed, the whole debate has consisted of such refocusings, each side highlighting and essentialising different dimensions of the cycle of agonistic panics and counter-panics (on this process in scientific discourse more generally see Strathern 1991).

As the affair continued, it became clear that Muslim religious feelings were not protected under the British blasphemy law. British Muslims discovered that their religion could be violated and mocked without the law affording them any protection. In response, they reconstructed English society and essentialised it as hostile and unfeeling. At the same time, they reconstituted themselves as a community of suffering.

Yet in reality, the solidarity generated by the Rushdie affair was relatively brief. The 'normal' politics of South Asian Muslims in Britain is factional and internally divisive. While the broad protest movement which came to be known as 'the Rushdie affair' asserted the autonomy of the Muslims of Britain and demanded that Islam be accorded an equal place in British society, this unity has been on the whole, in most British cities, an elusive, exceptional moment. Pakistani local-level factional politics leads, not to increasing autonomy and independence but, paradoxically, to a *loss* of autonomy and increased dependence on the British state and its forces of law and order (the police, the courts, the local authority, even the Pakistan High Commission). Rather than self-sufficiency, the 'internal' affairs of the community constantly reach impasses which require outside intervention.

A fundamental aporia is implied here: on the one hand, factional politics revitalises communal values through acts of identification which make them loci of intense competition. Competition continuously valorises ethnic-specific projects, while participation in internal ethnic contestations marks the limits of community as a distinct, *known* collectivity. Yet the political passions motivating factional claims to honour and recognition precipitate conflicts which communal leaders are unable to control. Hence the very valorisation of distinctiveness and autonomy leads to its own negation, as the impossibility of conflict resolution generates an increasing dependency on agencies beyond the community. This aporetic trajectory may be conceived of as one of *internal colonialisation*. To understand the dialectical nature of what, quite often, is a highly self-destructive process, we need to appreciate how diasporic factional alliances work both to knit communal social spaces together, and to divide and undermine communal unity.

Why study micropolitics?

Micropolitics, once the mainstay of political anthropological analyses, has come to be regarded stereotypically as an archaism, based upon obsolete utilitarian approaches and individual actor-centred models. As theory has shifted towards decentring discursive approaches, 'real' actors with their strategies, manipulations and passions have been replaced by 'subject positions' (according to gender, class, race, nation, and so forth). Historiographically, the intricacies of micropolitical representation are hard to follow, seeming to lose the wood for the trees. Yet the social dramas and factional analyses of Turner or Bailey anticipated by many years current discussions of local/global relations, precisely because these analyses positioned 'the local' within the regional and the national and highlighted the way in which the minute and recurrent processes of the everyday world are articulated with large-scale social change (see R. Werbner 1990). In a sense, microdramas are both historical and exemplary: they deconstruct essentialised cultural and social categories (lineage, gender, class, etc.) in order to reveal underlying structural contradictions and external interventions. They can also show – as in the present account – how what seems to be fragmented is systematically linked.

The social drama which unfolded in Manchester over a period of five years, from 1986 to 1991, can only be understood in relation to the ceremonial events which have dominated this book and which gathered groups and factions for collective celebrations or protests. Somewhat arbitrarily (because there were others) I have chosen several key protagonists as prime movers of the factional conflicts which shook Pakistani Mancunians from 1980 to 1991: Chaudhry Amin, an ex-factory worker and trade unionist turned small manufacturer, a Gujar Jhelmi with a strong sense of honour, leader for a while of a faction which attempted to challenge the hegemony of the ruling faction; Seth Saheb, a member of the triumvirate of men leading the ruling faction, a wealthy wholesaler, a committed man, a patriot and a pious Muslim, centrally placed in the East Punjabi Arain *biradari*; Khaddam Saheb, a dapper, sophisticated and urbane man, highly educated and intelligent, a voluntary social worker, a radical socialist and a committed Islamist with an activist agenda, who was a member of the Shi'a community; and the third member of the triumvirate, Maulana Saheb, a shadowy presence behind the scenes of communal politics, *maulvi* of the Central Mosque until his defeat in 1991, a villainous yet (as we shall see) tragic anti-hero: handsome, charismatic, an educated man with a good command of English, a passionate Barelvi militant, but above all, a highly political man determined to retain his monopolistic hold over the Central Mosque at all costs. He was appointed as *maulvi* by the hegemonic 'patti' (faction) which had ruled the mosque/community since its foundation. Ironically, this group (along with other groups and individuals which joined it) spent the rest of the decade trying to get rid of the Maulana. During this period they were increasingly marginalised as *the* elite of the community, as more and more actors and groups came to be involved in the politics of the Central Mosque.

My fable, of the rise and fall of a *maulvi*, is inevitably a constructed one, yet it evokes parallel processes in South Asia itself. Like the *mullah* of Wazirastan (Ahmed 1991a), the *maulvi* of the Central Manchester Mosque is an embattled figure, a man poised on the edge of greatness yet unable to overcome the structural contradictions that determine his positioning. These arise primarily from the ambivalent status accorded to Muslim clerics in the popular religious imagination, their often miserly salaries and poor working conditions.

Urban religion in Western societies depends upon trained religious experts who also undertake a pastoral, caring role. Such experts need to be accorded the dignity and status due to men of learning if they themselves are to take their religious knowledge seriously, in all its subtle complexity. Maulana Saheb knew only that he would not bow to the rich and mighty. He appreciated, in other words, that his scholarship would not protect him from subservience. He continued to battle with the *'ulama* of other sects and to engage in – whenever necessary – potentially violent factional politics.

Factions & communalism

The term faction is perhaps best reserved for political alliances which cut across class interests, lack a coherent ideological platform or compete *within* class-based political parties. As vertical political alliances, factional rivalries undermine both the solidarity of propertied dominant groups in the society and the potential unity of their clients and dependants. Rather than paternalism, patronage seems to reign supreme. Such pragmatism, combined with a politics of honour and shame, appeared to characterise the changing constellation of factional alliances among Pakistani settlers in Manchester. What the social drama presented here has also shown, however, is that, where the politics of honour and shame, mixed with sheer pragmatism, is allowed to dominate, a small number of committed activists promoting essentialist attachments to language, religion or ethnicity, may capture the leadership of factions, and come to dominate broader political agendas. Even when this does not occur, ethnic, religious or linguistic divisions may set limits to the membership of factional alliances or political parties. The Central Mosque of Manchester, nominally the property of the whole 'Muslim' community, came to be dominated in effect first by Pakistanis and, in the long run, by Barelvis. Similarly, Jones (1974) reports that in Indore, Brahmins as a caste group were divided between two opposing factions but each faction was united on an ethnic/linguistic basis. In post-independence Punjabi politics, Sikhs shifted between the Akali Dal and Congress, but it is unlikely that many Hindus chose to be members of the Akali Dal.

Sometimes it is the sheer impotence of factional politics to have an impact on long-term trends which was most striking. In Manchester, while local leaders engaged in internecine power struggles over sectarian issues, the various religious leaders who had figured at one time or another in these factional disputes built up a formidable array of Islamic institutions. Each *maulvi* who resigned or abandoned the Central Mosque subsequently set up a new viable alternative to it. While erstwhile factional leaders have long been forgotten, and past disputes mainly buried, these religious institutions have grown and flourished. Potential class solidarities among British Pakistanis are constantly penetrated by sectarian, kinship, caste or regional loyalties.

Lindholm (1982) points out that among the Swat Pathans, the antagonism between close collaterals, members of opposed political blocs, is suppressed in cases of homicide perpetrated by outsiders: a man will not remain an ally of a person who murders a close consanguineous relative (a brother or first cousin), even though he himself is feuding with his first cousins. The system thus reverts in exceptional circumstances to a more classic segmentary pattern of fission and fusion. Similarly, at the other extreme, an existential threat to the entire ethnic group may rally the two opposed blocs behind a unified leadership. The rise of the Pathan *badshah* (ruler) exemplified this process: he overcame apparently endemic internal factionalism and succeeded to power by effectively confronting an external threat to the integrity of the Swat state (Akbar Ahmed 1976; see also Barth 1985). The Rushdie affair mobilised the usually divided Pakistani and Bangladeshi communities in Britain. Maulana Saheb, the militant Barelvi cleric of the Central Mosque, told me:

> Rushdie was a good thing. I said in a speech which I made in London that I was grateful to Rushdie for bringing our young people back to Islam. They were leaving us. We, the Muslims, were united [against him]. I even joined with those others [the Wahabis, Deobandis, and Shi'ites he normally brands as non-Muslims].... Did you see the demonstration in London? 100,000 people marched together....

Such unities are usually fleeting, however. Yet the suppression of internal divisions in the face of perceived external attacks or violence may foster an atmosphere in which pragmatism is displaced by 'vertical' ethnic and communal ideologies, often progressively radical. On the positive side, it can also (as happened in Manchester) unite erstwhile factional enemies in an attempt to control the source of violence. Violence and the fear of violence set limits to the utilitarian shifting of individuals and small groups back and forth between factions, as bonds of substance and kinship are evoked, linking protagonists to the victims of violence. Internal violence may be part of the everyday politics of honour and shame, but once violence is constructed as having a particular source (an individual, such as the Maulana or his ally) or as an external threat (posed by 'Wahabis' or the 'West', for example), this leads over time to a realignment. When this happens, interpersonal rivalries and the pragmatics of alliance change. Either, as happened in Manchester, divided leaders bury the hatchet temporarily to rid themselves of a troublemaker or, if this fails, factional politics is displaced by a politics of fear subsisting on emotional rallying of supporters in the name of primordially constructed identities. It was in the interest of Maulana Saheb and his closest allies to perpetuate the violence, partly in order to intimidate the opposition but mainly to draw the lines between loyal supporters and opponents more sharply and to reconstruct this division in moral terms, as marking a divide between true and false Muslims.

The polarisation that emerges as a result of a politics of violence suppresses economic antagonisms between classes because it is animated by a sense of threatened subjectivities. At its most pernicious, violence bifurcates the community along communal lines, defined by kinship, caste, religious sect or ethnicity. Factions may not be ideological but they are never the only actors in the political arena: they exist alongside other political organisations which foster coherent class or ascriptive ideologies and build up, sometimes almost surreptitiously, organisations which are *not* fractionised but are highly unified and ideologically committed (especially during their formative stages). In an atmosphere of pragmatic power manipulations and compromises, even small committed cadres may shatter the *status quo*. In Egypt, for example, as Gaffney's study shows, radical Islamist groups were allowed by a weak local state to use violent tactics over an extended period of time to polarise Muslims and Coptic Christians and to undermine their peaceful co-existence (see Gaffney 1994, especially Chap. 4). It is often easier to mobilise supporters under nationalist, caste or ethnic banners: Hardiman's (1982) own discussion of anti-colonial mobilisation shows that it was not 'class' but Indian national liberty (or Patidar solidarity) which was the rallying cry of subaltern leaders, even though the groups mobilised were peasant farmers.

Such displacements may, as a consequence, prevent the emergence of inter-communal class solidarities. Above all, however, it is the fuzziness of factional agendas, appealing to many diverse interests and constituencies, which makes them more vulnerable than explicitly class-based parties to a rhetoric which evokes people's fears and sense of threatened identities, and allows for the rise of unscrupulous politicians, out to gain power at the expense of internal and external communal consensus. This was evident in the politics of the Central Mosque of Manchester during the 1980s which provoked internal disunity while making rhetorical claims to Islamic unity in the face of Wahabis or the West. Yet what was also striking about the conflicts in this diasporic arena was the class consciousness of the vast majority of faction leaders and their ideological commitment to particular political agendas.

The problem was that in the face of constructed 'external' threats, moderate pragmatist leaders for a long time lost out to 'extremists' in their efforts to rally supporters.[1] Their ability to unite was also undermined by past fights and remembered public offences which divided them from their potentially moderate allies. The complexity of this micropolitical arena may thus afford us some insight into the way communalism in India and Sri Lanka or ethno-nationalism in Pakistan works through a transmutation of factional alliances and political parties, pragmatically constructed, and often grounded in legitimate class griev-ances, to promote communal violence. Neo-fascist groups in Europe similarly use violence to transmute class grievances into ethnic conflicts.

The mosque elections

This trajectory may seem irreversible. In the elections to the Mosque Committee which took place in Manchester in August 1989, a powerful alliance of erstwhile rivals had been constructed to oust the allegedly villainous *maulvi*. The alliance included the founding group which had built the mosque, the Arain businessmen and several of their allies who had displaced them; Chaudhry Amin and his supporters from Longsight and Whalley Range; and at least one of the rival Barelvi mosque groups in the city (which claimed, however, to remain 'neutral'; despite this group's deep hostility to Maulana Saheb, prominent members expressed the fear that the Central Mosque might be taken over by 'Deobandis'). This faction (*patti*) was aligned against the Maulana and his

---

[1] I define moderation as a tolerance of divergent points of view, and an attempt to work within a broad consensual framework. Extremism is defined as a commitment to a specific ideology as the only legitimate truth, which others must conform to, or be excluded altogether.

supporters. Prominent among the latter were Khaddam Saheb, the radical activist and his entourage, the Deputy Chairman from Whalley Range, Association B from Longsight and at least one of the UK Islamic Mission mosques (despite the fact that the members of this group, aligned with *Jama'at-i Islami*, were normally branded 'non-Muslim' 'Wahabis' by Maulana Saheb in his conversations with me). The opposition faction united the Arain activists, normally fractionised by internal animosities, and included virtually all the big businessmen and early pioneers, including Seth Saheb, who had at one time or another controlled the mosque, and most of the representative voluntary associations in the city. The groundwork for the elections had been extensive and vast sums had been spent by all the leaders on enrolling their members (the opposition faction was said to have enrolled 3,000 voters).

The elections to the Central Mosque took place on Friday, 11 August 1989. By the time I arrived, the factional leaders had already begun to gather, sorting out last-minute arrangements for what promised to be a long day of voting. Throughout that morning the tension in the courtyard outside the mosque was so tangible it could be cut with a knife. It seemed that a tiny incident might spark a major conflagration. The police were out in full force. Indeed, the community liaison police officer told me that they had been planning this election for months (it had been delayed six months on various pretences, as the factions first went to court, then on *hajj*). The elections were being organised, not by members of the community, but by a special London-based English electoral firm. Community leaders maintained constant vigilance as lines of men queued up to vote. The slightest disputes were brought before the community liaison police officer for arbitration.

In the mosque, Maulana Saheb was delivering the Friday sermon. He had been warned not to electioneer. It was the month of Ashura, and the battle of Karbala was the main theme of the sermon. The sermon stressed the holiness of the Prophet's family, *Ahl-e Rasool*, and the Maulana dwelt at some length on the heroic martyrdom of Ali, son-in-law of the Prophet and Husain, his martyred grandson. He explained to the congregation that Husain had told his followers to escape during the night before it was too late. But they had refused:

> They all wanted to stay with Imam Husain. They all said: 'We left our cities, homes and children and joined you, and if we leave you now, how can we face the Prophet, Peace Be Upon Him, and Allah? We swear to God, even if we are slashed into small pieces, we shall never turn our backs on you and never leave you alone. We are ready to fight with our swords and arrows. We can even fight with stones for your sake.'
>
> In the morning Shimr (the Caliph's evil commander) brought them a letter of protection issued by Ubaid Allah Ibn Ziyad (the governor of Kufa who ordered the attack) and called up Hazrat Abbas because he was Shimr's nephew. Hazrat Abbas told him: 'Curse on your protection and upon he who has issued you with this letter! You wish to kill Hazrat Husain by granting me protection? I will not leave Hazrat Husain and I do not want your protection!'

Maulana Saheb went on to relate another episode involving Husain's sister: Husain's head was brought before her impaled on an arrow, and Ibn Ziyad struck at Husain's teeth with his stick. He was stopped by one of the commanders of the enemy army who said: 'This is the face which the Prophet Muhammad, Peace Be Upon Him, used to kiss.' 'Now Husain's name is bright,' the Maulana continued, 'and he is remembered for his courage and because he was killed for no reason. He was on the side of right but the wicked king of that time killed him. And those people who killed him, we do not think of them as Muslims.'

The story of Husain's martyrdom is clearly an allegory invoking the loyalty of supporters who remain constant even when they are promised immunity. Maulana Saheb now moved on to decipher the allegory:

> Today you people have come with an aim which is to cast your vote. This is your responsibility: to choose those people who are able to work for you [represent you]. If the people who share my sentiments are elected then I will stay [as the *maulvi* of the mosque] but if they are not elected I will resign. During the past years in which I have been working in the mosque, if I hurt anybody's feelings then please forgive me. Whatever I have done, I did the best I could, and I did it with sincerity. I have spread the word of Islam throughout Europe, not only in Manchester. I believe that everyone in Europe, in every school [i.e. every sect] has heard of the Central Mosque of Manchester. Many groups have come here [to visit the mosque] and I have guided them along the righteous path. I have represented this mosque in all the [religious] movements.
>
> This election is your secret referendum for me. In these two groups [factional alliances] there are some people who refuse even to shake hands with me. If they win, how could I lead the prayer with them [standing behind me]? May God make my friends successful. If they [his group] win, I shall lead the morning prayers, and if your vote goes on the other side [against me], then my night prayer [tonight] will be my last. If someone's heart has been hurt, then I am sorry. I ask for forgiveness. If the decision is against you [i.e. against his supporters] then you will have to accept it without making or causing any trouble. The same request comes from the other group as well: that you co-operate in the future so that there will be no trouble [fighting]. We should work in peace and we should come to the mosque as much as possible.

This speech can only be understood in its full pathos if one appreciates the depth of identification the *maulvi* feels with the Central Mosque, his domain for the past ten years. As he told me:

> You know, they [the businessmen, his enemies] invited the Keeper of the Ka'ba from Saudi Arabia to come and talk here, in my mosque. I left the mosque, I refused to hear him. He showed no respect, he should have approached me and asked permission – from me. I am the *maulvi* here.

The Central Mosque is 'his' mosque, a space from which he has excluded at will all preachers and community leaders who do not share his particular brand of Islam, as well as anyone who had crossed him. The mosque has been his command centre, from which he has organised the campaigns to take over the Community Centre or other mosques. He compels the audience to recognise (what they already know) that the election is about him, not about the management of the mosque, and that if he loses, he will be fired. Hence he threatens to resign. His vulnerability is exposed as a personal affliction: he is the victim of hatred despite his good work for the sake of Islam and the community. Like Husain, he is a martyr wrongly attacked.

Most significant about his speech is the insight it provides into the motives behind his aggressive public persona. To an outsider he appeared to have reached the apogee of success: he drove around Manchester in a white Mercedes; he spoke with dignity and assurance; he made speeches in the Town Hall before visiting dignitaries; he met schoolteachers and race relations representatives. He was not treated as an ignorant man by outsiders: his English was relatively fluent and he was well educated in Arabic and Qur'anic studies. Yet this man who seemed to have reached the zenith of his career felt that his honour was not assured, and he articulated his vulnerability in *class* terms. Although he had repeatedly explained to me the Barelvi creed that accords respect to any Sayyid descendant of the Prophet, regardless of his occupation ('Even a poor man', he told me. 'You saw me just now, sitting with that old man. I kissed his hand. He is just a taxi-driver but I respect him because he is from the family of the Prophet'), he nevertheless was determined that his own honour should not be compromised by his position as a *maulvi*. The irony was that in England he could in fact have gained respect and honour from members of the community simply by providing pastoral services to those in need and by instructing them in the intricacies of their faith. Instead, he continued to fight the spectre of failure and subservience as though he was still working in Pakistan.

After the *jumaa* prayers he emerged from the mosque, dressed in white, a flamboyant white turban on his head. He sat alongside the members of the ruling faction still loyal to him, where he was surrounded by supporters. He had infringed the rules laid down before the elections, and had got away with it.

The community liaison police officer explained to me that he admired the community:

Mind you, the organisation of the elections leaves much to be desired. There were a lot of loose ends to be negotiated. It wasn't at all well prepared. These people are learning about democracy here. Do you know that this is the only mosque in the whole of Britain that holds such elections? Even the mosques in London don't hold them – they all belong to some country, Pakistan or something, which gave the money to build those mosques. And Pakistan itself hasn't had much democracy, they've mainly had dictatorships, haven't they? So these people are having to learn about democracy. [I commented that perhaps the mosque needed a constitution. He laughed.] No, I think on balance it's better off without a constitution, it would probably only complicate matters more. It's probably better to continue as now to resolve problems through negotiation with both sides. They all come to me – I have to resolve matters but there's usually justice on both sides, I can see both points of view, it's very difficult to come to a decision.

But I like them. They are a very law-abiding community. They are very co-operative, they have principles, and they bring their children up very well to be God-fearing, good Muslims. The family is very strong. They support the family, are very family-oriented; in some ways they remind me of the Jewish community. They are having some problems now with their young people. They [the youth] are rebelling, flexing their muscles, and they [the parents] expect the police to deal with them, but of course we can't.

The problem here is [in a hushed voice] that there is a lot of money which flows through this mosque every week and it's not very well accounted for. But I like [Maulana Saheb]. I could spend hours just listening to him. There is quite a lot of tension here. There's cheating on both sides. People might vote twice, or vote in someone else's name. They are marking their fingers with red, but it can be washed off. They can give a fictitious work place [which makes them eligible to vote in Manchester; it was said that many of the voters had come from as far afield as Nelson].

He explained that there had been some argument about the trusteeship a few moments before, but it had been ignored.

[Do you like your job? He laughed.] Well, I'm getting on towards retirement now, I've been in the police for more than 26 years and after 30 years I retire. I've been in police

headquarters and I know that the management there is no good. I don't just suspect it –
I know it. And it affects the morale of the bobby on the beat. They don't get the support
they need. Oh, I enjoy this job of dealing with the community. You know, they [the police]
work under pressure, I don't like to use the word stress. And then they do things they
shouldn't. Like the other day a Mr X. phoned the police because he had had his front
windscreen smashed. It was evening. When the policeman came an hour and a half later
he complained that he had been called out on such a trivial matter. He could have
apologised and explained that he had been very busy dealing with very serious matters,
one after the other, but instead he was rude and X. rang me up to complain. You have to
be tactful but the problem is with the [police] management really.

Despite his involvement in the preparations he remained somewhat puzzled
by the factional complexities of alliances and counter-alliances. At one point he
drew me aside and said:

I wonder if you could explain something to me? There is one thing I don't understand:
why are the current committee members fighting against their own committee?...

As the afternoon wore on, a festive, carnival spirit replaced the more tangible
tension of the morning. A lot of people relaxed. Cases of Coca-Cola were produced and distributed. It was a beautiful warm afternoon. Food was handed out.
It now seemed more likely that the day would pass without a fight. One little
incident which flared up involved the plump young welfare officer of the ruling
faction. The leaders of both sides rushed forward to control their supporters, to
quieten them down. More tangible even than the tension was the consciousness
both sides displayed that tension should be avoided at all costs. Only a few,
especially one group on Maulana Saheb's side, seemed willing to let things get
out of control. But key leaders on that side too seemed determined to maintain
order. As evening approached, the courtyard filled with men, and, as it grew
dark, there was a sense once more that if something flared up, an explosion
could follow. But the atmosphere remained calm and, indeed, full of camaraderie
and goodwill. The young men lined up peacefully and patiently, waiting their
turn to vote, chatting to friends. There was some discussion about when polling
should cease. It had started late: instead of at 9 am as had been advertised, it
began at 10.15, and this gave an excuse to keep the gates open after 9 pm, the
official closing time. In fact, everyone who came to vote was given the chance to
do so. At 9.30 pm when the gates to the mosque courtyard were finally closed,
and policemen stationed to guard them, there was no-one left outside. The
queue was still quite long but eventually, at about 10.05, everyone had voted,
and the doors were shut (see Plate 9.2).

The results of the elections were announced the following morning. The
Maulana's faction had won by a handful of votes. Altogether, 1,150 votes had
been cast. The ruling faction had received some 615 votes, the opposition about
530, a difference of 85 votes, 47.8 per cent cast for the opposition, 52.2 per cent
for the ruling faction. Chaudhry Amin whom I saw that evening was exhausted
and disgusted. 'Most people never bothered to turn up,' he complained. A small-
time leader, he knew the defeat probably spelt the end of his political career.

A few days later, when I went to talk to the *maulvi*, I found him still
triumphant, basking in glory. He had routed the opposition and he expressed no
magnanimity or willingness to forgive his opponents. He would not, he told me,
'bend down his neck so that rich businessmen could step over it'. Ironically, of

course, he had worked closely in alliance with some of the most prominent Arain businessmen in the community for many years; they had turned against him only recently to join with their former Arain factional opponents. Now, however, the battle lines were clearly drawn:

> There are people in Manchester who do not believe at all. They are the businessmen. All they want is a *maulvi* who will submit to them.... They want me to bend my neck but I refuse to bend my neck. I am a man with education. I have a BA, and an MA in Islamic Studies, and I have shown them! [triumphantly] I respect people, even taxi-drivers, not because they are rich but only if they come from the family of the Prophet. That is the most blessed family.

'Did you hear my speech?' he asked me. 'Did you see them? There were young people crying there, my supporters were all crying when I said I would resign.'

I asked him why some people were so against him. He responded with a harangue, accusing most members of the community of not being Sunnis, of being Wahabi, not true Muslims:

> You know, I never go into a Shi'a mosque, I have nothing to do with the Shi'ites. And then there are others that are not Sunni; they are Wahabi, followers of Saudi Arabia. I never agree to stand behind them in Mecca, because they are not real Muslims.
> (Q.) Who? The Islamic Academy? The UK Islamic Mission?
> Yes, all of those.
> I tried again: 'How do you envisage your role in the community?'
> My role is to bring the message of Islam to people and the wider society, but not by going around begging, knocking on doors. Only if I am invited, or if someone – like you – comes and wants to learn. Not to crawl. I was invited to give a talk the other night to the Rotary Club. I talked for about two hours.

In some ways Maulana Saheb fits Gaffney's portrayal of the *mujahid* preacher, an embattled warrior for the cause of Islam, connected metonymically to the sources of sanctity (the Qur'an, the Prophet's descendants) (Gaffney 1994: 53). Yet like all Barelvi preachers, his hermeneutical abilities were remarkable: I had indeed learnt a good deal from his imaginative and often penetrating interpretations of the Qur'an and Hadith as symbolic allegories. His understanding of Islam combined both metaphor *and* metonym, ritual practice *and* interpretation. In this respect he was neither an Islamist nor a fundamentalist. Yet he shared many of their political sentiments and attitudes.

He left me with the sense that here was an embattled individual, who, even in victory, was quite unable to assume a caring, pastoral role in relation to the community at large, or to acknowledge his responsibility for all its members. As far as he was concerned, the moment of victory was not a moment for healing communal divisions; nor did he feel that the mosque, corporately owned by the community, should rightfully be accessible to all its members, irrespective of religious approach. He conveyed no sense that he should assume the role of religious head of the whole Muslim community of Manchester. The sectarian battle, like the class battle, was an ongoing one. He could not unlock the chains which bound him to partisan causes. Indeed, he appeared to have no desire to do so.

Two years later, in 1991, while I was away from England, Maulana Saheb was finally defeated. The battle against him was led this time by a local *pir* (Muslim saint), a pious reformist with Deobandi tendencies who led his troops to elections under the banner 'defeat evil'. Among his allies, I was told, was the *maulvi* of one of the UK Islamic Mission mosques who had switched sides after being excluded from the Central Mosque when he wished to pray there at the death of a close relative.

And so the 'evil' Maulana was finally removed from his throne. Yet even the new religious leader, whose slogan was communal peace, failed to institute the *majlas al shura*, the assembly of elders, which he had promised he would set up to unite the community. Other attempts to create a Council of Mosques, initiated during the Rushdie affair, had also all failed and had eventually collapsed (Scantlebury 1995: 429). Ultimately, this living saint too appears to have been defeated and the mosque limped on with revelations of corruption and regular fighting, all of which required the involvement of outside agencies: the police, the courts, the High Commission. A central democratic institution of the community as a corporate body, it was still seeking a religious leader who could span all the interests, sects and groups in the community and recreate a prior moral amity. The Maulana, I was told, had left for Pakistan in 1995 amid allegations of fraud and corruption (he was later to return).

The aftermath of violence

After the death in Whalley Range, it had seemed to me that the violent divisions within the Manchester Pakistani community which emerged during 1987 would create a spiral of further violence. Subsequent events proved that this assumption was too simplistic. The death in Whalley Range, following the earlier death at the Central Mosque and the election *halagula* at the Community Centre, appeared to drive home the cost of violence to the community and its reputation. Leaders embarked on a cautious reappraisal of strategy and a greater consciousness of the consequences of spontaneous physical aggression. They began to preach self-control. Events during the following year were marked by careful and considered preparations. Elections were universally felt to be best held by means of the ballot-box rather than by a show of hands. An attempt was made to settle election results by compromise before the actual event.

Four potentially violent events took place peacefully. The first – the elections to the Community Centre – started rather badly with abuse and shouting matches between factional leaders during pre-election meetings. In the upshot, however, the losing faction decided to accept with good grace what amounted to a technical constitutional defeat. They did this, despite the fact that they had spent a good deal of time and money in mobilising support. In the following event – the second elections of a Longsight Community Representative for the Race Sub-Committee – the two main candidates reached a dramatic compromise agreement minutes before the elections were due to be held.

The third event, the election of a Whalley Range Community Representative, was bitterly contested. It ended quite remarkably in a dead heat with both candidates receiving exactly the same number of votes. There was a handful of ambiguous spoilt ballots. One of the factions did, however, win the *Deputy* Community Representative seat, by one vote (!). Here was a potentially explosive situation. Among the people who had gathered outside the church hall where the elections had been held to hear the results were men supporting the two rival factions spanning both Whalley Range and Longsight, as well as other parts of the city. A great deal of time and effort had been invested in the election campaign. The result was highly ambiguous, the animosities deeply felt. Yet here too the participants restrained themselves. There was no violence and no shouting. I was told later that elections to the Central Mosque were being delayed in order to avoid violence, and to prepare for a peaceful and orderly campaign.

The fourth and most important testing event, the mosque elections, had also passed off peacefully. The results were announced on the following morning. It was a bright and pleasant day. Outside the mosque, it was mainly the activists who gathered to hear the results. One of them greeted me: 'You saw the elections, they were peaceful, democratic.' I stood around, chatting with one of the men from the opposition group. Suddenly the other group broke into shouts of 'Nare Takbir' ('Say, He is Great'). There was a rush forward and shouting. My companion, whose father had been one of the founding members of the community, said: 'It looks as though they've won.' Some of the leaders of the winning faction quieted the shouters, saying: 'No, no, none of this.' The winning chairman made a little speech saying that the elections had been conducted peacefully and that he was now calling on the other party to join them. There was a big show of peace. The chairman came forward and embraced a leading member of the losing faction. Other men embraced each other, while, in the meantime, the results were brought out and people crowded around to inspect them. A man with a thin face whom I vaguely recognised gave me the results. Silently, the losers walked away, deflated.

After his ultimate defeat and the loss of his post at the Central Mosque, Maulana Saheb went back to Pakistan for a while, amid a cloud of allegations about financial misconduct. Later, he returned to Manchester. When I met him in February 2000, he was extremely friendly and affable. He told me mournfully that although he was still the *khalifa* and right-hand deputy of his London *pir*, all his attempts to gain a post as a *maulvi* in a major mosque in Britain had failed, despite his superior qualifications. I wondered whether the story of his infamous reign in Manchester had gone before him. Some months later, I was told that he had set up a new mosque of his own in Manchester, to add to the growing list of mosques established over the years by ex-'*ulama* of the Central Jami'a Mosque in the city.

Conclusion: Islamic dilemmas

Factional conflicts disguise long-term historical trends behind the facade of an apparently never-ending soap opera. People in Manchester, as elsewhere, fabulate the political history of their community retrospectively as a series of *personalised* leadership struggles, victories and downfalls. The details and personalities in these disputes all appear crucial to this historical narrative of community, and rather trivial and confusing to bystanders. But until quite recently the real historical process has been one of increasing *religious* domination (and choice). The enormous efflorescence of mosques and their growing influence in communal affairs has not been a peculiarly Mancunian phenomenon: it is evident throughout Britain, always apparently generated by local personal disputes. By

1995 there were 19 mosques within a radius of five miles from the city centre of Manchester (of which 11 were Pakistani), and they reflected the full national, linguistic and sectarian diversity in the Muslim community, as well as the factional rifts and the splits these had precipitated (see Appendix 2). The ideological divisions within South Asia have been reproduced in Britain, with the saintly *pirs* and *'ulama* who have spearheaded this ideological expansion ultimately bypassing the factional politics and political resistances they encountered. If there is a counter-movement, it is towards greater direct involvement in British national and local government electoral politics and the emergence, as we saw in the previous chapter, of popular forms of public protest and syncretic popular cultural celebration, the latter combining Islam with 'fun' and often dominated by women, sportsmen and youth.

The aporia of a (Muslim, Pakistani) community struggling to find itself is evident: because it needs to be democratic the community enmeshes itself in relations with external agencies which are asked to mediate internal conflicts. Clearly, it is impossible under the circumstances to speak of communal 'autonomy', although this is a constant theme of speeches made by lay preachers and activists. At the same time, it could be argued that this enmeshment with British institutions simply underlines the fact that Pakistanis are local citizens who exercise their rights in their adopted country. It does seem clear, however, that unified communities can be more effective in the broader public sphere. Bradford Pakistanis, united through a long-term pact between a Deobandi and Barelvi (Sher Azam and Pir Maroof) and having the Council of Mosques (set up and funded by the local authority) as a base, have been able to exert great influence in the national public sphere (see P. Lewis 1994 and 1997; Samad 1997).

If Islam is the identity which Pakistanis wish, above all, to defend and transmit to the next generation, then the Central Mosque of Manchester is the jewel in the crown, the highest value. Yet this crown has been tarnished by constant bickering and conflict, as well as by the sheer corruption of a few mosque officials. The younger generation would seem to be the main victims of this embattled atmosphere. At times they are used in factional confrontations to present a show of strength. But, on the whole, young men simply avoid the mosque altogether, finding the sectarian arguments and factional fights incomprehensible and unpleasant. A few join youth associations, the majority inspired by Islamist ideas and promoting global versions of Islam. For all these young men Islam seems far from being a religion of peace. Elders are well aware of this growing alienation of their young people. Yet at the same time there are important issues to settle in the democratic management of mosques, especially corporately owned ones like the Central Mosque of Manchester, which they cannot ignore. Both financial arrangements and the toleration by Islam in Britain of different interpretations and ritual practices are at stake in these factional disputes.

Many erstwhile factional leaders have turned to other, more global causes. Seth Saheb now devotes his energies to the Imran Khan appeal fund. Al Masoom had led the way towards new forms of fund-raising and Islamic celebration. There is a growing trend to bypass the politics of the mosque altogether by engaging directly in national secular politics, but secular politics too is necessarily enmeshed in factionalism. In the mid-1990s Pakistani diasporic politics in Manchester was still ultimately inseparable from religious politics.

Local members of the community can easily avoid factional disputes and, indeed, many choose to do so. But whenever they set foot in a Pakistani-controlled mosque they are making a *political* choice, whether they like it or not. As observant Muslims, and they are increasingly so, they cannot entirely escape from factional politics.

10
Conclusion
The diasporic public sphere

The political imaginaries of diaspora

The moral fables of diaspora are Janus-faced: they transform the pain and longing of exile into new political imaginaries centred on the social universe created by migrants-turned-settlers. In the case of Pakistan diasporas, the move is to the margins of three lived-in worlds: the South Asian, with its aesthetic of fun and laughter, of vivid colours and fragrances, of music and dance; the Islamic, with its utopian vision of a perfect moral order; and the Pakistani, with its roots in the soil, in family, community and national loyalties. The creative locus of the new imaginaries, I have argued in this study, is the diasporic public sphere. The identities evoked in the narratives – of nation, local community, religion and diaspora – are at times fused, at times kept strictly separated.

When we think of contemporary diasporas, the 'exemplary communities of the transnational moment' as Tololyan calls them (1996: 4), we need to think, this book has shown, beyond previous paradigms of transnationalism, of diasporas as dispersed ethnic, religious or national communities. Both the reach of the media today and their immediacy, the live coverage of events broadcast simultaneously in remote localities, mean that diasporas are now in large measure focused around such global news dramas. At the same time, individual diasporic communities remain deeply rooted in highly localised struggles for citizenship or in even more parochial factional struggles for power and honour. While we may distinguish analytically between these different scales of action and imaginative creativity, what remains important to disclose is the way local conflicts feed into and upon such global media events.

Tololyan makes the additional point that the semantic domain of diaspora as a discursive concept has expanded enormously in the past decade, appropriated both by Third World intellectuals and by theories challenging the separate autonomy of the nation-state (1996: 3–5). The stress in much of this literature is on the culturally hybrid, aesthetic and experiential dimensions of diaspora (for example, Bhabha 1994; Brah 1996). By contrast, my argument in this book has started from a definition which seeks to retain a prior emphasis on the compelling nature of *obligations* diasporans feel across space and national boundary. I thus defined diasporas as *communities of co-responsibility*, recognising not simply their loyalty but their existential connection with co-diasporics elsewhere, or in the home country. This sense of co-responsibility is expressed in tangible material

251

gestures of charitable giving and complex forms of political mobilisation. In this sense definitions of diaspora which recognise merely its aesthetic and experiential dimensions are to my mind too limited (see, for example, Gilroy 1993). It is the intersection of the political, aesthetic and moral sensibilities of diasporans, expressed in interpretive encounters and arguments of identity as these focus on public and global media events, which is the central theme of the present book. My aim throughout the book has been to understand the evolution of a key diasporic institution, the 'diasporic public sphere', a space in which different transnational political imaginaries are interpreted and argued over, where fables of diaspora are formulated and political mobilisation generated in response to global social dramas: September 11, the Gulf War, the Rushdie affair, Kashmir, Bosnia, Chechnya, Palestine, and the heroic or villainous protagonists that embody major global dramas – Usama bin Laden, Saddam Hussein, Salman Rushdie, Yassir Arafat. At the same time, however, the diasporic public sphere is a space where nation and citizenship come to be intertwined with these global dramas. My specific case is that of Pakistani migrant-settlers in Britain who are also culturally part of a wider South Asian diaspora and who also simultaneously recognise themselves as a *Muslim* diaspora.

I began by introducing the diasporic public sphere as an arena of conflict, argument and imaginative creativity. From being hidden, I argued, the Pakistani and Muslim public sphere in Britain came to be visibilised in response to the publication of *The Satanic Verses*, with both negative and positive effects. In some measure, the Rushdie affair highlighted the extent to which political imaginaries of diaspora remain utopian and millenarian, but it also pointed to the emergence of some practical agendas for justice and equal citizenship. Above all, I argued, the complexity of the diasporic public sphere which the Rushdie affair and its aftermath revealed is the outcome of different, and often clashing, meroscopic visions of the common good, enunciated by subaltern activists. This complexity has been further increased by diasporic women who have begun to demand an autonomous voice in communal affairs. Diasporic unity is therefore to be understood in transcendental terms: as the product of shared foci of passionate debate rather than internal homogeneity and agreement; of intermittently agreed procedural strategies for joint mobilisation rather than centralised control, or external definitions of identity imposed upon diasporas by the state.

The notion of meroscopia is central to my argument in this concluding chapter. I mean by it the partial, positioned, sited and inevitably perspectival visions of reality espoused by political actors in the public sphere. The neologism draws on Strathern's notion of 'merography' which she uses to highlight the partial, positioned meanings and connections of and between concepts (such as 'culture' and 'nature', for example) used in scholarly texts and discourses. 'Meroscopia' refers to a similar partiality which marks the often impassioned knowledges of the people we study. Indeed, a key feature of the diasporic public sphere is that, while procedures are often exceedingly formal, speeches reflect deeply held political passions.

My analysis of the diasporic public sphere has owed much to Sandria Freitag's theorisation of the emergence of public arenas in British India (Freitag 1988, 1989a & b), and to Don Handelman's exploration of the architectonics of public culture (Handelman 1990). Freitag demonstrates that a language of shared communal symbols evolved among the Muslims of India, despite and alongside persistent leadership rivalries, internal class divisions and factional or religious conflicts.

Public events and ceremonials, Handelman proposes, are 'framed' symbolically so as to set them apart from the everyday, while at the same time they draw upon quotidian props and are grounded in both explicit and implicit moral ideologies.

A third strand in my analysis accords with Nancy Frazer and Seyla Benhabib's reformulations of the modern, democratically plural public sphere (Frazer 1992; Benhabib 1992). In her critical revision, Benhabib stresses the 'porousness' of the modern public sphere and its increasing complexity which arises because 'neither access to it nor its agendas for debate can be predefined by criteria of moral or political homogeneity' (1992: 94). Frazer (1992), arguing against the singularity of the bourgeois public sphere described by Habermas, stresses the important democratic role of a pluralised public sphere: subaltern counterpublics, she argues, create new discursive spaces where marginalised interests can be debated and articulated. Hence, my aim has not been to reify a 'public'/'private' divide but, on the contrary, to show how new social movements, including ethnic, religious and gendered diasporic movements such as the one considered here, both sustain autonomous spaces of public debate and attempt to influence wider public political realms and centres of power. Crucially, then, 'the struggle over what gets included in the public sphere is itself a struggle for justice and freedom' (ibid.). Moreover, like Benhabib I stress that debates taking place in this network of multiple public spheres are not simply rational and legalistic but imaginatively creative as well.

But recognising the co-existence of a multiplicity of public arenas, as this book has done, still begs a critical question: why focus on obscure, localised disputes and arcane arguments of identity in hidden arenas in Manchester when at stake are global issues of postcolonial migration, racism and religious nationalism? Why study the local when the discourses enunciated are global, and are publicised and debated by both English and Urdu media? Indeed, why study 'the local' at all? This, of course, is an issue of some consequence for anthropology and subaltern studies more generally.

One answer to this question is to recognise the bias implicit in what is privileged as 'significant' and hence worthy of close interrogation. Clearly, an overriding consequence of mediatised 'global' images is to exaggerate the centrality of the West. But there are many contexts in which the encounter with the West is merely part of a much broader penumbra of concerns for protagonists. Their political passion is often directed towards obligations or injustices closer to home, perpetrated by their own leaders and ruling classes. In this vein, reflecting on the Urdu realist literary movement in the 1930s, Aijaz Ahmad has argued against Frederic Jameson's essentialist proposition that all 'Third World' literature is ultimately to be read as 'nationalist allegory' – a response to the 'experience of colonialism and imperialism'. The lumping together of all 'Third World' novels as the Other of the West, Ahmad argues, effaces the autonomous bases of non-Western literatures and effectively constitutes them as an 'absence', a negative mirroring (Ahmad 1992: 100 and *passim*). Yet not only, he says, is most literature outside the West not even written in English; even more crucially, far from being exclusively preoccupied with the confrontation of their nations with imperialism and colonialism, the agendas of the Urdu realist writers were often highly complex and internally focused, demanding that

a critique of others (anti-colonialism) be conducted in the perspective of an even more comprehensive, multifaceted critique of ourselves: our class structures, our familial ideologies, our management of bodies and sexualities, our idealisms, our silences. (ibid.: 118)

In other words, there can be no separation, Ahmad suggests, of the agonism of *internal* moral debates from broader ethnic or national confrontations. Similarly, we have seen that Pakistani diasporic ideas about nationalism and ethnicity emerge *dialectically* from a reworking and transcendence of local disputes among local Pakistanis, in the local negotiation of shared symbols of collective struggle or resistance.

Not only that. The focus on sites of subaltern struggle reiterates Renan's insight that nationalism is itself a 'daily plebiscite'. Analysing Latin American nationalism, Radcliffe and Westwood find that national identities are the product of 'quotidian ideological work' (Radcliffe and Westwood 1996: 164), 'reiterated by reference to the sites, apart from the nation, through which subjectivities [a]re constituted and expressed' (ibid.: 165). Local people, they claim, participate in the 'discursive process of imagining the nation', despite the fact that their 'ideas of nation and identity ... do not reach the reifying (and massifying) forms of newspapers, novels and the television screen' (ibid.). Pakistani subalterns in Manchester memorialise the local and situate themselves nationally and universally, we have seen, through ongoing fabulations of the past as future. They weave their collective loyalties out of multiple, sited affiliations and positionings. At times they fuse their different identities – South Asian, Muslim, Pakistani – in encompassing moral fables; conversely, they hedge these identities with taboos, separating the spaces of patriotism or high Islam from quotidian South Asian 'fun'.

In focusing on the local production of collective discourses, we need to remember as well that South Asian migration to Britain included a sizeable indigenous intelligentsia, not all of whom were versed in English but who nevertheless were able to 'challenge narratives that objectify diaspora Muslims as the proletarians or underclass of late capitalism' (Metcalf 1996a: 4; see also P. Lewis 1994). Indeed, many members of this intelligentsia have emerged locally, in response to local exigencies. This has been an important message to be drawn from my research in Manchester: to recognise the intellectual and aesthetic work performed by a buried Muslim diasporic intelligentsia, organic intellectuals operating beyond the objectifying gaze of social scientists and journalists alike, and belying simplistic profiles of Muslim underprivilege.

In 1987, when I first started my research on the diasporic public sphere in South Manchester, this sphere was almost entirely invisible to the wider public. With the exception of selectively invited politicians or civic leaders, not only were most non-Pakistanis and non-Muslims excluded from it; women too were entirely absent. This was a male domain of honour and politics, of civic virtue and public responsibility. The only times when the invisibility of the diasporic sphere was pierced was when violent clashes occasionally erupted between factions and the police were called in to settle matters. Otherwise public ceremonials and political meetings remained almost entirely hidden from view, a world of meroscopic political imaginings which I could only guess at from casual remarks made in passing by male acquaintances.

Originally, I had planned my study of the diasporic public sphere to be a window into this hidden, subterranean world of public political debate and passion; a dialogical and polyphonic text in which the oratorical achievements of the men making these invisible spaces were allowed a wider and different audience. But events caught up with my study and changed the nature of the project I had embarked upon. Anna Tsing remarks that she 'turned her fieldwork goals inside out – from learning about Meratus despite their marginality to writing about marginality itself' (Tsing 1993: 107). I started out to study invisible public spaces, voices and identities, and ended up disclosing the processes of their visibilisation. In a paradoxical sense, I found, that visibilisation, which first occurred in response to the publication of *The Satanic Verses*, highlighted a marginality that had not been there before, in the enclosed spaces of hidden civic debate. The cosiness of that closed world of honour and public dignity was shattered, perhaps irreparably, by the evident hostility of the public's response to Muslim anger.

The marginalisation was a double one: a scholarly apologetics described protesting Muslims as the poor, misunderstood, working-class victims of a racist society; and Muslims themselves were confronted with their political impotence in their newly adopted society, and confronted by it, paradoxically, at the very moment of their greatest empowerment. The mobilisation against the book and its author brought together rival Muslim sectarian groups and factions from all over the country, and its climax, the anti-Rushdie demonstration in London, reflected the combined mobilising strength of Muslim passions, the rage and offence of Islam.

Several contradictory social trajectories have resulted from that key historical moment when Muslims united publicly in a massive, global social movement spearheaded by South Asian settlers in Britain. The complex nature of these trajectories underlines the inadequacy of theories of marginality which start from notions of a fixed centrality, usually of 'the nation' and the widest public sphere that its cultural, financial and political elites command. To escape such commonsensical notions of centrality we need a theory of political imaginaries which allows for a relativist and shifting definition of where the centre lies, as it is constituted from different meroscopic perspectives and in different historical contexts (see also Brah 1996: 210).

Transnational migration creates new opportunities for the achievement of what Mines has aptly called civic individuality (Mines 1994). Individuality in South Asia is grasped as an accomplishment of those men who have distinguished themselves by their public service. The individual in this symbolic matrix is a person set apart from the masses and known for his generous giving for the public good. Hence individuality is conceived as a ranked quality, quite different from the universal egalitarianism envisaged by the philosophers of the Enlightenment. The men at the centre of communal affairs who stage and manage Pakistani national memorial days or community celebrations have achieved such individuality by assuming roles of civic responsibility which, in all likelihood, they would never have had the opportunity to command in Pakistan. Most of us, after all, are passive citizens of our respective nations. In Britain these men, who arrived penniless and single in the 1950s and 1960s, have, as this book shows, become active citizens within the diasporic public sphere and community spokesmen who routinely deal with ministers, members of parliament, civic leaders or police inspectors, and join forces with or against these state representatives in emancipatory struggles for multicultural or anti-racist citizenship in Britain.

So, although from one perspective the orators and political activists of the diasporic public sphere remain powerless and marginal strangers in a new land, excluded from the levers of power, from another perspective theirs has been the awesome task of making something new, of building a community that will last – socially, culturally, intellectually. They invent and narrate this community through moral fables which often place it at the centre of world events. 'Invention', rather than being a manipulative and self-interested exercise, strives above all to make sense of local predicaments by reaching out to the emotional, aesthetic, intellectual and ethical sensibilities of fellow-migrant settlers, as we have seen in this book.

Local leaders' tendency to globalise local predicaments reverses the direction stressed in globalisation theory, where the thrust is on the appropriation of the global by the local. By contrast, I have tried to stress the imaginative transposition of the local on to the global. The consequence of such a move is a magnification and centralisation of the local, transformed imaginatively into a central stage of global dramas, from which protagonists address world leaders and events. In constructing this imaginary drama, Pakistanis draw also on moral fables produced in other public spheres, such as the intercontinental Muslim or Asian press and media. Thus it is that the political imaginaries of diaspora come to be theories that travel (Said 1983).

For Manchester Pakistanis the world is multi-centred and shaped by flows of ideologies as well as of consumer goods, pilgrims, visiting kinsmen, ambassadors, pop stars, cricketers, religious experts, politicians and media images, the latter originating from Bombay, Mecca, Islamabad, London, New York or Hollywood (Appadurai 1990, 1993; Gillespie 1995). The diasporic world which is locally created appropriates and combines these travelling ideas and images into meaningful moral allegories.

It would be misleading, however, to argue that such processes of localisation and hybridisation lead merely to a relocalising of the global (Robertson 1995). Nor is it simply a matter of ethnic revivalism, a renewed stress on parochial loyalties which, Friedman has argued, has emerged in response to the weakening of the nation-state and its universalist ideals (Friedman 1997). There is undoubtedly a valid contrast to be drawn, as Hannerz does, between cosmopolitans and transnationals or locals who create culturally and socially encapsulated worlds wherever they migrate (Hannerz 1992). Against the trend to reduce working-class diasporans to mere ethnics, the need is to recognise the complexity of diasporic imaginative journeys.

In globalising their predicaments, transnationals reveal themselves to be imaginatively open to the world from within their enclosed ethnic spaces. In their public oratory Pakistanis consciously attack the cultural imperialism of the West, but they do so in order to reject its effects upon themselves – true Muslims, members of the working classes. They address the affairs of nations and states, world affairs, in a rhetoric that easily combines discourses of socialism, democracy, nationalism and human rights with a vision of Islamic utopias, a perfect moral order, the coming of the millennium. But they also simultaneously fight cut-throat *internal* battles with local rivals for honour and the right to define the collective good of the community. The point is that they can address these global ethical issues precisely because the diasporic public sphere they have created does not have a direct impact on world affairs. Paradoxically, then, it is a space of freedom, in the Kantian sense, a critical space of debate (see O'Neill 1989: 15–27 and *passim*). Hannah Arendt remarks that in the ancient *polis* to be free meant 'to leave the household and enter the political realm, where all were equals' (Arendt 1959: 30–1). Equality was a privileged status because

> far from being connected with justice, as in modern times, [it] was the very essence of freedom: to be free meant to be free from the inequality present in rulership and to move in a sphere where neither rule nor being ruled existed. (ibid.: 31)

The rise of a Muslim public sphere at the end of the nineteenth century in the Muslim world was associated with increasing transcultural communication (Salvatore 1997: 45). For the first time there was open debate beyond the confines of the 'ulama (ibid.). Armando Salvatore argues that the emergent field of discourse was marked by a reification of keywords such as *Shari'a, umma* or *Islam*, as these words came to be standardised and subordinated to the rules of public communication (1997: 46–7). In somewhat similar vein, Gerd Baumann (1996) also notes the public reification of communal and cultural labels in the rhetoric dominating South Asian local-level politics in Britain, although, unlike Salvatore, he explains this reification mainly in instrumental terms. Dominant discourses of culture and community, he argues, are self-serving responses by minority leaders claiming resources from the state and local government, or by civil servants attempting to define an administrative order (ibid., Chap. 7). Culture and identity as discrete phenomena are, according to this interpretation, the product of modernity and its reificatory discourses and modes of control.

The present book has attempted to show the limitations of such a reductive interpretation. Through a detailed study of the diasporic public sphere it reveals that the public play of ethnic labels and counter-labels disguises a complex, hidden world of sited subjectivities and subject positions, of people committed, though not exclusively, to their own unique 'life style and value system' (Lévi-Strauss 1994: 422).[1] This is a world of political passion grounded in compelling cultural imaginaries about community, honour and morality, not simply as discursive reifications but as desired and experientially lived realities. The very detachment of the diasporic public sphere from wider realms of power makes it a dialogical space of meroscopic visions and open debate. It is also a space of aesthetic production: speeches have to be carefully planned and eloquently and dramatically delivered. Compared with most ordinary citizens, then, Pakistani settlers have achieved a kind of centrality in their own eyes and in the eyes of their followers. The moral drama they enact is a universal fable of friends and foes, good and evil. What is often disguised, however, by this globalising rhetoric is local issues of racism, inequality and poverty for which speakers have no immediate solution.

The Rushdie affair & the visibilisation of British Islam

At least, this was so until the Rushdie affair. On the one hand, the agonistic moral panics which marked the affair and its essentialising discourses have created a legacy of anti-Muslim prejudice in Britain and globally which will take years of hard work to eradicate, as well as affecting race relations adversely

---

[1] Baumann also glosses over the very high rates of intra-marriage and even intercontinental marriages among second-generation, British-born diasporic Pakistanis which continuously reinforce cultural boundaries (see Shaw 2001).

throughout Europe (van der Veer 1997: 102). Islamophobia targets the Muslim community as fanatical and violent, a legitimising veneer which at its most virulent covers over deep-seated racialisms. Indeed, suspicions of Muslim religious zealotry are widespread even in liberal circles, undermining Muslim attempts to achieve full religious equality. Only in January 1998 did Muslims for the first time gain state recognition for grant-maintained Muslim schools after a lengthy, concerted campaign, despite the fact that Anglican, Catholic and Jewish schools have long had such recognition (Dwyer and Meyer 1996).[2] The prejudicial dark halo which specifically surrounds Pakistanis includes repeated allegations of corruption and vote-buying in the pursuit of segmental and factional interest politics (see Solomos and Back 1995). The negative effects of Islamophobia on job opportunities open to Muslims, and especially young, second-generation Pakistanis, are inestimable, and may be one of the worst legacies of the Rushdie affair. They are likely to exacerbate the growing polarisation apparent in the 1991 census, despite high rates of social mobility, between the affluent and the impoverished, the educated and the unskilled among British South Asian settlers (Ballard 1996; Eade et al. 1996). As a differentialist racialised discourse which has taken root in Britain, although less so perhaps than in the rest of Europe, Islamophobia marginalises Muslims and Pakistanis in their adopted countries, singling them out for opprobrium by contrast to other minorities – Indians, Chinese, Afro-Caribbeans (Modood 1997). Even worse, perhaps, than Islamophobia has been the sense of alienation the affair generated among the Muslim citizens of Britain, whether workers, businessmen or intellectuals, a feeling that the nation as community simply does not care (see the Runnymede Trust 1997).

Yet the Rushdie affair might be said to have had some important positive effects as well. It liberated Pakistani settler-citizens from the self-imposed burden of being a silent, well-behaved minority, whatever the provocation, and opened up the realm of activist, anti-racist and emancipatory citizenship politics. It also blocked the rising ascendancy of religious puritanism and Manichean occidentalism evident, as I show elsewhere (e.g. Werbner 1996a), in the speeches pronounced from public platforms in some sections of the community. Although London is now said to be the world centre of Islamic, mainly Arab, extremism, and some of the more radical movements are attractive to some young Pakistanis (Samad 1997), extremists from within the community are no longer able to intimidate the majority. The result has been an efflorescence of cultural and religious societies, gatherings, festivals and philanthropic drives for global diasporic causes. In these, local Pakistanis draw freely upon the full range of symbolic resources at their command – South Asian and English as well as Islamic. Muslim moderation and tolerance now thrive in Britain, it seems to me, as never before.

The Rushdie affair underlined the full implications of being a British citizen as a felt set of obligations and entitlements. On the one hand, there came to be a general acceptance that, as overseas Muslims outside the House of Islam, British Muslims were both duty-bound and obliged to respect the law of the land (on this see B. Lewis 1994; Shadid and van Koningsfeld 1996). On the other hand, the affair spurred the community on to create much more specific and achievable local agendas: recognition for Muslim schools, a reform of the Race Relations Act

---

[2] These two schools, previously financed through parental fees, are now entitled to full state support.

to protect religious minorities, a variety of local campaigns and projects. One such successful campaign which hit the headlines in 1996 was led by men in Birmingham, determined to rid their residential neighbourhood of prostitution. The legal change in the Race Relations Act, if achieved, could well have a lasting constitutional impact on the character of religious pluralism in Britain. Pakistani Muslims are now far more willing to confront issues related to racism squarely, to acknowledge their existence and to recognise the need to fight them vocally and openly. One might say that the shame of Islam generated by the Rushdie affair has been turned into a new strength, a new agenda for multiculturalism, for a fundamental revision of the national self-image of Britain as it moves to becoming a more self-consciously plural society. Muslims are both the victims and the torch-bearers of this movement (see Asad 1993, Chap. 7). Conceived thus, multiculturalism for most British Muslims is not primarily a matter of corporate representation for the sake of minor local government grants or representative positions, as is often assumed, but of a struggle for recognition and the respect for difference (Taylor 1992).

It might seem paradoxical that demands for respect should take the form of violent threats, but this reflects the aporia of powerlessness vulnerable minorities often face. There was a kind of residual triumph even in the public humiliation suffered during the affair since, as one preacher told his Manchester congregation in May 1989, Rushdie had, in effect, been incarcerated in self-imposed imprisonment:

> Look at Salman Rushdie. He has earned millions of pounds, but he is scared to death. The world is so vast but for him it has become very small because he has disgraced Allah's Beloved [i.e. the Prophet].

In the absence of legal protection for Islam, the protests were intended, above all, to issue a warning to future transgressors: Muslim honour will be redeemed.

Political imaginaries & transnational subjectivities

Once again we see here how centrality and marginality do not have fixed meanings; they are perspectival, a matter of merography (Strathern 1992), of the partial connections we make as ethnographers between these terms. To define oneself as defender of the faith or the bearer of an emancipatory mission, whatever that may be, is surely to define oneself as in some way a central actor on the national or global political stage. Indeed, theorists of social movements argue that the production and reappropriation of meaning are at the core of contemporary social conflicts. Such conflicts are waged, Alberto Melucci has proposed, against the standardising forces of a planetary information society which invades and attempts to shape even the most intimate realms of subjectivity,

> where individuals and groups lay claim to autonomy, where they conduct their search for identity by transforming them into a space where they reappropriate, self-realise, and themselves construct the meaning of what they are and what they do. (Melucci 1997: 58–60; see also Melucci 1996a & b)

Not only economic migrants or refugees but all of us, Melucci argues, are 'migrant animals in the labyrinths of the world metropolises', constantly shifting contexts and identities (1997: 61). Our task as ethnographers is thus to study processes of *individuation*, the way that the individuality of a multiple self becomes an autonomous, *responsible* subject (ibid.: 64 and *passim*).

But this process of identity definition presupposes, I have argued here, the existence of a dialogical or critical community of fellow travellers. Far from being a natural *Gemeinschaft* in the sense defined by Tönnies (1955), the critical community, according to Foucault, arises 'when the interruption, refusal or reversal of forms of a given community leads to the exposure of the tacit community which supports it' (Rajchman 1991: 102; see Foucault 1984: 384–6); in other words, when unseen practices of tacit power or ideology are laid bare. Muslims in Britain have been compelled over the past decade to engage in critical moments of self-reflection about themselves and the world in the face of events which have tested their taken-for-granted personal and collective loyalties and commitments.

Women & the expansion of the diasporic public sphere

One such test, we saw, has come from women demanding an equal voice in the diasporic public sphere. This challenge to male hegemony reflects the *ideological convergence* of a nascent women's Asian and Muslim social movement in Britain and worldwide (on ideological convergence in social movements see Werbner 1991a). The broad spectrum of Asian women's organisations in Britain demanding a say in public affairs includes secular activists, such as Southall's Black Sisters, protesting against Asian patriarchy and its more virulent effects (*Southall Black Sisters* 1990), Kashmiri women nationalists, Islamist feminists who wear the *hijab* while demanding the right to study, work and decide whom to marry, as well as the usual run of women's cultural or philanthropic organisations (Lyon 1995). In Bradford in the aftermath of the riots in 1995, eight women came together in a multi-faith, multi-ethnic peace march, standing between riot police and male protesters (Burlet and Reid 1996: 149–50). As in South Manchester, women in Bradford too have criticised the macho culture which produced the riots and the male ethos dominating communal affairs, to the exclusion of youth and women (ibid.: 151, 153). Demands by women in Manchester to have a voice in communal affairs were vehemently rejected by the men who dominate the diasporic public sphere. But the men finally acceded to the women's public right to a voice, in the face of mounting pressure. A contingent of women from Manchester constituted the only female presence at a national protest march in London in 1996, organised against the atrocities in Kashmir by the Pakistan People's Party. Rather than interpreting male defensiveness in culturalist terms, however, as stemming from conservative 'patriarchal' attitudes, it is perhaps better understood as the product of the men's sense of their own marginality in the wider public sphere of the nation. In Britain, the communal arena is the only one the men could control absolutely.

External marginalisation has been exacerbated in South Manchester in recent years by the absence of a single, highly respected leader or of grass-roots solidarity. These have been displaced, as this study shows, by internecine fighting, mismanagement of communal institutions and constant appeals for state handouts and recognition which have plagued communal affairs (see also Werbner 1991b). The intensity of such internal conflicts resulted, until the end of 1997, in both the Manchester Central Mosque and the Pakistani Community Centre being

Plate 10.1 'Women in Black' march in Manchester against atrocities in Bosnia and Kashmir

Plate 10.2 The Jami'a Central Mosque in Manchester

placed for a while under the guardianship of the Pakistan High Commissioner and his Vice-Consul in Manchester. This clearly represented a severe loss of communal autonomy. For a time it seemed as though the diasporic public sphere and the alternative civil order it symbolised had been irreparably shattered. Rather than creating a unified front against Islamophobia, Pakistanis appeared to be locked in perpetual relations of dependency, proving Fanon's theory that

> By throwing himself with all his force into the vendetta, the native tries to persuade himself that colonialism does not exist, that everything is going on as before, that history continues. (Fanon 1963/67: 42)

Might we not say, then, that the diasporic public sphere, which I have described here as a critical space of freedom, is in reality a space of delusions – at most, a 'talking shop' as the Jewish diasporic arena has acerbically been labelled (see Brooks 1990 on the British Board of Jewish Deputies)? This would be, I think, to underestimate the constructive power of political passion, and misconstrue the ebbs and flows of communal self-organisation which has had its moments of success and euphoria as well as its failures. One positive outcome of losing control over the Central Mosque has been to redirect the politics of community towards new spaces of voluntary action and leadership, and thus to open up new opportunities for women, young people and poets – those categories previously excluded from the official, masculinised high cultural spaces of community.

In *Weapons of the Weak* James Scott argues perceptively that,

> So long as men and women continue to justify their conduct by reference to values, the struggle for the symbolic high ground between groups and classes will remain an integral part of any conflict over power. (Scott 1985: 235)

Women in Manchester, we have seen, have had to battle to claim an official, legitimate voice in the diasporic public sphere. As doubly marginalised citizens, with inadequate class and cultural resources at their command, and excluded even from the diasporic public sphere, theirs has been a struggle to define themselves as active citizens both of the community and of the nation.

In *The Migration Process* (Werbner 1990a) I analysed the struggle of Punjabi Muslim women settlers in Britain to regain control of the gift economy and through it the inter-domestic domain of ritual and ceremonial exchange relations between families which they were used to controlling in Pakistan. Inter-domestic relations shape much of the quotidian activity and sociality of Punjabi society, both male and female, and underpin the reproduction of the social order and its celebration. On their arrival in Britain, one of the first battles Pakistani immigrant women thus fought was to reconstitute and recapture this domain of inter-familial sociality (Werbner 1990a; see also Eglar 1960; Bhachu 1995).

Although inter-domestic gatherings such as weddings or funerals can be extremely large, mobilising several hundreds and even thousands of men, women and children, the events remain focused around friendship networks and familial concerns and are in this respect 'private' and 'domestic'. By contrast, the diasporic public sphere is a space in which unrelated individuals meet to debate broader civic and political issues. In Britain, where civil society is open and fluid, the diasporic arena is a set-apart network of spaces, ambiguously placed within the broader public sphere of the nation – in this case, Britain – and its extra-territorial extensions – the Islamic community or *umma*, on the one hand, and

Pakistan, a relatively new postcolonial nation, on the other. What makes this arena of communal action a *public* sphere, I argue, is the fact that – in terms of Habermas's original definition (Habermas 1989) – it is a sphere in which private citizens gather to deliberate on issues of general public concern, whether this be citizenship and political democracy in Pakistan or the economic opportunities and problems facing the Asian business community in Britain. The diasporic arena is thus an 'alternative' public sphere, to use Paul Gilroy's term, created by emancipatory 'story-telling and music-making' (Gilroy 1993: 200), and leading to 'forms of community consciousness and solidarity that maintain identifications outside the national time/space in order to live inside, with a difference' (Clifford 1994: 308). It is the site of 'constant processes of struggle and negotiation', of 'constructing the collectivity and "its interest"' (Yuval-Davis 1997a: 193–4).

To break the male stranglehold on the diasporic public sphere women needed to capture the moral high ground. They did so in Manchester by becoming givers to international causes, and by appropriating global emancipatory discourses of human rights and gender equality. Above all, they moved out of the sheltered spaces of the home into the public world of the street, organising protest marches against the atrocities in Bosnia and in Kashmir.

Cultural performances: the marching season

The usual stereotypes of Muslim women in purdah, trapped in a restricted vision of the world like 'frogs in a well' (Jeffrey 1979), hardly fitted the images that these protest marches evoked. One particularly vivid memory I carry is of three ten-year-old girls, their faces glowing with enthusiasm, shouting loudly and rhythmically, as they marched in unison, the call to freedom: 'We want Freedom! We want Justice! We want Freedom! We want Justice!...' The girls, dressed in black (it was a 'Women in Black' march), formed part of a long procession of women from various British Pakistani and Kashmiri women's organisations demonstrating against genocide, rape and torture in Bosnia and Kashmir. Dressed in black, they seemed to fit media images of militant Islamic fundamentalists but this is misleading: they were moderates and democrats. At the same time, their feminist militancy and courage were unmistakable.

Another image I carry is of a 19-year-old young woman, the British daughter of Pakistani settlers and at the time a science undergraduate student at the University of Manchester, leading the march, her voice ringing out loud and clear, with urgency and determination, electrifying the women in the procession into forming a single voice, a single body: 'Stop the rape in Bosnia, Stop the torture of women and children!' The courage shown by this young woman who led a procession in public with such determination and dedication was quite awesome. In between her shouts, a strictly veiled woman called out the traditional refrain of Sufi marches – 'Nare Takbir!' 'Allah hu Akbar', the women answered in unison, as though programmed in advance, underlining the hybridity of the emancipatory discourses they deployed quite naturally which mixed the rhetoric of feminism and human rights with traditional Islamic chants.

Mrs Khan, the charismatic leader of Al Masoom, the women's association which organised the march, was in no doubt that this was a moment for the changing of the guard, for training a new cadre of women activists. In her speech, made in front of Manchester Town Hall at the end of the march, she turned to some of the younger marchers, speaking in Urdu:

> I am proud of you. Proud of our young girls.... Our time has almost finished. If we talk a little, our throats get dry. It is time for you younger girls to take over from us on this issue [of human rights' violations in Bosnia and Kashmir]. You protect yourselves, children. If you do not look after yourselves, nobody will. Unless you shout out loud and clear, no-one will look after you, or pay attention to you. This world is very cruel and its conscience is dead. Unless you shout very, very loud for your rights, nobody will listen to you.... So shout loud for your rights!'

She went on to appeal to the older generation ('my elder sisters') to allow their daughters and daughters-in-law to come forward and to take part in the organisation.

> Children, remember that Islam, Christianity and other religions of the world teach women to fight for their own rights. All cruelties are imposed by men. No woman is killing another woman in Kashmir and Bosnia. It is men who are responsible for the killing.
> Ladies, raise your voices and tell the world that we will not put up with this any longer. To put up with this is a sin, a great sin. Don't forget the Holocaust that took place in Germany less than one hundred years ago; and now, a second holocaust has started in this world. Say No! to the killings! Come out in protest, shout loud for this to be stopped.
> Children, remember! What does Islam teach us? What does Christianity teach us? What do the other religions teach us? That women should fight for their rights!
> We and our children have to do this. We have to stop the bloodshed. Our children have to stop it. Thank you!

Al Masoom is not a secularist women's organisation. Quite the contrary: as we have seen, its women members are pious Muslims who pray regularly, fast on Ramadan and give time voluntarily to teaching young children the Qur'an. But the organisation is fired by a conviction that Islam is an egalitarian religion that guarantees women's rights and that, indeed, this is the true message of all the great religions. This Sufi view that the spirit of religion, its true core meaning, transcends any scriptural formalities, allows the women to make Islam the rallying cry for women's rights.

Joining in the march was Gerald Kaufman, veteran Labour MP and long-term admirer of Al Masoom. His admiration went beyond mere political expediency and was related to the way Al Masoom – exceptionally in the arena of local ethnic politics – had been a donor to public causes rather than a mere recipient (taker) of state largesse. This is also what had allowed it to forge links with many different and varied organisations and persons beyond the community. Outside the Town Hall Kaufman congratulated the tired marchers on the important work they were doing for Bosnia and Kashmir (see Plate 7.2). His support was clearly rooted in a common commitment to the cause of human rights and citizenship.

Identity & performance

Studying public events and performances as this book has attempted to do takes us beyond reflections on identity, however insightful, gleaned from interviews with immigrants or their British-born children (see, for example, Modood et al. 1994; Jacobson 1998). While not neglecting what people say, the anthropological study of cultural performances as 'texts' opens a window into the embodied meanings and passions with which actors endow their culture situationally (Geertz 1973). Such textual meanings can only be gauged by considering a set of performances; each performance reflects on others in the social field obliquely; each may amplify or negate a prior event. Geertz calls this collocation of social situations or public performances a 'loose library of texts'. The present book suggests that they are more than that: they involve implicit structural oppositions – between the political 'right' and 'left', between male and female, between young and old and so forth. Intertextual meanings are critical for the study of complex identities in action.

Secondly, analysed in sequence, cultural performances plot 'social dramas' which reveal the hidden structural dimensions of social life, played out over time (Turner 1974). Finally, cultural performances highlight the subtle indexical play of back stage and front stage animating the micropolitics of diaspora, the fact, for example, that rhetorical declamations of universal moral messages may disguise specifically targeted social barbs directed against particular rivals, understood only by a select audience 'in the know'.

In all three senses, cultural performances are essentially political, an enactment and embodiment of historically contingent power relations and rival political imaginaries. They are conjunctural moments that both risk and test existing values. The present book discloses how the cultural performances of nation, community and religious and aesthetic diasporas staged by diasporic Pakistanis are enacted through localised micropolitical struggles for influence and leadership which also shape broader emancipatory protest movements.

Considered as a cultural performance, communal processing is for South Asians an emotive experience, we have seen, an expression of identity and community. Indeed, Sandria Freitag sees such communal marching as one of the explosive elements which contributed to communal outbreaks of violence in India under the Raj (Freitag 1988). Processing is often a religious act, and, as such, according to Inden, it is incompatible with modernity (Inden 1995). Yet in South Asia today political demonstrations have extended the remit of traditional processions to become a highly significant vehicle of mobilisation and protest, at times for reactionary communal causes such as the processing which converged on Ayodhya (van der Veer 1994). In Pakistan during the Zia era the Women's Action Forum led demonstrations against the Islamicisation programme initiated by the military regime (Mumtaz and Shaheed 1987). While men languished in jail, the women marched.

But which identities are negotiated in marching is not simply a given; it is a matter of the threat posed to the marchers' subjectivies. This became evident in an incident which occurred during a protest march against the atrocities in Kashmir. This time the procession was organised by APWA, the All Pakistan Women's Association. The women of Al Masoom were invited to join the demonstration in reciprocity for APWA's participation in their earlier protest march for Bosnia. On the surface, relations between the two organisations were cordial, reflecting the ability of the women in the city to maintain solidarity, unlike the men who are locked in endless factional disputes – sometimes in violent conflicts. It was evident, however, from the start that this march was really being organised by men, not women. My notes recall:

> We march along the streets of Manchester towards the Town Hall, both men and women this time, calling for freedom and justice. A friend, one of Al Masoom's leading women

activists, decides to move to the front of the procession with the Pakistani flag she is carrying. An APWA female organiser asks her to take the flag to the back. 'But this is our flag, the flag of our country, Pakistan,' my friend protests. The objector mobilises a local Pakistani Labour Councillor and a Pakistan People Party's activist to support her request. A furious argument ensues. After consulting Mrs Khan, my friend resolutely marches on in the second row, Pakistani flag held high. A very proud and beautiful woman in her forties, she normally avoids the public limelight, preferring to act behind the scenes. It must be hard for her to stand up to all those stares, all that pressure, I think.

The public humiliation caused by the flag incident precipitated a rift between Al Masoom and APWA, as well as with the Labour councillor along with the local Consulate. Respectable women among Pakistanis are not supposed to be reprimanded or shamed in public. The interference of the male councillor on some flimsy political pretence was regarded as unforgivable. APWA was exposed for the puppet organisation it really is – a female shadow of elite male dominance.

The 'flag affair' rippled through the community, the subject of endless gossip and moralising speculation. Was it right to put the national flag of Pakistan at the back of the march? (The argument for this was the pragmatic need to disguise from the media the Pakistani Government's hoped-for agenda of incorporating Indian Kashmir into the state once a plebiscite is held there.) Were the Al Masoom women right to disobey the directives of the organisers of the march? (They claimed that there should have been agreed guidelines, such as 'no flags', given in advance, not invented midway through the procession.) Was it all a matter of hidden feminine jealousy? (My friend, carrying the flag high, elegantly dressed, her long hair flying in the wind as she marched, was inevitably going to figure in the press pictures – as, indeed, she did.)

For Mrs Khan and the women of Al Masoom the argument was simple. 'We are Pakistanis. Pakistan is our country. We are proud of our flag.'

Several days later I saw my friend and congratulated her on her courage in holding the flag high and keeping her place despite the pressure on her to move to the back. 'I don't think I would have been brave enough to do what you did,' I speculated. She drew herself up to her full five feet four inches height and declared proudly: 'Yes! I proved to them that I am a true Pathan!' Her unexpected response pointed to the multiplicity of identities diasporan Pakistani women have. Particular identities are highlighted situationally. In the present instance, we had moved from the sphere of universal sisterhood, human rights and nationalist loyalties to the sphere of the personal: of essential qualities, of pedigree, breeding, caste, class. My friend is a Pathan, a tribe of proud warriors and a landowning Punjabi Muslim caste. A Pathan woman is not to be publicly slighted.

Multiple identities

Citizenship is often grasped as an exclusionary identity denoting singular loyalty to a particular national collectivity. In reality, however, as the flag affair showed, people bear multiple collective loyalties and quite often – as in the case of British Pakistanis – multiple formal citizenships. The claims, the duties and the rights attached to these memberships and loyalties are played out in complex ways in the public domain. The protest march in which the flag incident occurred was a demonstration by settler Pakistani women against the policies of the British

Government, their own government, in which they highlighted the particular predicament of Muslim women, citizens of India, to whom they felt attached both as women and as Muslims. But the march also asserted the marchers' citizenship in a third country, Pakistan, which had an historical stake in the Kashmir dispute and was, in addition, the women's homeland, a land to which they were attached by familial, sentimental and patriotic ties. This attachment was one of honour, underlined by the flag bearer's emphasis on her Muslim caste identity as a Pathan, a nation of fierce warriors who, moreover, were renowned for their resistance to British colonisation.

The women's claim to equality with men in the public domain was thus played out not only directly but indirectly, through their public appropriation of potent symbols of legitimate authority: Islam, Pakistan, the House of Commons (expressed through the support of the local MP), Pukhtun honour, while at the same time they challenged the right of men to be the sole owners of these symbols. Their message was that men have, in effect, abrogated these entitlements by failing to protect vulnerable women and children, proving the legitimate right of women to seize control over their own destiny, to re-imagine an alternative, non-masculinised national community (Radcliffe and Westwood 1996: 156).

Anne Phillips comments that 'typically in politics, each of us flits through a number of identities, forming and reforming tentative alliances that may not survive the issue at hand' (1991: 155). Similarly, Chantal Mouffe has argued that 'the subjectivity of a given social agent is always precariously and provisionally fixed or, to use the Lacanian term, sutured at the intersection of various discourses' (Mouffe 1988: 90). These statements, it must be stressed, are not intended to convey a kind of superficiality of commitments/identities, implied by some postmodernist accounts of alternative lifestyles since, as Mouffe in particular argues, identities both articulate and are constituted by social antagonisms and struggles.

Postmodernists who attack essentialist constructions of 'culture' miss the fact that identities matter, deeply, and are long-term. At the same time, they are not simply pre-given or inherited: they are formed, made and remade; they exist in practice, dialogically, through collective action and interaction. More than anything, identities constitute subjective narratives of virtue and moral commitment. The fact that a person has heterogeneous identities, a multiplicity of identities, does not imply contradiction, ambivalence or a lack of commitment, because identities matter *in context*. They are played out in different identity spaces and foregrounded oppositionally. Hence, the present book has highlighted the difference between *objectification*, the situational play of identities, and *reification*, the violent fixing of subordinated and excluded identities (see also Werbner 1997b). In the flag affair, surrounded by shouting men and menacing women, vulnerable and alone, what mattered most to my flag-carrying friend was not that she was a woman (some of her attackers were women), a Muslim (they were all Muslims), a Pakistani citizen (ditto), a Punjabi (ditto), a British citizen (ditto); what mattered was her pride, her tenacity, her unwillingness to cave in. In retrospect, wondering at her own temerity, she attributed it to an essential quality, something 'in her blood', so to speak, beyond rationality, inherited from her tribe. As a true Pathan, she could not allow those upstarts with no pedigree to humiliate her. But this was a post-factum reconstruction, an attempt to explain even to herself her unexpected boldness. It is, perhaps, significant that she did not attribute this boldness to her essential quality as an individual. She did not say to me: 'I am an individual.' She said: 'I am a Pathan.'

New-wave feminist literature has in recent years stressed the multiple identities that subjects bear, and that often drive a wedge within marginalised groups (e.g. hooks 1994; Haraway 1991; Young 1995). If women are united by gender, they are divided by class, race, ethnicity, lifestyle and so forth. Forming alliances in these circumstances becomes a major challenge, one of creating a 'cyborg' politics (Haraway 1990; Werbner 1997a). Yuval-Davis argues that in the face of such differences, transversal politics requires constant perspectival manoeuvring – 'rooting' and 'shifting', so that one does not abandon one's own positioning but nevertheless accords respect to that of one's interlocutor.

This has been the true challenge of the *Satanic Verses* affair: to create a space of dialogue with Muslims angered and outraged by the novel, while not abandoning one's own (liberal, modernist) convictions. Such a dialogue is painful because it requires a high degree of reflexivity and mutual awareness (Melucci 1997) but it is, I believe, possible; not least, as I show here, because the novel is open to alternative readings which highlight its serious engagement with Islam as a modern, humanist religion. Huntington's orientalist attempt to erect a civilisational barrier between Muslims and so-called Judaeo-Christians (Huntington 1993) obscures the three monotheistic religions' shared myths of origin and overstresses the relatively trivial nature of the doctrinal differences separating these 'Abrahamic' traditions (see Turner 1994: 22ff.). If there is a radical division, it lies elsewhere, cutting across such reified theistic labels, defined by the pragmatic willingness or unwillingness of protagonists to practise what Rorty has called 'tolerant reciprocity' (Rorty 1992a: 61).

The perception of an unbridgeable chasm has made the Muslim bid to full participation in the national public sphere particularly difficult. In general, the reason why the struggle for compensatory citizenship entitlements excludes minorities in moral terms from active citizenship stems from the definition of citizenship as the duty, *qua citizen*, to work for the sake of the wider public good, to aim 'towards a politics in which people will transcend their localised and partial concerns, getting beyond the narrow materialism of special interest to address the needs of the community instead' (Phillips 1995: 290).

Clearly, the aporia presented to disadvantaged ethnic minorities, as to women, by this precept is that their particularistic claims to compensation for historical underprivilege are constructed as narrow, selfish and divisive, yet a 'transcendence' of these claims would seem simply to perpetuate their current subordination.

Seen in this light the obstacles faced by Pakistani (Asian/Muslim) subaltern activists, men and women, young and old, do not stem from their inability to transcend the constraints of class or unchanging traditions; rather, the challenge they face is one of convincing a sceptical British public that theirs is a reasoned voice that deserves to be heard. The diversity of diasporic subaltern voices articulated in the present study is intended to confound prevalent stereotypes of Pakistani settlers in Britain as a helpless underclass, the 'ignorant masses', immersed in nepotistic *biradari* (clan) politics, fanatical and intransigent. The need is to recognise instead the cultural complexity revealed by diasporic political and religious commitments expressed by protagonists promoting different – and quite often opposed – ideological agendas.

This underscores the question raised by Spivak of how, and in what sense, we can recover a lost subaltern consciousness (Spivak 1987: 202–7; 1995). After all, most of the voices recorded here never reach the wider public sphere. They are yesterday's news, like the leftover samosa savouries after the celebratory party is over, barely remembered even by the protagonists themselves as they realign and enter the fray of new political battles. The *Jang* newspaper picture commemorating the event gathers dust, while the speeches lie buried in a pile of video tapes that no one watches, or are recorded over by the latest Hindi film.

Spivak suggests that Indian subaltern historians deploy a strategic essentialism to recover the subjectivity or agency of subordinate actors without an autonomous voice. But this presupposes an absence, a silence. Thus Pandey, writing about the Awadh Indian peasant insurgency movement, reflects that

> The peasants' view of the struggle will probably never be recovered; and whatever we may say about it at this stage must be very tentative. Yet it seems important to try to piece together some part of it, from the isolated statements of peasants found in the documents and from the only other evidence we have – the message contained in their action. (Pandey 1988: 240)

If anthropology as an ethnography of the present has a mission, it is precisely to open a window on to such hidden subaltern worlds and through contemporary research to reveal the tremendous complexity of the reflexive self-interrogation engaged in by protagonists. To the question 'Can the subaltern speak?' the answer must surely be that the subaltern can and does speak, although the constituencies she addresses may not be those we define as centrally important and her voice may leave no documentary trace. However tentative our understanding of emergent subaltern subjectivities (for they are plural), the challenge is to rewrite the margin as the centre of action.

Writing centrality

How can we, as anthropologists, *write* the 'centrality' of ethnic groups or of women doubly marginalised in hegemonic discourses? I was present when the women of Al Masoom set off on their first trip to Bosnia, laden with medicines, food and clothing, and taking with them an ambulance for the medical services of the refugee camps. The news from Bosnia at the time was of ethnic cleansing and genocide. As they parted tearfully from family and children we wondered whether we would ever see them again; the journey seemed so hazardous and the destination a wilderness.

Shaheen Khan, one of the travellers, later wrote an account of the trip which she attempted to publish, unsuccessfully, in the Urdu press. The following are extracts, translated from Urdu:

> As we left Whalley Range in Manchester the Al Masoom workers bade us farewell, praying for our safe journey. We waved goodbye while each of us wondered when we would see our husbands and children again.

She describes their travel all night through Germany to arrival finally in Austria:

> Austria is a beautiful country. As we journeyed through it, the snowcapped mountains glittered like silver in the moonlight. It was calm and very quiet. Not a living soul was in sight on that snowy night, but then, who would want to travel in such dreadful weather? It seemed as though we were journeying through the dwellings of jinns.

They had trouble with the Croatian officials.

In a way, who could blame them? We were certainly not the usual type of aid worker going to Bosnia, and it must have seemed incredible to them that our little group of middle-aged women and men (two drivers) had actually journeyed all the way from Britain.

They were in contact with an Islamic aid organisation caring for Bosnian refugees in Croatia. She describes their visits to the refugee camps:

Often, we found, the rooms were filled with survivors of many different families, all living together. There were no complete families in the camp.

... The Muslims of Bosnia are beautiful and affectionate people. Their children are so lovely and attractive that you feel like taking some home with you. But the Bosnians don't want them to disperse.

We met a very old, respectable lady. Even though she was very ill she mustered enough strength to tell us her tragic story. Her whole family, her sons, daughters and grandchildren had all been killed before her very eyes. She was left destitute. Every single person we met had her or his sad tale to tell us. We listened to them patiently, with great sorrow, and prayed together with them.

The visits to the camps left them 'so sad we could barely touch the food'. They met various officials, including the Bosnian ambassador, handed over the keys to the ambulance and all the food and prepared for the journey home.

On the journey back we all crowded into the single van, jammed together on foam mattresses, exhilarated but tired. The men sat in front, taking it in turns to drive. It was the night of Shabe Barat so we planned to sing *nateen* (songs in praise of the Prophet and God). We sang all night while the snowflakes outside fell incessantly like a silent refrain. Neither snow nor singing ceased – the songs and snow kept us company on the night's journey.

After an exhausting journey came a rough night crossing from Ostend which ended with the ferry being turned back to the Belgian shore. Back into the van, the group drove to Calais. 'As those renowned white cliffs emerged out of the gloom, we thanked God.'

I have quoted at length from this account in order to highlight the way that women, as active agents, weave their Islamic, familial and female identities with their political activism, their love of popular culture, music and 'fun', and their humanitarian faith into a whole fabric. Religion, this book has argued, is not merely a set of norms but a deeply experienced aesthetic.

I want to go beyond the view, however, that sees in creative allegories from the margins an expression of agency, and as such a substitute, in effect, for any real action in the world. This is an implicit flaw in some very fine recent ethnographies on counter-hegemonic creativity. It may be true that through artistic fabulations, subordinated minorities or women can overcome experienced paradoxes of everyday life (Abu-Lughod 1986 and 1993; Boddy 1989; Lavie 1991; Tsing 1993). Foucault in his later works saw aesthetic self-fashioning as the foundation for emancipatory politics and the achievement of a critical, autonomous subjectivity (Rajchman 1991: 98, 108–9; Foucault 1984: 45). But in the study of subaltern politics we need, I have argued here, to probe further, into what makes for key moments of social transition from fabulations to political mobilisation, from mere consciousness to emancipatory politics, from the grand oratory of the diasporic public sphere to open public protest.

Not all moral fabulations lead to practical outcomes of the type their orators envisage. The utopian imaginings of an Islamic millennium, the past recreated as the future, which were expressed during the Gulf War, underlined the gap between redemptive vision and reality which could only be bridged by a magical discourse. Yet as others too have argued (Kepel 1985, 1994; Roy 1994; Gellner 1994; Burke 1988), these speeches can be read as an ethical critique of the corruption and greed of Western and Muslim elites. Speakers' narratives draw on ideas about renewal and return that are foundational in Islam. Thus for Pakistanis nation and community are epitomised by their exemplary leaders: Quaid-i-Azam, Maulana Iqbal, Imran Khan and, ultimately, the Prophet. The next millennium will herald the coming of an apocalyptic moment leading towards the Day of Justice. In this sense grass-roots nationalism bears the distinctive stamp of local, historically evolved ethical and ideological conceptions of what constitutes community, a feature of nationalism underlined by recent studies of Indian nationalism (van der Veer 1994; Chatterjee 1986; Nandy 1988).

Islamist 'fundamentalist' discourses are fractured into a variety of different redemptive visions and projects, only some of them violent or revolutionary (see Kepel 1985; Burke and Lapidus 1988; Roy 1994, Werbner 1996a). This complex semiotic of redemption is only one further demonstration of the fact that culture, religion and community do not refer to fixed, totalising worldviews. Although sometimes reified by racists, policy-makers and ethnic 'leaders', these concepts are too important and too central to the anthropological project to be rubbished as mere fictions of scholarly research, collusive in a system of external colonial or neo-colonial domination.

Towards a theory of the heterogeneous community

Hence, despite the pervasive fear of essentialism, expressed in scholarly critiques on the very ideas of 'community' and 'culture' and the link between them (Abu-Lughod 1993; Caglar 1997; Baumann 1997), theorists of multiculturalism and the new feminist scholarship are reaching out towards a revised conceptualisation of community, one which allows for internal diversity and conflict, for cross-cutting ties, for the multiple identities citizens bear within a critical community. Such approaches define community as actively made and remade through the sited, meroscopic visions of its members as composite, complex and heterogeneous. A community is no longer grasped as a culturally homogeneous and harmonious *Gemeinschaft* but as a space of agonistic power relations and debate across difference. In line with postmodernist thinking what is envisaged is 'a new vision of justice which gives primacy to difference, to heterogeneity, to paradox and contradiction, and to local knowledge' (Turner 1994: 11–12).

This complexity has to be set against the fact, however, that diasporans, like postmoderns, face 'the challenge of responsibility for the Other' grounded in 'moral choice' (Bauman 1995: 1). Choices in a postmodern world, Bauman argues, are shot through and through with ambivalence and doubt, a predicament shared by South Asians and Muslim diasporans, Akbar Ahmed convincingly demonstrates (Ahmed 1992). It is clear, nevertheless, that political activists in the diasporic public arena are fired by deeply held political commitments and moral convictions. Even while these may be disputed and argued over, they rest on shared moral imperatives regarding responsibility for the Other, epitomised in the notion of *khidmat*, service for the community. What *is* in doubt, and endlessly scrutinised at public meetings, is the true character of rivals, the possible gap between self-declared moral intent and actual practice.

If we accept that ethnographies are partial truths, then merographic writing, Strathern (1992) suggests, reflects the shifting perspectives of texts, concepts and authors. The challenge is, I suggest, to relate these features of ethnographic *writing* to the meroscopias, the partial visions, of the *people* we study; to write those diverse visions, each paradoxically containing a unitary vision of the just society, so as to avoid essentialising constructions of fixed collectivities – of diaspora, nation, community, culture, society.

Conclusion: theories of ethnicity & diasporic studies

The question is, how can such a study of meroscopias contribute to the ongoing theoretical debate on ethnicity? We can trace the modern study of ethnic relations to early ethnographies of urbanism that theorised the city as the locus of fleeting encounters between strangers, of trans-ethnic cosmopolitan 'cultures', of 'intermezzo identities' (Back 1996). From the start such studies deployed tropes of order and disorder as the very object of analysis. Ethnicity, it was argued, rather than being a conservative force, was the modern product of urban interaction, framed by cognitive maps of city ethnoscapes (Mitchell 1956). The city, far from being an urban jungle, was thus, in reality, an ordered and predictable space. In this spirit, the Manchester and Chicago schools of urban research studied urban popular cultural performances, bohemian quarters or slums, immigrant ghettos and workplaces, political parties and ethnic joking relations.

But against the stress on the city as the heterotopic site of casual encounters between strangers has always been a counter-narrative of translocal and transnational 'communities' or 'diasporas'. The object of study in this case was the webs and flows of relations, goods and persons across boundaries, linking distant places and spaces; the journeys and cross-border communications valorised by diasporic migrant-traders-settlers across space and time. Such studies focused on 'dwelling, maintaining communities, having collective homes away from home' (Clifford 1994: 309). What defined these fields of sociality were very high levels of interpersonal and intercommunal investment and trust – economic, social, emotional and moral. Through investment ethnics and diasporans created identity spaces, set apart and framed by taboos and customs. Cities enabled the formation of such set-apart spaces. Thus, we have seen that most diasporan Pakistanis choose to keep the sacred spaces of high Islam they have established apart from the profane spaces of business or popular cultural celebration. They maintain a deliberate disjunction between different cultural modalities or lived-in worlds of sociality.

The counter-focus on boundary-crossing diasporan or ethnic networks must be an essential component of any theory of ethnicity because the study of fleeting encounters or of local-level 'identity politics' fails to disclose where translocal subjects locate long-term *value*. Despite the multi-ethnic hybridity of British youth culture, schoolfriends of different racial or cultural backgrounds tend to drift apart as they reach adulthood (Hewitt 1986). By contrast, a *diasporic* focus highlights the investments young Asians make as future adults in enduring, long-term relations of sociality (marriage, family, community), through which they define their subjectivities as moral individuals. It is these relations to which they turn for nurture, comfort and joyous celebrations and it is against these, as we have seen here, that they define their youthful struggles for autonomy. The price of belonging, however, is exacted in social conformity, a subjection to the ethical norms and restrictions of close-knit networks.

Against this subjection, cities open up spaces for cultural experimentation and identity switching. They mediate worlds of work and leisure, of privacy and publicity. Spatial heterotopias are places of escape from the moral order of close-knit community (Hetherington 1998). They constitute openings for new ethical imaginings and performances of what 'community' or 'culture' might mean in the future. These have an impact on existing diasporic worldviews without, however, negating or effacing them. A theory of ethnicity must confront this process which includes the reproduction of the moral order of community even as 'newness' emerges into the world.

Thus I have chosen in this study to highlight what may be conceived of as a series of neo-Durkheimian questions about value: about the compelling nature of social morality and the experience of sociality. The departure from Durkheim is in the awareness that such moralities are played out in the context of unequal power relations; that modernity is itself a powerfully determining, moralising force rather than simply a play of the free market; and that what is moral is the outcome of arguments of identity.

I have used meroscopia to refer to a situated political vision performed and defended from a specific subject position. The combined kaleidoscopic worldview of a 'community', its 'morality', the moral good it posits, is thus constituted, this study has argued, from the colliding meroscopic visions of its variously positioned members, locked in debate with one another. Ethnic groups and diasporas are not unified and homogeneous, any more than cultures or communities are. They are 'lived and re-lived through multiple modalities' as 'differentiated, heterogeneous and contested spaces, even as they are implicated in the construction of a common "we"' (Brah 1996: 184).

But this presumes a shared space of dialogue and, as I have suggested in this study, that space has to be created through voluntary efforts and investments. Within that space, communication may be conflictual and confrontational, the mutual accusations and recriminations bitter and condemnatory, the political and religious disagreements sharp and unbridgeable. But in being focused around shared celebrations, predicaments and places, these arguments create a bounded arena of focused communal value. The cross-cutting, multiple conflicts themselves create overarching unities. In this sense meroscopias first divide and then unite, to echo a famous dictum of the Manchester School. The plurality of radical disagreements within diasporic groups can nevertheless unite protagonists in an interpretive community. Arguments of identity divide diasporas over key ontological issues as Clifford (1994) and Yuval-Davis (1997a) have shown for the Jewish diaspora, or Gilroy (1993) for the Black diaspora. The semiotic of redemption characterising the Pakistani diaspora is thus, I propose, *dialectical* rather than homeostatic: conflicts and contradictions highlight the shared values competed over, framed in shared transcendent procedural and discursive unities.

An important theoretical point is at stake here, related to Barth's famous dictum that ethnic groups are defined by their 'boundaries', not the cultural 'stuff' these boundaries enclose (Barth 1969). The key insight which this classic anthropological view afforded stemmed from Evans-Pritchard's segmentary analysis of the Nuer: identities are essentially social rather than cultural, and they shift situationally; collective identities emerge in contestation, oppositionally. It is the boundary of contestation that marks identity, signalled by diacritical emblems, border posts that 'stand for' a group's distinctiveness. These differences may at times appear insignificant to outsiders. In Bosnia groups sharing the same language in one case, and the same religion in another, were willing to murder and rape neighbours marked by minor cultural differences. In Zimbabwe a black government embarked on a reign of terror against black citizens of the new nation who had participated in the liberation struggle along with them and who spoke a dialect of Shona, the language of the party in power (R. Werbner 1991).

In modern nation-states, however, 'bounded' collective identities and interests – and hence also conflictual relations – are often the product and construction of the 'centre': of a buried intelligentsia locked in arguments of identity among themselves. It is this debate that determines both the imagined boundaries of ethnic contestation and the imagination of the community as a bounded whole. Such definitions from the centre obscure the everyday, mundane reality that ethnic communal boundaries are shaped by quotidian networks of exchange and sociality, and are thus variable, changing, fuzzy and indeterminate. Rather than any sharp boundary defining the ethnic group, it is the centre that imagines the boundary. The political imaginaries marking out ethnic communities as 'bounded' are nurtured and publicised by organic intellectuals at the centre. In this specific sense it is the cultural 'stuff' of ethnicity, an unceasing argument of identities produced at the centre, which defines ethnic groups as distinct and separate, not the fuzzy boundaries these arguments mask. Thus America's immigrant communities, according to Walzer, are characterised by a

> centre of active participants ... and a much larger periphery of individuals and families who are little more than recipients of services generated at the centre. They are communities without boundaries, shading off into a residual mass of people who think of themselves simply as Americans. Borders and border guards are among the first products of a successful national liberation movement, but ethnic assertiveness has no similar outcome. There is no way for the various groups to prevent or regulate individual crossings. Nor can the state do this without the most radical coercion of individuals. (Walzer 1992: 150)

In the face of the fuzzy boundaries of modern-day ethnic groups, attempts to institute a corporate form of multiculturalism, as we demonstrate elsewhere (in Modood and Werbner 1997), simply cannot work. Nor are Pakistanis part of one single 'community'. Rather, they belong to a host of meroscopically generated moral, aesthetic and interpretive communities, uniting them with other Muslims, women, black people, South Asians, cricket lovers, Labour activists, businessmen and anti-racists, as well as with their fellow-Pakistanis.

The list points to the complex embeddedness of meroscopias in political and moral as well as socially determining subject positions. The tendency in the literature has been to stress the deterministic constraints of gender, race, age and class. The present study highlights that beyond these is also an engagement by ethnic activists with democratic values and human rights.

Chantal Mouffe argues, following de Tocqueville, for a recognition of the importance of the democratic revolution 'on the symbolic level':

As long as equality has not yet acquired ... its place of central significance in the social imagination of Western societies, struggles for this equality cannot exist. As soon as the principle of equality is admitted in one domain, however, *the eventual questioning of all possible forms of inequality is an ineluctable consequence.* Once begun, the democratic revolution has had, necessarily, to undermine all forms of power and domination, wherever they might be. (Mouffe 1988: 94, emphasis added)

Benedict Anderson writes about the independence movements in the Americas that they became, 'as soon as they were printed about', 'concepts', 'models', and indeed 'blueprints' which ultimately challenged entrenched institutions, such as slavery, even if this was not the original intent of the Creole nationalists (Anderson 1991: 81, see also 80, 49). Similarly, we may say of the French Revolution or the American Declaration of Independence that, in Ricoeur's terms, they are social texts which came to be detached from the moment of their enunciation and to open up new worlds (Ricoeur 1981: 208). Hence, when the women of Al Masoom say with utter conviction that Islam posits the equality of men and women, they are expressing the *Zeitgeist* of the times, rather than simply the truth of Islam at its foundational moment. As Mrs Khan told me:

People interpret Islam wrongly. Islam gives true rights to women, equal to men. The [bad] influence on the position of women has come from the Indian subcontinent (i.e. it's just a local custom). Read the Qur'an and you will find that men and women are no different, they are granted equal rights and equal opportunities. The only thing is that because women are physically weaker than men they are given extra protection.

Recognising that the idea of the individual and the notion of citizenship have both been expansive concepts, in terms of the range of social categories to which they have come to be applied, does not, however, tell us much about the meaning of the terms or their present limitations. The liberal tendency has been to think of the citizen as the individual stripped of all her/his attributes: of nation, ethnicity, class or gender. As James Donald puts it, 'the very principle of universality inherent in the idea of citizenship means that this status cannot be colonised by any claim to define it in cultural terms' (Donald 1996: 174). Since, according to this view, the abstract, disembodied individual is the locus of citizenship rights, it is the individual *qua citizen* who both defends and upholds the law and is granted freedom and equality by it. Put radically, 'the citizen occupies an empty place ... [which] can be occupied by anyone – occupied in the sense of being spoken from, not in the sense of being given a substantial identity' (ibid.).

Yet there is an alternative to positing the idea of the 'autonomous' individual or, in the communitarian version, the 'unique' individual or culture, as the foundational building block of democracy. For ultimately, the unique individual is produced by her/his dialogical relations with others in which s/he both transcends and expresses the multiple identities – gendered, generational, ethnic, religious, national – which make her/him a unique person. This notion is particularly explicit for Pakistanis who draw on Islam to articulate an other-oriented view of individual and society. Mrs Khan told me:

According to Muslim law you need to live for others. Your things are not yours – you have to share. Your life is not all yours. In my view, if I feel that my life, my money is just my own, what is the difference between me and an animal? [But by the same token] a man has no right to beat a woman; in my religion no human being can hurt another.

Even those who seem to be living selfishly only for themselves, who buy palatial houses in expensive suburbs, are in reality seeking to impress others.

> We live for society. We are not independent. [Hence] society has the right to control wrongdoers. If citizens were just individuals – why would they bother to vote? We are all tied together. Democracy is important. Everyone has the right to speak and choose for themselves what they think is good or bad.

Just as the individual citizen is a uniquely heterogeneous combination of identities, so too the nation-state as moral community can no longer be, if it ever was in the past, a single, culturally homogeneous whole. Today's nation-states can only be united *through their heterogeneity*: through the complex web of cross-cutting ties that link and divide their individual citizens by gender, generation, ethnicity, class, culture, religion, secularism, political conviction, sexuality, life-style, hobbies, occupation. Iris Young invokes the ideal of the heterogeneous community as an allegorical city, with the 'experience of difference ... always being inserted.... without walls.... having a sense of the beyond ... the "being-together" of strangers ... and yet acknowledging their contiguity in living and the contributions each makes to the others' (Young 1990: 318). In this respect multiculturalism is important as a political imaginary of heterogeneity, not as a practice of institutionalised corporate cultural pluralism. 'Critical' multicultural-ism (Turner 1993), like all ethnic pluralisms, implies a broader, encompassing sense of community (Lyon 1997).

Rejecting the study of elites in favour of a subaltern politics of the local, Edmund Burke argues that 'the more we look, the more [Muslim] micropolitics of protest appears an affair not of heroic poses and radical flourishes, but of bets artfully hedged, old grudges paid off in kind, and (sometimes) old solidarities re-emphasized' (1988: 23). My aim in this book has been to show that both the grudges and the heroic poses of subaltern ethnic and/or gendered activists are crucial factors to be taken into account in any analysis of the way global and local cultures are sustained as living, changing, *disunited* and open realities of the kind I have traced in this study. Through activism the very terms of citizenship and transnational political subjectivity can be reversed and those defined as passive victims can become the imaginative agents of their own destiny.

Bibliography

Abrahamian, Ervand. 1988. 'Ali Shari'ati: Ideologue of the Iranian Revolution', in Burke and Lapidus, pp. 289–98.

Abu-Lughod, Lila. 1986. *Veiled Sentiments: Honor and Poetry in a Bedouin Society.* Berkeley: University of California Press.

——— 1993. 'Writing Against Culture,' in R.G. Fox (ed.), *Recapturing Anthropology.* Santa Fe: School of American Research Press, pp. 137–62.

Ahmad, Aziz. 1967. *Islamic Modernism in India and Pakistan 1857–1964.* London: Oxford University Press for the Royal Institute of International Affairs.

——— 1972. 'Activism of the Ulama in Pakistan', in Keddie, pp. 257–72.

Ahmad, Aijaz. 1992. *In Theory: Classes, Nations, Literatures.* London: Verso.

Ahmad, Mumtaz. 1992. 'The Politics of War: Islamic Fundamentalisms in Pakistan', in Piscatori, pp. 155–85.

Ahmad, Ziaddun (ed.), 1976. *Muhammad Ali Jinnah: Founder of Pakistan.* Karachi: Ministry of Information and Broadcasting.

Ahmed, Akbar S. 1976. *Millennium and Charisma among Pathans: a Critical Essay in Social Anthropology.* London: Routledge and Kegan Paul.

——— 1980. *Pukhtun Economy and Society: Traditional Structure and Economic Development.* London: Routledge and Kegan Paul.

——— 1986. *Pakistan Society: Islam, Ethnicity and Leadership in South Asia.* Karachi: Oxford University Press.

——— 1991a [1983]. *Resistance and Control in Pakistan.* London: Routledge.

——— 1991b. 'Salman Rushdie: A New Chapter', *The Guardian,* 17 January.

——— 1991c. 'Islam: the Roots of Misperception', *History Today* 41, April.

——— 1992. *Postmodernism and Islam: Predicament and Promise.* London: Routledge.

——— 1997. *Jinnah.* London: Routledge.

Ahsan, M.M. and A.R. Kidawi (eds), 1992. *Sacrilege versus Civility: Muslim Perspectives on The Satanic Verses Affair.* Leicester: The Islamic Foundation.

Akhavi, Shahrough. 1983. 'Shariati's Social Thought', in Nikki R. Keddie (ed.). *Religion and Politics in Iran.* New Haven, CT: Yale University Press.

Akhtar, Shabir. 1989. *Be Careful with Muhammad! The Salman Rushdie Affair.* London: Bellew Publishing.

Alavi, Hamza. 1988. 'Pakistan and Islam: Ethnicity and Ideology', in Fred Halliday and Hamza Alavi (eds), *State and Ideology in the Middle East and Pakistan.* London: Macmillan, pp. 64–111.

278 Bibliography

—— 1997. 'Ironies of History: Contradictions of the Khilafat Movement', in Mushirul Hasan (ed.), *Muslim Identities in Plural Societies*. New Delhi: Manohar. Also published in *Comparative Studies of South Asia, Africa and the Middle East* XVII (1): 1–17.

Al-Azmeh, Aziz. 1993. *Islams and Modernities*. London: Verso.

Ali, Mashuq. 1989. 'Second Introductory Paper', CRE Discussion Paper 1.

Ali, Yasmin. 1992. 'Muslim Women and the Politics of Ethnicity and Culture in the North of England', in Gita Saghal and Nira Yuval Davis (eds), *Refusing Holy Orders*. London: Virago, pp. 101–23.

Anderson, Benedict. 1991 [1983]. *Imagined Communities*. London: Verso.

—— 1994. 'Exodus', *Critical Inquiry* 20 (2): 314–27.

Anthias, Floya. 1998. 'Evaluating "Diaspora": Beyond Ethnicity?' *Sociology* 3 (32): 557–80.

—— and Nira Yuval-Davis. 1992. *Racialized Boundaries: Race, Nation, Gender, Colour and Class and the Anti-Racist Struggle*. London and New York: Routledge.

Antze, Paul and Michael Lambek (eds) 1996. *Tense Past: Cultural Essays in Trauma and Memory*. London: Routledge.

Anwar, Muhammad. 1996. *British Pakistanis: Demographic, Social and Economic Position*. Warwick: University of Warwick Centre for Research in Ethnic Relations.

Appadurai, Arjun. 1988. 'Theme Issue on Place and Voice in Anthropological Theory', *Cultural Anthropology* 3 (1): 16–20.

—— 1990. 'Disjuncture and Difference in the Global Cultural Economy', *Theory, Culture and Society* 7: 295–310.

—— 1993. 'Global Ethnoscapes: Notes and Queries for a Transnational Anthropology', in Richard G. Fox (ed.), *Recapturing Anthropology: Working in the Present*. Santa Fe: School of American Research Press, pp. 191–210.

Appignanesi, Lisa and Sara Maitland (eds), 1989. *The Rushdie File*. London: Fourth Estate.

Arabia. 1985. 'Old Differences Make a New Start in *Eid* Violence', October.

Arendt, Hannah. 1959. *The Human Condition: A Study of the Central Dilemmas Facing Modern Man*. New York: Doubleday Anchor.

Aristotle. 1941. *The Basic Works of Aristotle*, (ed.) Richard McKeon. New York: Random House.

Armbrust, Walter. 1996. *Mass Culture and Modernism in Egypt*. Cambridge: Cambridge University Press.

Armstrong, Karen. 1988. *Holy War: The Crusades and their Impact on Today's World* (A Channel 4 Book). London: Macmillan.

Asad, Talal. 1972. 'Market Model, Class Structure and Consent: a Reconsideration of Swat Political Organisation' *Man* (NS) 7 (1): 74–94.

—— 1986. 'The Concept of Cultural Translation in British Social Anthropology', in Clifford and Marcus, pp. 141–64.

—— 1990a. 'Ethnography, Literature, and Politics: Some Readings and Uses of Salman Rushdie's *The Satanic Verses*', *Cultural Anthropology* 5 (3): 239–69.

—— 1990b. 'Multiculturalism and British Identity in the Wake of the Rushdie Affair', *Politics and Society* 18 (4): 455–76.

—— 1993. *Genealogies of Religion*. Baltimore, MD: Johns Hopkins University Press.

Back, Les. 1996. *New Ethnicities in Urban Culture*. London: UCL Press.

Badran, Margot. 1995. *Feminists, Islam, and the Nation: Gender and the Making of Postmodern Egypt*. Princeton, NJ: Princeton University Press.

Bailey, F.G. 1969. *Strategems and Spoils: a Social Anthropology of Politics*. Oxford: Blackwell.

Bakhtin, M. 1981. *The Dialogic Imagination*, trans. C. Emerson and M. Hosquist. Austin:

University of Texas Press.

—— 1984 [1965]. *Rabelais and His World*, trans. Helene Iswolsky. Bloomington: Indiana University Press.

Ballard, Roger. 1996. 'The Pakistanis: Stability and Introspection', in Ceri Peach (ed.), *Ethnicity in the 1991 Census*, Vol. II. London: HMSO, pp. 121–49.

Bar Hillel, Y. 1970. *Aspects of Language*. New York: Humanities Press.

Barth, Frederik. 1959. *Political Leadership among the Swat Pathans*. London: Athlone Press.

—— 1960. 'The System of Social Stratification in Swat, Northern Pakistan', in E.R. Leach (ed.), *Aspects of Caste in South India, Ceylon and North West Pakistan*. Cambridge Papers in Social Anthropology, 2. Cambridge: Cambridge University Press, pp. 113–46.

—— 1969. 'Introduction', in *Ethnic Groups and Boundaries: the Social Organisation of Cultural Difference*. London: George Allen & Unwin, pp. 9–38.

—— 1981 [1959]. 'Segmentary Opposition and the Theory of Games'. Reprinted in *Features of Person and Society in Swat: Collected Essays on Pathan*. London: Routledge and Kegan Paul.

—— 1985. *The Last Wali of Swat*. Oslo: Norwegian University Press, distributed by Oxford University Press.

Barthes, Roland. 1957. *Mythologies*. Boulder, CO: Paladin.

Bateson, Gregory. 1958 [1936]. *Naven*. Stanford, CA: Stanford University Press.

—— 1973. *Steps to an Ecology of the Mind*. London: Paladin.

Bauman, Richard and Charles L. Briggs. 1990. 'Poetics and Performance as Critical Perspectives on Language and Social Life', *Annual Review of Anthropology*, 19: 259–83.

Bauman, Zygmunt. 1990. *Modernity and the Holocaust*. London: Routledge.

—— 1992. *Intimations of Postmodernity*. London: Routledge.

—— 1993. *Postmodern Ethics*. Oxford: Blackwell.

—— 1995. *Life in Fragments: Essays in Postmodern Morality*. Oxford: Blackwell.

—— 1997. 'The Making and Unmaking of Strangers', in Werbner and Modood, pp. 46–57.

Baumann, Gerd. 1996. *Contesting Culture: Discourses of Identity in Multi-Ethnic London*. Cambridge: Cambridge University Press.

—— 1997. 'Dominant and Demotic Discourses of Culture: Their Relevance to Multi-Ethnic Alliances', in Werbner and Modood, pp. 209–25.

Becker, A.L. 1979. 'Text-Building, Epistemology, and the Aesthetics of Javanese Shadow Theatre', in A.L. Becker and Aram A. Yengoyen (eds), *The Imagination of Reality: Essays in Southeast Asian Coherence Systems*. Norwood, NJ: Ablex, pp. 211–43.

Beeman, William O. 1983. 'Images of the Great Satan: Representation of the United States in the Iranian Revolution', in Nikki R. Keddie (ed.), *Religion and Politics in Iran*. New Haven, CT: Yale University Press, pp. 191–217.

Ben-Ari, Eyal and Yoram Bilu (eds), 1997. *Grasping Land: Space and Place in Contemporary Israeli Discourse and Experience*. Albany, NY: SUNY Press.

Benhabib, Seyla. 1992. *Situating the Self: Gender, Community and Postmodernism in Contemporary Ethics*. Cambridge: Polity Press.

Bergman, Samuel H. and N. Rotenstreich. 1966. 'Introduction', in Immanuel Kant, *Critique of Pure Reason*. Jerusalem: Bialik Institute (Hebrew).

Berman, Marshall. 1992. 'Why Modernism Still Matters', in Scott Lash and Jonathan Friedman (eds), *Modernity and Identity*. Oxford: Blackwell, pp. 33–58.

Bhabha, Homi K. 1990. *Nation and Narration*. London: Routledge.

—— 1992. 'Postcolonial Authority and Postcolonial Guilt', Discussion, in Lawrence Grossberg, Cary Nelson and Paula Treichler (eds), *Cultural Studies*. London: Routledge.

—— 1994. *The Location of Culture*. London: Routledge, pp. 56–68.

Bhachu, Parminder. 1995. 'New Cultural Forms and Transnational South Asian Women: Culture, Class and Consumption among British Asian Women in the Diaspora', in Peter van der Veer (ed.), *Nation and Migration: the Politics of Space in the South Asian Diaspora*. Philadelphia, PA: University of Pennsylvania Press, pp. 222–44.

Binder, Leonard. 1961. *Religion and Politics in Pakistan*. Berkeley: University of California Press.

Black-Michaud, Jacob. 1975. *Cohesive Force: Feud in the Mediterranean and the Middle East*. Oxford: Blackwell.

Blake, William. 1946. *The Portable Blake*. London: Viking Press.

Boddy, Janice. 1989. *Wombs and Alien Spirits*. Madison: University of Wisconsin Press.

Bolitho, Hector. 1954. *Jinnah: Creator of Pakistan*. London: John Murray.

Bonacich, Edna. 1973. 'A Theory of Middleman Minorities', *American Sociological Review* 38: 583–94.

Bourdieu, Pierre. 1977 [1972]. *Outline of a Theory of Practice*, trans. Richard Nice. Cambridge: Cambridge University Press.

—— 1984. *Distinction*. London: Routledge.

—— 1985. 'The Social Space and the Genesis of Groups', *Theory and Society* 14: 723–44.

Bowen, John R. 1989. '*Salat* in Indonesia: the Social Meanings of an Islamic Ritual', *Man* (NS) 24: 299–318.

—— 1993. *Muslims Through Discourse: Religion and Ritual in Gayo Society*. Princeton, NJ: Princeton University Press.

Brah, Avtar. 1996. *Cartographies of Diaspora: Contesting Identities*. London: Routledge.

Brooke-Rose, Christine. 1992. 'Palimpsest History', in Umberto Eco and C. Stefan (eds), *Interpretation and Reinterpretation*, Cambridge: Cambridge University Press, pp. 125–38.

Brooks, Stephen. 1990 [1989]. *The Club: the Jews of Modern Britain*. London: Pan Books.

Bruner, Jerome. 1991. 'The Narrative Construction of Reality', *Critical Inquiry* 18: 1–21.

Burke, Edmund III. 1988. 'Islam and Social Movements: Methodological Reflections', in Burke and Lapidus, pp. 17–35.

—— and Ira M. Lapidus (eds), 1988. *Islam, Politics and Social Movements*. Berkeley: University of California Press.

Burlet, Stacey and Helen Reid. 1996. 'Riots, Representations and Responsibilities: the Role of Young Men in Pakistani-Heritage Communities', in W.A.R. Shadid and P.S. van Koningsveld (eds), *Political Participation and Identities of Muslims in Non-Muslim States*. Kampen, Netherlands: Kok Pharos, pp. 144–59.

Caglar, Ayse S. 1997. 'Hyphenated Identities and the Limits of "Culture"', in Modood and Werbner, pp. 169–85.

Caplan, Patricia. 1978. 'Women's Organisations in Madras City, India', in Patricia Caplan and Janet M. Bujra (eds), *Women United, Women Divided*. London: Tavistock, pp. 99–128.

Carrier, James G. 1992. 'Occidentalism: the World Turned Upside-Down', *American Ethnologist* 19 (2): 195–212.

Cassirer, Ernest. 1951. *The Philosophy of the Enlightenment*. Boston, MA: Beacon Press.

Castells, Manuel. 1983. *The City and the Grassroots: A Cross-Cultural Theory of Urban Social Movements*. London: Edward Arnold.

Castells, Manuel. 1997. *The Power of Identity (The Information Age: Economy, Society and Culture, Vol. II)*. Oxford: Blackwell.

—— 1998. *End of the Millenium (The Information Age: Economy, Society and Culture, Vol. III)*. Oxford: Blackwell.

CCCS. 1982. *The Empire Strikes Back*. London: Hutchinson.

Chatterjee, Partha 1986. *Nationalist Thought and the Colonial World: A Derivative Discourse.* London: Zed Books.

Chaudhary, Vivek. 1995. 'The Prince of Pakistan', *The Guardian*, 7 February.

Clark, Katerina and Michael Holquist. 1984. *Mikhail Bakhtin.* Cambridge, MA and London: The Belknap Press of Harvard University Press.

Clifford, Gay. 1974. *The Transformations of Allegory.* London: Routledge and Kegan Paul.

Clifford, James. 1986. 'Introduction: Partial Truths', in Clifford and Marcus, pp. 1–26.

—— 1988. *The Predicament of Culture.* Cambridge MA: Harvard University Press.

—— 1994. 'Diasporas'. *Cultural Anthropology* 9 (3): 302–38.

—— and George Marcus (eds), 1986. *Writing Culture.* Berkeley: University of California Press.

Cohen, Abner. 1965. *Arab Border Villages in Israel: a Study of Continuity and Change in Social Life.* Manchester: University of Manchester Press.

—— 1969. *Custom and Politics in Urban Africa.* London: Routledge.

—— 1981. *The Politics of Elite Culture.* Berkeley: University of California Press.

—— 1993. *Masquerade Politics: Explorations in the Structure of Urban Cultural Movements.* Oxford: Berg Publishers.

—— 1991. 'Drama and Politics in the Development of a London Carnival', in Pnina Werbner and Muhammad Anwar (eds), *Black and Ethnic Leaderships in Britain: the Cultural Dimensions of Political Action.* London: Routledge, pp. 170–202.

Cohen, Philip. 1988. 'The Perversion of Inheritance: Studies in the Making of Multi-Racist Britain', in Philip Cohen and Harwant S. Bains (eds), *Multi-Racist Britain.* London: Macmillan Education, pp. 9–118.

Cohen, Robin. 1995. *Global Diasporas: an Introduction.* London: UCL Press.

Cohen, Stanley. 1972. *Folk Devils and Moral Panics: the Creation of Mods and Rockers.* London: MacGibbon & Kee.

Colonna, Fanny. 1984. 'Cultural Resistance and Religious Legitimacy in Colonial Algeria', in Akbar S. Ahmed and David M. Hart (eds), *Islam in Tribal Societies.* London: Routledge and Kegan Paul, pp. 106–26.

Comaroff, Jean. 1985. *Body of Power, Spirit of Resistance: the Culture and History of a South African People.* Chicago: University of Chicago Press.

Connerton, Paul. 1989. *How Societies Remember.* Cambridge: Cambridge University Press

CRE Discussion Paper 1. 1989a. *Law, Blasphemy and the Multi-Faith Society.* London: CRE.

CRE Discussion Paper 2. 1989b. *Free Speech.* London: CRE.

CRE Discussion Paper 3. 1989c. *Britain: A Plural Society.* London: CRE.

Dickey, Sara. 1993. *Cinema and the Urban Poor in South India.* Cambridge: Cambridge University Press.

Dominguez, Virginia. 1989. *People as Subject, People as Object: Selfhood and Peoplehood in Contemporary Israel.* Madison: Wisconsin University Press.

Donald, James. 1996. 'The Citizen and the Man About Town', in Stuart Hall and Paul du Gay (eds), *Questions of Cultural Identity.* London: Sage, pp. 170–90.

Douglas, Mary. 1968. 'The Social Control of Cognition: Some Factors in Joke Perception', *Man* (NS) 3: 361–76.

Dumont, Louis. 1970. *Homo Hierarchicus: The Caste System and Its Implications.* Chicago: University of Chicago Press.

—— 1983. 'A Modified View of Our Origins: the Christian Beginnings of Modern Individualism', *Contributions to Indian Sociology* (NS), 17 (1): 1–26.

Durkheim, Emile. 1915. *The Elementary Forms of the Religious Life.* London: George Allen & Unwin.

282 Bibliography

Dwyer, Claire and Astrid Meyer. 1996. 'The Establishment of Islamic Schools: A Controversial Phenomenon in Three European Countries', in W.A.R. Shadid and P.S. van Koningsveld (eds), *Muslims in the Margin: Political Responses to the Presence of Islam in Western Europe*. Kampen, Netherlands: Kok Pharos, pp. 218–42.

Eade, John. 1991. 'The Political Construction of Class and Community: Bangladeshi Political Leadership in Tower Hamlets, East London', in Werbner and Anwar, pp. 34–109.

Eade, John, Tim Vamplew and Ceri Peach. 1996. 'The Bangladeshis: the Encapsulated Community', in Ceri Peach (ed.), *Ethnicity in the 1991 Census*, Vol. II. London: HMSO, pp. 150–60.

Eco, Umberto. 1989. *The Open Work*, trans. Anna Cancogni. Cambridge, MA: Harvard University Press.

—— 1992. *Interpretation and Overinterpretation*, edited by Stefan Collini. Cambridge: Cambridge University Press.

Eglar, Zekiye. 1960. *A Punjabi Village in Pakistan*. New York: Columbia University Press.

Eickelman, Dale F. 1976. *Moroccan Islam*. Austin: University of Texas Press.

—— and Jon W. Anderson. 1999. *New Media in the Muslim World: the Emerging Public Sphere*. Bloomington: Indiana University Press.

—— and James Piscatori. 1996. *Muslim Politics*. Princeton, NJ: Princeton University Press.

Elias, Norbert. 1978. *The Civilising Process*. Oxford: Blackwell.

Epstein, A.L. 1958. *Politics in an Urban African Community*. Manchester: Manchester University Press.

—— 1978. *Ethos and Identity*. London: Tavistock.

Eriksen, T.H. 1993. 'In Which Sense do Cultural Islands Exist?', *Social Anthropology* 1 (1B): 133–48.

Evans-Prichard, E.E. 1940. *The Nuer*. Oxford: Clarendon Press.

Ewing, Katherine Pratt. 1997. *Arguing Sainthood: Modernity, Psychoanalysis, and Islam*. Durham, NC: Duke University Press.

Fabian, Johannes. 1983. *Time and the Other*. New York: Columbia University Press.

Fanon, Frantz. 1963/67. *The Wretched of the Earth*. London: Penguin.

Featherstone, Mike. 1991. *Consumer Culture and Postmodernism*. London: Sage.

Ferguson, James and Akhil Gupta. 1992. 'Beyond Culture: Space, Identity and the Politics of Difference', *Cultural Anthropology* 7 (1): 6–23.

Fernandez, J.W. 1982. *Bwiti: an Ethnography of the Religious Imagination in Africa*. Princeton, NJ: Princeton University Press.

—— 1986. *Persuasions and Performances: the Play of Tropes in Culture*. Bloomington: Indiana University Press.

Fischer, Michael, M.J. 1986. 'Ethnicity and the Postmodern Arts of Memory', in Clifford and Marcus, pp. 196–233.

Fischer, Michael, M.J. and Mehdi Abedi. 1990. *Debating Muslims: Cultural Dialogues in Postmodernity and Tradition*. Madison: University of Wisconsin Press.

Fish, Stanley. 1992. 'There's No Such Thing as Free Speech and It's a Good Thing Too', *Boston Review* 17 (1), pp. 3–4, 23–6.

Foucault, Michel. 1977 [1975]. *Discipline and Punish*, trans. Alan Sheridan. London: Penguin.

—— 1984. *The Foucault Reader*, edited by Paul Rabinow. London: Penguin.

—— 1989 [1972]. *The Archaeology of Knowledge*. London: Routledge.

Frazer, Nancy. 1992. 'Rethinking the Public Sphere: a Contribution to the Critique of Actually Existing Democracy', in Craig Calhoun (ed.), *Habermas and the Public Sphere*.

Cambridge, MA: MIT Press, pp. 109–42.

Freitag, Sandria B. 1988. 'The Roots of Muslim Separatism in South Asia: Personal Practice and Public Structures in Kanpur and Bombay', in Burke and Lapidus, pp. 113–45.

—— 1989a. *Collective Action and Community: Public Arenas and the Emergence of Communalism in North India*. Berkeley: University of California Press.

—— (ed.), 1989b. *Culture and Power in Banaras: Community, Performance and Environment, 1800–1980*. Berkeley: University of California Press.

Friedman, Jonathan. 1992. 'The Past in the Future: History and the Politics of Identity', *American Anthropologist* 94 (4): 837–59.

—— 1997. 'Global Crises, the Struggle for Cultural Identity and Intellectual Pork-barrelling: Cosmopolitans Versus Locals, Ethnics and Nationals in an Era of De-Hegemonization', in Werbner and Modood, pp. 70–89.

Fuentes, Carlos. 1989. 'Words Apart', *The Guardian*, 24 February. Reprinted in Appignanesi and Maitland.

Fuss, Diana. 1989. *Essentially Speaking: Feminism, Nature and Difference*. London and New York: Routledge.

Gaffney, Patrick D. 1994. *The Prophet's Pulpit: Islamic Preaching in Contemporary Egypt*. Berkeley: University of California Press.

Garbett, Kingsley G. 1970. 'The Analysis of Social Situations', Malinowski Lecture, *Man* (NS) 5 (2): 214–27.

Garfinkel, Harold. 1967. *Studies in Ethnomethodology*. Englewood Cliffs, NJ: Prentice Hall.

Gearing, F. O. 1970. *The Face of the Fox*. Chicago: Aldine.

Geertz, Clifford. 1968. *Islam Observed*. New Haven, CT: Yale University Press.

—— 1973a. 'After the Revolution', in *The Interpretation of Cultures*. New York: Basic Books, pp. 234–311.

—— 1973b. 'Deep Play: Notes on a Balinese Cockfight', in *The Interpretation of Cultures*. London: Hutchinson, pp. 412–56.

—— 1993. [1983]. *Local Knowledge*. London: Fontana.

Gellner, Ernest. 1981. *Muslim Society*. Cambridge: Cambridge University Press.

—— 1992. *Postmodernism, Reason and Religion*. London: Routledge.

—— 1994. 'Foreword', in Akbar S. Ahmed and Hastings Donnan (eds), *Islam, Globalisation and Postmodernity*. London: Routledge, pp. xi–xiv.

Ghosh, Amitav. 1989. 'The Diaspora in Indian Culture', *Public Culture* 2 (1): 73–8.

Giddens, Anthony. 1987. 'Nation States and Violence', in *Social Theory and Modern Sociology*. Oxford: Polity Press.

Gillespie, Marie. 1995. *Television, Ethnicity and Cultural Change*. London: Routledge.

Gillis, John R. (ed.), 1994. *Commemorations: The Politics of National Identity*. Princeton, NJ: Princeton University Press.

Gilmartin, David. 1979. 'Religious Leadership and the Pakistan Movement in the Punjab', *Modern Asian Studies* 13 (3): 485–517.

—— 1984. 'Shrines, Succession and Sources of Moral Authority', in Barbara Daly Metcalf (ed.), *Moral Conduct and Authority*. Berkeley: University of California Press, pp. 221–40.

—— 1988. *Empire and Islam: Punjab and the Making of Pakistan*. London: I.B. Taurus.

Gilroy, Paul. 1990. 'The End of Anti-Racism', *New Community* 17 (1): 71–83.

—— 1993. *The Black Atlantic: Modernity and Double Consciousness*. London: Verso.

Gilsenan, Michael. 1982. *Recognising Islam: Religion and Society in the Modern Arab World*. New York: Pantheon Books.

Gluckman, Max. 1958/1940. *Analysis of a Social Situation in Modern Zululand*, Rhodes-

284 Bibliography

Livingstone Paper 28. Manchester: Manchester University Press.

—— 1956. *Custom and Conflict in Africa*. Oxford: Blackwell.

—— 1962. 'Les Rites de Passages', in Max Gluckman (ed.), *Essays on the Ritual of Social Relations*. Manchester: Manchester University Press, pp. 1–51.

Goering, John. 1993. 'Reclothing the Emperor While Avoiding Ideological Polarisation', *New Community* 19 (2): 336–48.

Goffman, Erving. 1959. *The Presentation of Self in Everyday Life*. Garden City, NY: Double-day-Anchor.

—— 1961. *Encounters*. Indianapolis: Bobbs-Merrill.

Gupta, Akhil and James Ferguson. 1992 'Beyond "Culture": Space, Identity, and the Politics of Difference', theme issue on 'Space, Identity, and the Politics of Difference', *Cultural Anthropology* 7 (1): 6–23.

Habermas, Jurgen. 1985. 'Modernity – An Incomplete Project', in Hal Foster (ed.), *Postmodern Culture*. London: Pluto.

—— 1987. [1981] *The Theory of Communicative Action*, Vol. II, trans. T. McCarthy. Cambridge: Polity Press.

—— 1989. [1962]. *The Structural Transformation of the Public Sphere*, trans. Thomas Burger. Cambridge: Polity Press.

—— 1992. 'Further Reflections on the Public Sphere', in Craig Calhoun (ed.), *Habermas and the Public Sphere*. Cambridge, MA: MIT Press, pp. 421–61.

—— 1994. 'Struggles for Recognition in the Democratic Constitutional State', in Amy Gutmann (ed.), *Multiculturalism: Examining the Politics of Recognition*. Princeton, NJ: Princeton University Press, pp. 107–48.

Halbwachs, Maurice. 1992. *On Collective Memory*, edited, translated and with an introduction by Louis Coser. Chicago: University of Chicago Press.

Hall, Stuart. 1990. 'Cultural Identity and Diaspora', in J. Rutherford (ed.), *Identity: Community, Culture, Difference*. London: Lawrence and Wishart, pp. 222–37.

—— 1991. 'Old and New Identities, Old and New Ethnicities', in A.D. King (ed.), *Culture, Globalisation and the World System*. London: Sage.

—— 1992. 'New Ethnicities', in J. Donald and A. Rattansi (eds), *Race, Culture and Difference*. London: Sage, pp. 252–9.

—— et al. 1978. *Policing the Crisis: Mugging, the State, and Law and Order*. London: Macmillan.

Handelman, Don. 1981. 'The Ritual Clown: Attributes and Affinities', *Anthropos* 76: 321–70.

—— 1990. *Models and Mirrors: Towards an Anthropology of Public Events*. Cambridge: Cambridge University Press.

—— and Lea Shamgar. 1997. 'The Presence of Absence: the Memorialism of National Death in Israel', in Ben-Ari and Bilu, pp. 61–84.

Hannerz, Ulf. 1990. 'Cosmopolitans and Locals in World Culture', *Theory, Culture and Society* 7 (2–3): 237–51.

—— 1992. *Cultural Complexity: Studies in the Social Organisation of Meaning*. New York: Columbia University Press.

Hannigan, John A. 1985. 'Alain Tourain, Manuel Castells and Social Movement Theory: A Critical Appraisal', *The Sociological Quarterly* 26 (4): 435–54.

Haraway, Donna J. 1991. *Simians, Cyborgs and Women: the Reinvention of Nature*. London: Free Association.

Hardiman, David. 1982. 'The Indian "Faction": A Political Theory Examined', in *Subaltern Studies I: Writings in South Asian History and Society*. New Delhi: Oxford University Press.

Hardy, P. 1972. *The Muslims of British India*. Cambridge: Cambridge University Press.

Hebdige, Dick. 1979. *Subculture: the Meaning of Style*. London: Methuen.

Hegland, Mary. 1983. 'The Two Images of Husain: Accommodation and Revolution in an Iranian Village', in Nikki R. Keddie (ed.), *Religion and Politics in Iran*. New Haven, CT: Yale University Press, pp. 218–37.

—— 1987. 'Conclusion: Religious Resurgence in Today's World', in Richard T. Antoun and Mary Elaine Hegland (eds), *Religious Resurgence*. Syracuse, NY: Syracuse University Press, pp. 223–32.

Heikal, Muhammad. 1992. *Illusions of Triumph*. London: HarperCollins.

Herzfeld, Michael. 1992. *The Social Production of Indifference: Exploring the Symbolic Roots of Western Democracy*. Chicago: University of Chicago Press.

Hetherington, Kevin. 1994. 'The Contemporary Significance of Schmalenbach's Concept of the Bund', *Sociological Review* 42 (1): 1–25.

—— 1998. *Expressions of Identity: Space, Performance, Politics*. London: Sage.

Hewitt, Roger. 1986. *Black Talk, White Talk: Inter-racial Friendship and Communication amongst Adolescents*. Cambridge: Cambridge University Press.

Hobsbawm, E.J. 1959. *Primitive Rebels*. Manchester: Manchester University Press.

—— and Terence Ranger (eds), 1983. *The Invention of Tradition*. Cambridge: Cambridge University Press.

Holub, Robert C. 1991. *Jurgen Habermas: Critic in the Public Sphere*. London: Routledge.

hooks, bell. 1994. *Outlaw Culture: Resisting Representation*. London: Routledge.

Huntington, Samuel P. 1993. 'The Clash of Civilizations?', *Foreign Affairs* 72 (3): 22–41.

Hutchinson, Sharon. 1996. *Nuer Dilemmas*. Berkeley: University of California Press.

Inden, Ronald. 1995. 'Embodying God: from Imperial Progresses to National Progress in India', *Economy and Society* 24 (2): 245–78.

Iqbal, Afzal. n.d. *Islamisation of Pakistan*. Lahore: Vanguard.

Jacobson, Jessica. 1998. *Islam in Transition: Religion and Identity among British Pakistani Youth*. London and New York: Routledge, for the London School of Economics.

Jallal, Ayesha. 1985. *The Sole Spokesman: Jinnah, the Muslim League and the Demand for Pakistan*. Cambridge: Cambridge University Press.

Jameson, Fredric. 1991. *Postmodernism: Or the Cultural Logic of Late Capitalism*. London: Verso.

Jayawardena, Kumari. 1986. *Feminism and Nationalism in the Third World*. London: Zed Books.

Jeffery, Patricia. 1979. *Frogs in the Well*. London: Zed Books.

Jones, Rodney W. 1974. *Urban Politics in India: Area, Power and Policy in a Penetrated System*. Berkeley: University of California Press.

Jones, Trevor. 1993. *Britain's Ethnic Minorities: an Analysis of the Labour Force Survey*. London: Policy Studies Institute.

Jussawala, Feroza. 1989. 'Resurrecting the Prophet: the Case of Salman, the Otherwise', *Public Culture* 2 (1): 106–17.

Kabbani, Rana. 1989. *Letter to Christendom*. London: Virago.

Kalka, Iris. 1991. 'Striking a Bargain: Political Radicalism in a Middle Class London Borough', in Werbner and Anwar, pp. 203–25.

Kandiyoti, Deniz (ed.), 1991. *Women, Islam and the State*. London: Macmillan.

Kant, Immanuel. 1952. *The Critique of Pure Judgement*. Oxford: Clarendon.

Kapferer, Bruce. 1983. *Celebration of Demons*. Bloomington: Indiana University Press.

—— 1988. *Legends of People, Myths of State: Violence, Intolerance and Political Culture in Sri Lanka and Australia*. Washington, DC: Smithsonian Institution Press.

—— 1997. *The Feast of the Sorcerer*, Chicago, Il: University of Chicago Press.

Keddie, Nikki R. (ed.), 1972. *Scholars, Saints and Sufis*. Berkeley: University of California Press.

Kepel, Gilles, 1985. *The Prophet and the Pharaoh: Muslim Extremism in Egypt*, trans. Jon Rothschild. Berkeley: University of California Press.

—— 1994. *The Revenge of God: the Resurgence of Islam, Christianity and Judaism in the Modern World*, trans. Alan Braley. Philadelphia, PA: Pennsylvania State University Press.

Kermode, Frank. 1980. 'Secrets and Narrative Sequence', in W.J.T. Mitchell.

Kratz, Corinne A. 1993. *Affecting Performance: Meaning, Movement and Experience in Okiek Women's Initiation*. Washington, DC: Smithsonian Institution Press.

Kumar, Nita. 1988. *The Artisans of Banaras: Popular Culture and Identity, 1880–1986*. Princeton, NJ: Princeton University Press.

Kurin, Richard. 1984. 'Morality, Personhood, and the Exemplary Life: Popular Conceptions of Muslims in Paradise', in Barbara Daly Metcalf (ed.), *Moral Conduct and Authority: the Place of Adab in South Asian Islam*. Berkeley: University of California Press.

Lambek, Michael. 1993. *Knowledge and Practice in Mayotte: Local Discourses of Islam, Sorcery and Spirit Possession*. Toronto: University of Toronto Press.

Laqueur, Thomas W. 1994. 'Memory and Naming in the Great War', in Gillis, pp. 150–67.

Launay, Robert. 1992. *Beyond the Stream: Islam and Society in a West African Town*. Berkeley: University of California Press.

Lavie, Smadar. 1990. *The Poetics of Military Occupation*. Berkeley: University of California Press.

Lee, Simon. 1990. *The Cost of Free Speech*. London: Faber and Faber.

Lefebvre, Henri. 1991. [1974] *The Production of Space*, trans. Donald Nicholson-Smith. Oxford: Blackwell.

Levinas, E. 1987. *Collected Philosophical Papers*, trans. Alphonso Lingis. Dordrecht: Martinus Nijhoff Publishers.

Lévi-Strauss, Claude. 1994. 'Anthropology, Race and Politics: a Conversation with Didier Eribon', in Robert Borowski (ed.), *Assessing Cultural Anthropology*. London: McGraw-Hill, pp. 420–9.

Lewis, Bernard. 1975. *History, Remembered, Recorded, Invented*. Princeton, NJ: Princeton University Press.

—— 1994. [1992] 'Legal and Historical Reflections on the Position of Muslim Populations under non-Muslim Rule', in Bernard Lewis and Dominique Schnapper (eds), *Muslims in Europe*. London: Pinter Publishers, pp. 1–18.

Lewis, Philip. 1994. *Islamic Britain: Religion, Politics and Identity among British Muslims*. London: I.B. Tauris.

—— 1997. 'Arenas of Ethnic Negotiation: Cooperation and Conflict in Bradford', in Tariq Modood and Pnina Werbner (eds), *The Politics of Multiculturalism in the New Europe*. London: Zed Books, pp. 126–46.

Lindholm, Charles. 1982. *Generosity and Jealousy: The Swat Pukhtun of Northern Pakistan*. New York: Columbia University Press.

—— 1990. 'Ambiguity and the Social Construction of Authority in Swat', in Pnina Werbner (ed.), *Person, Myth and Society in South Asian Islam*. Special edition of *Social Analysis*, 28. University of Adelaide.

—— 1996. *Frontier Perspectives: Essays in Comparative Anthropology*. New Delhi: Oxford University Press.

—— 1997. *The Islamic Middle East: an Historical Anthropology*. Oxford: Blackwell.

Longhurst, Brian and Mike Savage. 1997. 'Social Class, Consumption and the Influence of

Bourdieu: Some Critical Issues', in Stephen Edgell, Kevin Hetherington and Alan Warde (eds), *Consumption Matters*. Oxford: Blackwells Publishers for the *Sociological Review*, pp. 274–301.

Lyon, Wenonah. 1995. 'Islam and Islamic Women in Britain', *Women: A Cultural Review* 6, 1: 46–56.

—— 1997. 'Another way of Being British: Ethnicity, South Asians and England', in Modood and Werbner, pp. 186–206.

Lyotard, Jean-François. 1985. 'Histoire Universalle et Differences Culturelle', *Critique* 41, May.

—— 1986. [1977]. *The Postmodern Condition: a Report on Knowledge*. trans. Geoff Bennington and Brian Massumi. Manchester: Manchester University Press.

—— 1988. *Peregrinations: Law, Form, Event*. New York: Columbia University Press.

Malik, Jamal S. 1989. 'Legitimising Islamization – the case of the Council of Islamic Ideology in Pakistan, 1962–1981', *Orient* 30 (2): 251–68.

—— 1990. 'The Luminous Nurani: Charisma and Political Mobilisation among the Barelwis in Pakistan', in Pnina Werbner (ed.), *Person, Myth and Society in South Asian Islam*. Special issue of *Social Analysis*, 28. University of Adelaide, pp. 38–50.

—— 1998. *Colonialization of Islam: Dissolution of Traditional Institutions in Pakistan*. New Delhi: Manohar.

Malik, Sohail. 1995. 'Acheson Man', *Q News*, 20–27 January.

Malkki, Liisa. 1992. 'National Geographic: Rootings of People and the Territorialisation of National Identity among Scholars and Refugees', *Cultural Anthropology* 7 (1): 24–43.

—— 1995. *Purity and Exile: Violence, Memory, and National Cosmology among Hutu Refugees in Tanzania*. Chicago: University of Chicago Press.

Manchester Evening News. 1988. 'Man Dies from a Punch in the Chest', October.

Marcus, George and Michael M.J. Fischer. 1986. *Anthropology as Cultural Critique*. Chicago: University of Chicago Press.

Margalit, Avishai. 1996. *The Decent Society*. Cambridge, MA: Harvard University Press.

Marriott, McKim. 1976. 'Hindu Transactions: Diversity without Dualism', in Bruce Kapferer (ed.), *Transaction and Meaning*. Philadelphia, PA: ISHI, pp. 109–42

Mayer, Adrian C. 1981. 'Public Service and Individual Merit in a Town in Central India', in Adrian C. Mayer (ed.), *Culture and Morality: Essays in Honour of Christoph von Fuerer-Heimendorf*. New Delhi: Oxford University Press.

Mayer, Philip. 1961. *Townsmen and Tribesmen*. Cape Town: Oxford University Press.

Mazrui, Ali M. 1989. 'The Satanic Verses or a Satanic Novel? Moral Dilemmas of the Rushdie Affair', *Free Speech*. London: CRE.

McIntyre, Alisdair. 1988. *Whose Justice? Whose Rationality?* Notre Dame, IL: University of Notre Dame Press.

Melotti, Umberto. 1997. 'International Migration in Europe: Social Projects and Political Cultures', in Tariq Modood and Pnina Werbner (eds), *The Politics of Multiculturalism in the New Europe: Racism, Identity, Community*. London: Zed Books, pp. 73–92.

Melucci, Alberto. 1989. *Nomads of the Present: Social Movements and Individual Needs in Contemporary Societies*. London: Hutchinson Radius.

—— 1996a. *Challenging Codes: Collective Action in the Information Age*. Cambridge: Cambridge University Press.

—— 1996b. *The Playing Self: Person and Meaning in the Planetary Society*. Cambridge: Cambridge University Press.

—— 1997. 'Identity and Difference in a Globalized World', in Werbner and Modood (eds), pp. 58–69.

288 Bibliography

Mercer, Kobena. 1990. 'Welcome to the Jungle: Identity and Diversity in Postmodern Politics', in J. Rutherford (ed.), *Identity: Community, Culture, Difference*. London: Lawrence and Wishart, pp. 43–71.

—— 1992. '1968: Periodizing Politics and Identity', in Lawrence Grossberg, Cary Nelson and Paula Treichler (eds), *Cultural Studies*. London: Routledge, pp. 424–49.

Metcalf, Barbara D. 1982. *Islamic Revival in British India: Deoband, 1860–1900*. Princeton, NJ: Princeton University Press.

—— 1987. 'Islamic Arguments in Contemporary Pakistan', in William R. Roff (ed.), *Islam and the Political Economy of Meaning: Comparative Studies in Muslim Discourse*. Berkeley: University of California Press, pp. 132–60.

—— 1990. *Perfecting Women: Maulana Ashraf 'Ali Thanawi's Bihishti Zewar*. Berkeley: University of California Press.

—— (ed.) 1996a. *Making Muslim Space in North America and Europe*. Berkeley: University of California Press.

—— 1996b. 'Introduction: Sacred Words, Sanctional Practice, New Communities', in Metcalf, pp. 1–27.

—— 1996c. 'New Medinas: the Tablighi Jama'at in North America and Europe', in Metcalf, pp. 110–30.

Miles, Robert. 1993. *Racism after Race Relations*. London: Routledge.

—— 1994. 'A Rise of Racism and Fascism in Contemporary Europe? Some Sceptical Reflections on its Nature and Extent', *New Community* 20 (4): 547–62.

Miller, Daniel (ed.), 1995. *Worlds Apart: Modernity Through the Prism of the Local*. London: Routledge.

Mines, Mattison. 1994. *Public Faces, Private Voices: Community and Individuality in South India*. Berkeley: University of California Press.

Mitchell, J.C. 1956. *The Kalela Dance*. Manchester: Manchester University Press for the Rhodes-Livingstone Institute.

Mitchell, W.J.T. (ed.), 1980. *On Narrative*. Chicago: University of Chicago Press.

Modood, Tariq. 1988. '"Black", Racial Equality and Ethnic Identity', *New Community* XIV (3): 397–404.

—— 1990. 'British Asian Muslims and the Rushdie Affair', *The Political Quarterly* 61 (2): 143–60.

—— 1994a. 'Establishment, Multiculturalism and British Citizenship', *The Political Quarterly* 65 (1): 53–73.

—— 1994b. 'The End of a Hegemony: The Concept of "Black" and British Asians', in John Rex and B. Drury (eds), *Ethnic Mobilisation in a Multi-Cultural Europe*. Aldershot: Gower.

—— 1996. 'If Races do not Exist, Then What Does? Racial Categorisation and Ethnic Realities', in R. Barot (ed.), *The Racism Problematic: Contemporary Sociological Debates on Race and Ethnicity*. New York: Edwin Mellen Press.

—— 1997. '"Difference", Cultural Racism and Anti-Racism', in Werbner and Modood, pp. 134–72.

Modood, Tariq, Sharon Beishon and Satnam Virdee. 1994. *Changing Ethnic Identities*. London: Policy Studies Institute.

Modood, Tariq, Richard Berthoud et al. 1997. *Ethnic Minorities in Britain: Diversity and Disadvantage*. Fourth National Survey of Ethnic Minorities. London: Policy Studies Institute.

Modood, Tariq and Pnina Werbner (eds), 1997. *The Politics of Multiculturalism in the New Europe*. London: Zed Books.

Moodie, Dunbar T. 1975. *The Rise of Afrikanerdom: Power, Apartheid and the Afrikaner Civil Religion.* Los Angeles: University of California Press.

Mouffe, Chantal. 1988. 'Hegemony and New Political Subjects: Towards a New Concept of Democracy', in Cary Nelson and Lawrence Grossberg (eds), *From Marxism to the Interpretation of Culture.* Urbana, IL: University of Illinois Press, pp. 89–103.

—— 1993. *The Return of the Political.* London: Verso.

Mumtaz, Khawar and Farida Shaheed (eds), 1987. *Women of Pakistan: Two Steps Foward, One Step Back?* London: Zed Books.

Munir, Muhammad. n.d. *Pakistan: From Jinnah to Zia – A Study in Ideological Convulsions,* New Delhi: Document Press.

Najmabadi, Afsaneh. 1989. 'Hazards of Modernity and Morality: Women, State and Morality in Contemporary Iran', in Deniz Kandiyoti (ed.), *Women, Islam and the State.* London: Macmillan, pp. 48–76.

Nandy, Ashis. 1988. *The Intimate Enemy: Loss and Recovery of Self Under Colonialism.* New Delhi: Oxford University Press.

Nicholson, Reynold A. 1978. *Studies in Islamic Mysticism.* Cambridge: Cambridge University Press.

Nielsen, Jørgen S. 1988. 'Muslims in Britain and Local Authority Responses', in Tomas Gerholm and Yngre Georg Lithman (eds), *The New Islamic Presence in Western Europe.* London: Mansell, pp. 53–77.

—— 1992. 'Islam, Muslims, and British Local and Central Government: Structural Fluidity'. Paper presented at the Conference on 'European Islam: Societies and States', Turin, April.

Norris, Christopher. 1989. 'Reading Donald Davidson: Truth, Meaning and Right Interpretation', in Richard Shusterman (ed.), *Analytic Aesthetics.* Oxford: Blackwell.

—— 1991. *Uncritical Theory: Postmodernism, Intellectuals and the Gulf War.* London: Lawrence and Wishart.

O'Neill, Onora. 1989. *Constructions of Reason: Explorations in Kant's Practical Philosophy.* Cambridge: Cambridge University Press.

Ong, Aihwa and Donald Nonini. 1997. *Underground Empires: the Cultural Politics of Modern Chinese Transnationalism.* New York: Routledge.

Ortner, Sherry. 1984. 'Theory in Anthropology since the Sixties', *Comparative Studies in Society and History* 26: 126–66.

Paine, Robert. 1989. 'Israel: Jewish Identity and Competition over Tradition', in Elizabeth Tonkin, Maryon McDonald and Malcolm Chapman (eds), *History and Ethnicity.* ASA Monograph 27. London: Routledge, pp. 121–36.

Pandey, Gyanendra. 1988. 'Peasant Revolt and Indian Nationalism', in Ranajit Guha and Gyatri Chakravorty Spivak (eds), *Selected Subaltern Studies.* Oxford: Oxford University Press, pp. 233–87.

Papastergiadis, Nikos. 1993a. 'The Ends of Migration'. Keynote Lecture presented at the Art Gallery of New South Wales.

—— 1993b. *Modernity as Exile.* Manchester: Manchester University Press.

Parekh, Bikhu. 1989a. 'Between Holy Text and Moral Void', *New Statesman & Society,* 23 March.

—— 1989b. 'Reflections', in Appignanesi and Maitland.

—— 1994. 'Some Reflections on the Hindu Diaspora', *New Community,* 20 (4): 547–62.

Patel, Suresh. 1988. 'Insurance and Ethnic Business: an Emerging Crisis in the Inner City', *New Community* 15 (1): 79–90.

Peters, Emrys L. 1959. 'The Proliferation of Segments in the Lineages of the Bedouin of

Cyrenaica', Curl Bequest Essay, *Journal of the Royal Anthropological Institute* 90 (1): 29–53.

—— 1967. 'Some Structural Aspects of the Feud Among the Camel-herding Bedouin of Cyrenaica', *Africa* XXXVII (3): 261–82.

Pettigrew, Joyce. 1975. *Robber Noblemen: a Study of the Political System of the Sikh Jats.* London: Routledge and Kegan Paul.

Phillips, Anne. 1991. *Engendering Democracy*. Cambridge: Polity Press.

—— 1993. *Democracy and Difference*. Cambridge: Polity Press.

—— 1995. 'Democracy and Difference: Some Problems for Feminist Theory', in Will Kymlicka (ed.), *The Rights of Minority Cultures*. Oxford: Oxford University Press, pp. 288–99.

Piscatori, James (ed.), 1991. *Islamic Fundamentalisms and the Gulf Crisis*. Chicago: The Fundamentalist Project, American Academy of Arts and Science.

Pocock, David. 1957. 'The Bases of Faction in Gujerat', *British Journal of Sociology* 8: 295–306.

Pomorska, Krystyna. 1984. 'Prologue', in Bakhtin.

Quilligan, Maureen. 1979. *The Language of Allegory: Defining the Genre*. Ithaca, NY: Cornell University Press.

Radcliffe, Sarah and Sallie Westwood. 1996. *Remaking the Nation: Place, Identity and Politics in Latin America*. London: Routledge.

Raheja, Gloria Goodwin and Ann Grodzins Gold. 1994. *Listen to the Heron's Words: Reimagining Gender and Kinship in North India*. Berkeley: University of California Press.

Rajchman, John. 1991. *Truth and Eros: Foucault, Lacan and the Question of Ethics*. London and New York: Routledge.

Rapport, Nigel. 1993. *Diverse World-Views in an English Village*. Edinburgh: Edinburgh University Press.

Rex, John. 1986. 'The Role of Class Analysis in the Study of Race Relations: a Weberian Perspective', in Rex and Mason, pp. 64–83.

—— 1992. *Ethnic Identity and Ethnic Mobilisation in Britain*. Monographs in Ethnic Relations 5. London: CRER for the ESRC.

—— and D. Mason (eds), 1986. *Theories of Race and Ethnic Relations*. Cambridge: Cambridge University Press.

Ricoeur, Paul. 1980. 'Narrative Time', in W.J.T. Mitchell.

—— 1981. *Hermeneutics and the Human Sciences*, ed. J.B. Thompson. Cambridge: Cambridge University Press.

Rimmon-Kenan, S. 1983. *Narrative Fiction, Contemporary Poetics*. London: Methuen.

Robertson, Roland. 1995. 'Glocalisation: Time-Space and Homogeneity-Heterogeneity', in Mike Featherstone, Scott Lash and Roland Robertson (eds), *Global Modernities*. London: Sage, pp. 25–44.

Rodman, Margaret C. 1992. 'Empowering Place: Multilocality and Multivocality', *American Anthropologist* 94 (3): 640–56.

Rogers, Alisdair and Steven Vertovec (eds), 1995. 'Introduction', in Alisdair Rogers and Steven Vertovec (eds), *The Urban Context: Ethnicity, Social Networks and Situational Analysis*. Oxford: Berg, pp. 1–34.

Rorty, Richard. 1992a. 'Cosmopolitanism without Emancipation: a Response to Lyotard', in Scott Lash and Jonathan Friedman (eds), *Modernity and Identity*. Oxford: Blackwell, pp. 59–72.

—— 1992b. 'The Pragmatist's Progress', in Eco, pp. 89–108.

Rosaldo, Renato. 1989. *Culture and Truth*. Boston, MA: Beacon Press.

Roy, Olivier. 1994. *The Failure of Political Islam*, trans. Carol Volk. Cambridge, MA: Harvard University Press.

Runnymede Trust. 1997. *Islamophobia: A Challenge for Us All*. London: Runnymede Trust.

Rushdie, Salman. 1988. *The Satanic Verses*. London: Viking.

—— 1991a. *Imaginary Homelands 1981–1990: Essays and Criticism*. London: Granta Books.

—— 1991b. 'One Man in a Doomed Balloon', *The Guardian*, 13 December.

Ruthven, Malise. 1990. *A Satanic Affair: Salman Rushdie and the Wrath of Islam*. London: Hogarth Press.

Safran, William. 1991. 'Diasporas in Modern Societies: Myths of Homeland and Return', *Diaspora* 1 (1): 83–99.

Saghal, Gita and Nira Yuval-Davis (eds), 1992. *Refusing Holy Orders; Women and Fundamentalism in Britain*. London: Virago.

Sahlins, Marshall. 1985. *Islands of History*, London: Tavistock Publications.

Said, Edward W. 1983a. 'Opponents, Audiences, Constituencies and Community' in Hal Foster (ed.), *Post Modern Culture*. London: Pluto Press, 135–59.

—— 1983b. *The World, the Text and the Critic*. London: Vintage.

Salvatore, Armando. 1997. *Islam and the Political Discourse of Modernity*. London: Ithaca Press.

Samad, A.Y. 1992. 'Book Burning and Race Relations: Political Mobilisation of Bradford Muslims', *New Community* 18 (4): 507–19.

Samad, Yunas. 1997. 'The Plural Guises of Multiculturalism: Conceptualising a Fragmented Paradigm', in Tariq Modood and Pnina Werbner (eds), *The Politics of Multiculturalism in the New Europe: Racism, Identity, Community*. London: Zed Books, pp. 240–60.

Scantlebury, E. 1995. 'Muslims in Manchester: the Depiction of a Religious Community', *New Community* 21 (3): 425–36.

Schutz, Alfred. 1944. 'The Stranger: an Essay in Social Psychology', *American Journal of Sociology* 49 (6): 499–507.

Scott, James C. 1985. *Weapons of the Weak: Everyday Forms of Peasant Resistance*. New Haven, CT: Yale University Press.

—— 1992. *Domination and the Arts of Resistance: Hidden Transcripts*. New Haven, CT: Yale University Press.

Shadid, Wasif and Sjoerd van Koningsveld. 1996. 'Loyalty to a non-Muslim Government: an Analysis of Islamic Normative Discussions and of the Views of some Contemporary Islamists', in W.A.R. Shadid and P.S. van Koningsveld (eds), *Political Participation and Identities of Muslims in Non-Muslim Countries*. Kampen, Netherlands: Kok Pharos, pp. 84–114.

Sharma, Sanjay, John Hutnyk and Shwami Sharma (eds), 1996. *Dis-Orienting Rhythms: the Politics of the New Asian Dance Music*. London: Zed Books.

Shaw, Alison. 2001. 'Kinship, Cultural Preference and Immigration: Consanguineous Marriage among British Pakistanis', *JRAI (incorporating Man)* 7 (2): 315–35.

Sherani, S. Rahman. 1991. 'Ulema and Pir in the Politics of Pakistan', in Hastings Donnan and Pnina Werbner (eds), *Economy and Culture in Pakistan*. London: Macmillan, pp. 216–41.

Shulman, David D. 1985. *The King and the Clown in South Indian Myth and Poetry*. Princeton, NJ: Princeton University Press.

Simmel, Georg. 1950. 'The Stranger', in K.H. Wolff (ed.), *The Sociology of Georg Simmel*. New York: Free Press, pp. 402–8.

Simon, Roger. 1991. *Gramsci's Political Thought: An Introduction*. London: Lawrence and Wishart.

Singer, Milton. 1972. *When a Great Tradition Modernises*. London: Pall Mall Press.

Sivanandan, A. 1989. 'All that Melts into Air is Solid: the Hokum of New Times', *Race and Class* 31 (3): 1–30.

—— 1990. *Communities of Resistance: Writings on Black Struggles for Socialism*. London: Verso.

Solomos, John and Les Back. 1995. *Race, Politics and Social Change*. London: Routledge.

Southall Black Sisters. 1990. *Against the Grain: Southall Black Sisters 1979–1989, A Celebration of Survival and Struggle*. London: Southall Black Sisters.

Spivak, Gayatri Chakravorty. 1987. *In Other Worlds: Essays in Cultural Politics*. New York: Methuen.

—— 1995. 'Can the Subaltern Speak?', in Bill Ashcroft, Gareth Griffiths and Helen Tiffin (eds), *The Postcolonial Reader*. London: Routledge, pp. 24–8.

Strathern, Marilyn. 1987a. 'An Awkward Relationship: the Case of Feminism and Anthropology', *Signs* 12: 276–92.

—— 1987b. 'Out of Context: The Persuasive Fictions of Anthropology' (Frazer Lecture), *Current Anthropology* 28: 251–81.

—— 1991. *Partial Connections*. Savage, MD: Rowman and Littlefields.

—— 1992. *After Nature: English Kinship in the Late 20th Century*. Cambridge: Cambridge University Press.

Swartz, Marc J. 1969. *Local-Level Politics: Social and Cultural Perspectives*. London: Athlone Press.

Tambiah, Stanley. 1985. *Culture, Thought, and Social Action: an Anthropological Perspective*. Cambridge, MA: Harvard University Press.

Taylor, Charles. 1992. *Multiculturalism and 'The Politics of Recognition'*. Princeton, NJ: Princeton University Press.

Taylor, Philip M. 1992. *War and the Media*. Manchester: Manchester University Press.

Thomas, Nicholas. 1992. 'The Inversion of Tradition', *American Ethnologist* 19 (2): 213–32.

Thompson, E.P. 1971. 'The Moral Economy of the English Crowd in the Eighteenth Century', *Past and Present* 50: 76–136.

—— 1980 [1963]. *The Making of the English Working Class*. London: Pelican.

Thompson, Leonard. 1985. *The Political Mythology of Apartheid*, New Haven, CT and London: Yale University Press.

Tololyan, Khachig. 1991. 'The Nation-State and its Other: in Lieu of a Preface', *Diaspora: A Journal of Transnational Studies* 1 (1): 3–7.

—— 1996. 'Rethinking Diaspora(s): Stateless Power in the Transnational Moment', *Diaspora* 5 (1): 3–36.

Tönnies, Ferdinand. 1955. *Community and Association*, trans. by Charles P. Loomis. London: Routledge and Kegan Paul.

Touraine, Alain. 1981. [1978] *The Voice and the Eye: An Analysis of Social Movements*, trans. Alan Duff. Cambridge: Cambridge University Press.

Tsing, Anna L. 1993. *In the Realm of the Diamond Queen*. Princeton, NJ: Princeton University Press.

Turner, Bryan S. 1990. 'Outline of a Theory of Citizenship', *Sociology* 24 (2): 189–218.

—— 1992. 'Ideology and Utopia in the Formation of an Intelligentsia: Reflections on the English Cultural Conduit', *Theory, Culture and Society* 9 (1): 159–82.

—— 1994. *Orientalism, Postmodernism and Globalism*. London: Routledge.

Turner, Terence. 1993. 'Anthropology and Multiculturalism: What is Anthropology that Multiculturalists Should be Mindful of It?', *Cultural Anthropology* 8 (4): 411–29.

Turner, Victor. 1974. *Dramas, Fields, and Metaphors: Symbolic Action in Human Society*. Ithaca, NY: Cornell University Press.

—— 1980. 'Social Dramas and Theories about them', in W.J.T. Mitchell.

Van der Veer, Peter. 1989. 'Satanic or Angelic: The Politics of Literary and Religious Inspiration', *Public Culture* 2 (1): 100–5.

—— 1994. *Religious Nationalism: Hindus and Muslims in India*. Berkeley: University of California Press.

—— 1995. 'Introduction: the Diasporic Imagination', in Peter van der Veer (ed.), *Nation and Migration: the Politics of Space in the South Asian Diaspora*. Philadelphia, PA: University of Pennsylvania Press, pp. 1–16.

—— 1996. 'Response' to 'Allegories of Sacred Imperfection: Magic, Hermeneutics and Passion in *The Satanic Verses*', by Pnina Werbner, *Current Anthropology*, Special Issue on 'Anthropology in Public', Vol. 37 supplement: S55–S86.

—— 1997. '"The Enigma of Arrival": Hybridity and Multiplicity in the Global Space', in Werbner and Modood, pp. 90–105.

Voll, John O. 1987. 'Islamic Renewal and the "Failure of the West"', in Richard T. Antoun and Mary E. Hegland (eds), *Religious Resurgence*. Syracuse, NY: Syracuse University Press: pp. 127–44.

Wallman, Sandra. 1986. 'Ethnicity and the Boundary Process in Context', in Rex and Mason, pp. 226–45.

Walzer, Michael. 1992. 'Comment', in Charles Taylor, pp. 99–105.

Weldon, Fay. 1989. *Sacred Cows: A Portrait of Britain, Post-Rushdie, Pre-Utopia*. Counterblast 4. London: Chatto & Windus.

Webster, Richard. 1990. *A Brief History of Blasphemy: Liberalism, Censorship and 'The Satanic Verses'*. London: Orwell Press.

Werbner, Pnina. 1990a. *The Migration Process: Capital, Gifts and Offerings among British Pakistanis*. Oxford: Berg Publishers.

—— 1990b. 'Renewing an Industrial Past: British Pakistani Entrepreneurship in Manchester', *Migration*, 8, pp. 1–39.

—— 1990c. 'Exemplary Personhood and the Political Mythology of Overseas Pakistanis', in Pnina Werbner (ed.), *Person, Myth and Society in South Asian Islam*, Special Issue of *Social Analysis* 28. University of Adelaide, pp. 51–69.

—— 1991a. 'Black and Ethnic Leaderships in Britain: a Theoretical Overview', in Werbner and Anwar, pp. 15–40.

—— 1991b. 'The Fiction of Unity in Ethnic Politics: Aspects of Representation and the State among Manchester Pakistanis', in Werbner and Anwar, pp. 113–45.

—— 1991c. 'Factionalism and Violence in the Communal Politics of British Overseas Pakistanis', in Hastings Donnan and Pnina Werbner (eds), *Economy and Culture in Pakistan: Migrants and Cities in a Muslim Society*. London: Macmillan, pp. 188–215.

—— 1991d. 'Shattered Bridges: the Dialectics of Progress and Alienation Among British Muslims', *New Community* 17 (3): 331–46.

—— 1994. 'Diaspora and Millennium: British Pakistani Local-Global Fabulations of the Gulf War', in Akbar S. Ahmed and Hastings Donnan (eds), *Islam, Globalization and Postmodernity*. London: Routledge, pp. 213–36.

—— 1996a. 'The Making of Muslim Dissent: Hybridized Discourses, Lay Preachers and Radical Rhetoric among British Pakistanis', *American Ethnologist* 23 (1): 102–22.

—— 1996b. 'Stamping the Earth with the Name of Allah: Zikr and the Sacralising of Space among British Muslims', *Cultural Anthropology* 11 (3): 309–38.

—— 1996c. 'The Fusion of Identities: Political Passion and the Poetics of Performance among British Pakistanis', in Lionel Caplan, David Parkin and Humphrey Fisher (eds), *The Politics of Cultural Performance*. Oxford: Berghahn Publishers, pp. 81–100.

—— 1996d. 'Allegories of Sacred Imperfection: Magic, Hermeneutics and Passion in *The Satanic Verses*', *Current Anthropology*, Special Issue on 'Anthropology in Public', Vol. 37 supplement: S55–S86.

—— 1996e. 'Fun Spaces: on Identity and Social Empowerment among British Pakistanis', *Theory, Culture and Society* 13 (4): 53–80.

—— 1997a. 'Introduction: the Dialectics of Cultural Hybridity', in Werbner and Modood, pp. 1–26.

—— 1997b. 'Essentialising Essentialism, Essentialising "Silence": Ambivalence and Multiculturalism in the Constructions of Racism and Ethnicity', in Werbner and Modood, pp. 226–54.

—— 1997c. '"The Lion of Lahore": Anthropology, Cultural Performance and Imran Khan', in Stephen Nugent and Cris Shore (eds), *Anthropology and Cultural Studies*. London: Pluto Press, pp. 34–67.

—— 1998. 'Diasporic Political Imaginaries: a Sphere of Freedom or a Sphere of Illusions?', *Communal/Plural: Journal of Transnational and Crosscultural Studies* 6 (1): 11–31.

—— 1999. 'Political Motherhood and the Feminisation of Citizenship: Women's Activism and the Transformation of the Public Sphere', in Nira Yuval-Davis and Pnina Werbner (eds), *Women, Citizenship and Difference*. London: Zed Books, pp. 221–45.

—— 2000a. 'Introduction: The Materiality of Diaspora – Between Aesthetic and "Real" Politics,' *Diaspora* 9 (1): 5–20.

—— 2000b. 'Divided Loyalties, Empowered Citizenship? Muslims in Britain', *Citizenship Studies* 4 (1): 307–24.

—— 2001. 'The Limits of Cultural Hybridity: on Ritual Monsters, Poetic Licence, and Contested Postcolonial Purification', *JRAI (incorporating Man)* 7 (1): 133–52.

Werbner, Pnina and Muhammad Anwar (eds). 1991. *Black and Ethnic Leaderships in Britain: the Cultural Dimensions of Political Action*. London: Routledge.

Werbner, Pnina and Tariq Modood (eds). 1997. *Debating Cultural Hybridity: Multi-Cultural Identities and the Politics of Anti-Racism*. London: Zed Books.

Werbner, Pnina and Nira Yuval-Davis. 1999. 'Introduction: Women and the New Discourse of Citizenship', in Nira Yuval-Davis and Pnina Werbner (eds), *Women, Citizenship and Difference*. London: Zed Books, pp. 1–37.

Werbner, Richard P. 1989. *Ritual Passage, Sacred Journey*. Washington, DC: Smithsonian Institution Press.

—— 1991. *Tears of the Dead*. Washington, DC: Smithsonian Institution Press.

—— 1995. 'Human Rights and Moral Knowledge: Arguments of Accountability in Zimbabwe', in Marilyn Strathern (ed.), *Shifting Contexts*. ASA Monographs. London: Routledge, pp. 99–116.

—— 1996. 'Introduction: Multiple Identities, Plural Arenas', in Richard Werbner and Terence Ranger (eds), *Postcolonial Identities in Africa*. London: Zed Books, pp. 1–26.

—— (ed.), 1998a. *Memory and the Postcolony: African Anthropology and the Critique of Power*. London: Zed Books.

—— 1998b. 'Smoke from the Barrel of a Gun: Postwars of the Dead, Memory and Reinscription', in Richard Werbner 1998a, pp. 71–102.

White, Hayden. 1980. 'The Value of Narrativity in the Representation of Reality', in W.J.T. Mitchell, pp. 1–24.

Wieviorka, Michel. 1997. 'Is It So Difficult To Be an Anti-Racist?', in Werbner and Modood, pp. 139–53.

Wilson, A.N. 1991. *Against Religion*. Counterblast 19. London: Chatto & Windus.

Wolpert, Stanley. 1984. *Jinnah of Pakistan*. Karachi: Oxford University Press.

Young, Iris Marion. 1990. 'The Ideal of Community and the Politics of Difference', in Linda J. Nicholson (ed.), *Feminism/Postmodernism*. London: Routledge, pp. 300–23.

—— 1995. 'Togetherness in Difference: Transforming the Logic of Group Political Conflict', in Will Kymlicka (ed.), *The Rights of Minority Cultures*. Oxford: Oxford University Press, pp. 155–76.

Yuval-Davis, Nira. 1997a. 'Ethnicity, Gender Relations and Multiculturalism', in Werbner and Modood, pp. 193–208.

—— 1997b. *Gender and Nation*. London: Sage.

Zizek, Slavoj. 1994. 'Identity and its Vicissitudes: Hegel's "Logic of Essence" as a Theory of Ideology', in Ernesto Laclau (ed.), *The Making of Political Identities*. London: Verso, pp. 40–75.

Appendix 1
Factional Alliances, 1987–8

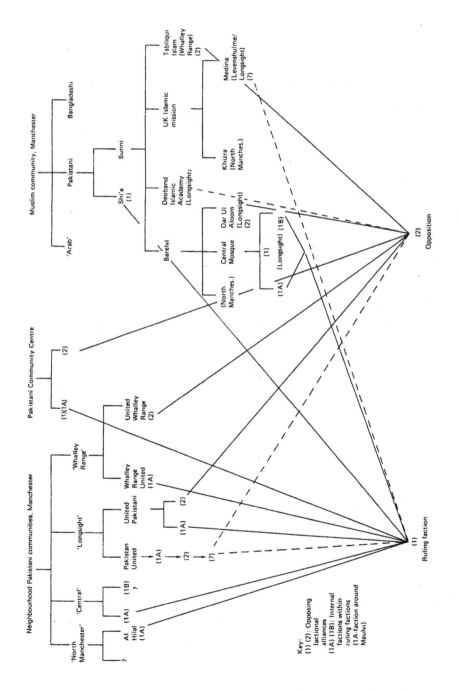

Appendix 2

Official Mosques in Manchester

(Roughly in chronological order of their foundation)

Mosque	Location	Main group	School of thought
Central Mosque	Victoria Park	Pakistani	Barelvi
Shah Jala Masjid	Rusholme	Bangladeshi	Barelvi
Shah Jalal Masjid	West Didsbury	Arab	N/A
Islamic Academy	Ancoats	Pakistani	Deobandi
Bellot Street	Cheetham Hill	Iraqi	Shi'a
Imamia Masjid	Moss Side	Pakistani	Shi'a
Madina Masjid	Levenshulme	Pakistani	UK Islamic Mission
Al Hilal Masjid	Cheetham Hill	Pakistani	UK Islamic Mission
Jamia Mosque	Cheetham Hill	Pakistani	Barelvi
Hijra Masjid	Old Trafford	Gujerati-Indian	Deobandi
Masjid Nur	Old Trafford	Gujerati-Indian	Deobandi
Zakaria Mosque	Whalley Range	Pakistani	Tablighi-Jama'at
Dar-ul Uloom	Longsight	Pakistani	Barelvi
Makki Masjid	Longsight	Pakistani	Ahl-i-Hadith
Muhammadia Masjid	Longsight	Pakistani	Barelvi
Farooqi Mosque (now Naqshbandia Mujaddidiya)	Fallowfield (moved to Ladybarn)	Pakistani	Barelvi/Deobandi
Eccles Mosque	Eccles	Yemeni	N/A
Muslim Youth	City Centre	H/A	'non-sectarian' Foundation (Islamist)
Salford Mosque	Salford University	N/A	N/A

(Derived from Scantlebury 1995)

Index